**Southern Italy**

N

0   50 km
0   50 miles

IONIAN SEA

MEDITERRANEAN SEA

Calabria

Capo Colonna
Isola di Capo Rizzuto
Capo Rizzuto
Golfo di Squillace
Catanzaro
Squillace
Soverato
Monasterace Marina
Punta Stilo
Capo Spartivento
Locri
Gerace
Bovalino
Capo Bruzzano
Melito di Porto Salvo
Reggio di Calabria
Parco Nazionale dell'Aspromonte
1955
Villa San Giovanni
Scilla
Palmi
Gioia Tauro
Rosarno
Capo Vaticano
Tropea
Briàtico
Pizzo
Mileto
Vibo Valentia
Golfo di Sant'Eufemia
Gizzaria Lido
Lamezia Terme
Catanzaro Lido
Taverna
Isola Sua
Petilia (Policastro)
Petilia
E45
A3
Stretto di Messina
Capo Rasocolmo
Punta del Faro
Isola Stromboli
Ísole Eolie o Lípari
Isola Alicudi
Isola Filicudi
Isola Panarea
Isola Salina
Isola Lipari
Lipari
Isola Vulcano
page 315

Messina
Monti Peloritani
Milazzo
Capo d'Orlando
Sant'Àgata di Militello
Taormina
Giarre
Acireale
Mascali
Monti Nebrodi
Randazzo
Bronte
Catania
Golfo di Catania
Adrano
Nicolosi
3323
Paternò
Leonforte
Troina
Nicosia
Castelbuono
Cefalù
Termini Imerese
Bagheria
Palermo
Monte Pellegrino
Monreale
Carini
Alcamo
Partinico
A29
E90
A19
E90
page 272
A20
Capo San Vito
Castellammare del Golfo
Trapani
Ísole Égadi
Marsala
Mazara del Vallo
Capo Granitola
Castelvetrano
Campobello di Mazara
Salemi
Calatafimi
Gibellina
Menfi
Sciacca
Ribera
Porto Empedocle
Agrigento
Aragona
Canicattì
Palma di Montechiaro
Licata
Gela
Golfo di Gela
Caltanissetta
San Cataldo
Mussomeli
Riesi
Enna
Piazza Armerina
Mazzarino
Caltagirone
Grammichele
Vittoria
Còmiso
Ragusa
Scicli
Pozzallo
Monti Iblei
Modica
Noto
Avola
Pachino
Portopalo di Capo Passero
Capo Passero
Golfo di Noto
Siracusa
Augusta
Golfo di Augusta
Lentini
Sorino
Melilli
Scordia
Palazzolo Acreide
Capo Santa Croce

Sicilia

Canale di Sicilia

Isola di Ustica

Ísole Pelagie
Ísola di Linosa
Isolotto di Lampione
Ísola di Lampedusa
Lampedusa
page 288-89

Isola di Pantelleria
Pantelleria

MALTA
Gozo
Victoria
Comino
Valletta
Malta

page 240
page 315
page 288-89

# INSIGHT GUIDES

# SOUTHERN ITALY

Part of the Langenscheidt Publishing Group

## INSIGHT GUIDE
# SOUTHERN
# ITALY

### Editorial
*Project Editor*
**Roger Williams**
*Managing Editor*
**Cathy Muscat**
*Editorial Director*
**Brian Bell**

### Distribution

*UK & Ireland*
**GeoCenter International Ltd**
Meridian House, Churchill Way West
Basingstoke, Hampshire RG21 6YR
Fax: (44) 1256 817988

*United States*
**Langenscheidt Publishers, Inc.**
36–36 33rd Street 4th Floor
Long Island City, NY 11106
Fax: 1 (718) 784 0640

*Australia*
**Universal Publishers**
1 Waterloo Road
Macquarie Park, NSW 2113
Fax: (61) 2 9888 9074

*New Zealand*
**Hema Maps New Zealand Ltd (HNZ)**
Unit D, 24 Ra ORA Drive
East Tamaki, Auckland
Fax: (64) 9 273 6479

*Worldwide*
**Apa Publications GmbH & Co.**
**Verlag KG (Singapore branch)**
38 Joo Koon Road, Singapore 628990
Tel: (65) 6865 1600. Fax: (65) 6861 6438

### Printing

**Insight Print Services (Pte) Ltd**
38 Joo Koon Road, Singapore 628990
Tel: (65) 6865 1600. Fax: (65) 6861 6438

©2007 Apa Publications GmbH & Co.
Verlag KG (Singapore branch)
*All Rights Reserved*
*First Edition (updated) 2006*
*(reprinted with revisions) 2007*

### CONTACTING THE EDITORS
We would appreciate it if readers
would alert us to errors or out-
dated information by writing to:
**Insight Guides, P.O. Box 7910,**
**London SE1 1WE, England.**
**Fax: (44) 20 7403 0290.**
**insight@apaguide.co.uk**

**www.insightguides.com**
*In North America:*
**www.insighttravelguides.com**

# ABOUT THIS BOOK

The first Insight Guide pioneered the use of creative full-colour photography in travel guides in 1970. Since then, we have expanded our range to cater for our readers' need not only for reliable information about their chosen des-tination but also for a real under-standing of the culture and workings of that destination. Now, when the internet can supply inexhaustible (but not always reliable) facts, our books marry text and pictures to provide those much more elusive qualities: knowledge and dis-cernment. To achieve this, they rely heavily on the authority of locally based writers and photographers.

*Insight Guide: Southern Italy* is carefully structured to convey an understand-ing of the region and its culture as well as to guide readers through its many sights and activities:

◆ The **Features** section, indicated by a yellow bar at the top of each page, covers the history and culture of the country in a series of infor-mative essays.

◆ The main **Places** section, indi-cated by a blue bar, is a complete guide to all the sights and areas worth visiting. Places of special interest are coordinated by number with the maps.

◆ The **Travel Tips** list-ings section, with an orange bar, provides a handy point of ref-erence for useful information on travel, hotels, shops, restau-rants and more.

## Map Legend

| | |
|---|---|
| ▬ ▪ ▬ | International Boundary |
| ▬ ▬ ▬ ▬ | Regional/Province Boundary |
| ▬ ▪ ▬ ▪ | National Park/Reserve |
| ▬ ▬ ▬ ▬ | Ferry Route |
| ✈ ✈ | Airport: International/Regional |
| 🚌 | Bus Station |
| ❶ | Tourist Information |
| ✉ | Post Office |
| ✝ ✝ ✝ | Church/Ruins |
| ✝ | Monastery |
| ☪ | Mosque |
| ✡ | Synagogue |
| 🏰 🏚 | Castle/Ruins |
| ∴ | Archaeological Site |
| ∩ | Cave |
| 🗿 | Statue/Monument |
| ★ | Place of Interest |

### The contributors

Nobody knows everything about a destination, and it is Insight Guides' policy to seek out expert writers, locally based whenever possible, who can write with wit and authority about their speciality. This book has assembled such a team.

**Lisa Gerard-Sharp**, a writer with a special interest in Italy and the principal author of several Insight Guides to the country's cities and regions, contributed the original features on Pleasure Seekers, Movies, Music, Literature, Saints and Superstitions and wrote the chapters on Sicily and its islands.

The history and architecture chapters are by the writer **Jonathan Keates**, whose knowledge of Italy has won acclaim, particularly for his book *Italian Journeys*.

**Bruce Johnston**, former Rome correspondent of London's *Daily Telegraph* wrote the inside story of the Mafia, revealed the secrets of daily life among Southern Italians and gave his assessment of the economics of the South. These features and the modern history chapter were brought up to date for this edition by Lisa Gerard-Sharp.

Food writer and broadcaster **Ursula Ferrigno** wrote the food chapter and wine expert **Jim Budd** wrote the chapter on wine.

The Volcanoes and Wild Places chapters are by **Carla Lionello**, who also wrote all but one of the mainland Places chapters. Lionello left her native Venice for Rome in 1989, where she has lived ever since. The chapter she missed out on was Puglia, written by **John Heseltine**, who looked at the region with a photographer's eye and contributed his pictures to the book. Travel Tips are by **Jon Eldan**, who bought a one-way ticket to Europe in 1994, finally settling in Italy.

**Marc Zakian**, travel writer and regular contributor to a number of newspapers on all things Italian, updated the Places chapters and the Travel Tips for this edition.

Many of the pictures are by **Bill Wassman**, a veteran contributor to Insight Guides. Other photographers whose work features include **Herb Hartmann** and **Gregory Wrona**.

The book was proofread by **Jan Wiltshire** and indexed by **Penny Phenix**. The project editor was **Roger Williams**, who has lived and taught in Southern Italy. His novel, *Lunch With Elizabeth David*, is based on the life of Norman Douglas, the eccentric English travel writer often quoted in this book.

The main places of interest in the Places section are coordinated by number with a full-colour map (e.g. ❶), and a symbol at the top of every right-hand page tells you where to find the map.

## INSIGHT GUIDE
# SOUTHERN ITALY

## Maps

Trulli houses in
Alberobello, Puglia

### Travel Tips

### Places

# PASSIONS AND PALACES

*The Mezzogiorno, the least known part of Italy,*
*combines timeless holiday favourites with a wild interior*

The south of Italy is the most Latin region of Europe. This is the *Mezzogiorno*, the midday region, where beneath the high sun passions burn, voices rise, and the excitement of living is so uncontainable that it has to be expressed not just in words, but in gestures. Warm and extrovert, the people of the coast and cities are accustomed to tourists, as they have been accustomed to a variety of foreign rulers.

Pleasure seekers have been coming to *Campania felix*, the happy country, since the heydays of Rome when the hedonistic highlights were, as now, to be found around the Bay of Naples and the islands of Capri, Ischia and Procida. They were only following in the steps of the Greeks who had earlier settled such communities as Sybaris in Calabria, where the behaviour of its inhabitants gave us the word "sybaritic", meaning a delight in excessive sensual pleasure.

Although this southern land has been enjoyed since the arrival of civilisation, its corners, its hill villages and off-beat towns are among the most remote in Europe. Travellers in parts of Basilicata, Puglia and Calabria today often find themselves fixed by the stares of people unused to seeing strangers. Ancient Greek still peppers dialects, an Albanian culture has survived intact after more than 400 years, and Sicily's southern flanks are tinged with Arabic. It is no surprise that remote communities in Campania were selected for gene trials in recent years; the families here have lived for so long in one place that they have become a curiosity for science.

Life is not always easy. Crime is ever present, in particular in the shape of the Mafia and its sister organisations, and with it comes institutionalised corruption. Around the puffing volcanoes of Vesuvius and Etna and between seismic shudders, natural disasters are a further burden, to be heaped on the neglect and scorn frequently offered by the more prosperous north. But this harshness of life, which in the past century and a half drove many to emigrate, has kept the landscape raw and unmolested, and allowed wildlife to flourish and wolves to roam.

What keeps people healthy, however, as well as demonstrably happy, is undoubtedly a diet of fish and vegetables, pasta and olive oil, which produces a sense of optimism and wellbeing that wealthier nations can only struggle to emulate. The fact that the less well off have such a healthy diet is one of a number of contradictions that rule the south: friendly welcomes do not disguise endemic criminal practices; unemployment is high but signs of actual poverty are few; palatial buildings can be found in the poorest parts of towns; and the most hidebound male enclaves can vote for a woman mayor. ❏

**PRECEDING PAGES:** Belvedere of Infinity, Villa Cimbrone, Ravello; taking the air in Troina, Sicily's loftiest town, with Mt Etna behind; the old harbour of Lípari, Aeolian Islands; landscape in Sciacca, Sicily.
**LEFT:** Spaccanapoli, the heart of Naples' old town.

# Decisive Dates

## PREHISTORY 5000–1000 BC

Earliest settlers include Samnites of Campania, Lucanians in Basilicata, Bruttians in Calabria, Darians in Puglia and Sicani and Siculi in Sicily. They trade with Minoans and Phoenicians.

## ANCIENT GREECE AND ROME, TO AD 410

**11th–8th centuries BC** The beginnings of Magna Graecia (Great Greece). Foundation of Greek colonies in southern Italy, including the town of Parthenope, later Neapolis (Naples).

**753 BC** Foundation of Rome.
**540 BC** Pythagoras establishes philosophy school at Crotone (ancient Kroton) in Calabria.
**510 BC** Crotone's army, led by the legendary athlete Milo, destroys Sybaris.
**6th–5th centuries BC** Building of the temples at Paestum. Siracusa (Syracuse) in southeastern Sicily becomes the greatest city in Europe.
**326 BC** Romans conquer Naples.
**282 BC** Pyrrhus of Epirus invades southern Italy and is defeated by Romans at Benevento in 275.
**264 BC** First Punic War (Rome against Carthage) begins.
**216 BC** Hannibal defeats Romans at Cannae.
**212 BC** Archimedes killed in siege of Siracusa.

*Circa* **280 BC** Completion of Via Appia from Rome to Brindisi.
**146 BC** The Punic Wars end with destruction of Carthage by the Romans.
**73 BC** Revolt of Spartacus begins at Cumae.
**65 BC** The poet Horace born in Venosa, in Puglia.
**43 BC** Roman poet Ovid (Publius Ovidius Naso) born at Sulmona, in Abruzzo.
**26 BC** Emperor Tiberius retires to Capri.
**AD 79** Eruption of Vesuvius destroys Pompeii and Herculaneum.
**324** Constantinople (Istanbul) founded as capital of the Roman Empire by Constantine, the first Christian Roman Emperor. Christianity becomes the dominant religion in southern Italy.
**393** Roman Empire divided into Eastern (Rome) and Western (Constantinople) halves.
**410** Sack of Rome by Alaric, King of the Goths, who dies two years later at Cosenza.

## LONGOBARDS AND BYZANTIUM 6TH–10TH CENTURIES

**535** Emperor Justinian brings all Italy within rule of Eastern Empire.
**568** Longobards (Lombards), a Germanic tribe, start to overrun Italy. The *Mezzogiorno* is divided between Byzantine and Longobard rulers.
**800** Pope declares Charlemagne the Holy Roman Emperor.
**965** The entire island of Sicily falls under Arab domination after three centuries of attacks on coastal cities by Muslim raiders ("Saracens" or Moors) from North Africa.

## NORMANS 1042–1194

**1042** William, son of Tancred of Hauteville (Normandy), becomes Count of Puglia.
**1053** William's oldest son, Robert Guiscard, is Duke of Puglia and conquers all southern Italy.
**1071** William's youngest son, Roger, takes Palermo and becomes The Great Count of Sicily.
**1130** Roger II, son of Roger, is proclaimed King of Sicily after conquest of Naples and Amalfi.

## HOHENSTAUFEN 1194–1266

**1194** Fall of the Norman monarchy. Henry VI of Germany becomes King of Naples.
**1197–1250** Emperor Frederick II, *Stupor Mundi*, brings good government and a cultural renaissance to his southern domains.

## ANGEVIN DYNASTY 1266–1442

**1266** After a power vacuum, Charles of Anjou becomes King of Sicily and Naples.

**1268** Conradin, the rightful heir to the throne, is cruelly executed by Charles in Naples.

**1309–43** Robert The Wise brings Giotto and Petrarch to the court of Naples.

## HOUSE OF ARAGON 1282–1496

**1282** Popular uprising on Easter Monday in Palermo (the Sicilian Vespers) brings Spanish House of Aragon.

**1435** The Angevin kingdom of Naples passes to Alfonso of Aragon who seven years later reunites Naples and Sicily as King of Two Sicilies.

**1453** Conquest of Constantinople by Turks ends Eastern Roman Empire.

**1468** Albanians arrive after their country is overrun by Turks, and they thrive here.

## SPANISH VICEROYS 1503–1707

**1503** Southern Italy becomes part of the Spanish Empire.

**1647** Revolt of Masaniello against the Spanish government in Naples.

**1669** Mount Etna erupts violently, destroying towns on the east coast of Sicily.

**1693** Earthquake in eastern Sicily.

## HABSBURGS 1707–48

**1713** Treaty of Utrecht awards the southern kingdom to Austria.

**1737** Teatro San Carlo, Naples, begun.

## BOURBONS 1748–1860

**1748** Charles III of Bourbon is crowned King in Palermo and defeats the Austrians at Vietri.

**1748** Excavations begin at Pompeii and Herculaneum.

**1759** Charles III dies and is succeeded by Ferdinand IV.

**1790** Museo Nazionale in Naples founded with royal collection of pictures and antiquities.

**1799** Revolution in Naples: "the Parthenopean Republic" is crushed by Lord Nelson and Cardinal Ruffo.

**1805** The Neapolitan royal family flee to Sicily.

**1808** Joachim Murat becomes King of Naples.

**1816** Murat is shot in Calabria and Ferdinand is restored as Ferdinand I of The Two Sicilies.

---

**PRECEDING PAGES:** Neapolitan macaroni makers, 1880.
**LEFT:** King Solomon in the 12th-century floor mosaic from the nave of the cathedral of Otranto, Puglia.
**RIGHT:** *Vesuvius Erupting* from Sir William Hamilton's *Campi Phlegraeiae* (1779).

## HOUSE OF SAVOY 1861–1944

**1860** Giuseppe Garibaldi lands in Sicily with a force of 1,000, meeting up with the troops of Victor Emmanuel II of Savoy in Teano, Calabria. Francis II, grandson of Ferdinand I, is deposed. The south becomes part of the Kingdom of Italy under King Victor Emmanuel II.

**1870** Rome becomes the capital of Italy.

**1908** Messina earthquake leaves 84,000 dead.

**1915** Italy joins Allies in World War I.

**1922** Mussolini comes to power.

**1940** Italy joins Germany in World War II.

**1943** Allies land in Sicily and Salerno; Italy surrenders. Germans retreat from Naples.

## THE REPUBLIC, FROM 1946

**1957** Sicily granted regional autonomy. Italy one of the 6 founders of the Common Market (now the EU).

**1980** Severe earthquake in Campania.

**1992** Mount Etna erupts. Murder of judges Falcone and Borsellino. The tide turns against Mafia.

**1990s** Conflict drives Albanian refugees into Italy.

**2002** Euro replaces the Lira.

**2004** Prime Minister Berlusconi is cleared of corruption after four-year trial.

**2006** Mafia Godfather Bernardo Provenzano is captured. Election of a centre-left coalition under Romano Prodi. Election of southerner and former communist, Giorgio Napolitano, as President.

**2007** Forest fires sweep across southern Italy. ❑

# GREEKS AND ROMANS

*The Greeks were the first to find a sybaritic lifestyle in these*
*fertile lands, but their prosperity soon attracted rivals*

A few dolmens in Puglia are about the sum of the remnants of southern Italy's prehistoric inhabitants. When the colonising Greeks arrived, the east coast of the mainland was inhabited by Apulians and the central Apennines by Samnians. Campanians, Lucanians (in Basilicata) and Bruttians of the west coast spoke a common Oscan language. In Sicily the Elymni, Sicani and Siculi held sway.

The Greeks were the first to make a major cultural impact on the region. They had been driven westwards by a shortage of arable land and were seeking fresh markets to trade their metal goods. Soon after 750 BC, a series of settlements began to spring up along the bay of Naples, on the Calabrian coast and in the Gulf of Taranto. Neapolis, Rhegium and Siracusa expanded to become the regional capitals of Naples, Reggio Calabria and Syracuse, but there were equally important cities, such as Cumae, Sybaris and Metapontum, which would sink into insignificance or be abandoned.

## Magna Graecia

The Greek colonists came from the cities in mainland Greece, Asia Minor and the islands of the Aegean, and they brought their religion, laws, ceremonies and customs. Temples, such as those at Paestum *(see page 106)*, were raised to a variety of deities. Theatres were built for the performance of tragedies by Aeschylus and Euripides, the one at Siracusa seating 15,000, and skilled painters decorated houses, tombs and public buildings with murals showing mythological scenes or glimpses of daily life.

Despite a shared cultural heritage and common language, the colonies were fiercely competitive, particularly over trade with the peoples of the north and the Carthaginians in North Africa. Their economy was based on an immensely profitable agriculture, centred on the production

of wine and olive oil, and exports included earthenware, jewellery, weapons, textiles and the beautifully painted vases which characterise this Greek civilisation in the Italian south.

Later, the Romans designated this scatter of harbours and markets in Italy's heel and toe as Magna Graecia, "Great Greece", which had

become so prosperous by the 5th century BC that its cities were more affluent than their founding communities in Greece. In Calabria, Sybaris grew famously rich from fisheries, wool and livestock. Crowing cocks and noisy market traders were banned from the city limits, and the pampered citizens were known for their decadent habits of taking steam baths and dining in the company of their wives. Their skins, it was said, were so sensitive that contact with a rose petal could bring them out in blisters. The word "sybaritic" has come to mean a delight in excessive sensual pleasure.

At the same time, Syracuse (Siracusa) in Sicily became the largest city in all Europe.

**LEFT:** Greek warrior, found in the sea in Riace in 1973 and now in the Museo Nazionale, Reggio Calabria.
**RIGHT:** Tiberius, who retired to run the Roman Empire from his villa in Capri.

Wherever the Greeks travelled, they took their culture with them, and the cities of Magna Graecia nurtured rich traditions of philosophy, poetry and drama. Many distinguished writers and scientists came here as refugees from Greece. In 531 BC the mathematician, philosopher and teacher Pythagoras, from the island of Samos, arrived at Crotone on the Tyrrhenian Sea, where he attracted an enthusiastic following of young disciples keen to investigate his ideas on science, music and the nature of the soul. During the 5th century BC the great poet Pindar, whose odes celebrated the winners of athletic championships and chariot races, vis-

Carthage on the North African coast, founded by Queen Dido who led refugees here from the kingdom of the Phoenicians in present-day Lebanon. The Carthaginians established trading bases in Spain, overran western Sicily, and started to look longingly towards the Italian mainland where a new power was starting to make its influence felt.

By the middle of the 4th century BC the republican state of Rome had become feared among its immediate neighbours for its superbly trained army, a formidable fighting machine which had subdued the great strongholds of the Etruscans in the central regions of

ited the Calabrian town of Locri, praising it as a pioneer of good government, the first city in the Greek-speaking world, according to him, to have its own written code of laws.

How much the inhabitants of these towns appreciated beautiful things can be seen in the bronzes of Riace, found near Reggio Calabria in 1972. Superbly proportioned sculptures of bearded male nudes, they were probably the work of a talented 5th-century BC Athenian sculptor, such as Phidias or Polycleites, and may have been intended for a local temple.

Inevitably, the prosperity of Magna Graecia attracted the envy of states elsewhere in the Mediterranean. Among the most successful was

Lazio and Tuscany. When the Romans turned their attention to Magna Graecia, around 282 BC, several of its cities, led by the wealthy port of Tarentum (Taranto), turned for help to a powerful and charismatic leader, Pyrrhus, ruler of the northern Greek kingdom of Epirus.

### The original Pyrrhic victory

Brave, ambitious and skilful in battle, Pyrrhus had become a semi-mythical figure by the time the Tarentines sought his aid. A mere touch of his big toe was said to cure diseases of the spleen, while his whole body was rumoured to be untouchable by fire. He got off to a poor start, however, losing most of his expedition in a storm and arriving at Tarentum with a handful of cavalry and just two out of an original 20 elephants. The king then shocked the pleasure-loving citizens by closing all places of amusement, putting an end to drunken parties and conscripting every adult male capable of holding a sword or a spear. This business-like approach reaped its rewards in several victories over the Roman armies, but Pyrrhus pushed his luck too far. His costly victories over the Romans brought him more losses than his enemy, which led to the

### ISLAND OF PLENTY

"Sicily is the Republic's granary, the nurse at whose breast the Roman people is fed."

— CATO THE ELDER (234–149 BC)

trading power and began to cast an eye on fertile and prosperous Sicily. In 264 BC, mercenaries known as the Mamertines, who controlled the key Sicilian port of Messana (Messina), sought an alliance with Rome. This was a chance for the Romans to head off any possible Carthaginian incursion and the alliance provoked the first of the Punic Wars ("Punic" is from the Latin Punicus, meaning Phoenician or Carthaginian), which Romans won only after building a battle fleet to boost their sea power.

expression "Pyrrhic victory". In AD 275, he was defeated near Benevento, Campania, and he abandoned Magna Graecia to its new masters.

Having dealt with Pyrrhus, the Romans could concentrate on neutralising and ultimately annihilating the Carthaginians, who were by now their major commercial rivals in the western Mediterranean. Though the two peoples were nominally united by a series of friendship treaties begun in 509 BC, tension started to develop when Rome expanded as a

**LEFT:** painting from the Tomb of the Diver, Paestum, 475 BC. **ABOVE:** a mosaic from Pompeii showing a group of philosophers from the Athens Academy.

Defeated on the mainland and in Sicily, the Carthaginians retreated to the territories they controlled in Spain, where they determined to strike back at the Romans. Hannibal, son of vanquished general Hamilcar Barca, led Carthage into the Second Punic War (218–201 BC). His march from Spain across the Pyrenees and over the Alps into Italy with a vast army and elephants became the stuff of legend, and in 216 BC he inflicted a crushing defeat on the Roman army at Cannae, near the modern town of Canosa di Puglia. The Roman force of 100,000 was twice the size of Hannibal's, but the Carthaginians quickly routed the cavalry and then charged the infantry legions who were waiting in the rear for the signal to advance. The huge army scattered and its commander, Aemilius Paulus, was taken prisoner. Nothing now lay between Hannibal and the city of Rome, but instead of turning north towards this ultimate prize, he chose to march west into the fertile province of Campania, to take up winter quarters at Capua, near Naples. The Carthaginians were seduced by the city's opulence and good living, and the Romans were able to capture it after a prolonged siege.

Hannibal had failed to take Rome, and returned to Africa, where he was finally defeated by Publius Cornelius Scipio at the battle of Zama in 201 BC.

## The Romans march in

The cities of Magna Graecia had seen Hannibal's arrival in southern Italy as their last chance to maintain independence from the Roman Empire. When Rome seized control of the region, after a third and final Punic War which resulted in Carthage's total destruction in 146 BC, the many Greek-speaking towns of Calabria, Puglia and Campania lost much of their importance. The new masters, absentee patricians, turned the countryside into ranch-style estates known as *latifundia*, run with slave labour, forcing peasants from the land and creating desolation through overgrazing. The

### THE GREATEST SCIENTIST OF THE ANCIENT WORLD

The great Greek scientist Archimedes was the son of an astronomer from Syracuse (Siracusa), where he was born in 287 BC. Famously, if apocryphally, he jumped naked from a public bath and ran through the streets of the city shouting "*Eureka!*" (I've found it) after devising a way of measuring the volume of the crown of Hieron II of Syracuse, and thus determining that it was not made of real gold.

Archimedes was an intensely practical scientist and his theories and inventions are still in use today, notably the Archimedes screw, which raises underground water. He was such a master of the techniques of leverage that his maxim "Give me a place to stand and I will move the world"

became well known. Rising to a challenge and using a series of pulleys, he once apparently pulled a laden merchant ship across the sand using one hand. He was immensely useful to the king, and to Syracuse, especially in the defence of the city against the Romans, who had no doubt that they were up against a master of ingenuity.

Their siege began in 215 BC and lasted three years, largely through Archimedes' efforts. He devised catapults and cranes and huge lenses that deflected the sun and set fire to their ships. When the city succumbed, Archimedes was killed by a soldier who did not know who he was. The Romans had, understandably, wanted to take him alive.

slaves were often badly treated, and in 73 BC their discontents and those of the dispossessed small farmers found a spokesman in a former gladiator from Capua named Spartacus. Raising an army of more than 100,000, he swept north into central Italy, before turning back to devastate the southern province of Lucania (modern Basilicata).

Here he was finally defeated by Marcus Licinius Crassus, who crucified all surviving rebels, though the body of Spartacus, killed in the battle, was never found. Admired as much for his competent leadership and sense of fairness as for his personal courage, the rebel

Ancient Roman Florida, with luxury villas, seaside resorts and fashionable health spas developing both on the mainland and on the islands of Capri and Ischia. Capri was chosen by Tiberius for the site of an immense villa, where his orgies became the subject of lurid gossip among historians, while a beachside residence at Baiae near Naples was selected by the Emperor Nero as an ideal setting for the murder of his mother, the domineering Agrippina.

The south, during this early phase of empire, became a favourite haunt of Roman poets such as Virgil, Ovid and Horace, who were fond of its landscapes and keen to absorb the atmos-

leader became a symbol of proletarian revolt and the subject of one of the most successful of Hollywood's epics.

Once pacified, southern Italy became a tourist destination and an ideal spot for Roman holiday homes. The lush volcanic terrain of Campania, surrounding the ancient city of Neapolis, was particularly welcoming, and during the first century AD, in the reigns of the emperors Augustus and Tiberius, the whole area bordering the Bay of Naples became an

phere of Greek culture lingering from an earlier age. Virgil was buried at Naples in 19 BC, after dying at Brindisi of a fever caught while on a trip to Greece (though the monument traditionally shown to visitors as his tomb probably contains someone else's remains). Horace, who came from the Apulian town of Venosa, loved his native countryside and wrote affectionately of its streams, woods and mountains.

## Ancient terrors

Southern Italy and its neighbouring islands of Sicily and Stromboli are the only area of the Mediterranean to contain active volcanoes, and these smoking mountains were contemplated

**LEFT:** Archimedes works out how to measure the gold in the king's crown (16th-century woodcut).
**ABOVE:** Pompeii painting, Museo Nazionale, Naples.

with awe and terror by the Greeks and Romans. Beliefs associated with them grew from ancient myths of imprisoned giants, who could raise storms and earthquakes. Among the Phlegraean Fields, a volcanic area around Puteoli (Pozzuoli), was the entrance to the Underworld, through an extinct crater named Avernus, from the Greek phrase "where no birds fly".

A real danger lay in the looming presence of Mount Vesuvius, dominating the skyline surrounding the Bay of Naples. Suspicions of a likely eruption, following an earthquake in AD 62, were discounted by the people of Pompeii, an ancient city lying in the volcano's shadow, who had spent large sums on refurbishing their temples, theatre and amphitheatre. The speed with which the disaster overtook them, on 24 August AD 79, was the result of a pyroclastic explosion, which suffocated many of those trying to escape the hail of volcanic debris and buried them under a 7-metre (23-ft) layer of ash and pumice stone. Further destruction awaited the neighbouring town of Herculaneum. It was engulfed in a torrent of boiling mud mixed with ashes and stones, which formed a hardened crust that obliterated the whole settled area even more thoroughly than at Pompeii. The ruins of both

## THE DAY THE WHOLE WORLD PERISHED

A letter by Pliny the Younger (Gaius Plinius Secundus) to the historian Cornelius Tacitus recalls the catastrophic eruption of Vesuvius in AD 79. Staying with his uncle, the naturalist and scientist Pliny the Elder, he watched as a dense cloud covered the bay of Naples and the rain of ash started to fall. "Darkness came down, not the dark of a moonless night, but as though a lamp were extinguished in a shuttered room. You could hear the shrieks of women, the wailing of children and the cries of men." As the boy and his mother fled, the elder Pliny ordered a ship to be made ready and set off down the bay to try to rescue friends living closer to Vesuvius. "Ashes were already falling, followed by pumice and stones charred and cracked by the flames," wrote the young Pliny, but the rescuers came on shore and his uncle calmed everybody's fears by going to sleep in a nearby house, his snores resounding through the rattling hail of pumice.

When flames and a stink of sulphur warned of the approaching lava flow, he hurried back to the beach, but the fumes finally choked him to death. After 48 hours of total darkness, his body was recovered "looking more like somebody asleep than that of a dead man."

His young nephew recalled, "I believed the whole world was perishing with me and I along with it."

cities and their remarkable evidence of daily life and customs under the Roman Empire lay buried until excavations in the early 18th century began revealing this tragic yet always astonishing survival of an ancient civilisation at the height of its splendour *(see page 157)*.

The final break-up of the Roman Empire began after Emperor Constantine transferred the imperial capital from Rome to Byzantium in AD 330 and Germanic tribes began invading from the north. In 410 Rome was sacked by the Goths under Alaric. After a week of looting, they moved south through Campania, plundering Naples and other towns as they went.

Alaric looked forward to conquering Sicily and moving on to Africa, Rome's richest imperial province, but he died from malaria at the Calabrian town of Cosenza. At his extraordinary funeral, the Goths diverted the nearby River Busento in order to bury the king in its bed along with huge heaps of Roman treasure and art works. The river was then restored to its natural channel and the local slaves who had dug the grave were said to have been massacred to preserve its secret location.

## Byzantium follows Rome

With the collapse of imperial government, stability and local law was often left to the Christian church and its embryo communities. For the next five centuries, the Italian south came under different spheres of political influence. The Eastern Roman Empire of Byzantium annexed parts of Calabria and Puglia, which were ruled by governors appointed from Constantinople. The towns of Otranto and Bari became flourishing Byzantine provincial capitals, graced with fine buildings and maintaining a vigorous trade with other Italian cities such as Pisa, Lucca and Genoa. Naples, too, came under the Byzantine Empire and in due course was allowed to appoint its own Dux.

Northern Italy, meantime, fell under the control of the Germanic Longobards, who moved south and established an independent duchy at Benevento, Campania, which lasted 500 years.

### APOPLECTIC POPE

Always hospitable, Neapolitans tolerated Muslim Saracen invaders, which so angered Pope John VIII he excommunicated the entire city.

Such conflicting influences turned the south into a racial and linguistic melting pot. Traces of Byzantine Greek can still be detected in the dialect of remote mountain villages, while blond hair, fair skin and blue eyes, in contrast to the characteristic southern swarthiness, is held to indicate descent from north European invaders.

In the early 8th century, a fresh ingredient was added to the brew when the Muslim armies which had swept into Sicily from North Africa pushed across the Straits of Messina and seized key fortresses and towns.

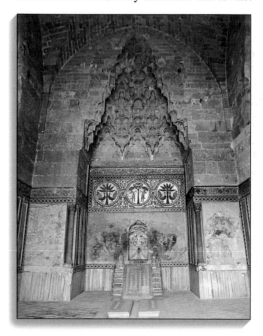

An Islamic culture hung on in various areas of the south until well into the 13th century. The Moorish style influenced agriculture, with the introduction of carob trees, prickly pears and citrus fruits, and brought a new sophistication to local decorative arts in ceramics and metalwork. It also profoundly affected the urban layout and lifestyle in southern towns. From a distance many still have the flat-roofed, whitewashed look of a Middle Eastern or North African *medina*, and the emphasis on cool shade among courtyards and alleyways, with houses placed close together, is a further indicator of this Saracen thread in the complex patchwork of local history. ❑

**LEFT:** a wall painting in Pompeii from the Museo Nazionale Archeologico in Naples.
**RIGHT:** Islamic architecture from Palermo, Sicily.

# THE TWO KINGDOMS

*From the arrival of the Normans to the rise of Napoleon, the crowns of Sicily and Naples were passed among German, Spanish and French kings*

**D**uring the 11th century a drastic overhaul took place of the existing structures of political power in southern Italy. A chance encounter in 1016 between a group of pilgrims to a shrine on Monte Gargano and a local Longobard warlord bent on raising a rebellion against the Byzantine imperial government, brought a band of Norman mercenaries into the south, whose military prowess made them unafraid of changing sides whenever it should suit them.

Over the next hundred years the Normans – relatives of those who conquered England in 1066 – succeeded in eliminating Byzantine rule in Apulia and Calabria as well as dislodging most, though not all, of their Islamic communities. The effect was to bind the whole area more closely to Catholic Christendom, breaking cultural and economic links with Constantinople and creating a powerful new state, which might become a useful ally or a dangerous enemy in the continuing political struggle for supremacy between the Papacy on the one hand and the Holy Roman Empire, founded by Charlemagne, King of the Francs, on the other.

## A cosmopolitan court

Though the Norman kingdom eventually settled its capital in Sicily, at Palermo, the mainland provinces were of vital importance in the business of resisting the Papacy's territorial greed. Successive popes did not forget that in 1084 a mixed Norman and Saracen force had looted Rome before setting it on fire. Perhaps the most important feature of Norman rule, in terms of an enduring cultural influence on the south, was its monarchs' complete acceptance of a polyglot, multiracial, multi-faith society. Kings such as Roger II (1130–54) reigned in the context of a court which included Muslim, Jewish and Greek Orthodox worshippers, and

**LEFT:** Frederick II (1194–1250) grants an Italian city a privilege, from an illuminated manuscript, *circa* 1300.
**RIGHT:** Roger II (1130–54) receives a petitioner in Palermo's Capella Palatina.

the atmosphere was suitably cosmopolitan. Even the strongly Byzantine city of Bari had its character and traditions preserved rather than destroyed by the Normans.

A period of relative stability during the late 12th century was interrupted by the death in 1189 of William II, King of Sicily, and the

resulting struggle for power between his bastard cousin, Tancred of Lecce, and Henry VI, Holy Roman Emperor, who was married to William's aunt Constance. In 1194 Constance gave birth to Frederick, who became King of Sicily, and was crowned emperor as Frederick II in 1220. One of the most forceful personalities of his age, he combined the best qualities of his double inheritance, from Italianised Normans on his mother's side and German warriors on his father's. He was a poet, a scholar and a cosmopolitan in tastes and outlook, something of a Renaissance man long before the Renaissance, a shrewd diplomat and an energetic and successful leader of armies. Such a combination of qualities in a single man was calculated to alarm the rulers of neighbouring states, led by Pope Innocent III (1198–1216) who had done more than any of his predecessors to bolster the papacy's political power and influence. For most of his 30-year reign Frederick found himself in direct conflict with Innocent or his papal successor Gregory IX, and in 1241 a third pope, Innocent IV, excommunicated Frederick.

## A rare benevolence

Whatever the feelings of his subjects as to the emperor's refusal to submit to papal authority, they admired him as a benevolent ruler, who brought to the Mezzogiorno one of the few periods of good government it was ever to know. In the so-called "Constitutions" he issued at Melfi in Basilicata in 1231, he made a serious attempt to codify the kingdom's laws, as well as to ensure fair and regular taxation, together with standardised weights and measures and an efficient customs service. By founding a university at Naples, Frederick aimed to develop a new class of properly trained civil servants to administer the everyday processes of government.

Unfortunately, the success of this experiment was undermined by a serious drain on his

### FREDERICK, THE WONDER OF THE WORLD

When not campaigning against power-hungry popes, German barons and rebellious Italian cities, or using diplomacy to reconcile crusaders and Muslims in the Middle East, Emperor Frederick II devoted himself to writing poetry and books on science and hunting.

Some of the earliest extant literature in the Italian language derives from his exotic court, peopled with Greeks, Arabs, Jews and even the occasional Englishman, surrounding him at his castles and palaces in such towns as Lucera, Trani, Foggia and Bari, or at the majestic octagonal Castel del Monte near Andria in Puglia, an image in stone of the harmony Frederick tried to bring to his empire in an age of bigotry and bloodshed. Frederick's own poems, their medieval Italian still easy to read nearly eight centuries later, used Arabic verse forms, made references to classical Greek myths and echoed the style of the aristocratic troubadours of France and Germany. Mostly about love, they were written for sheer amusement, but their elegance made them models for other poets, including Dante, who called Frederick "the father of Italian poetry". A keen bird-watcher, he also wrote a definitive book on falconry.

Admired for his skills as warrior, law-maker, politician, architect, scientist and musician, the emperor was hailed as *Stupor Mundi* – "The Wonder of the World".

finances as the constant military struggle with the popes continued. Frederick's sudden death in 1150 of a fever, near the Puglian town of Lucera, plunged southern Italy into confusion. While Frederick's legitimate heir Conrad succeeded as emperor, a bastard son Manfred was allotted the kingdom of Sicily and southern Italy, but when Conrad died four years later, Manfred found himself in direct conflict with the papal armies. Routing them easily enough, he concentrated on building up his power base through alliances with different rulers.

> **SICILIAN VESPERS**
>
> The uprising supposedly began when a French captain grasped the bosom of a woman while searching the Easter procession. She fainted in the arms of her husband who cried out, "Death to the French!"

As a rival candidate for the throne, the Pope chose Charles of Anjou, brother of the King of France, who gathered an army and advanced on the city of Benevento, where he defeated Manfred in 1266. Instead of exploiting his southern victory, however, Charles began developing a grandiose scheme for seizing the Byzantine Empire, an enterprise supported by a heavier taxation on the south than Frederick had ever imposed. The Greek emperor Michael Palaeologus, realising what was afoot, encouraged Manfred's daughter Constance and her husband the Spanish King Pedro of Aragon to seize the Sicilian throne by fair means or foul, and on Easter Monday 1282 a wholesale massacre of Charles's French troops in Palermo – the so-called Sicilian Vespers – sparked off a war which lasted 20 years. The upshot was the separation of the kingdom into two halves. While Sicily was awarded to the Aragonese, the Mezzogiorno was henceforth to be ruled by Charles's descendants, the Angevins.

## The Angevin kings

The solution may not have been perfect, but it ought at least to have guaranteed prosperity and stability to the whole war-torn region. As it happened, the Angevin kings, from their court at Naples, were keen to renew the cultural activities promoted by Emperor Frederick in the previous century, and the city attracted poets and artists from elsewhere in Italy, including Giovanni Boccaccio, author of the

*Decameron*, and the great Tuscan painter Giotto. The countryside, on the other hand, had suffered drastically from the effects of war, with much depopulation and a serious decline in agriculture. Areas once rich from growing wheat and barley were now turned over to pasture, and the feudal lords of the great estates into which most of the south was divided turned to plunder of herds and flocks, banditry and small-scale warfare with their neighbours in order to sustain their families and their

castles. The seeds had been planted of a social mentality which persists to this day throughout the Mezzogiorno, in which the rule of law, the sense of a common good and the idea of civic responsibility are far less important than clan loyalty, maintenance of status and a show of strength sufficient to intimidate enemies or competitors.

When the crowns of Naples and Sicily were reunited by the Aragonese monarch Alfonso the Magnanimous in 1442, he was forced to make a serious concession of rights and privileges to the feudal barons, with a consequent lightening of the tax burden on the aristocracy at the expense of the peasants. The revolts

**LEFT:** Frederick II and his falcon master, from his own book, *The Art of Hunting with Birds*, 1232.
**RIGHT:** the "Sicilian Vespers", an uprising in Palermo at Easter in 1242, divided the kingdom in two.

which followed throughout Calabria as a consequence were savagely repressed. Tightening their grip on both the countryside and the market towns of the south, the barons offered a significant threat to royal authority and in 1484 they felt sufficiently strong and united to declare open rebellion against the king.

Though they were temporarily crushed, an invasion of Italy 10 years later by King Charles VIII of France, leading a formidable army equipped with state-of-the-art weaponry, gave the signal for a further assault on the beleaguered Aragonese monarchy by its own nobles. In 1500 diplomatic attempts were made to

once more to the kingdom, known by now as "The Two Sicilies", a name it would bear until its dissolution in 1860.

## A Spanish colony

To many observers it nevertheless became clear that the area was becoming little more than a colonial dependency of Spain, exploited for its agricultural produce, hardly benefiting from the wealth created by Spanish imperial expansion in South America and grossly overburdened with new taxes. Spanish culture, meanwhile, made a significant impact on all aspects of southern life. Naples was dominated by a Span-

divide the realm once more, this time between France and the newly united kingdom of Spain created from the marriage of Ferdinand of Aragon to Isabella of Castile.

Eventually Spain's sheer military might succeeded in clawing back Naples and southern Italy, and the coronation of Ferdinand and Isabella's son Charles V as Holy Roman Emperor in 1530 effectively sealed the Mezzogiorno's destiny for the next 200 years as a dominion of the Spanish crown. Charles was as forceful a personality on the 16th century scene as Frederick II had been in the 13th century, and what seemed at first to be a framework of good order and legality brought peace

ish-speaking nobility and the use of the honorific "Don" as a title for men of influence quickly established itself, as did the custom of formally addressing others with the phrase "Your honour", together with verbs in the third person. This habit survives in modern Italian.

The Spanish viceroys of Naples saw it as their duty to impose the iron will of the monarch on a restless and potentially anarchic populace, yet at the same time they respected the local barons' determination to hang on to at least some of their ancient powers. The Holy Office, better known to us as the Inquisition, was never introduced into the mainland portion of the kingdom, despite its proven success as an instrument of government in Spain and Sicily. The nobles, meanwhile, were permitted to keep their elected assembly, which vetted the application of all fresh taxes. In an extensive rebuilding programme of cathedrals, monasteries and parish churches, the Church reaffirmed its wealth and importance, symbolised also in its considerable landholdings throughout the realm.

This combined authority of the crown, the nobility and the church fostered a smouldering resentment among ordinary citizens which

**YOUR FEMALE HONOUR**

Italians today address each other as "she" rather than "you", a legacy of the Spanish *merced*, a feminine word meaning honour.

conflict known as the Thirty Years' War, the need for fighting men, food to provision them and cash to pay them proved an intolerable drain on the south's resources.

Among other desperate stratagems for raising money, the viceroys resorted to selling feudal privileges and land rights, with accompanying titles of nobility, so that the Neapolitan aristocracy, its numbers already inflated, became the most numerous in any European state, the throng of princes, dukes, marquises, counts and barons running into hundreds.

grew more hostile as the Spanish monarchy entered a prolonged financial crisis towards the end of the 16th century.

## Bandits and revolutionaries

Banditry now became a regular feature of southern life, sometimes involving whole villages and pitched battles. One viceroy condemned 18,000 people to death for this crime alone, while completely failing to stamp it out. As the early 1600s saw Spain and its satellites being drawn into the

LEFT: detail from the cloister of Santa Chiara, Naples.
ABOVE: the Aragonese fleet entering Naples' port in 1442, attributed to Francesco Rosselli (1445–1513).

Harassed by press gangs and tax collectors, the people rose in revolt in the summer of 1647. Their leader was a young Neapolitan fisherman Tommaso Aniello, known as Masaniello, originally the spokesman of an infuriated crowd gathering to demonstrate against a new levy on fruit and vegetables. The rioters soon banded together under his championship, invoking the patronage of the Virgin Mary, and unrest spread quickly to other cities, fanned by foreign *agents provocateurs* and those with personal grudges against local overlords. The barons were slow to assemble an adequate counter-insurgency force, but meanwhile a group of Neapolitan nobles dispatched hired assassins to murder

Masaniello. It was more than a year before the revolt was successfully quashed. Masaniello's name by now resounded throughout Europe as a popular hero, and in later ages he became the subject of novels, operas and feature films.

## Bourbon grandeur

The Treaty of Utrecht in 1714, ending the War of the Spanish Succession, awarded the Kingdom of the Two Sicilies to Austria, but in 1734 the state once more achieved full independence, with Charles of Bourbon, Duke of Parma, becoming the first king of its new ruling dynasty. Wealthy and ambitious, Charles, as

befitted a descendant of France's Sun King Louis XIV, had an exalted idea of his family's importance and laboured to create a suitably grandiose context at Naples for a Bourbon monarch and his court, building vast new palaces at Caserta and Capodimonte.

All the 18th century's enlightened despots were concerned to establish a reputation as reformers, and the king quickly gathered around him a series of capable administrators, devoted to overhauling the antiquated, inefficient and corrupt machinery of government inherited from the Spanish viceroys. Charles's reforms, spearheaded by zealous ministers such as Bernardo Tanucci, struck first at the power and wealth of the Church, and then attempted to remove several of the more offensive feudal privileges of the barons. Perhaps inevitably, such efforts at limiting aristocratic power had less success, and under Charles's son Ferdinand the whole impetus of reform ground to a halt.

Naples nevertheless became a lively and exciting city during the second half of the 18th century. Its intellectual life, more or less dead since the arrival of the Spaniards, revived as a result of greater press freedom, less interference by the Church and improved communications with other European cities.

Always fond of music, the Neapolitans had enthusiastically welcomed opera from Venice and Rome, and they now began developing their own special variety, a type of operatic comedy which introduced local dialect and familiar figures from everyday life. A whole group of talented southern composers concentrated on expanding the possibilities of this form, known to musicians as *"opera buffa"*.

### HORATIO NELSON, THE DEMON LOVER

It was on a visit to Naples in 1798, after defeating Napoleon's fleet at the battle of the Nile, that Nelson met and fell in love with the bewitching Emma Hamilton.

Her husband, Sir William, the English ambassador to Ferdinand I, was a wealthy connoisseur, internationally famous as an expert on Greek vases and as an enthusiastic amateur geologist. Emma was a Cheshire blacksmith's daughter, who had worked in a London brothel called The Temple of Health. She had been his nephew's mistress, and they married in 1791 when Sir William was 60 and she was 26. At Naples she gained favour with Queen Maria Carolina and was admired by foreign visitors for her "Attitudes", classi-

cal poses imitating Greek vase painting, in which she appeared as flimsily dressed as possible.

Hamilton seems to have encouraged Emma's passion for Nelson, and the King and Queen were delighted with the arrangement, especially when the British admiral helped them to suppress the 1799 "Parthenopean Republic". While her lover hanged the rebel leader, Prince Caracciolo, at the yardarm of his flagship, Emma dealt harshly with petitions for mercy from wives of other revolutionaries. Accompanied by the Hamiltons, Nelson returned to a hero's welcome in London. For the Neapolitans, however, he and Emma became demonised as the agents of tyranny and reaction.

The best of them, such as Domenico Cimarosa and Giovanni Paisiello, were to influence such great international masters of operatic comedy as Mozart and Rossini.

## Height of the Grand Tour

The area around Vesuvius also witnessed one of the most important events of 18th-century European culture in the gradual excavation of the buried Roman cities of Pompeii and Herculaneum, an enterprise begun by King Charles. Naples had established itself as one of the most important centres of the Grand Tour, the extended educational visit to Italy which

structure for the whole state. Unfortunately his son Ferdinand was a less intelligent monarch, fond of hunting and practical jokes, a king whose reactionary instincts were encouraged by his wife Maria Carolina of Austria, aided by her English lover Admiral Acton. Incensed by the execution in Paris of her sister Queen Marie Antoinette, she urged Ferdinand to join an alliance against the French, but when Napoleon's armies invaded Italy four years later the royal family fled to Sicily, along with their friends the English ambassador Sir William Hamilton and his wife Emma.

In 1799 revolutionaries in Naples proclaimed

became obligatory for young European aristocrats. Collecting antiques, particularly Greek and Roman statuary and vases, became a passion with visiting noblemen, and Neapolitans were able to make a profitable business out of selling curios and *objets d'art*.

The liberal tone of life in Bourbon Naples encouraged many people to hope that, at the outbreak of the French Revolution in 1789, the reforms begun by King Charles would at length accommodate a more democratic political

**LEFT:** Masaniello, who led a popular revolt against the despotic Spanish monarchy in 1647.
**ABOVE:** a lithograph of the Teatro di San Carlo, 1840.

the so-called Parthenopean Republic (Parthenope was one of the city's ancient Greek names) led by high-minded intellectuals and freethinking aristocrats. Lasting only five months, it was finally overwhelmed by a combination of a Calabrian peasant army led by Cardinal Fabrizio Ruffo and the English fleet commanded by Lady Hamilton's lover, no less a figure than Lord Horatio Nelson. The terms of an honourable surrender were violated when Nelson, egged on by Lady Hamilton and Queen Maria Carolina, hanged the revolutionary leaders, and the massacres and reactionary repression which followed had a disastrous impact on the Bourbon monarchy's image throughout Europe. ❑

# ONE NATION

*With unification, the "Two Sicilies" joined the rest of Italy.*
*But its history lingered in a culture too complex to be quickly assimilated*

The rule of the restored Bourbons after the Parthenopean Republic's collapse was unsurprisingly short. On 14 June 1800 a French army under Napoleon Bonaparte won a decisive victory over the Austrians at Marengo in northern Italy, and soon afterwards a full-scale occupation of the Italian states by French troops began. The whole political map was now redrawn, with the north being transformed into the Kingdom of Italy, governed by a viceroy in Milan, Tuscany given to Napoleon's sister Elisa, and his brother Joseph made King of Naples. Afterwards sent to rule in Spain, Joseph was replaced by Joachim Murat, husband of the Emperor's sister Caroline.

## Napoleonic rule

While the Bourbons had returned to Sicily, guarded by British warships, the Kingdom of Naples enjoyed what was probably the best government since the days of Emperor Frederick II. Under Napoleonic rule, new centralised bureaucracy and the wholesale abolition of feudal privileges brought with them an impartial administration, supported by the French Civil Code, which standardised legal procedure, introduced a fair taxation system and established adequate policing throughout the nation.

Unfortunately, this new regime, while sweeping away old abuses, did little to alter the social status quo, since the barons were still guaranteed ownership of their estates. Such fresh lands as became available were bought by the bourgeoisie who were created from the new ministerial class engaged in carrying out French reforms.

Napoleon was keen to encourage young Italians to join his armies, and for many this offered an excellent opportunity to improve their status and financial prospects while seeing something of the world during the Emperor's military campaigns. When Joachim Murat, as

**LEFT:** results of the plebiscite to unify Italy are announced in Naples, 1860.
**RIGHT:** Garibaldi, hero of Italian unification.

King of Naples, cut loose from his brother-in-law's empire in 1814, several Neapolitan army officers, familiar by now with other models of government, demanded a constitution in return for their support. Secret societies devoted to political reform, known as the Carbonari, had sprung up in various regiments, but Murat,

hitherto a wise and practical sovereign, preferred to repress them rather than capitalise on their potential support following Napoleon's defeat at Leipzig and exile to Elba. Austrian troops meanwhile closed in on the kingdom, defeating Murat's army at Tolentino in the Papal States in 1815. After fleeing to Corsica, he made a last desperate bid to regain his kingdom, landing in Calabria at the head of a small body of volunteers, but he was captured and executed by an Austrian firing squad.

Memories of Murat's reign and of his dream of unifying Italy under a single monarch lingered during the subsequent Bourbon restoration. The new Kingdom of the Two Sicilies brought together what had technically been two separate realms, with King Ferdinand IV becoming Ferdinand I at the head of his new state. During residence in Sicily he had granted the island a constitution, but once properly reinstated he abandoned his constitutional experiment, provoking anger among the new class of educated professionals. In July 1820 rioting broke out in the city of Nola and spread to other provinces, forcing the king to renew his former pledges. When rebel factions began quarrelling with each other, Ferdinand brought an Austrian force from the mainland, scattered the constitutionalists and restored the status quo.

To outsiders, the kingdom's apparent security, internal or external, scarcely concealed the poverty and lawlessness rife in much of the south beyond Naples and Campania. The restoration of the monarchy in 1815 had entailed the return of frontiers and customs barriers, with a resultant increase in smuggling of all kinds.

Owing partly to the unemployment caused by a depressed agriculture and the amalgamation of small farms into big ranch-style estates, banditry now resumed a greater significance in rural life than ever, and travellers ventured at their peril through the wilder reaches of Calabria, Puglia and the Abruzzi. The bandits

After Ferdinand's death in 1825, the Kingdom of the Two Sicilies slumbered in a climate of reaction and repression under the rule of his son Francis I and his grandson Ferdinand II. Neither was quite the fool or the ogre the rest of Europe liked to believe them to be, and many ordinary citizens were content with a despotic regime which ensured tranquillity and a semblance of order through press censorship, police informers and severe penalties for any activity remotely hinting at political dissent. Ferdinand II's remark that his realm was "safe between salt water and holy water" (referring to his fellow sovereign, the Pope) reflects a complacency echoed by many of his subjects.

themselves were often romanticised by local communities as Robin Hood figures protecting the poor against rich oppressors. One of them, known as Fra Diavolo, achieved international fame when in 1830 the French composer Daniel Auber made him the subject of an opera.

## Italy united

Whatever the slowness of communications in 19th-century Italy, and despite the Bourbon government's suppression of any kind of political activism, the cause of Italian unity began gathering support among the professional class of doctors, lawyers and civil servants, as well as finding favour with a small number of liberal aristocrats and army officers. It was inevitable that even so conservative and backward a society as that of the Two Sicilies would feel the effects of growing unrest among other Italian states, as the movement towards unification, known to historians as the Risorgimento, shifted from theoretical to practical objectives.

In 1846 the ultra-reactionary Pope Gregory XIII died, and was succeeded by the comparatively young and apparently liberal Pius IX. Many anticipated a dawning of freedom and democracy, with the new pope as Italy's spiritual leader. The momentum of revolution was now unstoppable, and after demonstrations took place in Naples, full-scale revolution broke out in Sicily during February 1848. King Ferdinand, hastily granting a constitution as his father had done, waited on events. His new liberal ministers proved unequal to their task, and it was easy enough for the king to re-establish control by the age-old device of appealing to the *lazzaroni*, the Neapolitan mob of sailors, fisherfolk and beggars, whose support for the Bourbon regime could always be relied upon.

## A haven for reactionaries

After mopping up whatever opposition remained, Ferdinand was able to present his kingdom as a haven for other sovereigns fleeing from their revolutionary subjects, such as Pope Pius IX and Grand Duke Leopold of Tuscany. Even the mildest political dissidents were now condemned to fester in jail, while the Church was persuaded to allow its priests to act as police informers and press censorship was tightened.

Such measures were no worse than those adopted in other European states at the time, but it was a visitor from Britain, a country which did not imprison its liberals and muzzle its newspapers, who turned Ferdinand and his kingdom into headline news. In 1851 the future Prime Minister William Ewart Gladstone, while staying in Naples, made enquiries into the repressive treatment of political prisoners and when he returned to London he published an indignant account of his findings. His pamphlets drew attention to the corruption and injustice which had prevailed in southern Italy and Sicily since the monarchy's restoration. When and whether this same monarchy would fall was more doubtful. An attempt at an uprising in 1857, near Sapri on the Calabrian coast, was crushed by local peasants, but by the time Ferdinand II died in 1859, to be succeeded by his dim, unimaginative son Francis II, events were preparing to reshape Italy for ever. The war breaking out that year between France and Austria was

fought largely in northern Italy, resulting in the creation of an Italian monarchy under King Victor Emmanuel of Piedmont, which other states such as Tuscany and Modena, deposing their sovereign dukes, hastened to join.

## Garibaldi's expedition

While southern Italy remained largely loyal to King Francis II, Sicily welcomed the 1860 expedition of the "liberator" Giuseppe Garibaldi and his "Mille" (Thousand) who freed the island from Bourbon rule. Garibaldi now pushed on into Calabria, his tiny force of 3,000 scattering the defenders of even such larger towns as Reggio. When he entered

**LEFT:** detail of an anonymous painting of an 1848 revolutionary, from Galleria Nazionale, Capodimonte.
**RIGHT:** Francis II, the last foreign regent of Naples.

Naples in triumph on 7 September, the Bourbon garrison turned out to salute him.

King Francis was still able to depend on the support of the large force he had mustered on the Volturno river, between Naples and Rome. He might have won the ensuing two-day battle with Garibaldi's troops, had he not insisted on taking full command of the army, deploying them in a complex pincer movement which broke down almost immediately. The king retreated to the fortress of Gaeta, and his young wife, Maria Adelaide, inspired the stronghold's defenders during a siege carried on for nearly a year, which gave the royal couple a kind of tragic dignity admired even among those most applauding the Bourbons' downfall.

## Birth of the secret societies

The plebiscite by which the territory of the Two Sicilies signified its adherence to the new Kingdom of Italy was a democratic charade, rigged with the help of the Neapolitan secret society known as the Camorra. Like those of the Sicilian Mafia, the Camorra's origins are obscure, but during the late 19th century it emerged as a significant force in local politics, with a developing criminal arm whose influence grew more menacing as the city's urban problems

## GARIBALDI'S MOST FAMOUS WAR WOUND

As the champion of liberty, admired for his courage, leadership and integrity, Giuseppe Garibaldi was a hero for most Italians, but not for Italy's first king, Victor Emmanuel, and his conservative ministers. Jealous of his success in Sicily and the south, and terrified lest his republicanism encouraged a revolt against the monarchy, they sought to exploit his potential as an icon of independence. The king encouraged him to invade the Papal States, but he soon worried that the enterprise would get out of control, and he sent an army into Calabria under General Cialdini to round up the invasion force and arrest Garibaldi. A battle on the slopes of the rugged Aspromonte mountain lasted 10 minutes, since Garibaldi's men had orders not to shoot at their fellow Italians. One of the only casualties was the hero himself, so badly wounded in the leg that it took 15 hours to get him down the mountain to the coast, where Cialdini had him hoisted aboard a gunboat. His foot had swollen so much that the bullet could not be located, and only after three months' examination by 23 surgeons from various countries was he saved from an amputation. Lying on an adjustable invalid bed sent to him by the wife of British Prime Minister Lord Palmerston, Garibaldi became more newsworthy than ever, while Aspromonte, the bandit-haunted Calabrian mountain, gained international fame.

increased. A similar organisation, the 'Ndrangheta, existed in Calabria, and this too gained in power, infiltrating all areas of regional government and economy.

As with the Mafia, both societies first evolved as a means of protecting the rural working class against oppression by feudal landlords and as an alternative to the injustices and incompetence of the Bourbon government. The new Italian kingdom, which lasted until 1946, did little to improve such matters throughout the south, and living standards in many small communities

> ### IDEALLY SPEAKING
>
> "We have created a nation. Now our task is to shape the people."
> — GIUSEPPE GARIBALDI

south after the political unrest that followed Italy's entry into World War I in 1915. The economy benefited from vigorous promotion of areas such as the Bay of Naples, the Costa Amalfitana and the islands of Capri and Ischia as tourist resorts, boosted by a vogue for sunbathing and Mediterranean cruises.

Mussolini's obsessions, however, included the so-called "Battle for Wheat" designed to make Italy self-sufficient in food, and it was the Mezzogiorno which bore the brunt of Fascist agricultural reforms, with the clearance of

remained at more or less the same level on the eve of World War II as they had been at the time of Garibaldi's expedition. For many villagers the only alternative to grinding poverty was emigration to the New World, taking with them the values of family cohesiveness and suspicion of the law which had always lain deeply ingrained in the life of the Mezzogiorno.

Benito Mussolini's seizure of power as Italian Prime Minister in 1922 was hailed by many as a chance to restore order and legality to the

**LEFT:** Garibaldi and his "Mille" (Thousand) land in Sicily to free the island from Bourbon rule.
**ABOVE:** swaggering anti-Camorra vigilantes, 1890.

valuable pastureland, olive groves and orchards to fulfil Il Duce's demands. Fascism could nevertheless count on widespread support from the politically conservative south, where Mussolini's pact with Hitler and his commitment of Italian forces to World War II was greeted with much enthusiasm.

In the weeks before the war, the exodus of foreigners from honeypots such as Capri was compensated for by an influx of Italians. The foreign minister, Count Ciano, packed off his children and his wife Edda, Mussolini's daughter, to Villa Ciano, their island retreat. The move was seen by many as an example to follow. War against Britain and France was declared in September and Italy invaded Greece. The Allies targetted ports and railheads in the south and the surprise air attack on Taranto in November is said to have so impressed the Japanese that they took the idea to Pearl Harbor.

After their success in Africa, the Allies chose Sicily as the landing stage for bringing the war against Hitler back to Europe. In 1943 the Americans landed on the island's west coast, the British and Canadians on the east coast. Troops had meantime landed in Taranto after bombardment

## ALLIED ATTACKS

"I am glad that Naples is having such severe nights. The breed will harden, the war will make of the Neapolitans a Nordic race."
– BENITO MUSSOLINI, July 1943

by the British Navy, and General Alexander later made Churchill a gift of the Union Jack hoisted there – the first Allied flag flown in Europe since Britain's withdrawal from France at Dunkirk.

On the morning of 8 September the German garrison on Capri awoke to see the horizon crowded with men-of-war, and soon the whole Bay of Salerno, was crammed with ships and landing vessels. By the end of the afternoon Italian radio announced the country's unconditional surrender. Four days later Rear Admiral

## TASTE OF VICTORY

The people of Naples were starving by the time the Allies arrived. They had been banned from fishing in the mine-filled bay and the departing Germans were rumoured to have polluted their water supply. Many were reduced to eating barnacles and grass. But when the Allies arrived, they proved perfect hosts, laying on a banquet for the joint forces commander, General Mark Clark, in the splendid Renaissance Palazzo Cuomo. The main course was an ingenious creation: a steak of manatee, a herbivorous sea mammal, from Naples' famous aquarium, cooked in a garlic sauce. It was all that was left. The other exhibits had long been consumed.

Sir Anthony Morse settled himself into Villa Ciano as temporary governor of Capri.

Naples had suffered comparatively little bombardment prior to the Allied landing, but the Germans had blown up a number of key points in the city as they retreated, and the people were on the brink of starvation. For many Allied servicemen, Naples became a symbol of the resilience of the Italian south and its ancient civilisation across the centuries.

## The postwar republic

Such resilience was to be tested in different ways during the late 20th century. The new Italian republic which came into being in 1946 merely succeeded in widening the already con-siderable gap which existed psychologically and economically between the Mezzogiorno and northern Italy.

The nation's substantially corrupt political system, supported by the US as a bastion against communism during the Cold War, encouraged the creation in the south of a con-servative fiefdom ruled by local bosses of the right-wing Christian Democrat Party. A culture of cynicism and apathy was accompanied by the misuse of public funds on a grand scale, the failure to maintain an adequate infrastructure in either urban or rural areas, the spread of

ing. Even so, the south faces major challenges: state neglect and maladministration, endemic corruption, high unemployment and a brain drain as many of the most skilled leave for better eco-nomic prospects in the north. As for illegal immi-gration, the break-up of Yugoslavia in the 1990s brought an influx of refugees, beginning with waves of Kosovan Albanians, and putting huge pressure on the Adriatic ports and the commu-nities of Puglia.

Silvio Berlusconi's flawed administration rep-resented a low point in the fortunes of the south, despite promises that grand infrastructure pro-jects would kick-start the sluggish economy.

violent mafia-related crime, and a general sense that little, after all, had changed since the days of the barons and the Bourbons.

The end of the Cold War also loosened the US grip on Italian politics during the 1990s and a genuinely representative system was allowed to develop. The attitude in certain parts of the south became more optimistic, with signs that even such a deeply rooted resignation as that of the Mezzogiorno was ultimately capable of chang-

Instead, cynics emphasised political corruption in the south, and pointed to the curious fact that in the 2001 general elections every single Sicil-ian seat was won by Berlusconi.

The tables turned in 2006, with the incoming left-leaning administration promising to tackle deep-rooted southern problems. Even so, it may be a Pyrrhic victory for the left, forced to reveal that the good times are over – good times that many in the south have never seen. Even so, the election of a southerner as president has helped restore pride and status to the neglected Mezzo-giorno. Neapolitan-born Giorgio Napolitano has seven years in which to act as a beacon for his cynical southern compatriots.                              ❏

**Left:** the 20th century began with emigration to America from the impoverished south.
**Above:** it ended with conflict in Yugoslavia and the arrival of thousands of Albanian refugees.

# PLEASURE SEEKERS

*"It was all purple wine, all art and song, and nobody a grain the worse. It was fireworks and conversation, civilisation and amenity" – Henry James*

The normally taut prose of Henry James was tinged purple by a surfeit of sun and nostalgia in Sorrento when he wrote the above lines in 1881. The myth of Mediterranean plenty and the blazing vitality of southern life have caused many northern puritans to succumb to dreams of simplicity and flight. Other writers have been intoxicated by the romance of the south, from classical landscapes to the lost civilisation of Pompeii or the imperial palaces that once belonged to Nero, Caligula and Tiberius.

In his 1820 ode, *To Naples*, Percy Bysshe Shelley strikes a bittersweet tone, recording a "Metropolis of a ruined paradise / Long lost, late won, and yet but half regained!" In Pompeii some 20 years later, Frances Trollope, an inveterate traveller, evokes "the well-used curb-stone, against which the ear almost fancies it can catch the grating of a Roman chariot wheel".

## Romantic Grand Tourists

The 18th-century Grand Tourists simplified the south yet were deeply affected by it. Romantic visitors were concerned with experiencing the pathos, transience and futility of existence, a spirit which, in the Victorian era, became transmuted into restlessness and a longing for release from repressive northern climes.

Travel was imbued with lofty aspirations and couched in the language of self-denial. Frances Cobbe criticised her fellow countrywomen for abandoning "the noble strife" of English life for "the lotus-eater life of the south". For repressed northerners, no idle malingering was acceptable, including travel for its own sake, particularly since morals were thought to decline as the climate improved.

The climate prompted northerners to follow the flock, migrating south in autumn and north in spring. The recommended cure for consumption was a spell in southern climes but, as

**LEFT:** visitors being shown Virgil's tomb, detail of a 19th-century painting, Neapolitan School.
**RIGHT:** cartoon of early tourists ascending Vesuvius.

William Chambers noted in 1870, "Fashion, ennui and love of gaiety seem to send quite as many abroad as absolutely bad health." If the exodus to the south began as a whim of the artistic and cultural elite, social climbers and pleasure seekers soon followed. Even if the avowed reasons for travel were classical pil-

grimage and health, southern Italy became an escape from the sterile intellectualism of northern society.

Visitors steeped in classical lore had read Theocritus and Virgil and, uplifted by it all, they scoured Sicily and Campania, in thrall to the romance of ruins. In an atmosphere saturated with classical association, the southern landscape was invested with symbolic power. The biographer James Boswell indulged in the Grand Tour in the 1760s and he gushed over the classical associations of Naples: "Is it possible to conceive a richer scene than the finest bay diversified with islands and bordered by fields where Virgil's Muses charmed the creation, where the renowned of ancient Rome enjoyed the luxury of glorious retreat and the true flow of soul which they valued as much as triumphs?"

The classical ruins appealed to the Romantics' predilection for civilisations in decay. Faced with the panoply of classical culture, however, northerners experienced a sense of cultural inferiority. Norman Douglas, the connoisseur of southern culture, puts it in his inimitable way: "Most of us come to Italy too undiscerning, too reverent, in the pre-coital and pre-humorous stages... too stuffed with Renaissance ideals and Classical lore."

*Unprotected Females in Sicily and Calabria,* published in 1859, concluded that Calabria had no more than "a little peppering of danger to give romance".

But hers was not the general view. The Grand Tour usually went no further than Paestum, and lands beyond remained wild and apparently uncivilised well into the 20th century. Occasional intrepid travellers set off alone. In 1824 Craufurd Tait Ramage, tutor to the sons of the British Consul in Naples, went in search of southern Italy's "ancient remains and modern superstitions". For this purpose, he was "well furnished with capacious pockets, into which I

## Violence, passion and daily life

The Grand Tour represented both an intense exposure to classical heritage and a cultural finishing school. Grand Tourists also went in search of exalted emotions, from moral edification to spiritual enlightenment. Another more secret purpose was to sense the violence of natural forces, sample southern passions and experience the intensity of everyday life. The risks posed by earthquakes, volcanic eruptions and the odd violent encounter with brigands simply added a frisson of excitement to travel.

Women travellers, in particular, enjoyed testing their increasing sense of independence by venturing south. The anonymous authoress of

have stuffed my maps and notebooks: nankeen trousers, a large-brimmed straw hat, white shoes and an umbrella, a most valuable article to protect me from the sun's rays."

A century later, Augustus Hare wrote in *Cities of Southern Italy*: "The vastness and ugliness of the districts to be traversed, the bareness and filth of the inns, the roughness of the natives, the torment of the mosquitoes, the terror of earthquakes, the insecurity of roads from brigands, and the far more serious risk of malaria or typhoid from the bad water, are natural causes which have hitherto frightened strangers away from the south." To this he added one more item to be avoided, the *pizza napoletana*, which he described as "a horrible condiment made of dough baked with garlic, rancid bacon and strong cheese".

It was much safer to look at the classical remains in the shops and galleries around Naples. Priceless Roman statuary was appraised by foreign visitors with the acquisitive gaze of thrifty auctioneers. After a remorseless regime of galleries, churches and ancient ruins, Grand Tourists settled upon Neapolitan coral and cameos, Sicilian mosaics and alabaster replicas of Roman busts, returning home laden

**INDISCRETIONS**

"The wealthy English adulterers are the attraction of the place."
— J. H. NEWMAN, 1833

barren mountains, all thrown together in a most romantic confusion." And in his southern letters, the normally restrained Henry James was not above "the gush and cant" he deplored in his fellow travellers: "I wish I could send you a patch of the blue sea that stretches away to Naples and Capri – a few square feet of the pale purple that covers the gentle-looking flanks of Vesuvius."

The 19th-century Anglo-American elite swiftly succumbed to the enchantments of winter in Naples, but the city had too much

with what Charles Dickens called "an infinite variety of lumber".

The picturesque nature of southern scenery, especially the Bay of Naples, was a distinct source of pleasure for Grand Tourists. The 18th-century Irish philosopher George Berkeley was entranced by Ischia, an island whose praises were sung by Homer and Virgil: "The island is an epitome of the whole earth containing within the compass of 18 miles a wonderful variety of hills, vales, ragged rocks, fruitful plains, and

---

**LEFT:** *Forum at Pompeii* by Lapira (19th century).
**ABOVE:** detail from *View of Naples from Capodimonte* by Lapira. Vesuvius is always in the picture.

character and self-confidence to become an archetypal anglophone colony. According to the contemporary Australian writer Peter Robb, "Naples gave the world ice cream, pizza, *opera buffa* and transvestism as an art form. Naples ravished Virgil, Boccaccio, Stendhal, shocked and disgusted de Sade, Ruskin and Sartre. Naples filled the paintings of the visitor Caravaggio and the operas of Mozart."

However, this picaresque city also had a well-deserved reputation for warmth and wickedness, enhancing its appeal as a canvas for foreign eccentricity, eroticism or elopement.

Goethe, at large in Italy in the 1780s, had his own private sexual agenda in the south but his

*Italian Journeys* contain tamer public pronouncements, including praise of Taormina as "a patch of paradise on earth". At the same time as the German poet was extolling the wonders of Sicily, his compatriots from the Prussian court came to paint picturesque, virtually photographic views.

From the 18th century, pastiches of landscapes were custom-made for the collecting mania of the European aristocracy and appealed to such connoisseurs as the Englishman, William Beckford: "I viewed Vesuvius, rising distinct into the blue ether, with all that world of gardens and casinos which are scattered about the sea, just like a Greek temple, and light, light, light everywhere". This idyll was evoked in *The Story of San Michele*, published in 1929, which became an international bestseller.

## The Vesuvius show

Landscape artists were drawn to the sublime spectacles of Vesuvius or Etna erupting, scenes which naturally appealed to the heightened sensibilities of the Romantics. The volcanoes provoked a mixture of awe and ghoulishness in earlier visitors. In the 1670 edition of *Voyage of Italy*, Richard Lassels records that the guide to Vesuvius "will show

its base". From admiration, it was but a small step to the acquisition of paintings and antiquities, complete with villa and views.

In Capri, the writer Maxim Gorky was at the heart of a Russian revolutionary set who played chess at the Caffè Morgano. A "School of Revolutionary Technique for the scientific preparation of propagandists of Russian Socialism" was set up in 1908 and Lenin paid a visit.

Axel Munthe, the Swedish writer and collector, incorporated the remains of a Roman villa into his eclectic Edwardian museum piece, stuffed with Etruscan and Roman statuary. His romantic vision for Villa San Michele was of a home "open to the sun, wind, and the voice of

you a channel in which from that spewing hill had run a filthy green matter mingled together of brimstone, alum, iron, water, saltpeter and sulphur". In the days of the Grand Tour, the ascent of Vesuvius was first made by mule, but later superseded by cable car, until it was destroyed by the 1944 eruption, an event witnessed by an enthralled Norman Lewis. "The shape of the eruption that obliterated Pompeii reminded Pliny of a pine tree, and he probably stood here at Posillipo across the bay, where I was standing now, and where Nelson and Emma Hamilton stood to view the eruption of their day, and the shape was indeed like that of a many-branching tree".

Henry James witnessed "stricken Ischia", which was just recovering from the earthquake in 1883, but he preferred to focus on the romantic vision of the Bay of Naples: "Sorrento and Vesuvius were over against you; Naples furthest off, melted in the middle of the picture, into shimmering vagueness and innocence."

The discoveries and excavations at Pompeii and Herculaneum encouraged 18th-century foreign visitors to flock to the sites. With classical texts in hand, they sought out the most macabre tableaux to satisfy their morbid

> **TOURIST TRAP**
>
> "American and German tourists are popped systematically into the orifice of the Blue Grotto."
>
> – HENRY JAMES

instinctual humanity of the Italian people. John Steinbeck, visiting Positano in 1953, idealised the natives as "Positano's greatest commodity – characters who have lived in America and come home again to bask in the moral, physical, political and sartorial freedoms which flourish in their birth town."

Harold Acton (1904–94), the Anglo-Italian writer and aesthete, was prone to celebrating southern manhood, including the *lazzaroni*, the street urchins of Naples: "They were children of nature, sturdy, excitable,

curiosity. Samuel Rogers, exploring Pompeii in 1815, felt "a strange and not unpleasing sadness", a sentiment shared by modern travellers. Evelyn Waugh, visiting Palermo's Cappuccini Catacombs in the 1950s, relished the surreal vision of the dead and the "delicious" perfume emanating from the desiccated corpses.

Apart from the classical sites and transcendent landscape, travellers were drawn to the

**FAR LEFT:** on Capri in 1908 Lenin plays chess with Bogdanov while Maxim Gorky looks on.
**LEFT:** Axel Munthe in his Villa San Michele, inspiration for his bestselling book. **ABOVE:** a Capri boy poses for the German artist C.W. Allers in 1890.

apparently cheerful and carefree, proliferating in primitive simplicity, sufficient unto the day, the passing minute walking and sporting on the seashore naked, with no more shame than Adam in his primal innocence, and thanks to the climate, content with little and sleeping under the stars most of the year."

## A synonym for Sodom

But such idealised "primal innocence" was not a feature shared by predatory foreign visitors. Southern Italy has long been a place favourable to foreign and native vices, with all sexual proclivities catered for. On Capri, Tacitus delights in tales of the dissolute Roman emperor Tiberius (*circa* AD 70–140) who had a penchant for "secret orgies, or idle malevolent thoughts". Suetonius also speaks of the Emperor's "goatish" antics: "On retiring to Capri, he made himself a private sporting-house, where sexual extravagances were practised for his secret pleasure".

Describing early 20th-century Sicily, Harold Acton pronounced Taormina "a polite synonym for Sodom". The camp city, founded during a period of Greek decadence, has, like Capri, long been a homosexual haunt. Otto Geleng, the 19th-century landscape artist, was

one of several German aesthetes who promoted Taormina to "the flower of European pederasty". Although married to a Sicilian, Geleng was a believer in the dictum of girls for procreation, boys for pleasure.

As well as participating in nightly orgies, his fellow reveller, Oscar Wilde, helped create kitsch photographic compositions, crowning the languorous peasant boy models with laurels or posing naked but for Pan's pipes.

### Film-star appeal

In the 1940s Taormina was the glamorous haunt of such screen goddesses as Marlene Dietrich, Rita Hayworth and Joan Crawford,

who danced until dawn at the parties of Gaylord Hauser, the Hollywood dietician to the stars. His credo was: "Taormina enchants, seduces, but above all rejuvenates". Over a period of 30 years, Hauser regularly rejuvenated Greta Garbo, the reclusive star, in his villa. (Although the prime secret of rejuvenation seemed to be seduction, a diet of lettuce and cultural pilgrimages were also part of the recipe for eternal youth.) It was after a lengthy stay on Taormina that Garbo decided to abandon cinematic stardom for seclusion.

Truman Capote and Tennessee Williams also indulged their wild-boy reputations in Taormina, before alcohol and drugs wreaked havoc with their writing. By comparison, D. H. Lawrence led a dull, sheltered life on the island, confining himself to writing *Lady Chatterley's Lover*, based on the sexual exploits of his wife Frieda with a Sicilian muleteer.

Peter Robb, a former Naples resident and the author of *Midnight in Sicily*, is briefly captivated by the pastoral idyll of the south: "For a nanosecond I thought I saw now an interior Sicily of poetry and sex, pipes and panic, light and shade that lingered in a few old poems". Then he realised that, like Theocritus, whose 3rd-century BC *Idylls* were ultimately exercises in nostalgia, he too had succumbed to escapist dreams of pastoral simplicity.

In reality, Sicily's Hellenistic golden age also witnessed great atrocities, as did the Sicilian Moorish heyday 1,300 years later. Yet these exiled Arabs, like their Greek predecessors, praised their adoptive homeland in nostalgic poetry, painting Sicily purple with the dreamlike patina of memory. Modern visitors to the south are equally prone to false-memory syndrome, whether on an archaeological "Trail of Tiberius" or on a package tour of "The Picturesque Amalfi Coast".

Since the south is a canvas for the projection of northern passions, it is primarily a playground for the soul and senses. Doubling as a realm of repose and a realm of the senses, it symbolises both innocence and experience, a sunlit holiday and a seductive haven. ❑

**LEFT:** *Palermo*, by Carl Friedrich Heinrich Werner, 1839.
**RIGHT:** *Fishermen Mending Nets in Capri* (detail), by Theodor Leopold, 1892.

# THE SOUTHERN ITALIANS

*A welcoming people with organised crime, a male society which elects women mayors… it's the contradictions that rule in the south*

People who visit Southern Italy expecting to see Godfathers in dark glasses, or bare-footed street urchins, swindlers, wailing widows dressed in black, and other stereotypes, may come away feeling short-changed. Such images of the south, while still evident to a degree, are now often clichés. Visitors can instead expect to see traipsing across a rather chaotic and reckless stage the entire human spectrum, often depicted in powerful primary colours.

Southern Italy is full of cultivated, educated, courageous, scrupulous and genuinely warm and welcoming people. But it is also home to no fewer than four organised crime associations, whose membership programme amounts to a satanic way of life, and which is based on silence and fear. Tourists will remark on the poverty, squalor and air of lawlessness. But they will also note the innumerable signs of wealth. And, as Charles Richards in his book *The New Italians* wryly observed, the urchins still exist in Naples – but now they have shoes.

The truth is that Southern Italy, like its cuisine, is a land of strong contrasts and contradictions. It is a riddle. Everything seems true – and also the contrary.

## Dangerous but dapper

Greater Naples is a dangerous port and urban sprawl with one of the worst levels of juvenile crime in western Europe. But it is also the hub of a former kingdom, it has an aristocracy, and it is the port for the nearby charmed isle of Capri, which remains a popular haven for chic jet-setters. Naples, where innocent passers-by are accidentally killed or wounded by stray bullets fired by teenage Mafia hitmen high on cocaine, boasts Italy's finest tailors. Its manners are elegant, and there is a lively intellectual and theatre tradition. The city is home to the late great dramatist Eduardo De Filippo, the

PRECEDING PAGES: a wedding in Ravello; card players on the streets of Naples.
LEFT: a slow news day on the Amalfi coast.
RIGHT: ice cream seller in Sorrento.

legendary tenor Enrico Caruso, the San Carlo opera house, as well as to the Pizza Margherita. There is an unusually rich and old tradition of popular song, and an impressive local school of contemporary blues-inspired music.

Palermo is the Mafia capital; but it is also the anti-Mafia capital, where housewives defied

the Mafia by the symbolic mass-hanging from their windows and balconies of white sheets. There, the Mob-busting magistrates are protected by cool bodyguards, and have enjoyed the fame of minor pop stars. A centre of intellectual activity, Palermo has some top restaurants and contemporary art galleries, a major opera house (even if it took 23 years to restore), intellectual salons, and a host of small but inspired and dynamic publishing houses. Southern Italy has for years been a hothouse for cultural creativity, producing some of the country's finest authors.

Italy's highest and lowest achievements both stem from the south. Such contrasts and contradictions run deep through southern society where the politics are both progressive and reactionary. Local food is a celebration of sweet and sour experiences. In Palermo, Capri or Bari, you are as likely to be greeted by a cornucopia of culinary aromas wafting up from a kitchen as you are to be hit with the stench of foul drains. The ravages of 1960s Mafia building speculation in Palermo are still all too painfully evident, but appear side by side with the preserved and newly restored palaces of a decayed nobility.

> **GHOST TOWN**
>
> In Naples, an entire new town was recently found to exist without planning permission.

Mingling among fine buildings and dramatically beautiful countryside, almost everywhere in the south the visitor will find houses in an often indescribably ugly, unfinished state, unrendered, and with steel cables poking up out of the concrete pillars, as if these were poised to have another floor added to them tomorrow. The reason is not only *abusivismo*, or illegal housing, which is a widespread phenomenon. Another explanation offered by locals – although it sounds a little too innocent – is that each floor is added for each new child in a family, as a way of looking after the individuals of a brood, by providing them with a nest egg for when they get older. The truth, however, is that, as often as not, tomorrow never seems to come, meaning that many of the houses are in a permanent state of construction.

In the south, signs of religion and intellectuality abound, but are often juxtaposed with those of a cultural desert, and the fetid subculture of the criminal world. When Piero Aglieri, a fast-rising Sicilian Mafia boss, was flushed out of his lair on the edge of Palermo and arrested in 1997, police found a wealth of religious objects inside. There were indications that he had had private Mass celebrated in his hideout. A priest had become his confessor in hiding, and as a result briefly faced charges after Aglieri's arrest. As in the hideouts of several bosses of the Naples Camorra, copies of great works of literature were on the shelves, together with a much-used copy of the Bible.

## Fear of emasculation

In the north, the well-to-do tend to take an active role in society. In the south, they will often have no part in it at all. They are two separate societies. In the south, men still rule the roost, and can often be insanely jealous of their wives, and harbour old-fashioned and potentially dangerous attitudes. Often these are a barrier to women's independence, and the tension between the two viewpoints is a common cause of violence and even tragedy in the home.

Stories of men shooting their wives and children and then themselves for a variety of domestic and personal reasons provide a staple diet for newspapers. The underlying message is often one of emasculation in the face of creeping social change.

But, by the same token, the seaside town of Cefalù, a short distance from Palermo, is virtually run by women, beginning with the mayor and the police chief, and including the unemployment office, education, and the local entertainment industry. In San Giuseppe Jato – considered, along with the nearby town of Corleone, the historic centre of the Sicilian Mafia, and where the age-old code of silence, or *omertà*, continues to reign supreme – the local council is run by an inspired, left-wing woman mayor. But in another neighbouring town, Monreale, the local clergy has been investigated for rubbing shoulders with and even harbouring the *crème de la crème* of the Mafia.

The friendly and welcoming nature of the people of the south is a commonly overlooked trait. But it strongly contrasts with the frequent blood-letting of organised crime.

On the face of it, however, there may be little separating southerners from people living in any big city around the world. Stereotypical attitudes to sex, love and religion rarely now apply. Southern Italian children will now dress much the same as yours. And they will listen to more or less the same music, watch the same television shows, and suffer from many of the same problems and fears. Young people in the south, just as in the north, can now be

towns, and the countryside, it is the old culture that remains dominant.

## The Mob is not what it was

While the Mafia has a ubiquitous presence, many locals treat it as if it didn't exist. This tendency to ignore the phenomenon is, however, truer of the areas of Campania, Puglia and Calabria, where the Mafia has a less pyramidal and hence less obvious structure. But in Sicily, where the Mafia is more deeply embedded in the culture, and where the Mafia outrages of 1992–93 triggered a remarkable outcry, the phrase "anti-Mafia" is resonant in school class-

seen kissing in the street, and in many other ways are much more modern than a newcomer might expect.

But here, too, there are the inevitable contrasts. People in Palermo, as in London or New York, will live together without being married. But at the same time, they will also be driven by a culture and a set of rules which seem totally ancient. In the south, the rich and poor still often have almost as much chance of blending together as they might be expected to do in India. And in small villages and

rooms and civic functions. At the same time, some people shake their heads, and lament at the way the Mafia is "no longer what it was". The old Mafia was full of honourable men. Now it kills children and women.

Still another contradiction is that despite the south's traditional poverty and joblessness – unemployment is roughly 25 percent, or twice the national average – extreme poverty is rarely evident on the scale expected. The reason is that parents tend to help their children in the south more than elsewhere. For this reason, it's hard to find a single, thirty-something person who doesn't live at home. Without overheads, the southern youth thus

**LEFT:** tending an olive tree in late autumn.
**ABOVE:** hunters on Capri.

has an unexpectedly high buying power. This, and the sometimes superficial aspect of modern southern society, help to account for the high percentage of luxury cars driven by people whom we are told are out of work.

Reggio Calabria, ostensibly a dusty, rather broken town for a major city, is said to have the highest percentage of mobile phones in Italy. Many young people do in any case have some kind of work, but it is not declared, so that officially unemployment is high. Southern families substitute the State, making up for

the lack of a job, money and accommodation. It is a means of survival and, like the way of finding work in the south when technically there is none to be had, part of the philosophy which Neapolitans have developed into an art – *l'arte di arrangiarsi*, or the art of making do.

Continuing the southern tradition for education and intellectual creativity – much of Italian literature has its roots in the south – many young people get degrees compared to elsewhere in Italy, since there is more drive to get work. But the culture also has a tendency to lean towards the controversial, the detached, and the levantine.

> **STATELESS**
>
> One has the sensation that something is missing here. It is the lack of prescence of the State.

One of the most noticeable things about Southern Italy is that there one has the sensation that something is missing. It is not always easy to pin down what it is. It is the State. Throughout the south, there is a glaring lack of landmarks of civilisation as we know it, which traditionally serve to soothe and allay the fears of the newcomer. Schools, police stations, traffic wardens, sports fields, libraries, pedestrian crossings, and many other institutional signs, are all in short supply in the south. Indications of social tissue are little evident.

Filling the void, there is sometimes an uneasy sense of emptiness that may feel oppressive to the unaccustomed outsider. It is easy to confuse this sensation with the presence, lurking in the shadows, of organised criminals, and to mistake everyone who is swarthy and wearing sunglasses as threatening.

The lack of an identifiable presence of the State provides the fertile soil upon which the Mafia most feeds, apart from unemployment. The Mafia is many things, but it is also the local response – run riot – to the State's weakness. In Catania, Naples, and elsewhere, the Mafia finds it easy to engage the services of unemployed young people, who are prepared to commit serious crimes – and even murder – for the price of a second-hand moped.

## A life without stress

However, this lack of significant State activity often provides an alibi, and many young people who arguably could go north in search of work simply don't. Instead, they prefer to continue the unstressed lifestyle of a provincial existence, which, apart from friends and a favoured climate, offers little to a society.

For all its modern veneer, the south continues to give the impression, even to aware southerners, of a place where people prefer to take it easy, and to be helped, and to be waiting for a handout. There is little entrepreneurial spirit, although that is also changing. But is it changing enough? In Italy, there have been signs that the economy of the south is finally beginning to pick up. But at the same time, the bad news is that the north-south economic divide in the country is widening as never before. ❏

**LEFT:** a countryman from Puglia.

# A Woman from Reggio Calabria

Laura is in her mid-20s and comes from Reggio Calabria. She now works in Rome, where she can look back with some objectivity on her formative years in the provincial capital of the south.

Life in her home town was, she says, surprisingly pleasant, despite the dust, crime levels, lack of presence of the State, and the vertiginous unemployment figures, which show that almost two out of three young adults in the area is without work. In Reggio, a place that comes to life in summer, everyone seems to know each other, though the population is now approaching 2 million.

There are a number of film festivals and the night spots are bright. Even the fishermen's caves of the nearby town of Scilla are being turned into nightclubs, discos and fashionable cafés. Many families have two houses. Laura's family have three. Young adults living at home – Laura can think of no one who does not – once upon a time used to make love in their parents' cars. Now they do so in their summer houses. When Laura was in Reggio, she was hardly ever at home, although she tried to be there for lunch, or, better still, to have dinner if she was going to go out to a discotheque.

Like foreigners, she, too, says she would turn and stare if confronted by the spectacle of a black-clad woman carrying a bundle on her head – once an all too common sight in the south. Such sights can still be seen in the smaller villages, including Bova Marina and Bova Alta, where street signs continue to bear names in both Greek and Italian. Parts of Calabria are among the most remote in all of Italy but the women who carry on these traditions are mostly elderly, and thus such traditions seem unlikely to survive long into the 21st century. In the large towns, the process of modernisation has already set into the social fabric.

There was a time when Laura's grandmother spent all her mornings slaving over a hot stove. Now her mother, who is also a housewife, spends just 10 minutes doing the same thing. As a result of the influence of her children, she relies on pressure cookers and microwaves to produce food more quickly, though she continues to pride herself on using fresh produce. The difference is

**RIGHT:** young women in the south. Those who go north may miss the comforts and support of home.

that it no longer comes from daily trips to the market, but rather from once- or twice-weekly visits to the supermarket.

Like many fellow southern Italians who have gone north, Laura is highly motivated, which is why she has given up her easy life in order to get ahead on her own. In Rome, she misses the life that she had down South, where her doting mother saw to it that she never had to pay for a thing, or iron a stitch of her own clothing, let alone wash it.

Her mother still goes to church, but her father does not, while her father's brother is a Communist and an atheist. Laura does not go to church, but others in her age group still do, and on Sundays the

churches in and around Reggio continue to be full. Laura's father is now retired after working all his life as a state employee. Her sister, however, is a high-powered economist, with a top job in the capital. Laura is herself a degree holder in political science, and she speaks both English and French.

Reggio has a Serie A football team, a similarly well-rated basketball team, and also a volleyball team. All this brings people in from outside, and helps them to circulate more.

Southern men, Laura says, are more chivalrous, and southern people in general are warmer and more generous than people who are from the north. And never, ever, would anyone think of "going Dutch" in a bar. ❑

# A HANDY GUIDE TO LOCAL GESTURES

*Rituals, recriminations and rackets are all signalled by gestures seen in everyday life, as are displays of affection and betrayal*

Beggars rapping their chins constantly with their right hands is a sign for hunger; emptying an imaginary waistcoat pocket conveys to a market seller that one considers the price too dear; supporting an elbow with one hand, while making a limp-wristed movement with the other indicates a simpleton. Centuries of struggle have versed southern Italians in the art of survival, so it is hardly surprising that many gestures are bound up in a subtly subversive system of respect and honour. The language is entirely democratic: coercive or ingratiating gestures are as likely to be made by market traders or *mafiosi*, black-clad widows or chic lawyers flashing gold accessories.

## MOTHERS AND MANHOOD

Only in the south can the simple act of making coffee become charged with hidden pleas, taunts, and complicity, depending on accompanying looks and gestures. The hand-kissing of powerful men still exists, a legacy of *clientelismo*, an ingrained Bourbon culture of self-serving friendships and protection. Gestures concerned with gullibility and cunning are commonplace. Manhood and mothers are sacred, and a foolhardy gesture of abuse can result in a fight. Touching of testicles is the superstitious male response to any impending doom. A two-fingered salute refers to a cuckold, but the gesture has a broader meaning: the fingers pointing downwards invoke bad luck, while making this gesture at someone else brings them bad luck.

"Do you see what I mean or have I got to spell it out for you?" In this conversational device fingers are tight together, stabbing the air, to make the point.

△ THAT'S LIFE

"*La vita è così* – that's life – What do you expect? All politicians are thieves and liars." Hands are spread apart in a shrug of world-weary resignation.

▷ MAFIA THREAT

At a Sicilian Mafia trial, a *mafiosi* defendant warns the Supergrasses: "*Tieni la bocca chiusa*" – Keep your mouth shut or I'll cut your tongue out.

◁ HANDS IN WAITING

The parishioners do the talking. While the priest listens, his hands remain silent, preparing their response.

## MANNERS ON THE ROAD

Hand signals, particularly rude ones, are an integral part of the southern Italian's vocabulary. Street signals, however, are there merely to be considered, and a queue at traffic lights may only encourage motorists and moped riders to mount the pavement. Streetwise kids, known as *muschilli*, "little flies", thanks to their moped skills, add to the chaos as they speed about their nefarious business.

Blaring horns serve to signal frustration or fury, appreciation or celebration, rather than to point out an illegal manoeuvre. If you're driving too slowly on a quiet country road, expect to be shaken by a blaring horn and a car right on your tail. Driving slowly is a sign of a lack of virility and prowess, just as the wearing of seatbelts may be considered a slur on the driver's skills. It marks the driver out as a timorous foreigner or northern Italian, equally worthy of derision.

◁ **QUESTION TIME**
"*Che cavolo vuoi?* – What on earth do you want? And what am I expected to do about the water shortage?" An open palm, raised and lowered, comes with the questions.

▷ **I TELL YOU THIS**
"So then my granddaughter decided to get married." Daily conversation, even for the most sedentary, requires the exertion of hand movements.

◁ **JUST KIDDING**
A *scugnizzo*, a street kid, cheekily displays the *cornuto*, an aggressive two-fingered salute and a symbol of sexual infidelity.

▷ **ON THE TOWN**
"*La vita è bella* – Life's great. Let's hit the town before my shades steam up." Urban life is intensely visual and lived out on the streets.

# MANY MAFIA

*Each region has its organised crime, but the crackdown on Cosa Nostra*

*has met with some success. However, other groups are taking its place*

In Italy the word "mafia" can mean either the Sicilian organisation, which is sometimes known as Cosa Nostra (literally, "Our Thing"); or the other crime groups of the south – namely the Camorra of Naples; the unpronounceable and fearful sounding 'Ndrangheta of Calabria; or the newer upstart relative, Sacra Corona Unita, or Holy United Crown, of the Puglia region.

Yet, while the various mafias are distinguishable by their geographical origin, they are not by any means confined to them. All are represented elsewhere in Italy, largely by southerners who have emigrated north. Milan is a favourite colony, but other places that are becoming popular may come as more of a surprise – Tuscany, for example.

## A state of mind

But what the Mafia really is, most of all, is a state of mind. Its influence can be experienced throughout Italy – especially in the way that real or expected threats can still succeed in dissuading a person from going to the police – but it is prevalent in the south. Sicilians often surprise outsiders by freely admitting that people on their island "all have a little something of the mafia" in them.

While hard to describe, such a state of mind can be unmistakeable when expressed in everyday life. Several years ago, a few journalists visited Corleone, the hillside "capital" of the dominant Corleone Mafia family, which inspired Mario Puzo in his book *The Godfather* to name his central character Don Vito Corleone. As the reporters, one of whom was an attractive blonde, strolled into a crowded bar filled with ancient men, the animated buzz of conversation died, and every eye became trained on the newcomers. After consuming their drinks, the visitors went to pay, only to be

solemnly informed by a barman with downcast eyes: "The bill's been settled." He did not say by whom. Nor did any of the dozens of staring people in the bar, in which a deadly silence reigned.

It would be unfair to label such an act as mafioso; and the likelihood that there was a member of the mob in the bar at the time was

slim. But the key elements of the Mafia were all there: secrecy, silence, complicity if not conspiracy, and a dark sort of gallantry, where the subliminal message was about power. Imagine the same scene, but where the gesture is negative, or violent, and it is easy to understand how, as a local citizen, you might find this hard to report to the police.

The main distinction between Cosa Nostra and the other mafias, which are dominated by it, is that the first is the only one that is a real organisation, with rules, even though these are now fast eroding.

While Sicily's Mafia is based on a pyramid of power, with a ruling commission, its cousin

**LEFT:** the wreckage of the bomb that killed Judge Paolo Borsellino in Palermo, 1992.
**RIGHT:** police standing in front of anti-mafia banners at the Piazza Palermo.

the Camorra is a more informal collection of families, and its rules are much less cast in stone. The 'Ndrangheta is a stricter organisation than the Camorra, and horizontally arranged. It is more difficult for the police to penetrate than Cosa Nostra, since it is broken up into tiny, loosely strung together and apparently autonomous units, although bosses do meet from time to time for summits. The Sicilian Mafia itself used to have this form of organisation, and is now returning to it in a bid to survive attacks on it by the state.

Such changes mean that, out of fear of members turning state's evidence, bosses no longer

## Evidence of an organisation

Until the 1990s, many people in Italy, including even some politicians, claimed that the Mafia did not exist as an organisation at all. By demonstrating how the members of the Commission took collegiate decisions, the late Tommaso Buscetta, the first important Mafioso to turn state's evidence, helped judges to establish for the first time that the Mafia did exist as an organisation after all, in which individual decision-making members could be held to be jointly and severally liable for crimes they did not actually commit.

But while the old Mafia mentality has long

discuss business in the presence of *mafiosi* of lesser rank – for example, their drivers. Total trust is now confined to relatives or friends of equal standing. Ironically, however, as the State for years concentrated its efforts on the Mafia, its rougher cousin the 'Ndrangheta has profited and grown, and now represents an arguably much bigger threat than even Cosa Nostra. By contrast, the Sicilian Mafia has merely become leaner and meaner by eschewing high-profile violence in favour of racketeering, politicking for public contracts, recycling of toxic waste, money laundering and investment in legitimate businesses, particularly in health care.

existed, its current expression as an indiscriminately violent organisation in Sicily is relatively new. To understand, one must delve into the "industrial revolution" of Sicilian crime, the postwar transition from an organisation that was once linked to the land, into one that got rich from drugs and urban property speculation.

Until the mid 1970s, the Sicilian Mafia had been much as it always had been: a rough, rural, shadowy club. It is said to have had its roots in secret brotherhoods that were first pledged to honour, and to defend against corruption, foreign oppression, and feudal misdeeds typical of Bourbon misrule. Eventually becoming anti-government in nature, it was they who provided men, arms and money to Garibaldi and his Thousand. The sects were otherwise mainly connected to the land.

In World War II, it was the Mafia that ensured that the Allied troops were able to invade Sicily almost without a shot being fired, mainly through the good offices of the American gangster Lucky Luciano. He later stayed on in the old country and introduced heroin refining to Naples, a change that would have a profound effect on both the organisation and Italy.

**BACK TO SCHOOL**

Wary of electronic eavesdropping, Mafia communication now recalls the classroom: notes on scraps of paper known as *pizzini* are delivered only by trusted helpers.

into a cold-blooded organisation bent on power and profit gained through the lucrative new heroin trade, which systematically began to wipe out its opponents.

However, the Mafia at the peak of an earlier clan war in 1963 had already suffered a crisis for much the same reason, when Salvatore Greco, the then Godfather, unexpectedly stood down, dissolved the Commission or board of governors of the Mafia, and went to live abroad.

According to Tommaso Buscetta, what made

Back in Sicily after the war, local Godfathers were thanked by the Allies for their work, by being appointed mayors of no fewer than 95 towns. But the island-based organisation remained rural until the mid-1970s, when tobacco smuggling based in Palermo developed into the trafficking of drugs, and the Mafia hardened its ties with Rome.

In fact, it was the bloody rise in Palermo of the Corleonesi – a family from the town of Corleone – in the late 1970s and early 1980s which radically altered the face of the Mafia, turning it

**Left:** Camorra victim in the streets of Naples, 1890.
**Above:** Mafia suspects arrive in court, Palermo.

Greco throw in the towel "was the realisation that the Mafia was abandoning its traditional principles, in order to transform itself into a criminal organisation."

The cause of the crisis was Luciano Liggio, a young peasant and "lieutenant" in the Corleone clan. He murdered a country doctor called Michele Navarra in 1958 without referring the matter to the Commission. The murder opened the way for Liggio to mount an attack to gain supremacy of the port, market and city of Palermo. After Liggio's arrest in Milan in 1964, his two "lieutenants", Bernardo Provenzano and Salvatore "Toto" Riina, took up the reins of the family, which had yet to rise to supremacy within the Mafia. Soon after, Riina entered into a triumvirate with two other Godfathers, who were suddenly arrested.

In 1971, with the other two Godfathers in jail, and Liggio again in Palermo and on the run, the Corleonesi killed Pietro Scalgione, a magistrate, and his driver – the first time in Italy that a magistrate had been killed. Riina and Liggio were suspected of having personally taken part in the murder, the motive of which was to punish Scalgione for sending a rival family of the Corleonesi to trial.

The Corleone war of Mafia supremacy followed Liggio's arrest in 1974. It is said to have

left 1,000 dead and peaked in the 1980s with the murder of dozens of "illustrious corpses" of magistrates, police chiefs and local politicians. In 1992–93, the situation deteriorated along with the organisation, when it began to wage war on the Italian state.

"The cause of the wellbeing of most members of Cosa Nostra is simple," Stefano Bontate, an old-fashioned Godfather who died of unnatural causes, confided to Tommaso Buscetta when the two were in jail. "The root of all the new wealth is trafficking in drugs. But it will be Cosa Nostra's downfall."

The reason for dropping tobacco smuggling for that of heroin in 1978 was that there had

just been an unprecedented state crackdown on the former. By the early 1980s, Sicily supplied a third of the entire US market. "With the sale of drugs, all of the rules of behaviour of Cosa Nostra were re-opened for discussion." Fabrizio Calvi, an author of a key book on the inner workings of the Mafia, wrote: "the division of labour changed, and for the first time, everyone in the Mafia could now deal in what and with whom they liked, even with people outside the organisation."

## State's witnesses

Thanks to *pentiti*, or mafiosi who have turned state's witness in trials and investigations, many of the key figures of the organisation have been jailed. The trend began in 1984 when Tommaso Buscetta revealed to investigators how the old families of Palermo had gone into drugs. A major roundup of criminals ensued, followed by a "maxi-trial" in Palermo in 1986, when almost 500 mafiosi were put in the dock.

The life imprisonment of a number of people at the top of the organisation showed for the first time that the Mafia not only existed, but could be dealt a severe blow. The supreme court confirmation in 1991 of 19 life sentences rubber-stamped this, but soon triggered a complex series of events that included the spectacular murder of the anti-Mafia magistrate Giovanni Falcone and Judge Paolo Borsellino, and the detonation of bombs in Florence, Rome and Milan, which appeared to have political as well as Mafia overtones. The overriding symbol of such collusion between Mafia and the state, although he was acquitted at the end of a huge first trial in Palermo, was Giulio Andreotti, Italy's seven-times former prime minister and leading light of the once dominant (and Mafia-tainted) Christian Democrats.

## Turncoats turn tail

Although Andreotti was twice acquitted of collusion (on appeal), due to lack of evidence, the judges concluded that he had known members of the Mafia. They also gave credence to evidence of vote-rigging, which key "turncoats" claimed was central to both sides.

The trying of Andreotti was popularly interpreted as the high point of a revolution in Italy, since for decades the so-called "prince of darkness" had stood for a corrupt system of power, in which Rome was seen to have handed over economic aid earmarked for the south to organised criminals, in return for votes. However, a strong public reaction, which began with an outcry over the 1992 murder of the judges Falcone and Borsellino and a successive wave of Mafia violence outside Sicily, has now largely subsided.

**'NDRANGHETA HIDEOUT**

In 2004, during Italy's biggest anti-Mafia operation for a decade, the Calabrian Mafia were discovered to have built an underground village deep in the Aspromonte mountains.

The rush of mafiosi willing to abandon the Mob and turn state's evidence has now dangerously slowed, and the institution of *"pentiti"* has been undermined by a smear campaign conducted by the Mafia itself.

While it is tempting to draw the conclusion that the war against the Mafia has been lost, those in the front line insist that some key ground has been won. There have been tentative victories for public probity, helped by anti-Mafia legislation aimed at breaking the link between organised crime and politicians.

Recent legislation has paved the way for the confiscation of the Godfathers' assets and the re-assignment of land to civic use. The town of Corleone, in particular, seemed to forge a new start, symbolised by the provocative "Mafia Museum", a research centre dedicated to the study of organised crime.

But the Mafia is far from being a museum piece: 2004 saw bloody Camorra turf wars in Naples and heavy police reinforcements, though this alone cannot solve the poverty and gangster culture feeding organised crime. The state is cracking down nationally and sweeping arrests have been made, including that of 'Ndrangheta boss Giuseppe Morabito. Even so, in Locri, Calabria, the vice-president of the region was gunned down in 2005, representing the most blatant Mafia murder since the assassination of magistrates Falcone and Borsellino. Widespread public revulsion was the only solace to be had from the affair, with anti-Mafia protests in Calabria continuing.

Whether by sheer chance or shameless symbolism, the state's greatest recent coup coincided with the results of the Italian general elections. In 2006, Bernardo Provenzano, Cosa

Nostra's ageing *capo di tutti capi* was finally captured, after being discovered living close to his family home in Corleone. (His hitherto unimpeachable wife accidentally revealed his whereabouts, despite being a model Mafia wife in every other respect, both money laundering and running a real laundry, while barely leaving the house except to visit her lawyers).

Yet within the Sicilian Mafia, a power struggle is predicted, which will determine whether the crime syndicate changes tack and reverts

to violence, or maintains its carefully cultivated low profile. Either way, while Provenzano's newly released henchmen are vying to fill the power vacuum, protection rackets continue to flourish.

Nevertheless, there are signs of hope in such initiatives as the Addiopizzo association, which numbers over 7,000 consumers who agree only to shop at places that don't pay *pizzo*, protection money. As Leoluca Orlando, former Mayor of Palermo, says: "The fight against the Mafia is like a cart with two wheels – law enforcement and civic education; if they don't both turn at the same speed, the cart goes round in circles." ❏

**LEFT:** Marlon Brando in *The Godfather*, a romanticised Hollywood movie about the Mafia, made in 1972.
**RIGHT:** Bernardo Provenzano, the last senior figure in Cosa Nostra still at liberty, is arrested.

# THE ECONOMY

*The precarious southern economy has some distinctive characteristics,
such as "cathedrals in the desert" and protection rackets*

The south is characterised by glaring contradictions, and nowhere more so than in Naples and Sicily, where economic data are as reliable as eruption patterns on Mount Etna. Naples itself feels vibrant and creative, as proved by its new reputation as one of Italy's capitals of contemporary art. Yet a provocative poster for the city's 2006 mayoral campaign highlights the problems behind the scenes: "Our mayor should work here" runs the slogan, showing the mayoral throne in the middle of rubbish dumps, chaotic traffic and squalid slums. Naples was once dubbed "the most dangerous city in Italy"; the city responded by introducing community policing and extra officers to police the main tourist areas. Nowadays, occasional pickpocketing aside, most visitors feel safe yet exhilarated in the city, with Neapolitan warmth swiftly dispelling any fears.

Yet mystery surrounds how many of these warm-hearted citizens are actually contributing to the economy. The southern Italian economy must surely rank as one of the wonders of the modern world. Officially, an astonishing 24 percent of people there are unemployed, a figure that often reaches 50 percent among the young. Yet in 1997 the local GDP overtook the national average while the north-south divide was said to be widening. Much of the explanation lies in the fact that the south's huge submerged economy took off then, exacerbated by the lack of any sense of national citizenship, and allied to a mistrust of officialdom, illegal immigration and crime, all prevalent in a part of · the world dominated by the Mafia.

If Italy's black economy can be held by the World Bank to account for 27 percent of the national economy, then imagine what it must represent in the south, where entirely clandestine companies abound, despite being considered serious producers. Even companies that toe the line by being registered often evade tax, or dodge paying employees' contributions.

**LEFT:** the industrial port of Salerno.
**RIGHT:** street sellers in Naples.

## Just getting by

The south's black economy flourishes, especially in areas where people are given work to do at home and particularly in the province of Naples, which has a long tradition of handcrafted products, and where *arrangiarsi* ("getting by") is considered an art. The region has as

high a population density as Hong Kong, and the average earnings are the same as a standard state employee's in Milan, despite the unemployment statistics.

Local examples of such a contradictory wellbeing are in no way as isolated as one might think. Rather, they are representative of an alternative system for conducting business. In the greater Naples province, especially the northeast, and in Calabria, there are whole networks of such commerce.

Large yet illegal companies producing vast quantities of shoes, clothes or toys frequently thrive as a result of farming out work to people outside, a common tax-avoidance ruse.

There are now swathes of the south where the bosses of these firms bosses deal with buyers from the north, who establish a fixed standard of quality and price, as with any legitimate business. Each stage in the manufacturing process is contracted out, with costs well defined, even though the label may be unknown, or a fake of a well-known brand.

This applies to the whole province of Naples, where between a fifth and a third of the economy is submerged – hence, in part at least, the unregulated growth of the southern economy, which is nonetheless suffering from Chinese competition. (Ironically, the only

## Cathedrals in the desert

The above are the scant results of the planning that went on in the 1960s, and are the "noble relations" of the "cathedrals in the desert", a perfect term used to describe white elephants which could once be found all over the south, as obscenely large amounts of money were indiscriminately poured in.

The "desert cathedral" of all time was surely Gioia Tauro, a huge port completed at the end of the 1970s with public funding, but which became operational only in 1994 thanks to the enterprise of a Genoese entrepreneur. It has now become the largest transshipment port in

clothing suppliers who can undercut the Mafia are Chinese, who now run illegal factories and warehouses near Naples.) By stark contrast, the signs of industry in the lower half of Italy are desperately few. In Melfi, Basilicata, where Fiat makes its Punto and Lancia cars, the impressively high-tech plant is ringed liked a medieval fort with the factories and warehouses of the suppliers of the components.

In downtrodden Gela, Sicily, a petrochemical complex refines the small quantities of oil that the island produces, but is in part converted into a desalination plant. Other complexes exist in Taranto, in Puglia, and in the Campania region around Naples.

the Mediterranean, and, after Rotterdam, the second largest in Europe.

Its new lease of life as a container port is ideal; the lack of any local infrastructure is of little importance, since its business merely comes and goes. The local railway is pitifully poor – but who cares? The same applies to the Autostrada del Sole, the main motorway artery running down the boot of Italy, which, while passing the port, is always hopelessly overcrowded. But Gioia Tauro has little need of it. The downside of such splendid isolation is that the creeping tentacles of the Mafia, or 'Ndrangheta as the local organisation in Calabria is called, have stretched out and snatched many port services. As a result, Gioia Tauro has become a vital employer for almost every Mafia family in this part of Calabria.

However much its economy warms up, and no matter how many firms may be lured to the area with tax incentives, the glaring lack of infrastructure in the south will always seriously hamper its growth. During Italy's postwar boom years, funding was indiscriminately poured into the south, but the gravy train has since come to a halt. The lack of public investment has taken its toll and

### FAMILY BUSINESS

Gioio Tauro, Europe's second largest port, has become a vital employer for nearly every Mafia family in Calabria.

Similarly, despite over half a century of development policies, the "energy deficit" is so bad in some places in the south that it is almost impossible to run factories. Apart from having to spend large amounts of money to transport raw materials from the north, and often factoring in *pizzo*, or protection money to the Mafia (most firms find it advisable to pay up), producers in the south also have to invest in "stabilisers" in order to cope with the sporadic, fluctuating electricity levels.

strangles the south, smothering southern initiative. The sad truth is that while money once poured into the south in torrents – only to be wasted through negligence or political bribes – no one thought of providing aqueducts where they were badly needed. As a result, water continues to be rationed across the lower half of Italy, just as in times of war. Running businesses with such a sporadic supply is difficult, to say the least.

**LEFT:** Gioia Tauro, the largest transshipment port in the Mediterranean, is exploited by the 'Ndrangheta.
**ABOVE:** railway in Puglia. Road and rail networks remain underfunded.

## Couch economy

From the start of the 1990s, however, pockets of the south have seen traditions strengthened, often impressively, with the creation of *poli creativi*, "creative poles", industrial zones or sciences parks. The best-known is "*polo divani*", the "Sofa Valley" – of the Altamura-Matera area straddling Puglia and Basilicata.

"Sofa Valley" is dominated by a company called Natuzzi, the world leader in the sofa business and one of the few southern Italian companies quoted on the New York Stock Exchange. The firm has suffered from international competition and falling demand recently but is essentially sound. Altamura has other international giants in the field while, near Naples, another thriving "valley" specialises in the manufacture of fibre optics.

Sardinia spawned its own international success story with the creation of Tiscali, one of the world's largest internet companies, now merged as Tiscali-World Online. The island, whose main industry used to be kidnapping, has become a centre of the world service-provider industry. Not that the south dare rest on its laurels. As respected Sardinian footballer Gianfranco Zola says, "We are far from the cen-

### SOFA VALLEY
Natuzzi, quoted on the New York Stock exchange, dominates the world's sofa business.

tres of power and we have been penalised for that. Life isn't easy here as there are no big industries, but we want to prove we are capable of great things."

However, organised crime, which is a redistributor rather than a producer of resources, and which is rumoured to have disposed of its enemies in the cement pylons of motorways and others that prop up the "cathedrals in the desert", has developed its own answer to the *polo creativo* – drug trafficking. In Calabria and Campania, legions of young people seem to hang around, as befits a place where almost one in three is technically out of work.

But every so often, such a youth may take a package to Milan by car, and returns at the wheel of a much bigger car. He is today's answer to the *"casalinghe di Palermo"*, the housewives of Palermo, who in the 1970s were flown as mules to New York with packets of heroin secreted all over them. In the US, they were treated like queens, and on their return to Palermo were given a new kitchen by the local Mafia boss.

The Mafia helps to buoy up the economy in Caserta, near Naples, where the Camorra reigns, and can undercut competitors by 90 percent.

## Ecological time bomb

The transformation of the area from a rural economy to one based on the production of building materials, and then construction, meant that the holes that were dug in the area to extract the sand could now be refilled with toxic waste, now largely the preserve of the so-called eco-mafia.

Toxic waste is a new threat, ranging from asbestos and battery acid to chemical sludge and nuclear waste. Throughout Italy, tougher legislation demanding the proper treatment, disposal and labelling of waste has inadvertently spawned a lucrative illlicit trade. Instead of being disposed of properly in accordance with the law – a costly procedure – shipments of toxic waste are transported from north to south and dumped into the holes in Calabria or Sicily, or even burnt openly on the lower slopes of Mount Vesuvius, near Naples.

The obvious ecological consequences of such a foul practice in an area like Naples province, where half of the entire population of the south resides, would never bother the organised criminal or, for that matter, the average southerner. For the civic sense which drives his society is dangerously backward. And this despite the proven health hazards: toxic-waste dumping and toxic pollutants are blamed for the four-fold increase in cancer in the area in recent years. As for food production, farmers in the Caserta area fear that their crops will become contaminated.

Yet signs of optimism can be seen in a recent backlash against the south's treatment as a nuclear dumping ground. In 2003, the whole of Matera province went on strike, blocking roads and railways, in protest against plans to bury nuclear waste in Basilicata, forcing the government into an embarrassing about-turn. Fuelling the anger was the public perception that the country's waste was being unloaded in the south because its leaders did not dare find a site in the prosperous north. Increased public awareness and a newly politicised south can only help the entire region prosper.

## Cautious optimism

There may even be progress with the rebirth of the "cathedrals in the desert". Naples' Bagnoli steelworks, sited between the sea and the ancient hot springs, was the most wanton act of disdain to the environment in the south's

Beyond the classic tourist attractions, astute new schemes encourage the locals to care more about their cultural heritage. In addition, certain neglected areas, such as troglodytic Matera, have been boosted by films shot there – in Matera's case it was the harrowing *Passion of the Christ*. The Campania and Sicilian Film Commissions have also been doing their best to attract movie-shooting to the south.

Even so, there is a tendency to think that tourism can solve the south's ills. This view fails to face the stark reality that industrial output in the south continues to fall, with its craft sector faring even worse. As it is, the south only con-

modern history. Now, however, the site welcomes a science park, as well as Naples' summer nightlife, and there are plans for an "urban park", with new cultural centres attached. This belated environmental awareness has positive spin-offs for the tourism industry. Eco-tourism has increased by 10 percent, particularly in Molise, in Cilento in Salerno province, the Gargano in Puglia, and the Sila in Calabria. Tourism generally is on an upward curve, with a rise of around 20 percent in 2006.

**LEFT:** Pasquale Natuzzi, founder of the furniture giant.
**ABOVE:** fashion duo Domenico Dolce (right) and Stefano Gabbana found inspiration in Dolce's Sicilian roots.

tributes around 10 percent of Italian exports and fails to market its superb agricultural produce abroad. As for the broader picture, if the south's slide is to stop, Italy's debt, lacklustre public services and gaping north-south divide all need to be addressed. There are even fears that Italy may be forced out of the Eurozone within a decade. Then there is always the spectre of new "cathedrals in the desert", such as the mooted bridge over the Straits, stretching from Calabria to Sicily. The faithless south needs more inspirational bridges to the future than this one. As political commentator John Lloyd says, "Italy's left and right have both lost old faiths – finding new ones is an indispensable task." ❑

# MOVIES

*Southern Italy is a self-conscious movie in the making. Intensely visual,*
*it is a backdrop of extremes, of exquisite morality and cold-blooded Mafia murder*

Southern Italy has long been a source of inspiration for film-makers, with turbulent stories and settings presented on a plate. The dramatic landscape, melodramatic society and passionate people make the south a gift to directors, from Luchino Visconti and Francesco Rosi to foreigners such as Francis

Ford Coppola and Anthony Minghella.

Yet within the south, locations are shamelessly transposed: "Film directors are magpies who plunder landscapes, corrupt geography, redraw maps, invent villages," Anthony Minghella admits to the liberties taken on *The Talented Mr Ripley.* His film was set in the Bay of Naples in that transitional time when postwar Italy meets the *dolce vita* boom of the 1950s. While the island of Procida stars as itself, Naples opera house, Palermitan churches and the island of Ischia masquerade as cornerstones of other cities.

In Mel Gibson's controversial *The Passion of Christ* (2004), depicting the last twelve hours of Christ's life, Palestine was replicated by

Basilicata, and the poignant Crucifixion scenes shot in Matera. The Italian tone extends to the southern Italian crew and Monica Bellucci in the starring role of Mary Magdalene. Filmgoers may be unconvinced, but the Pope gave it his seal of approval: "It was as it was".

The sun-bleached image of Sicily is second-nature to cinema-goers as the land of *The Godfather.* The Mafia capital, Corleone, lends its jagged rocks and sullen populace to the trilogy. But, in recent years, Hollywood's infatuation with the glamour of gangsterland has been matched by the nostalgic, more whimsical appeal of such films as *Cinema Paradiso* and *Il Postino.* Yet, cinematically, the two poles of attraction remain Sicily and Naples, confirming their cultural superiority in the region.

## Italian classics

There is an honourable tradition of memorable Italian films set in the south. Roberto Rossellini set part of *Paisa* (1946) in Naples, featuring the friendship between an American GI and a Neapolitan street kid. His unsentimental *Viaggio in Italia* (Italian Journey, 1953), shot entirely in Naples, features a distressed couple, with the city acting as a metaphor for an unhappy marriage. While the man discovers his weakness (infidelity on Capri), his wife, played by Ingrid Bergman, discovers her strength (meaning of life in the cemetery); the couple appropriately break up in Pompeii.

The natural beauty of Sicily's Aeolian islands has always attracted film crews. Film buffs will recognise Panarea as the setting for Antonioni's *L'Avventura*, while Rossellini's *Stromboli* (1950) is set on the most volcanic island of all. Stromboli sparked off the romance between Roberto Rossellini and his star, Ingrid Bergman, an affair as doomed as the brooding melodrama of the movie. In the film, Bergman's character goes into hysterics with each volcanic eruption while in real life the lunar landscape ruined her hairstyle and humour; volcanic dust was a passion killer.

More recently, the island of Lipari features

in *Kaos* (1984), a Taviani brothers epic that conjured a Pirandellian universe of legends and lost loves. Equally distinctive is Nanni Moretti's charming and quirky *Caro Diario* (Dear Diary, 1994), shot on various offshore islands, including Salina, as was Michael Radford's Oscar-winning *Il Postino* (1994), a lyrical look at life in a delightful backwater. The only recent southern film to make an impact overseas is *Respiro* (2003), Emanuele Crialese's award-winning take on traditional family values, set in the lustrous landscape of Lampedusa.

The Neapolitan film industry has flourished since the 1900s, from the era of silent films to lightweight commercial successes and the halcyon days of Italian neo-realism. The strength of this realistic tradition survives in the work of contemporary Neapolitan directors, who manage to express the vibrancy of everyday life at the same time as facing up to the negative undercurrents in southern society.

Italian cinema has also been enriched by the presence of fine Neapolitan actors, from the expressive slapstick of Toto, Italy's Charlie Chaplin, to Sophia Loren. The two starred in De Sica's *Oro di Napoli* (The Gold of Naples, 1954), with Loren as a pizza-maker.

The Neapolitan director Francesco Rosi served his apprenticeship with De Sica in the heyday of Italian neo-realism and has made a career out of examining the underbelly of southern society. *La Sfida* (The Challenge, 1957), shot in the style of an American gangster movie, tackles the Camorra's corrupt control of the city markets, while *Mani sulla Città* (Hands on the City, 1963) deals with dubious property speculation in the city.

## Magnet for directors

Sicily is not slow to respond to its rival's cinematic tradition. Maria Grazia Cuccinotta starred in *Il Postino*, and in the James Bond action film, *The World is Not Enough*. The island has always acted as a magnet for renowned directors. Luchino Visconti, one of the masters of postwar Italian cinema, set several films on the island to great effect. His epic *Il Gattopardo* (The Leopard, 1963) is worthy of di Lampedusa's novel of the same name. Giuseppe Tornatore is

the best-known contemporary Sicilian director, thanks to the Oscar-winning success of *Cinema Paradiso* (1990). This nostalgic slice of Sicilian history, which shows the arrival of the Talkies in a benighted backwater, was shot in the village of Palazzo Adriano, near Palermo. The autobiographical film celebrates Sicilian exuberance with a bittersweet humour that mocks the grinding poverty. In the United States, the film broke box-office records for a foreign film.

Tornatore chose Siracusa as a beguiling backdrop for *Malena* (2000), his spirited romance set in Fascist times. The film also depicts a dramatic re-enactment of the Allied Landing on Pachino's

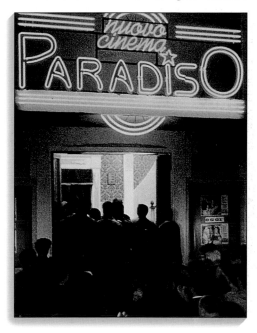

beaches, the same location chosen by rival director Fabio Conversi for *C'era una Volta in Sicilia* (Once Upon a Time in Sicily, 2000), about the landing of Garibaldi's troops in Sicily.

There is no mistaking the most popular theme in the Sicilian film canon. Leonardo Sciascia's anti-Mafia fiction has long inspired directors, but the finest Mafia portrayal is, heretically, American: Coppola's *Godfather* trilogy, featuring Marlon Brando and Al Pacino. Inspired by the internecine Mafia wars in Castellammare during the 1950s, the infamous town of Corleone lent its name to the Godfather. Coppola, a visionary maverick, orchestrates Sicily in celluloid. ❑

---

**LEFT:** Sophia Loren, who famously grew up in Naples' slums and became the Neapolitans' favourite star.
**RIGHT:** *Cinema Paradiso*, a 1990 Oscar winner.

# MUSIC

*Naples' opera is world famous. It grew out of a strong*
*musical tradition which is still lively today*

**M**usic is a mainstay of southern life and the Neapolitans' natural forte. Henry James said: "Neapolitan song has been blown well about the world, and it is late in the day to arrive with a ravished ear for it." His judgment is unfair: melodramatic love songs, *bel canto* opera, dance music and urban blues

still sound fresh in this most southern of cities. Although the rest of the south is musically overshadowed by Naples, operatic Sicily responds with Scarlatti and Bellini, two of Italy's greatest composers.

The 18th century was the golden age of Neapolitan music thanks to Scarlatti and the creation of the superb San Carlo opera house in 1737. Samuel Sharp attended a performance there in 1763 and was struck by the noisiness of the audience during the music but their rapt attention to the dancing. He was informed: "The Neapolitans go to see, not to hear an opera." Exuberance aside, noisy Naples has one of Italy's most prestigious opera houses,

second only to La Scala in Milan. Alessandro Scarlatti (1660–1725), one of the greatest southern composers, was born in Sicily but founded the Neapolitan school of music. He was a master of *opera seria*, which was inspired by mythological or historical themes and characterised by recitatives, which advanced the plot, and arias, which crystallised emotions. Scarlatti can also be considered the father of *bel canto*, a lyrical style which stresses the melodic line and carries a great emotional charge.

As one of the liveliest courts in Europe, Naples was also the birthplace of *opera buffa*, a light-hearted response to *opera seria*, situation comedies dependent on drama and improvisation. One of the best known Neapolitan composers of *opera buffa* was Domenico Cimarosa (1749–1801), whose many operas included *Il Matrimonio Segreto* (The Secret Marriage). Naples also possessed conservatoires where the finest *castrati*, such as Farinelli, were trained in both male and female roles.

## Romantic opera

While Sicily does not have a musical tradition to rival Naples or Milan, it has an operatic passion out of proportion to its achievements. Bellini (1801–35), born in Catania, personifies the enchanting art of *bel canto*, and is considered the founder of romantic opera. *Norma* is the best example of the genre, a *bel canto* masterpiece noted for its fine tone and ornamentation.

In spite of modest past musical accomplishments, Palermo has always felt entitled to expect an opera house worthy of any in Catania, Naples or Venice. The recently re-opened Teatro Massimo lives up to expectations, both an eclectic white elephant and a potent symbol of Sicily's cultural renaissance.

Not that southern achievements are restricted to opera. Neapolitan songs date back to the time of the troubadours and are characterised by their sweetness, melody, lyricism and poetic lilt. While the best-known songs tend to be 19th-century and are assured a place in the southern canon, the rest are still valued, particularly since the creation of the Compagnia di Canto Popolare folk society in the 1970s. If Neapolitan ballads are world famous, it is also thanks to opera stars such as Enrico Caruso, who did not restrict themselves to a classical repertoire. Today, Roberto Murolo is the greatest exponent of such traditional ballads as *O Sole Mio*, *Funiculì-Funiculà*, and *Torna a Surriento* (Return to Sorrento).

Southern musicians have a talent for improvisation and inspired borrowing, confirmed by the fact that many songs depend on a key-note similar to the traditional blue note in jazz. The Arab and African influences in the south have

Travel, a virtuoso Neapolitan band, won the San Remo song contest, Italy's musical showcase, in 2000, with their mix of rock, chamber music and Mediterranean melodies.

At best, southern dance, like southern music, manages to be both accessible and elitist. The tarantella, a boisterous folk dance originating from Campania, is currently enjoying a revival, with squares in the historic centre of Naples welcoming nightly hordes of talented dancing fans. Accompanied by guitar and tambourines, the dancers weave and twirl around the musicians, often clicking castanets. The city produces percussion instruments that do not exist

also enriched the musical tradition so that while jazz and rock rhythms fail to work in standard Italian, they ring true in Neapolitan. Among the talented singer-songwriters from the south, Pino Daniele is known for his Neapolitan urban blues. Sicilian singers also graft southern songs and music on to blues, rap or classical music. The Palermitan Giovanni Sollima is one of the best-known contemporary Italian composers, who combines classical and cutting-edge sounds in the manner of Philip Glass. Avion

elsewhere, as well as characteristic flutes, mandolins and tambourines.

In the 1870s, Henry James enjoyed a musical evening in Sorrento, entertained by an impromptu quartet of barber, tailor, saddle-maker and carpenter who played the violin, guitar and flute high on a splendid Sorrento terrace. "And so the afternoon waned, the purple wine flowed, the golden light faded, and song and dance grew free." The romance of southern dance is at one with images of the sun and the wine-dark sea. But as night falls, the summer dancing is sure to give way to the love, longing and melancholy embodied by traditional Neapolitan songs. ❑

**LEFT:** Domenico Cimarosa, composer of *opera buffa*.
**ABOVE:** Neapolitan tarantella, in an 1840 lithograph. The dance is enjoying a revival.

# LITERATURE

*Neapolitan theatre is the most dynamic in the country,*
*while Sicilian writing has produced an impressive canon of work*

Southern Italian literature is dominated by Sicilian genius in all genres, and by the theatricality of the Neapolitans. The richness of both traditions owes much to the cultural melting pot that is the south. Naples was founded by the Greeks, and it is not too fatuous to see a link between the citizens' ancient ori-

gins and a love of drama. The climate of tolerance and cosmopolitan culture in Naples has also enriched the city's literary life. Sicily might not claim the verbal virtuosity of Naples but it has an even more cosmopolitan literary canon, with Greek, Arab and mainstream European influences. Yet, whether politically committed or languidly sensuous, Sicilian writing has a distinctive spirit, and a powerful sense of identity rivalled only by the Neapolitan tradition.

Given the vivacity of the people and their passion for language and public performance, it is natural that the Neapolitan literary impulse finds its truest expression in the theatre. However, given the overlap between words and music in the city, the theatrical output ranges from audience participation and sung fables to musicals and mime. The *sceneggiata*, for instance, is popular melodrama with musical elements, a traditional Neapolitan genre successfully revived in the 1970s.

Neapolitan showmanship is traced back to the 17th-century *commedia dell'arte* character of Pulcinella, which in turn inspired Mr Punch. This masked, white-robed figure falls between comedy and tragedy, and is often seen as a metaphor for Naples itself. Although a victim of unrequited love and cruel treatment by his master, Pulcinella survives thanks to his irrepressible spirit and native cunning.

## The Neapolitan character

Eduardo De Filippo (1900–84), the city's greatest actor and dramatist, was born into a theatrical family, but was inspired both by Pulcinella and by Pirandello, with whom he worked in the 1930s. Although De Filippo's themes and settings are typically Neapolitan, the universal quality of his comic mockery transcends the narrow world of Christmas cribs and city dialect. His black comedy, *Filumena Marturano*, which deals with death and duty, strikes a chord with all Neapolitans. The plot revolves around the wish of an elderly courtesan for her lover to marry her, a ploy to prevent him from leaving for a younger rival. According to traditional Neapolitan logic, respect for death is paramount, if self-interested, since only the dead can pave the way for the living in the hereafter and, in the here and now, help loved ones to win the lottery, a local obsession.

"The theatre must be a picture which draws its life from reality, a reality which is at the same time prophetic," says one of De Filippo's characters – a view that could be the playwright's own credo. Yet De Filippo's realism and mockery are outweighed by his humanity and compassion, qualities singled out as truly Neapolitan by a lesser, much feted writer, Luciano De Crescenzo. As the city's best-known contemporary writer and media figure,

De Crescenzo goes on to offer an insight into the warped Neapolitan mind, with its familiar dicing with death: "And what about the orange light?" he asks an old man who spends his days at traffic lights waiting for accidents. "The orange? That doesn't mean anything. We keep it to brighten the place up."

## The Sicilian spirit

Native writers have used Sicily as a rich seam, mined for raw material and welded into Italy's most vibrant literary tradition. Despite the diversity, the common thread is the elusive yet unmistakeable Sicilian spirit. In particular, people from Agrigento are a mysterious breed, often called "*né carne né pesce*", neither fish nor fowl. Yet this curious province has produced exceptional Sicilian writers: Empedocles, the pre-Socratic philosopher; Pirandello, the Nobel prize-winning playwright; and Sciascia, the political novelist. Di Lampedusa, the author of *The Leopard*, also had his ancestral estate here. All these writers were gifted mavericks who shared a bittersweet relationship with their homeland. Empedocles committed suicide on Etna while Pirandello was the master of split personalities. Sciascia called his land a "wicked step-mother" yet rarely left, while Lampedusa was a languorous Sicilian prince who still produced a posthumous masterpiece, the greatest Italian novel ever.

Pirandello (1867–1936) is Italy's greatest dramatist, a writer who unites petty, provincial Sicily with universal themes of identity and loss. Just outside Agrigento, in the hamlet of Caos, is Pirandello's birthplace. The irony was not wasted on the master of the absurd, who called himself a "son of chaos". As one of Italy's most versatile writers, Pirandello covered philosophy, novellas, drama and comedy. His work paints a bleak picture of Sicily as a volcanic, violent, bestial land, yet one also ridden with bourgeois convention, from pursed lips and stiff-back chairs to arranged marriages.

Whereas Pirandello was an innovator, Giuseppe Tomasi di Lampedusa (1896–1957) was a traditionalist, with a poetic style steeped in Sicilian culture, aristocratic decadence and oriental fatalism. He is famous for producing a

novel which E.M. Forster calls "one of the great lonely books". *Il Gattopardo* (The Leopard) is the work of a nostalgic prince who described the absurdity of progress and optimism ("Nowhere has truth so short a life as in Sicily"). The fictional prince revels in the "voluptuous torpor" of a "lovely, faithless land" that dooms all new initiatives, even love, which is "flames for a year, ashes for thirty". Behind the bustle of the story is the concept of life as the forge of memory: one lives in order to remember. Death is ever-present even in the midst of pleasure, and visible in Sicilian excess and sensuality.

Leonardo Sciascia (1921–89) represents the opposing, realistic strand in Sicilian literature, considering himself a freethinker in an enslaved country. As one of many southern writers committed to social and political engagement, he denounced the abuses of power and the subterfuge at the heart of Italian politics. He tried to stir slumbering public opinion to protest against the abuse of power by the state or the Mafia. Di Lampedusa would have told the polemical novelist that he was wasting his breath: "Sleep is what Sicilians want." Yet, while both literary traditions are true of Sicily, in recent years Sciascia would have been more vindicated than his princely predecessor. ❑

**LEFT:** Pulcinella, a figure from the *commedia dell'arte*, is often seen as a metaphor for Naples.
**RIGHT:** a city book stall.

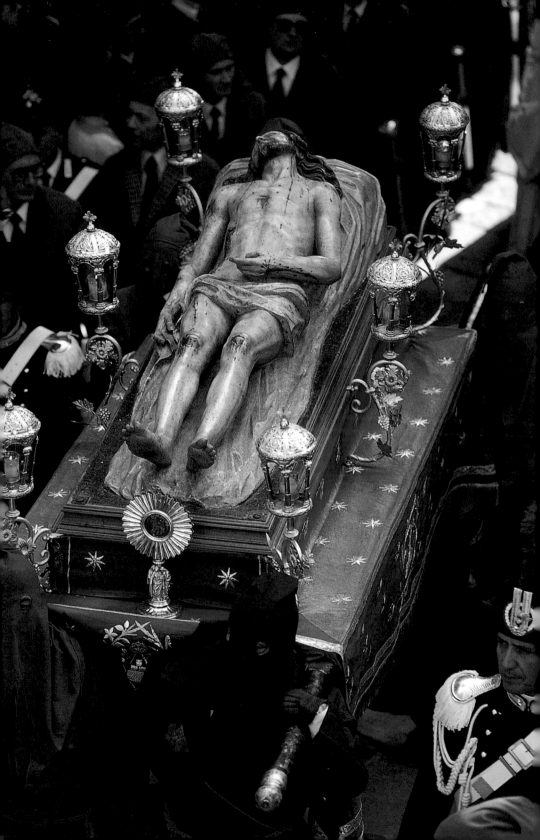

# SAINTS AND SUPERSTITIONS

*A deep belief in religion and strong superstition have created*
*a society of unusual customs and credos*

While cast in the role of stereotypically sunny Italians, the southerners are deeply superstitious. "Under the purest of skies," wrote Goethe, "lie the most uncertain of souls." A deceptive serenity masks a fear engendered by the scourges of eruptions and earthquakes, epidemics and invasions, emigration and unemployment, crime and poverty.

In such a climate of uncertainty, it is hardly surprising if salvation is seen in terms of self-denial or self-preservation rather than selffulfilment. Yet the spectacle of superstition, embracing miraculous apparitions and cabbalistic rituals, self-flagellation and paganistic festivals, only serves to deepen the southerners' genuine Catholic faith.

The south shelters a broad Church, instinctive and individualistic enough to ignore the Vatican's unease about unsanctioned practices, from the cabbala to the casting of spells, from ancestor worship to modern idolatry, or diabolical dancing and mortification of the flesh. In Sicily, for instance, the gory realism of the Easter re-enactments comes complete with penitential lashings. Even the *mafiosi* choose this moment to "make peace with God", or at least sign a short truce.

## Charm offensive

Homes and cars are often adorned with amulets, dangling Madonnas, and assorted charms, while chapels are stuffed with bones and skulls, as well as the most impressive reliquaries in Christendom. Amid the grimacing statues and ghoulish skulls, there are enough pieces of the True Cross − many brought back through the crusader ports of Bari and Brindisi − to create a forest. In religion but not in business, people are happy to stretch their credulity, especially when traditional faith shifts to the far shores of the supernatural. These are the same rational citizens who visit charlatans as an insurance

policy against the "evil eye". Southerners also remain fascinated by unsolved, and preferably blood-stained, miracles, from the celebrated liquefaction of St Gennaro's blood to sundry Madonnas shedding red-tinted tears and even, such as in the case of the Madonna from Carinola, an abundance of milk.

In Naples, the blood of St Gennaro has liquefied, with a few telling exceptions, since 1389. Yet among the more convincing miracles, the so-called "Madonna detectives" have unmasked charlatans happy to produce valves of red liquid designed to be placed behind the relevant statue's eyes; triggered by a remote command, the statue then weeps blood. The Vatican does its best to play down such phenomena, but to no avail: such "miracles" capture the public imagination.

San Biagio is the quarter famous in Naples for selling religious paraphernalia, from chalices and figurines to gilded saints and kitsch twinkling Madonnas. Esoteric perfumed candle

**LEFT:** Good Friday procession in Molfetta, Puglia.
**RIGHT:** skull in Santa Maria delle Anime del Purgatorio, where a cult of the dead flourishes.

shops include models that supposedly ward off evil spirits, as well as potions and remedies against the "evil eye", and personal talismans fashioned to your own requirements. But in typical double-edged Neapolitan tradition, there are also potions and manuals to guide dabblers in the occult through the intricacies of casting spells and curses. Southerners have a long tradition of casting spells. Remedies against the evils of the *jettatore*, or spellcaster, include touching a tiny horn of gold, silver or coral

> ## NUMBERS GAME
>
> In *La Smorfia*, a book of divination, numbers have different meanings: 19 represents both January and laughter; 17 simply means bad luck.

Armeno, the paraphernalia of the lottery are clearly visible, with wicker baskets ready for the magical numbers, and the lottery symbols written in both Neapolitan and standard Italian. *La Smorfia*, invented at about the same time as the lottery, is a mystical book of divination. In it, every dream is associated with a particular number, from 1 to 90, and used to predict the winning lottery numbers. The Church used to spur gamblers on by suggesting that all events were acts of divine providence, and disreputable clerics filled their coffers by confirming a link between divine grace and donations of specific sums of money.

## Cults of life and death

Since it is considered impossible to win the jackpot without the intercession of the dead, the lottery encourages dealings with latter-day soothsayers, mediums in touch with spirits in the afterlife. The Fontanella cemetery in Naples represents the overlap of the worlds of the living and the dead, and the place to consult the spirit world. Thousands of skulls and bones are lined up "ready for adoption" by people who have the time to devote to prayers for an anonymous, orphan soul. In return, and there is always a return according to local logic, the dead souls should watch over the living, helping them fulfil their dreams, and guiding them when it is time to "cross over to the other side".

*(pictured on page 86).* Folklore aside, southern cities still celebrate their patron saint's day with a fervour bordering on idolatry. To play a pallbearer's role at a festival is considered one of the greatest honours in life.

## Lottery and lucky numbers

Many southern Italians are slaves to the lottery, which has variously been seen as a way of rising above present circumstances, or as a chance to challenge fate and laugh in the face of the gods. Based on the Jewish cabbala, this Genoese import has been popular since the 16th century. In Naples, the numbers are drawn every Saturday. In atmospheric streets such as San Gregorio

The church of Santa Maria delle Anime del Purgatorio in Naples is a testament to the importance of the cult of death. The entrance is marked by three columns surmounted by a bronze skull, besides which are placed fresh carnations daily. This baroque church is built over an underground cemetery and ossuary where the skulls stacked in niches testify to the longevity of this curious cult. The church still belongs to an early 17th-century confraternity that was founded to collect alms to pay for Masses for the souls of the dead, thus speeding them on their way from purgatory to paradise. Although this practice of praying for trapped souls was officially banned by the Church in 1967, the cult still survives, as do such macabre funerary motifs as the winged skull.

The wishes of the dying and care of the deceased are considered sacrosanct. All Saints Day, on 1 November, signals a bout of serious ancestor worship all over the south, with visits to the graves of loved ones on All Souls, *I Morti*, the Day of the Dead. After the tombs have been inspected and spruced up, special food such as *torroni dei morti* nougat is eaten. In the south, symbolic foods enliven the most sombre of occasions. Although this is a culture impregnated with death, the day is a festive occasion, with presents for children, and, in certain cases, propitiatory gifts to the gods. In Sicily, a rock-hard sugar doll, known as a *pupa*, is presented to the deceased before being ceremonially eaten by the living, in a cheerful form of cannibalism. The living soul symbolically

on walls communicate the news with the minimum of fuss, so pink or blue ribbons placed by a communal entrance indicate the sex of the latest arrival in the apartment block.

## Greek beginnings

The south also represents the melding of different civilisations, each bringing its own set of superstitions and gods yet also displaying the essential vitality of southern culture. Fortune telling goes back to the time of the Greeks. At Cumae is the Antro della Sibilla, the sacred cave of the prophetess Sibyl, who was consulted by emperors and by Virgil, and foretold of the sack

takes on the spirit of the beloved, thereby assuming power over life and death.

Since southern Italians are also people of the here and now, the cult of the living is equally compelling. After a respectful nod to the deceased, a good Neapolitan takes the precaution of saying "*Salute a noi*", essentially a plea for a selfishly long and healthy life. The strength and immediacy of southern lives are clear in the confident public rituals regarding birth and death. Just as funeral notices pasted

of Rome. Greek language and ritual were not generally suppressed in the south until the 12th century, and vestiges of it remain. Indeed the cult of the Madonna is seen by some to be descended from the cult of the great Greek goddesses such as Athena and Persephone.

In Sicily, the fertility cult is still celebrated in Enna, the site of the temple of Demeter, goddess of agriculture and fertility, and of her daughter Persephone's banishment to the Underworld. The origins of the tarantella, Naples' signature dance, supposedly date back to Greek times when the Three Graces created a seductive dance to entice Ulysses back after he had narrowly escaped falling under the spell

**LEFT:** the casket containing the blood of San Gennaro, which liquefies three times a year.
**ABOVE:** services for the liquefaction are well attended.

of the song of the sirens, who lived in the siren lands, around the coast of Sorrento.

In the northeast of Sicily, the stretch of coast off Messina and Milazzo is awash with Greek-inspired myths: known as Mylae in classical times, Milazzo is the legendary site of Ulysses' shipwreck. Sailors north of Messina were wary of the twin demons of Charybdis, the whirlpool, and Scylla, the six-headed sea monster. It took an 18th-century scientist to demystify the whirlpools as the

meeting of clashing currents. Marsala, set on Sicily's west coast, provides equally compelling classical allusions: by the shore of ancient Lilybaeum is a church built over a grotto to Sibilla Sicula, Apollo's prophetess. Her rock sanctuary is set over a sacred spring where, according to the cult of the sibyl, maidens drank her water and uttered incantations which the sibyl interpreted. This damp Delphic oracle still inspires devotion, from lovelorn girls to joyous citizens celebrating the Ferragosto summer festival.

Despite the grandeur of the Greek legacy, many southern myths and superstitions are far more ancient and atavistic. The central, most powerful, piece of myth-making is connected with the life-threatening forces of Vesuvius and Etna, and the mountain gods who must be appeased at all costs. Adrano, set on the slopes of Etna, was the Greek city of Adranon, celebrated for its sanctuary to Adranus, the Siculi god of fire. Still today, during the bizarre August festival, a child dressed as an angel "flies" along a cord linking the old city powers: the castle, town hall and a statue of the god of fire himself. So far, Adranus has kept his city safe from fiery Etna.

The sense of appeasing the mountain gods survives in Zafferana Etnea, a hiking village and ski resort which found itself in the path of the 1992 and 2002 volcanic eruptions. Before abandoning his farmhouse to the volcano, Giuseppe Fichera, a local farmer, left bread, cheese and wine to satisfy "the tired and hungry mountain". Even gods of destruction need food and rest.

To present-day Sicilians, Etna is still an atavistic god. The city of Catania is a comfortable, commercial success yet feels distinctly uneasy living in Etna's shadow. In AD 253, Sant' Agata, the city's beloved patron saint, suffered martyrdom by being rolled in hot coals and having her breasts cut off. A February festival records her horrendous fate and she is tastelessly commemorated by breast-shaped jellies and cakes. Sant'Agata's statue or veil are still traditionally used to ward off impending lava flows, with mixed results.

## Miracles and flying monks

Some miracle-working clerics have been seen to have power over volcanoes. Alfonso di Liguori, the 18th-century founder of the Redemptorist order, is said to have stifled Vesuvius and, like other saintly southerners, he also raised the dead. Miracle workers in the 19th century included Fra Edidio of Taranto who brought back to life more than half a ton of eels (they are only sold live), and resurrected a butchered cow. In Calabria Francesco di Paulo raised 15 people from the dead while he was still only a boy.

Raising the dead was one miraculous power. Another saintly trait was flying, a particular 17th-century attribute. Most famous was Father Joseph, the Flying Monk of Copertino, who flew not just around his native Apulian town, but elsewhere in Italy, even appearing before an astonished Spanish Ambassador, a spectacle which apparently caused the Ambassador's wife to faint.

The miracles of these saints lived after them in the form of relics and images, which were used to repeat their supernatural feats.

Perhaps the most celebrated modern miracle worker is Saint Padre Pio di Pietrelcina, canonised by Pope John Paul II in 2002. He is one of more than 300, including St Francis of Assisi, who have claimed to have borne the stigmata – the wounds of Christ crucified *(see*

wants him." He called this process "a prolongation of the personality".

A great number of miracle workers in Puglia and Calabria have been made saints, and 10 popes came from the region. Reliquaries also abound. The 19th-century traveller Craufurd Tait Ramage wrote, "The quantity of holy relics in this part of the world is astonishing." He cites the monastery at Belforte as having a finger of Stephen (the first Christian martyr), a piece of the Holy Cross, the sepulchre in which Jesus was buried, and a fragment of the rod of Aaron, while the village of Soriano had a statue of St Dominic brought personally from Spain in 1530

*page 204)*. Padro Pio's stigmata first appeared in 1918 while he was praying in the monastery at San Giovanni Rotondo on the Gargano peninsula. Like his flying predecessors, he had the ability to appear elsewhere: before the pope in Rome, and during World War II when his sky-borne image guided a lost American pilot to his base on the Italian coast.

Padre Pio believed that a person could be in two places at once. "One minute he is here," he said, "and the next moment he is where God

by the Virgin Mary. Bari, on the other hand, claims to have the bones of St Nicholas, the original Father Christmas, which were brought here from Asia Minor and are now asked to work miracles among pilgrims.

The most famous pilgrimage site in the south is the shrine to the Archangel Michael on Monte Sant' Angelo. This crusader outpost was also the inspiration behind the creation of Mont Saint Michel in France. The spring water (now dried up) in his cave was undoubtedly once associated with dragon myths, as water is everywhere in the south, and it is not surprising that the dragon-slaying archangel should have found a home here. ❑

**LEFT:** lucky horns on sale, to protect against spellcasters known as *jettatori*.
**ABOVE:** Padre Pio on a balcony, San Giovanni Rotondo.

# FESTIVALS AND THE PAGEANTS OF HISTORY

*On land and sea, the south is cheered up with festivals for every season, celebrating local saints, glory days, wine harvests and the passing year*

"There had been no bland evenings," wrote Henry James on a visit to Sorrento, "that, somewhere or other, on the hills or by the sea, the white glow and the red dust didn't rise to the dim stars. Dust, perspiration, illumination, conversation, plenty of fireworks, plenty of talk. That's all they want." The festivals that take place throughout the year all over southern Italy are a mix of pagan and Christian, historical, cultural and agricultural. With music, costume and special food, they are all a matter of great local pride.

## COSTUMES AND CARNIVAL

Food festivals are a feature of Salerno and, at Christmas, Naples. Pre-Lenten carnivals are held notably in Sciacca in Sicily, which is particularly rich with events. Easter sees the most activity in the streets, with hooded penitents from medieval fraternities and processions lasting up to 20 hours. Many towns celebrate their patron saints and Albanians hold their own festivals *(see page 258)*. The past is re-enacted in a number of historical pageants, recalling days of former glory. In August the Saracen invasions are recalled in Positano, and Amalfi does not forget it was once a wealthy maritime republic. A palio at Orio, near Brindisi, puts on Swabian costume for the re-enactment of the wedding of Frederick II.

▷ **BUN FIGHT**
Festival bread, shaped like saints, is distributed in Agrigento on the first and second Sundays in June in honour of San Calogero, the town's patron saint.

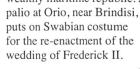

▷ **FEBRUARY SONG**
Musicians from Sagra del Mandorlo in Fiore, Agrigento's celebration of almond blossom.

◁ **ST NICHOLAS SETS SAIL**
In May, the Bishop of Bari blesses the boat that will take the statue of St Nicholas, the town's patron saint, out to sea, accompanied by a flotilla of boats (far left).

△ **MEDIEVAL FRATERNITY**
One of the fraternities of St Nicholas in Bari, which date back to medieval times. The procession leads from the cathedral where St Nicholas' relics are kept.

# THE WARRIOR PUPPETS OF SICILY

Travelling puppet shows have provided entertainment in Sicily for centuries, telling tales of saints, bandits and heroes, but most commonly the Paladins, the knights of Charlemagne's court, and their battles against the Saracens. The Christians traditionally strut on the left of the stage, the turbanned, baggy-trousered Saracens on the right. The audience knows all the characters – the knights Orlando and Rinaldo, the beautiful Angelica and the traitor Gano di Magonza – who are as familiar as characters in a soap opera. Feelings run high, especially in the noisy battle scenes.

Almost life-size, the puppets are up to 1.5 metres (5 ft tall) and exquisitely attired (*the ones pictured above are on sale in Taormina*). A great puppeteer is judged by his skill in directing the battle, and by his sound effects, including commentary in an archaic dialect.

◁ **AMALFI'S GLORY**
The festival of Sant'Andrea in Amalfi in June celebrates the town's glorious past with costumes, fireworks and music.

▷ **PALERMO'S PATRON**
Santa Rosalia, the patron saint of Palermo, is celebrated in the town's glittering festival of U Fistinu in July. The processions, fireworks and mayhem last six days.

◁ **CARNIVAL CHARACTERS**
Elaborate floats and figures in Sciacca, on the southeast coast of Sicily, make up one of the liveliest pre-Lent carnival parades in the south.

▷ **VILLAGE FIGURES**
Easter penitents in Montescagliosa, a hill village near Matera in Basilicata.

# FOOD

*Vegetables abound and there is pasta aplenty, but each*

*region retains its own distinctive cuisine*

**S**outhern Italy is so very different in character from both the northern and central regions of the country. It is truly a Mediterranean land dominated by the presence of the sea and specialising in hearty, spicy food – pasta, tomatoes, aubergines, fish, lamb and pork.

Campania is famous for Naples and its incomparable pizzas *(see page 96)*. Calabria is a proud mountain area where life is simple, and frugal, too, in parts. Basilicata, another mountainous region, is different – there the hunter tradition mingles with an Eastern influence to produce interesting dishes of lamb and pork. In Puglia, by way of contrast, vegetables and pasta predominate. Most of the great civilisations of the Mediterranean have left their mark on Sicily, the rich wheat basket of the Roman Empire, where pies were first made.

## Campania

"The difference between the king and me is that the king eats as much spaghetti as he likes, while I eat as much as I've got." This old Neapolitan saying illustrates the unique character of Campanian cuisine: popular traditions and aristocratic traditions, having overcome ancient differences, find that they have a common bond in the higher ideal of pasta.

All Neapolitans are united in the name of macaroni and spaghetti, and the phenomenon appears to be quite contagious. This simple and natural food has conquered the rest of the country and become the dominant feature of Italy's gastronomic culture. Without spaghetti and tomato sauce or macaroni and meat sauce (two of the specialities of this region), something very important is lacking and there is likely to be a feeling of unease and unhappiness.

This is not simply an old wives' tale or representation of a stereotype. It is part of a real need for an identity. Consequently a betrayal of,

or offence against, spaghetti on the part of the cook is naturally not to be tolerated. A plate of inferior spaghetti, overcooked with an unsatisfactory sauce, causes frustration and disappointment and, like a character in a romantic serial, an Italian who suffers such an offence never forgets.

## Calabria

A string of mountains between the Tyrrhenian and Ionian Seas, with only nine percent of its area low-lying, where "the rivers are torrents, the mountain slopes subject to landslides, the forests destroyed" – this is a description of Calabria, the most southerly point of the Italian peninsula, at the beginning of the 20th century. Travellers were struck by the violence of nature here, and by the theme of escape which seemed to dominate the character of the people.

When trade flourished in the Greek colonies of Crotone and Sybaris, the Calabrians began leaving the mountains to move down to the sea. Subsequently they returned to the mountains to

**LEFT:** pasta making. The wheat fields of Sicily made the first macaroni, in classical times.
**RIGHT:** fish soup in Aci Trezza, Sicily.

escape the Saracen pirates, and when it became safe they went down once more to the sea and beyond in search of a better life. An isolated, patriarchal society held families together in the course of this displacement, so that each generation lived exactly the same way as the one before, even when it migrated abroad.

The only secure possession the people of Calabria could take with them and rely on in a foreign country was the dietary tradition of their ancestors. As soon as finances permitted, they recreated the lost atmosphere of their homeland around substantial quantities of *ragu* (beef larded with *pancetta* and cooked in wine with carrots, leeks, dried mushrooms, onions, tomatoes, nutmeg and cloves).

Calabrian cuisine is therefore a function of a collective memory, in which the dishes are evidence of time recaptured. How far back, for example, can we trace the taste of their cabbage soups or *pancotto* (broth, stale bread, garlic, bay leaves, celery and parsley) or mushroom soup or *lagane* (handmade *fettuccine* cooked in milk and sprinkled with *pecorino*, a hard cheese)? Each dish speaks of seasons' harvests and simple living on the edge of survival, where natural fruits of the earth and sea (snails, fish, game, figs, olives and almonds) were

## BUFFALO CHEESE

In the terraced houses that line the winding streets of Naples, and in the farm kitchens of the rugged southern Italian countryside of Campania, with its fertile, volcanic soil, *mozzarella* has long been a staple part of the local diet. No one knows exactly how long the cheese has been made in the south of Italy, but in AD 60 the Romans are recorded as making similar food, curdling fresh milk with rennet extracted from the stomach of a sheep or goat.

Legend also has it that the monks of San Lorenzo di Capua gave bread and *mozza* cheese to the hungry who came knocking on the convent door in the 3rd century. Eventually, the soft *mozza* cheese reputedly made by the

monks became known as *mozzarella*. The word derives from the Italian verb *mozzare*, to cut off, the action of breaking the cheese curd into more manageable portions.

The transition of *mozzarella* made from sheep's milk to what is now considered the real thing made from the creamy milk of buffaloes came many centuries after the monks of San Lorenzo earned a reputation for their cheese. Indian water buffaloes, which roam wild in Southeast Asia, were introduced to southern Italy in the 16th century. They thrive in the mild dry climate, producing a rich, flavoursome milk from which the cheesemakers in the provincial capital, Naples, make *mozzarella di bufala*, buffalo *mozzarella*.

considered signs of the benevolence of the gods. Similarly, kid meat and cheeses recall the lives of the shepherds, while the many varieties of home-made pasta call to mind images of the family gathered around the table as the women of the household worked the dough.

The aubergine, too, the most used vegetable in this region, belongs to the same culinary world, whether it is cooked in vinegar and sugar or sautéed with garlic, stuffed or baked with cheese.

## Basilicata

The region of Basilicata has two different names. Lucania is derived from the Lucanians, the earliest inhabitants of the area. The other is more recent, dating to the time of the Greek-Byzantine domination of the area; *basileus* is the Greek word for king, and the name Basilicata meant a province of the Byzantine Empire. Thus the original pastoral-warrior civilisation was replaced by the sophisticated and decadent Eastern tradition – with note-worthy results in the kitchen.

On the one hand, there are some ancient recipes, typical of a primitive society of hunters, such as hare marinated in wine and flavoured with garlic and bay leaves, and partridge cooked with olives. On the other hand, there are flavour and taste combinations from the Middle East that have come into general use in dishes such as *tagliolini*, made either with milk and saffron or with almond milk flavoured with cinnamon.

Another feature of Lucanian cuisine is that it has remained a private affair within the family or, at very most, the village. This is because the region is all hills and mountains, with isolated villages clinging to their tips. Poor communication in the past often meant that people could not leave the village even if they wished. Hence the traditions of the local cuisine have remained in the custody of household kitchens.

Two of the most popular dishes are boned lamb with celery, onions and rosemary and *gnumariddi*, lamb offal and sweetbreads cooked with garlic, onions and cheese. As in inland Puglia, lamb is the principal meat. Then there is pork, which is also made into sausages and hams of some repute, and for special occa-

sions such as weddings, christenings and religious ceremonies, chicken stuffed with *pecorino*, eggs and chicken livers.

The remainder of the diet consists mainly of vegetables, baked in the oven and eaten in vast quantities as a substitute for meat, which is too costly for family budgets. Aubergines and olives, anchovies and capers, potatoes baked with onions and *pecorino*, mixed dishes of vegetables including peppers, courgettes, broccoli and tomatoes. Or else pasta, hard wheat *fusilli* with ricotta cheese, and *strascinati* – traditional pasta served with a sauce of chickpeas, green peas or lentils.

## Puglia

Puglian cuisine is something of an anomaly in relation to the other regional cuisines. The pasta-meat-vegetable relationship here is, in fact, reversed; vegetables produced in vast quantities throughout the region come first and the other foods then follow. Peppers, aubergines, broccoli, spinach, artichokes, broad beans, tomatoes, peas and other produce unquestionably have the leading role in the Puglian diet, with the other foods making up the entourage.

The tutelary deity linking the many-faceted vegetable world with the lesser world of the other foods is olive oil, more acidic and therefore stronger flavoured than the better-known Tuscan oil. So what does one eat with the vegetables? Pasta first of all, in particular *orecchiette*. The women make these "little ears" of wheat-and-water dough following a ritual that goes back many hundreds of years.

Vegetables are also used in soups, notably the *maritata*, for which chicory, fennel, celery and *escarole* are boiled, layered alternately with *pecorino* and pepper and covered with broth; in *calzoni* and *panzerotti*, pastry rolls with various fillings that are baked in the oven or fried; or in the impressive pies made with kid meat, chicken, beef, potatoes, onions, courgettes,

tomatoes and cheese, which may be served as either first or second courses.

This cuisine has the same basic structure as that of Naples, with a baroque overlay; the dishes are complex, and preparation is lengthy and often done in several stages. The Apulians even go so far as to stuff figs, and fillings feature in all their traditional cakes and pastries for religious and agricultural festivals, including Christmas and Easter. The plentiful fish, molluscs and crustaceans of this region are known for their quality; the waters are largely pollution-free and teeming with life. Italy's major oyster beds are located here in Taranto, the oysters being brought into the harbour from the larger bay every season.

Even fish do not escape the pie pan, where they are alternated with layers of vegetables and flavourings from the Middle East. Cheeses – *mozzarella*, *scamorza*, *caciocavallo* and *pecorino* – are produced in large quantities inland, as is lamb which is cooked with garlic and herbs as it has been since ancient times.

## Sicily

Sicily is a racial melting pot. Through the centuries, Norman, Islamic, Greek, Spanish and German cultures have left their mark and been distilled into a unique way of life. Over Sicilian cuisine float the fragrant aromas of aniseed, cloves, mint and cinnamon. It has been said that Sicily is a continent not an island, because there are elements in its geography and history that are unique and unrelated to the rest of Italy.

Located in the centre of the Mediterranean, Sicily has seen a succession of great civilisations: Greek, Carthaginian, Roman, Byzantine, Arab, Norman, French, Spanish and post-unification Italian. These civilisations accumulated one on top of the other, none of them actually disappearing, so that the economic, social and cultural structure of the island is the sum of all those that have preceded it over 2,000 years.

Its cooking is another aspect of this age-old baroque construction, composed of successive strata. The first and oldest is occupied by pasta; this is where wheat was first cultivated and made into flour, and where it was first mixed into the dough from which macaroni is made. Pastry making, known throughout the Mediterranean in Plato's time, was invented in Sicily. It was here that the seeds of the orange and lemon trees, pistachio nuts and dishes such as

### A ZEST FOR LEMONS

Whether as juice or grated zest, the lemon is utilised a thousand times a day. Covered with a vibrant peel, offering incomparable qualities, this "prince of fruits" was discovered on the slopes of the Himalayas and taken to Mesopotamia, the vast land between the Tigris and Euphrates. The Jewish people learned to cultivate the lemon during the famine of Babylon and then imported it into Palestine. When the Roman Empire extended into the East, lemons began to be grown in Sicily. Nevertheless, knowledge of the lemon did not spread to the rest of Italy until the 4th century, and did not reach France and Spain until the Middle Ages.

*couscous* (tiny balls of semolina steamed with oil and then added to a rock fish broth) arrived from the Arab world. This is the birthplace of pasta with sardines, perhaps the most famous dish of the region. Recipes such as *caponata* from Spain and *stoccafisso* (salt cod) from Norway were elaborated here. The list could go on.

In simple terms, the cuisine of Sicily can be divided into "dinners for the rich and food for the poor" as the historian of Sicilian folklore, Giuseppe Pitrè, wrote at the beginning of the 20th century. From all the island's specialities, "*fricasées, fricandea, ragouts* etc", and for desserts sorbets flavoured with peaches, figs and oranges.

The cooking typical of Sicily today is a combination of the eating traditions of the rich and the poor with additional differences imposed by the changing seasons. Sowing, threshing, the grape harvest, Christmas, Lent, Easter or the festivities of patron saints are ritually accompanied by gastronomic customs that have been handed down from father to son. On Christmas Eve, women

## CLASSIC DISHES

Siracusa was the gastronomic capital of the classical world, and here in the 5th century Mithaecus wrote *Lost Art of Cooking,* the first cookbook in the West.

him we learn that the peasants lived mainly on bread: bread with onions, with broad beans, with olives, with cheese and, when they could afford it, with soup containing pasta or vegetables. To this basic diet, the fisherfolk added fish, mainly sardines, and tuna and swordfish for special occasions. And if worst came to worst, from August to December the entire island could count on prickly pears. The nobility, on the other hand, dined in a luxury that left foreign visitors open-mouthed; plates and cups of gold and silver, innumerable courses of

still make *caponata* (so called because it is the traditional accompaniment to capon). On Sunday they still make pasta by hand; grape harvest time is still an occasion for eating roast peppers; and the return of the *paranze* (fishing boats) is celebrated with the wonderful taste of freshly caught sardines cooked on a spit. Sicilians continue to eat *cannoli* made with flakey pastry at Carnival time, and meat pies at Easter; the saying "be frugal with salt because it hardens the brain and the heart" still goes, and the aroma of garlic, bay leaves, aniseed, mint, cinnamon and cloves still dominates Sicilian cooking.     ❏

● *For a list of local dishes, see Travel Tips pages 363–4.*

**LEFT:** lemons for sale in Amalfi.
**ABOVE:** lunch is a meal to be taken seriously.

# The Perfect Pizza

Neapolitans lay claim to the birthplace of pizza. The author Elizabeth Romer describes the Neapolitan passion for pizza as a cult in Naples. It is an apt description, for in Naples mythology, passion and pizza entwine.

Naples was at its height in the 1780s, full of Bourbon wealth and spirit. Street vendors bought pizzas from small stands and roamed the city, selling slivers from a lidded metal box or a *tavolino*, a narrow board. The stands made pizza to order with simple, seasonal ingredients, including the newly

discovered tomato. It was at this time that *pizza marinara,* with its topping of tomatoes, garlic, oregano and olive oil, was born. A pizza delivered to King Ferdinando I and Queen Maria Carolina from Taverna de Cerriglio was said to be so well received that the king had a red-tiled pizza oven built at the Capodimonte Palace; another version of the story is that Maria Carolina, a Habsburg princess, would not allow pizza in the palace, so the king, tiring of going out for his favourite fare, built his own oven.

In 1830, Antica Pizzeria Port'Alba, the first *pizzeria*, opened in the heart of Naples. It quickly became a meeting place for the man in the street. For those who could afford it, there were pizzas topped with fish, shellfish and seafood, buffalo

mozzarella, cured meats and sometimes *cecinielli*, tiny white fish that are no more than larvae. The *Masturicola, a* popular pizza that no longer exists, was topped with lard, grated *pecorino* cheese and basil. Oregano and basil were the favoured herbs, as today. But because so many of the patrons were artists, students or workers living on shoestrings, the most common pizza was seasoned simply with oil and garlic.

The *pizzeria* developed a system for payment called *pizza a otto*; eat now, pay eight days later. The local joke became the question of whether pizza might be a man's last meal – if he died before he paid. Pizza was sold to passers-by, along with deep-fried bits of dough studded with *prosciutto* ham, herbs or pieces of cheese and shaped into a variety of forms that were easy to carry and eat. These were originally made from odds and ends of dough but eventually evolved into a new form, fried pizza, which can still be found in some *pizzerie*.

Ask a Neapolitan what their favourite pizza is (*"Qual'è la tua pizza preferita?"*) and the chances are they will say, "*La mia preferita è la pizza Margherita.*" As the story goes, the first classic pizza Margherita was made or at least named by Raffaele Esposito of the Pietro il Pizzaiolo *pizzeria*, now called Pizzeria Brandi. In 1889 Esposito was invited to the palace to create three pizzas for the visit of King Umberto and Queen Margherita of Savoy. The queen declared that her favourite was the patriotic one resembling the Italian flag with its colours of red (tomatoes), white (mozzarella) and green (basil). The pizza quickly became a Neapolitan classic and has been called *Pizza Margherita* after the queen to this day.

In the late 19th century, life was extremely hard for the Italian peasantry. By the end of the century, 5 million had made their way to America, 80 percent of them from the south. Their culture and their cuisine went with them. In pizza's migration, the crust has thinned and thickened, the shape has taken many forms and the toppings have stretched the culinary imagination. Few developed countries are without pizza and every culture has made its own stamp, from lotus-root-topped pizzas in Japan to pizza chain restaurants in Moscow.

In the 1950s and 1960s, as southern Italian families moved to the industrialised north seeking work, they brought with them their favourite food. Today the total sales of *pizzerie* exceed the sales of Fiat, the country's largest car manufacturer, and an estimated 7 million pizzas are produced every day. Local pizzas have become as accepted as the other indigenous foods of the area, incorporating regional ingredients and variations to provide a new tradition.

In Naples, it was only in the last two decades of the 20th century that the *pizzeria* evolved into a sit-down dining establishment. Now even some of the finest restaurants have a wood-burning oven to offer pizzas as a first course, while some *pizzerie* have begun to add other courses to their pizza menus. The colourful streets of Naples are still sprinkled with little stands selling pizzas by the slice, folded in half, a *libretto*, "like a book".

Neapolitans firmly believe that their original pizza is the best. And indeed it is. The water, flour, humidity and yeast combine to make excellent dough. Sunshine-ripened local tomatoes, which grow particularly well in rich volcanic ash, and delicious, dripping *mozzarella* cheese are impossible to beat.

In the mid-1990s a group of local *pizzaioli* or pizza-makers decided to create an organisation to defend the integrity of their product. *Associazione Vera Pizza Napoletana* has instituted courses and awards a diploma. Their logo is an image of the Neapolitan character Pulcinella, "Punch", holding a pizza paddle. Display of the emblem indicates that a *pizzeria* serves *vera pizza Napoletana,* a true Neapolitan pizza.

Their standards are based on the work of Carlo Mangoni, Professor of Physiology and Nutrition at the Second University of Naples. In alliance with the city of Naples, Professor Mangoni was asked to provide some research to establish the traditional ingredients and methods used to make a true Neapolitan pizza. The result was a 42-page document that outlined the historical roots of pizza, explored the traditional ingredients and the precise preparation and cooking process, and concluded with a detailed nutritional analysis.

This report was the first step in attempting to establish a DOC for pizza. The *Denominazione di Origine Controllata* (denomination of controlled origin) determines the geographic origin of specific foods and wines, outlines permitted ingredients and defines the production process.

The perfect pizza, DOC style, is based on three elements:
● First, the "crust", which is the simple combination of flour, water, salt and yeast. The Neapoli-

tans say that of all the components in their product, this makes it unique. The secret is in the overall rising time – at least six hours. Very little yeast is used for this slow rise and the result is a dough which is moist and very soft.
● Second, Neapolitan pizzas are scantily dressed. Crushed San Marzano tomatoes, slices of *mozzarella*, a few leaves of basil and a sprinkle of salt are added. All the ingredients used are raw, as the temperature of the pizza oven is high and the cooking time is quick. The final touch is a drizzle of oil from the *agliara*, dialect for the brass oil-can found on every pizza-maker's marble counter.
● Third, the oven: pizzas must be cooked in a

wood-burning oven. In a Naples *pizzeria*, the fire is almost never out. The oven stays warm with embers until the next kindling.  ❑

### Traditional DOC Pizza
**Verace Pizza Napolitana Marinara** Garnished with tomatoes, oil, oregano and garlic.
**Verace Pizza Napolitana Margherita** Garnished with tomatoes, oil, *mozzarella* and basil.
**Verace Pizza Napolitana Margherita Classica** Garnished with tomatoes, oil, *mozzarella*, basil and grated *Parmigiano-Reggiano.*
**Verace Pizza Napolitana Margherita Extra** Garnished with tomatoes, fresh cherry tomatoes, *mozzarella*, oil and basil.

**LEFT:** chef Silvio Martorano tosses the dough at the Gemma Pizzeria in Capri.
**RIGHT:** *pizzeria* in Naples, home of the ubiquitous dish.

# WINE

*Investors are increasingly interested in harnessing the bulk wine-producing regions and using local grape varieties to make top-class wines*

A lthough Southern Italy has a proud wine tradition that dates back to the ancient Greeks, it has long been known for producing low-quality, bulk wine. As in so many other aspects of Italian life, the famous wine names come from the north of the country. Marsala, the fortified wine from western Sicily, is the only Southern Italian wine that many people will know. Sadly, this is often because Marsala is widely used in cooking.

Since the beginning of the 1990s, however, this has begun to change and there are now many exciting developments. Local producers are increasingly turning from high-volume production to making quality wines, while investors both from other parts of Italy and the rest of the world are starting to take an interest in the south, especially in Puglia and Sicily.

Bulk wine production does, however, remain very important. Less than 5 percent of the wine produced in Southern Italy is bottled in the region rather than being sold off in bulk. Throughout Southern Italy only a small percentage of the vineyards are classified as Denominazione di Origine Controllata (DOC), the Italian version of the French *appellation contrôlée* system. There are a number of the best producers, especially in Sicily, who prefer to label their wines Indicazione Geografica Tipica (IGT), the Italian equivalent of the French *vins de pays* classification.

Local grape varieties are well adapted to the hot, dry conditions of Southern Italy *(see Grape Varieties, page 102)* and they produce many interesting wines which are welcome in a world of Chardonnay and Cabernet Sauvignon.

## Campania

Campania includes Naples, Pompeii and the islands of Capri and Ischia. Of the 48,000 hectares (120,000 acres) of vines planted only just over 1,000 are classified as DOC. The best

**LEFT:** winemakers Giusto Occhipinti and Giambattista Cilia in their Sicilian vineyard.
**RIGHT:** wine from the Amalfi coast.

wine is Taurasi, a red made chiefly from Aglianico. It is made in the hills near to the town of Avellino and is the south's first DOCG wine. DOCG is Italy's top wine classification and, so far, only 18 wines have this distinction. Taurasi develops complexity as it ages. The two leading companies are Feudi di San Gregorio and Mas-

tro-beradino. From Avellino also comes Fiano di Avellino, a white made from Fiano, possibly the best white variety of Southern Italy. Also from this area is another white, Greco di Tufo.

## Basilicata

This is an area of long rolling hills and deep valleys. Basilicata is not obviously picturesque like much of Tuscany, but it has an understated upland, rural charm. The vineyards are well inland and vines are planted up to around 600 metres (2,000 ft) above sea level. Because of the altitude the nights are cool even during the height of summer, which preserves the grapes' aromas and flavours. The region can suffer from violent summer storms. In June hailstones the size of golf balls can sometimes be seen cascading off tiled roofs as though they were bouncing along a fairway.

Aglianico del Vulture-is the only DOC of Basilicata. It has a long established reputation and has for many years been considered among the best red wines produced in Southern Italy. There are 1,200 hectares (3,000 acres) in the DOC centring on the small town of Rionero and the village of Barile. This wine is spicy and powerful and can be kept successfully for about 10 years. Paternoster is the best of the established producers.

## Puglia

Along with Sicily, Puglia has been Italy's leading bulk wine-producing region. Now that the bulk wine market has declined and European Union subsidies are more tightly regulated, the region is turning more and more to producing less but of a higher quality, as is Sicily.

Puglia is easily the largest wine producer of the mainland south, churning out around 800,000 million hectolitres a year. The vast majority of this is bulk wine, which still accounts for around 98 percent of the production. Only a small percentage is bottled as DOC. The main DOCs in northern Puglia are Castel

## DOC WINES

*Denominazione di Origine Controllata* (DOC) denotes a delimited wine region, and the following are the DOC regions in Southern Italy.

**Aglianico del Vulture**, Basilicata. Potentially one of Italy's finest reds. Paternoster is the leading company.

**Castel del Monte**, Puglia. This northern Puglian appellation produces variable wines in all three colours. Rivera is the best producer.

**Cirò**, Calabria. The best red from Calabria and made from Gaglioppo. Leading producers: Librandi and San Francesco.

**Marsala**, Sicily. Fortified wine "invented" by a Liverpool wine merchant, John Woodhouse, in 1773. Some of the

production is high volume, low quality at a cheap price. De Bartoli is the best producer; look out for his Vecchio Samperi, a VDT. Florio is also recommended.

**Salice** Salento, Puglia. Red appellation close to Taranto, with a growing reputation for powerful, easy drinking wines.

**Taurasi**, Campania. High-quality red made from Aglianico. Mastroberadino is the leading producer.

*Vino di Tavola* (VDT) is the day-to-day quaffing wine, like the ubiquitous Lacrima Cristi del Vesuvio, which comes from the vineyards in the area around Vesuvius.

Most Italians dining out will simply settle for a carafe of the local or house wine *(vino locale* or *vino della casa).*

del Monte, Locotondo and San Severo. Castel del Monte comes in all three colours and is named after the imposing and geometrically intriguing octagonal Norman castle that dominates the northern Apulian plain, a rather featureless stony flatland sloping gradually towards the Adriatic.

There is a move towards making quality wines by reducing the yields and, as elsewhere in Italy, increasing the density of plantation. However, standards remain variable here. Rivera at Andria, a well-established company, is the most dynamic and quality-conscious in the area. The company was founded in 1950 by

which is built around a steep, limestone ravine. Here an eponymous white DOC wine is made from Greco and Malvasia. Also in this part of Puglia is the cooperative of Locorotondo. DOC Locorotondo is solely for lemon- and lime-flavoured whites which can be made from Verdeca, Bianco d'Alessano and Fiano.

Wines from the hot Salento peninsula have a growing reputation, in particular the powerful Salice Salentino reds made from Negromaro and Malvasia Nera and also Copertino made from Negromaro. Around Manduria, Primitivo, which used to be used for blending, is now increasingly being bottled, giving big, juicy

the de Corato family, who have long been bottling their wines. Their top red is the complex Il Falcone, which shows what can be achieved here. DOC San Severo comes from north of Foggia. All three colours are made, and one of the leading producers is Alfonso di Sorda.

The land to the south and southeast of Bari is more undulating and interesting. This is the area characterised by white huts called *trulli* centred around the town of Alberobello. Near the border with Basilicata is the town of Gravina,

opulent wines. Leading producers in southern Puglia include Francesco Candido, the co-operative of Copertino, Leone de Castris and Cosimo Taurino.

## Calabria

Much of Calabria, the long toe of Italy, is too mountainous to be suitable for growing grapes and there are few areas suitable along its very long coastline where vineyards can be established before the mountains rise.

Cirò, produced on the Ionian Sea coast, is the best-known wine of Calabria. A little white Cirò is made from Greco, but most of the production is red from the Gaglioppo grape. From

**LEFT:** Puglian vineyard with *trulli* farm buildings.
**ABOVE:** vines thrive particularly well in the volcanic soil around Mount Etna.

a producer such as Librandi or San Francesco, Cirò is an attractive red that is probably best drunk within five or six years of the vintage. Greco di Bianco is a sweet wine made from semi-dried grapes from the town of Bianco in the deep south of Calabria. Across on the Ionian coast there are some interesting wines being made around Lamezia.

## Sicily

Although blisteringly hot in July and August, Sicily has a number of natural advantages that make it possible to produce good-quality wines. There are many hillside sites with thin, poor soils that, with the sun and low rainfall, make them ideal for growing vines. There are vineyards planted up to 900 metres (3,000 ft) above sea level. This moderates the heat of summer and means that the nights are cooler than on the plains. Both factors help to preserve the grapes' aromas and flavours.

However, until recently Sicily concentrated on high-volume grape production for the bulk wine market. Much of the island's production was destined to be made into grape concentrate or sent for compulsory distillation. The emphasis is now clearly shifting towards making quality wines. The Duca de Salaparuta, a large modern winery just to the east of Palermo, is one example. Their Duca Enrico is one of Sicily's best reds. Other notable producers include Regaleali and Terre di Ginestra, both in the Palermo region. Sicily's most high-profile foreign investor is the Australian company BRL Hardy, whose d'Istinto range is produced in their Calatrasi winery in Palermo.

Marsala is made at the extreme western end of Sicily. This fortified wine is made mainly from Catarratto, Grillo and Inzolia grape varieties. There are various grades of quality; the highest being Marsala Vergine or Solera. This is lightly fortified and has to be aged for at least five years. There is much indifferent Marsala made, but it can occasionally be amongst the finest fortified wines of the world.

The island of Pantelleria, just off the Tunisian coast, is known for its sweet Moscatos. Look out for Moscato Passito di Pantelleria. ❑

**LEFT:** vintage Marsala, Sicily's fortified wine.
**RIGHT:** the cellars of Carlo Pelleorino in Marsala.

---

## GRAPE VARIETIES

**Red**
*Aglianico:* responsible for the two best reds of Southern Italy – Aglianico del Vulture (Basilicata) and Taurasi (Campania).
*Gaglioppo:* widely planted in Calabria. It is a long ripening variety and is not harvested until early October.
*Magliocco:* planted in Calabria and believed to be an ancient Roman variety.
*Negromaro:* most popular red variety of Puglia, producing powerful and deep coloured wines. It is most successful in Salice Salentino and Copertino.
*Nero d'Avola:* Sicilian variety, makes the island's best reds.

*Primitivo:* linked with Zinfandel of California, there remains a dispute about whether Primitivo was taken over to the United States from Italy in the 19th century or whether Italian immigrants returning to Southern Italy imported Zinfandel which became known as Primitivo. Makes powerful, spicy wines in Puglia, especially at Manduria.

**White**
*Fiano:* perhaps Southern Italy's best white grape.
*Greco:* used to make successful whites in Basilicata and Calabria because it manages to keep sufficient acidity and aroma.

# ARCHITECTURE

*The extraordinary diversity of architecture includes a blending
and extending of styles found nowhere else in Europe*

The earliest surviving buildings of any significance in Southern Italy belong to the period of Greek colonisation during the 5th and 6th centuries BC. These are the three remarkably well-preserved temples at Paestum, a city whose prosperity and importance under both Greeks and Romans are mirrored in the extent and variety of its ruins.

There were once many more temples, but the grandeur of those which remain, the so-called Basilica, originally dedicated to the goddess Hera, the Temple of Ceres, actually built as a shrine to Pallas Athene, and the imposing Temple of Neptune, bears witness to the sophistication of architecture in Magna Graecia generally, even if elsewhere the evidence for this is rather more fragmentary. In towns such as Taranto, Locri and Crotone, the sites of major Greek buildings are identifiable, but their actual stones were removed long ago, to be reused in churches, castles and palaces, while the columns which formed a key element in classical architecture are often to be found in the nave of a cathedral, on either side of a doorway or built into the wall of a house.

## Roman landmarks

The Romans, in occupying the southern cities after winning the Punic Wars, tended to respect the existing structures, enlarging the central *agora* or marketplace to create a colonnaded forum with adjacent law courts and baths. To the larger towns they also added amphitheatres, as at Capua (now Santa Maria Capua Vetere) which boasted the empire's second biggest after the Colosseum in Rome. Another characteristic feature of the Roman townscape which survives here and there is the triumphal arch, raised to celebrate the conquests of a reigning emperor and decorated with relief sculpture, inscriptions and busts. The grandest of these, essentially a fusion of the most elegant classical style with a

sequence of political propaganda statements in the form of inscriptions and friezes, is the Arch of Trajan at Benevento, built in the emperor's honour around the mid-2nd century AD.

Roman domestic building is best seen during a visit to Pompeii and Herculaneum *(see page 157)*, the cities preserved for centuries under the crust of lava from Mount Vesuvius's catastrophic eruption in AD 79. The typical house of the period tended to concentrate on an inner atrium or courtyard surrounded by colonnades, with rooms leading off this, and an additional quadrangle, known as the *peristyle*, containing a garden and opening via a portico on to the street. Many of the Pompeiian houses reveal the highly developed lifestyle of ordinary people in the Roman Empire, with their frescoed rooms, heating systems and water supply created from catching rainwater in the *compluvium* or basin at the centre of the courtyard.

With the spread of Christianity throughout the empire, churches sprang up all over Southern

**LEFT:** building the cathedral in Otranto, from the 12th-century floor mosaic in the nave.
**RIGHT:** Valley of the Temples, Agrigento.

Italy, but only a few traces of such buildings from this period (2nd–5th centuries AD) remain, at Naples for instance, in the church of San Gennaro extra Moenia, with its nearby catacombs (underground chambers for Christian worship), and in the chapel of Santa Matrona at San Prisco near Capua.

A much stronger imprint on Christian architecture throughout the south was left by the Byzantine Empire, mostly in the form of small churches on a typically Greek plan, involving a central dome with four smaller domes clustered around it. The church of San Marco at Rossano, above the Gulf of Taranto, offers a good exam-

ple of late work in this style, while high up in the hills of southeastern Calabria, the Cattolica of Stilo is an almost perfect example of Byzantine architecture, with frescoes and re-utilised classical columns turned upside down to show Christianity's triumph over pagan superstition.

## The Normans and Romanesque

The arrival of Robert Guiscard and his conquering Norman army during the 11th century brought with it the new style of architecture known to us as Romanesque, which had taken hold all over Europe, from France and Germany to the cities of Northern Italy. A typical

### PAESTUM'S INFLUENCE ON WORLD ARCHITECTURE

The temples of Paestum represent some of the most influential buildings in the entire history of world architecture. Though travellers in the region had known about the ruins and the famous roses which had flourished here since the days of the Greeks, it was not until the mid-18th century that the site was "discovered" by connoisseurs living in Naples and Rome. Count Felice Gazzola, one of Charles III's ministers, encouraged foreign visitors to make the hazardous journey across the wild, malarial terrain surrounding the temples, and by 1787, when the German poet Goethe set out from Salerno to see them, a law had been passed to prevent coachmen overcharging such aesthetic

enthusiasts. Though Goethe was frightened by the blood-red eyes of the local buffaloes "which looked like hippopotamuses", his reaction on first seeing the temples was typical. "At first sight they excited nothing but stupefaction. I found myself in a world which was completely strange to me. Only by walking through them and around them can one attune one's life to theirs." Echoes of Paestum's magnificent Doric colonnades can be found everywhere, from Boston and Philadelphia, Paris and Moscow, to London's British Museum and the work of Scottish architects such as Glasgow's 19th-century genius "Greek" Thompson and Edinburgh's "Athenian" Stuart.

Romanesque church features an imposing portico, its columns resting on crouching lions and its bands of carving around the doorway adorned with figures from myth and folklore, as well as dragons and peacocks. Small, round-arched windows look down on a nave containing an ornate mosaic floor (as in Otranto Cathedral) from which steps rise to a presbytery and the high altar, with the bishop's throne behind it and an apse beyond. On either side of this part of the church are decorated pulpits *(ambones)* for the

the relics of St Nicholas, recently looted from the Byzantine city of Myra in Asia Minor (Turkey). Sicily has the most splendid examples in the cathedral at Cefalù and the monastery of Monreale in Palermo.

In the late 12th century, the Romanesque style began to give way to Gothic, with its emphasis on greater height and volume in the overall design of large buildings, its more elaborate style of vaulting in the construction of church roofs and its fondness for decoration and ornament, in forms such as the

reading of the epistle and gospel at Mass, and below the whole structure runs a crypt, its columns intricately carved with religious scenes or fanciful ensembles of leaves and grotesque faces.

Examples of this style are found everywhere in the Mezzogiorno, from Canosa, Ruvo di Puglia and Bitonto to L'Aquila, Acerenza and Salerno, though the dominant model for them all was probably Bari's great, fortress-like church of San Nicola, begun in 1087 to house

LEFT: the Temple of Neptune, Paestum.
ABOVE: Monreale Cathedral, an apogee of the Sicilian mix of Arabic, Byzantine and Romanesque styles.

ogival arch, the rose window or the crocketed finial. Though we tend to associate Gothic more obviously with Europe north of the Alps, Southern Italy possesses several splendid examples of this type of architecture. The great abbey of Fossanova is among the most outstanding. Built by Cistercian monks in the late 12th century, in an idiom clearly deriving from their order's homeland in eastern France, its nave and aisles are separated by pointed arches resting on clustered columns, from which shafts rise towards a cross-vaulted ceiling.

In Naples, the strong French influence in a variety of Gothic buildings was due to the Angevin monarchs ruling the kingdom between

1268 and 1442. Many of the major churches, including the Duomo, San Lorenzo Maggiore, Santa Maria Incoronata and above all San Domenico, retain their medieval aspect, despite later monuments and decorative detail.

The city also has two important secular buildings dating from the period of Norman and Angevin domination, the Castel dell'Ovo, a fortress built by William I of Sicily in 1154, and the Castel Nuovo or Maschio Angioino, the chief fortress of Naples, begun in 1279.

### SPAGNOLISMO

The Spanish aristocracy of Palermo delighted in *spagnolismo*, a love of ostentation, which was reflected in the Sicilian city's showy baroque architecture.

Frederick's castle at Lucera in Puglia is equally impressive, with walls a mile long that encircled his palace, treasury, mint, harems, zoo and, at one time, housed his 20,000-strong Saracen army.

From the Renaissance period (roughly 1400–1600) almost nothing of any real architectural significance exists in the Mezzogiorno to rival the outstanding achievements of northern and central Italy. There are several reasons for this. None of the southern towns enjoyed the same degree of independence and mercantile wealth as that of centres like Florence, Venice or Milan. The feudal nobility lacked the necessary public spirit to endow the building of churches, town halls or civic amenities such as loggias and fountains, and they showed little interest in planning handsome streets and squares to improve the appearance of the towns.

The Aragonese monarchy added minor embellishments to several cities during the 15th century, but the Spanish viceroys saw no reason to spend the kingdom's gradually diminishing resources on major architectural projects.

The most important examples of Renaissance building design in the Italian south are to be found in Naples. Though sculptors from Lombardy and Tuscany worked on the Triumphal Arch of Alfonso I, added in 1451 to the Maschio Angioino where the city council rules, the chief artists involved, Francesco Laurana and Domenico Gagini, were both firmly settled in Naples and helped to evolve a local sculptural style. The Arch is thoroughly representative of its period, displaying classical columns and entablature, allegorical figures in niches, carved relief panels and the figures of river gods in a pediment topped by a Corinthian column drum supporting the Archangel Michael dressed as a Roman warrior.

To the last years of the Renaissance belongs the Palazzo Reale, in Piazza del Plebiscito, the work of the Florentine architect Domenico Fontana, who began it in 1600, when it was hoped (in vain, as it turned out) that King Philip II of Spain would visit the city.

### Frederick's classic Gothic

The most remarkable building to have survived from the turbulent Middle Ages in southern Italy is the Castel del Monte, near the Apulian town of Andria. Raised around 1240 by Emperor Frederick II on a barren hilltop, this octagonal structure combined the functions of a castle and a palace. Its most striking qualities, apart from the overall balance of its proportions, is the fusion of Gothic detail in vaults and windows with touches of Classicism, which seem to anticipate the Renaissance, especially in the entrance porch, whose angled pediment and flanking columns are probably ideas from Roman buildings surviving at the time.

**LEFT:** Frederick's octagonal Castel Del Monte in Puglia, which anticipated the Renaissance.
**RIGHT:** Basilica Santa Croce in Lecce.

## Catholicism and baroque

With the onset, during the late 16th century, of the Counter-Reformation, the Catholic Church's initiative towards recovering spiritual territory lost to Protestantism and other heretical beliefs, much effort was devoted to beautifying and sometimes wholly reconstructing churches throughout the kingdom, as well as building many new ones, often dedicated to newly canonised saints such as St Teresa and St Philip Neri, whose cults were energetically promoted. In the early decades of the 17th century the style we know as baroque, outwardly majestic and imposing, while its interiors were fanciful and heavily detailed in design, began to take hold throughout Europe.

Southern Italian Catholicism, fervent, ecstatic, and embracing many elements of ancient paganism, took eagerly to this new architecture, more particularly because its exuberance ran counter to the rather more gloomy variety of religious devotion favoured by the ruling Spaniards, however scrupulous they were as practising Catholics.

Sometimes an entire town, not just in its churches and palaces, but in the decoration of ordinary houses and public buildings, might reflect this baroque enthusiasm, especially if

### IL BAROCCO LECCESE

Lecce's baroque palaces and churches are among the most memorable of Southern Italy's unexpected visual delights. The development of a local architectural style during the late 16th century, making use of motifs derived from buildings further north, in Naples and Rome, was based on the availability of a fine honey-coloured sandstone, easily sculpted into ornamental forms for use in the creation of stately doorways and elaborate windows. The balcony also plays an important part in the impact of this "southern baroque". A dominant feature in town houses of the Mezzogiorno, it sometimes reminds us of Spain, whose cultural influence on the whole region was so strong.

The word "baroque" is of obscure origin and loosely applied. In Lecce, where the style lasted until the end of the 18th century, it involves a use of fantasy and improvisation in forms derived from classical architecture – the column, the pediment, the frieze, the volute – to create an effect of wilful exuberance in the individual profile and detailing of the various buildings, almost as if the architects, such as Giuseppe Zimbalo and Gabriele Riccardi, were deliberately stretching the established rules of decorum to breaking point. The Leccesi themselves will tell you that the architecture reflects Puglia's sturdily independent character in this refusal to observe convention.

the locality offered a suitably workable stone. This was especially true of certain towns in southern Puglia, notably Lecce *(see page 109)* and Martina Franca, where a brilliant species of vernacular baroque evolved during the mid-18th century, wholly altering the appearance of streets and squares with its grandeur, fantasy and elegance. The style spread to smaller neighbouring communities, and we can catch hints of it in the extravagant ornament of windows, doorways or balconies throughout the region.

Once the Bourbon monarchy had established itself, after 1734, the need was felt for additional royal palaces in Naples, to emphasise the

Flemish Van Wittel), presents by far the most expansive statement of the late baroque palatial style anywhere in Italy. The building would have been grander still, with a central dome and flanking pavilions, but King Charles's successors were uninterested in completing the project as originally planned in 1752.

## Pompeii's legacy

The gradual shift in taste during the late 18th century towards a more austere interpretation of architecture's Greek and Roman heritage was much influenced by the rediscovery of Pompeii and Herculaneum which began taking

new king Charles III's status and to emulate his northern Italian fellow sovereign, the King of Savoy. Hence Charles built himself a summer hunting lodge, on a very grand scale despite its sober appearance, at Capodimonte (part of it now housing the Galleria Nazionale), with a park, a porcelain factory, an armoury and a sequence of handsome state apartments.

It was a second palace, at Caserta to the northeast of the city, which authenticated the Bourbons' significance among 18th-century rulers. Intended as a rural retreat in the unblushingly grandiose manner of Louis XIV's Versailles, Caserta, designed by the architect and painter Luigi Vanvitelli (an Italianised version of the

place at the same time. Architectural neoclassicism made comparatively little impression on the south, though a much admired example of the genre can be found in Pietro Bianchi's Neapolitan church of San Francesco di Paola (1817) based on the Pantheon in Rome, one of the most influential of ancient buildings in the inspirations it offered to European architects in the late 18th and early 19th centuries.

A significant new feature of Italian towns during the same period was the creation of theatres specifically designed to present performances of opera, the dominant musical form throughout Italy. These opera houses had an important social function as meeting places for the community, and during the occasional severe winter they had the added advantage of providing warmth in an age without adequate means of domestic heating. The traditional plan, involving a horseshoe auditorium arranged in tiers of boxes centred on a decorative proscenium arch, can be found in many southern cities from Salerno to Bari. Most distinguished among them is undoubtedly Naples' Teatro San Carlo, begun in 1737. Originally the back wall of this theatre could be removed to display a distant prospect of Mount

> **SOUND IDEA**
>
> When the San Carlo opera house was rebuilt after a fire in 1816, clay pitchers were inserted in the walls to improve the acoustics.

drained Pontine Marshes between Rome and Naples. Despite the discredited ideology which built them, their layout and architecture have been favourably reappraised in recent years. Industrialisation during the Fascist era did not improve the aspect of port cities such as Brindisi and Taranto, soon to be battered by repeated air attacks during World War II. After the war, little of any real distinction in the field of modern design was added to the average Southern Italian townscape. In recent decades exploitation by cowboy developers has

Vesuvius, which obliged with a minor eruption during the performance in 1827 of an opera entitled *The Last Days Of Pompeii*.

## Mussolini's style

After Italy's complete unification in 1870, the major towns of the Mezzogiorno lost their walls and gates, while suburbs spread around their historic centres, where street-widening often resulted in the ruthless demolition of ancient buildings. Under Mussolini, new towns were founded at Sabaudia and Latina, in the recently-

helped to disfigure whole areas, especially in Calabria. Perhaps the best symbol of genuine architectural progress in the Mezzogiorno is the award of the contract for Salerno's new regional courts of justice to the cutting-edge British architect David Chipperfield, noted for his concern for the relationship between buildings and the environment.

Only a change in the prevailing southern culture of corruption in local government is likely to generate similar projects elsewhere, in an area which has always lacked the money and the initiative to create the kind of architectural contexts which lend beauty and grandeur to the cities and landscapes of Northern Italy. ❏

**LEFT:** San Francesco di Paola, Naples, has classic grace.
**ABOVE:** modern departures in Vietri on the Amalfi coast.

# VOLCANOES AND EARTHQUAKES

*Ancient gods created them and tourists have flocked to see them.*
*The eruptions can be both spectacular and deadly, in this unquiet land*

One could hardly imagine a more frightening natural event than an earthquake or volcanic eruption. And yet for thousands of years people have lived in the midst of areas prone to such disasters. The eruption of Vesuvius on 22 March 1944 moved the special correspondent for the *Manchester Guardian* to write: "These Italians show a truly remarkable indifference in the face of disaster. I had expected scenes of panic, frantic ladies, crazed family men. There was nothing of the kind. They gathered in groups to observe the slow sacrifice of the village."

Italy's danger zone for earthquakes and volcanic activity extends from the east coast of Sicily to the central–southern section of the Apennines, an area that includes the most densely populated portion of the peninsula: the string of towns at the foot of Mt Vesuvius, in Campania, which are home to more than 600,000 people, and the nearby city of Naples. For Italians living in the shadow of a volcano, the local monolith is an object of myth, affection and fear, an ever-present and long-silent reminder of the natural forces that have shaped the region's past and at any moment might alter its present.

## Impotent science

Modern science has brought greater understanding of the causes of earthquakes, and organisation and technology can help to minimise their impact, using anti-seismic architecture, better and more efficient first aid, and rapid reconstruction after the event. But experts still cannot tell us when or with what force the disaster will strike.

As inescapable as the threat of these natural disasters is, when they actually occur, they also tend to reveal some of the less appealing sides of the culture of Southern Italy: the corruption,

bureaucratic morass and resigned fatalism of the south come into play and remain long after the lava flow and shaking have stopped. As always seems to be the case, it is the ordinary citizens who pay the price, many stuck for years and even decades in "temporary" shelters and prefabricated mobile homes. In the

scandalous aftermath of the earthquake that in 1968 hit the Valle del Belice, near Selinunte in Sicily, the 80,000 local residents lived in "emergency" housing for more than 20 years, as "interested" parties and Mafia contractors siphoned off government relief funds for reconstruction. The story of the earthquake which in 1980 shook the Irpinia area west of Naples is another notorious case of corruption and broken promises. After the earthquake, more than $30 billion earmarked for reconstruction never reached its destination.

Italy's enormous volcanic chain stretches, for the most part submerged, from Sicily to the Pontine Islands in Lazio along the western side

**LEFT:** lava flow from one of Mt Etna's last great eruptions, which lasted 473 days in 1991–93.
**RIGHT:** the Irpinia earthquake in Calabria in 1980 killed 6,000 and left 300,000 homeless.

of the peninsula. Most Italian volcanoes are long extinct; some have become lakes or were transformed into islands of charming beauty with post-volcanic activities such as the hot springs, geysers, pools of slightly radioactive mud and natural saunas of Ischia, Salina and Vulcano. Etna, Stromboli and Vulcano (all in Sicily), as well as Naples' Vesuvius, are all active volcanoes, and major tourist attractions.

With a height of 3,323 metres (10,900 ft), a base of nearly 1,600 sq. km (618 sq. miles) and a perimeter of 150 km (93 miles), Mt Etna is the largest volcano in Europe. By contrast, Vesuvius (from the Latin *vesbius*, meaning

"unextinguished"), only 1,277 metres (4,190 ft) high, is one of the smallest active volcanoes in the world. Vulcano and Stromboli, in the Aeolian Islands, are constantly active, emitting modest quantities of vapours, ash, pumice and lava, creating a unique spectacle, especially at night. The Solfatara, in the Phlegraean Fields, is an example of a half-extinct volcano with whistling geysers.

## Mythological meaning

Before being treated in a "scientific" way, volcanoes of the Mediterranean had a special place in classic mythology. For the Greeks, the Aeolian

### VESUVIUS ENTERS THE WAR

The 1944 eruption of Vesuvius surprised the Allied force who had just landed on the Campania coast and occupied Naples. The eruption caused them more damage than a bombing raid by the German air force could have done: an entire squadron of 88 B-25 bombers belonging to the American air force in a landing field near the town of Terzigno was quickly destroyed by the falling ash.

In *Naples 1944*, an extraordinarily vivid account of the time, an English Secret Service official, Norman Lewis, wrote: "March 19: Today Vesuvius erupted. It was the most majestic and terrible spectacle I have ever seen... The smoke from the crater seemed a solid mass as it oozed

slowly in a spiral... the cloud must have been 30 or 40 thousand feet high and it expanded for many miles... Periodically the crater shot snakes of red flame into the sky that flashed like lightning."

The story continued with the description of San Sebastiano, a town reached by the lava that slowly flowed along the main road, while a crowd dressed in black prayed on their knees in front of the danger, clutching at sacred images, among them St Gennaro brought in directly from Naples for the occasion.

Nearly 15,000 inhabitants of San Sebastiano, Somma Vesuviana and Cercola were evacuated by the Allies.

Islands in Sicily were the home of Aeolus, god of the winds, which he held in a grotto. According to legend, Aeolus forecast the weather by observing the vapours emerging from an active volcano (probably Stromboli); today it is known that the cloud formation over Stromboli is influenced by changes in the atmospheric pressure.

### ORIGINS OF LAVA

The word "lava", used to indicate the flow of magma on the earth's surface, originally comes from Neapolitan dialect.

Hephaestus, the Greek god of fire, kept his forge in the bowels of Etna, where he worked along with the Cyclops, giants whose single eye resembled a crater. The Roman god of fire who once lived around Vesuvius and Etna were not afraid to remain in their villages to combat the early effects of an eruption, sweeping the ashes from their roofs to avoid a collapse. The ancient inhabitants of the slopes of Etna, after protecting themselves from the heat by wearing wet sheepskins, used an iron stick to make holes in the surface of the still soft lava, so that a new lava flow was created underneath the surface, whose pressure would fracture the rocky crust; the liquid magma expanded and cooled, slowing its course and thus saving

was Vulcan, whose home was on the Aeolian island of the same name – the mountains of fire which we call volcanoes were named after him in the late Middle Ages.

The common belief that a volcano is a sort of "pressure cooker" that can "explode from one moment to the next" could not be further from the truth. Unlike an earthquake, a volcanic eruption is a phenomenon that can usually be predicted well in advance, and the initial signs do not present a danger. The ancient peoples

the houses and crops otherwise destined to be destroyed (this was the origin of the legend of Ulysses who pierced through Polyphemus-Etna's eye-crater with a spear).

Today, explosives are used on some volcanoes to alter the surface terrain in order to direct the flow of lava into an artificial canal to keep it away from inhabited centres, though on Vesuvius this strategy has always failed because of the high viscosity of its lava. In 2004, residents in the danger zone were offered 25,000 euros per household to leave the area. The offer was prompted by the risk that three million people may be affected by the next eruption. Few show signs of accepting the offer, however.

**LEFT:** figures in a fiery landscape, Etna, 1992.
**ABOVE:** Etna's lava surrounds a farmer's property, but in the end it will enrich the soil.

## Chronology of disasters

In the past 600 years, Italy has suffered 340 ruinous earthquakes and was the scene of spectacular and terrifying volcanic eruptions, including, in the modern era, the formation of a volcano in the Phlegraean Fields.
● AD 62 An earthquake destroyed nearly half of the Roman town of Pompeii *(see page 156).*
● AD 79 Vesuvius buried Pompeii, Herculaneum and Stabia.
● 1538 The youngest volcano in Europe, aptly called Monte Nuovo, was formed in the Phlegraean Fields on 29–30 September.
● 1614–24 The most prolonged eruption of

(12 in) of ash. The cone of the volcano dropped 168 metres (550 ft) and the diameter of the crater doubled.
● 1651–53 Etna destroyed the town of Bronte.
● 1669 One of the most frightening eruptions of Etna brought lava above the city walls of Catania, burying parts of the city; 11 days later the lava reached the sea.
● 1688 More than 1,500 were killed in an earthquake at Benevento, Campania.
● 1693 The earthquake of the Val di Noto, Sicily, on 11 January was the strongest in Italy's recorded history. The main jolt (there were more than 1,500) reached 7.7 on the Richter

Etna in recorded history poured forth a volume of material estimated to be 1,000 million cubic metres over 21 sq. km (8 sq. miles).
● 1627 An earthquake in Gargano, Puglia, obliterated San Severo and a good part of the nearby towns, claiming nearly 5,000 victims.
● 1631 Vesuvius, long inactive and by then covered with green vegetation, re-awoke with the most violent eruption of the past 1,000 years. The early signs were the same that preceded the eruption that destroyed Pompeii: thunder-like rumbling, earthquakes, and murky water in the wells. The damage was extensive: six towns buried by the lava and another nine by the mud; in Naples, roofs collapsed under 30 cm

### THE MESSINA QUAKE

At dawn on 28 December 1908, a sharp tremor struck the area of Messina and Reggio Calabria, followed by a violent tidal wave in the straits that divide the two cities. The boats and the military ships anchored in the port broke their moorings and smashed up against one another, and little remained of the beautiful ancient buildings and churches, nor of the famous Palazzata di Messina, the elegant row of 19th-century palaces that wound along the quay. The dead numbered 50,000, and funds were immediately raised among the expatriate community of Naples and Capri. Reconstruction began in 1911 with strict anti-seismic building codes.

scale, or at least 20 times the power of the earthquake that destroyed Messina in 1908. About 50 villages in a 550-sq. km (212-sq. mile) area were razed to the ground, and nearly 90,000 died. The beautiful baroque town of Noto was rebuilt from scratch 8 km (5 miles) south of the collapsed Noto.

● **1794** For the third time after 1631 and 1737, the lava of Vesuvius penetrated the streets, houses and the churches of Torre del Greco, and after crossing the city plunged into the sea.

● **1783** Several earthquakes hit southern Calabria; nearly 30,000 were killed.

● **1857** Earthquakes in Vulture (Basilicata) and

● **1944** Vesuvius's latest eruption *(see page 114)*.

● **1968** An earthquake in the Valle del Belice, Sicily, killed 300 and left 80,000 homeless.

● **1980** The Irpinia earthquake, Campania: the towns of Sant'Angelo dei Lombardi, Bagnoli Irpino and Nusco still show traces of the catastrophe that killed 6,000, injured 10,000 and left 300,000 homeless.

● **1983** On 14 May the lava flow of Etna was about to hit the towns of Nicolosi, Belpasso and Regalna. For the first time explosives were used to modify the natural beds of the volcano and direct the lava into an artificial basin.

● **1991–93** The eruption on Etna lasted 473 days,

Avellino (Campania) claimed 12,500 lives.

● **1883** Earthquake in Casamicciola, on Ischia, left 2,300 dead, among them many tourists.

● **1906** The lava of Vesuvius invaded Torre Annunziata and Boscotrecase; on 8 April, nearly a metre (3 ft) of slag and detritus fell on a church in San Giuseppe Vesuviano, killing 105 people who had sought refuge inside.

● **1908** The Messina earthquake *(see page 116)*.

● **1928** Mt Etna buries the city of Mascali.

● **1930** Irpinia earthquake: 1,500 killed.

**LEFT:** the earthquake in Messina in 1908.
**ABOVE:** the ruined town of Gibellina after an earthquake in the Valle del Bellice, Sicily, in 1968.

destroyed streets and farmhouses, and reached the edge of the village of Zafferana Etnea.

● **2002** Etna's (and Europe's) biggest eruption for centuries, destroying ski lifts and lodges, with quakes felt as far afield as Palermo and leading to the closure of Catania airport. Earthquake in the poor Campobasso area of Molise destroyed a school, killing 26 children.

● **2003** Stromboli eruption caused the collapse of the northwest flank of the volcano and provoked a *tsunami* giant wave which hit the island and had reverberations throughout the Aeolians.

● **2004–6** Dramatic activity on Etna and Stromboli, from high lava fountains to the opening of new craters. ❑

# WILD PLACES

*Spectacular, untamed landscapes in the protected areas of Calabria, Basilicata and Sicily can be explored along a network of hiking trails*

**M**ost of the southern Italian wilderness is found in protected areas, reserves and national parks. But these areas are not highly geared to tourism and visitors must often find their own way around. The wild parts of the south can be surprisingly green or predictably arid, with flora ranging from mountain evergreens to north African cacti and bushes. The protagonist along the coast and on the islands is the *macchia mediterranea*, scrubland of myrtle, mastic tree, rosemary, juniper, rock rose, broom, laurel, thyme and strawberry tree. Large populations of birds, including many predators, as well as rodents, foxes and wild boar, live side by side with increasing numbers of endangered species such as roe deer, wolves and otter.

The best time to enjoy the natural spaces is in the spring and autumn, the two most colourful seasons. The winter brings other charms: wolves' paw-prints left on the snow which falls on the highest mountains of Calabria, Basilicata and Sicily, and the possibility of skiing. Calabria and Sicily have the most to offer in both variety and extension of protected areas. Basilicata and Campania follow, but the latter's most spectacular landscapes are not to be found in protected areas. Puglia's one great contribution is the Gargano Promontory.

The **Sentiero Italia** is a national trail running all through the Mezzogiorno, beginning in Montalto, in Calabria's Parco dell'Aspromonte. It runs along the spine of the Apennines, passing from valley to valley, with refuges at strategic points along the way where hikers can stay the night. The trail, sponsored by the Club Alpino Italiano (CAI), reaches Umbria and will ultimately go as far as Trieste. (For more information, contact Nuove Frontiere based in Reggio Calabria, tel and fax: 0965-898295.)

Many of the **islands**, although not protected, have preserved their wild nature both above

**LEFT:** the Peregrine falcon inhabits the upper reaches of the Pollino massif. **RIGHT:** roe deer roam in the wilder southwestern corner of Pollino national park.

and below the water. This is particularly evident on the island of Maréttimo off western Sicily, on Filicudi and Alicudi in the Aeolian Islands, on Pantelleria and on Ustica, which has the most spectacular diving in the Tyrrhenian Sea and is one of the most important marine reserves in the Mediterranean.

## Campania

Campania is the most densely populated region in Italy, and its one protected area, the **Parco Nazionale del Cilento**, has little wilderness about it: expect a gorgeous piece of countryside covered with olive groves and wheat fields, with an endangered population of wolves and wild cats surviving in a few remote corners. Paradoxically, the chic island of **Capri** hosts some of the region's most impressive flora and fauna: beside the imported exotic agave, prickly pears and bougainvillea thrives the endemic and beautiful *macchia mediterranea*, which in the coves most protected from the wind leaves room for tiny forests of ilex. The southern coast between Punta Carena and Cala Ventroso and the area around the Arco Naturale are dotted with cluster-pines; the stretch of land between the Grotta Azzurra and Villa Jovis hosts the only palm which has spontaneously grown in Italy in the past 60 million years – the *Chamaerops humilis* – a remnant of the tropical climate that once reigned over the peninsula. The Faraglioni islands are home to the world's only blue common lizard, discovered in 1870.

## Basilicata and Calabria

Italy's largest national park and the richest repository of wildlife in Southern Italy is the

were awestruck by the enormous number of plants: *la macchia mediterranea* dominates the areas from the coast up to 800 metres (2,600 ft); the oak *(Quercus petraea)*, the Neapolitan alder *(Alnus cordata)*, turkey oak *(Quercus cerris)*, chestnut *(Castanea sativa)*, hornbeam *(Carpinus betulus)* and the Lobel maple *(Acer lobelii)* thrive at elevations up to 1,100 metres (3,600 ft); splendid forests of beech trees *(Fagus sylvatica)* extend above 1,000 metres (3,300 ft), all but filtering out the daylight from the ground below, together with the white fir tree *(Abies alba)* and black pine *(Pinus nigra)*.

But what renders the vegetation of the Pollino

**Parco Nazionale del Pollino**, which is equally split between Basilicata and Calabria. It covers 196,000 hectares (750 sq. miles) of mountainous territory in the provinces of Potenza and Cosenza. Its two main areas of interest are the **Pollino massif** in the centre and the wilder **Monti di Orsomarso** in the Calabrese southwest part of the park. Their isolated position and the mountain culture of the 170,000 residents keep the park pristine. Various grandiose projects to build concrete "touristic" resorts in the Pollino ended in 1993 with the official declaration of the Parco as a national park.

Botanists, who began by scientifically exploring the flora of the Pollino in the 19th century,

unique is the *pino loricato (Pinus leucodermis)*, which is only found here and in the Balkans. The emblem of the park, the *pino loricato* grows on the steeper and more rocky side of the Pollino massif and in the Orsomarso area where, at the foot of Mt Palanuda, the oldest specimens have reached a height of 40 metres (130 ft) and a width of a metre (3 ft). Sadly, the famous millenary *pino loricato* tree – the oldest living specimen – which stood at the Grande Porta del Pollino was burned down in 1993 by vandals who opposed the creation of the national park.

The tree takes its name from the unmistakable irregular pattern on its light grey bark, which reminded a local professor of the scales of the *lorica*, the scaled shield of the Roman legionaries. The highly resinous quality of the *pino loricato*'s fibres allows the trunk and branches to survive after the tree dies, becoming a sort of arboreal monument of great beauty against the bare rocks.

Even though it is thought that, on average, the park hosts only 15 percent of the fauna it could potentially hold, the presence of certain species is a good ecological indicator of the park's general environmental wellbeing. In particular, the unpolluted rivers are full of the pro-

**ANNUAL TIDY-UP**

On the third weekend of September every year, hundreds of volunteers carry out a big clean-up campaign in Italy's national parks.

among which the bright pink peony *(Paeonia mascula)* and the yellow orchid *(Dachtylorhiza sambucina)* stand out, attracting some 2,000 different species of insects. The steepest rocks make an ideal habitat for twelve species of predatory birds, including a few pairs of the majestic royal eagle *(Aquila chrysaetos)*, the more common royal kite *(Milvus milvus)* the astonishingly fast Peregrine falcon *(Falco peregrinus)*, which when it swoops down upon its prey reaches speeds of up to 300 km/h (190 mph). Their diet consists mainly of

tected river shrimp *(Austropotamobius pallipes)* and the endangered otter *(Lutra lutra)*, which was nearly brought to extinction in the 20th century by pollution and poachers, who sought its prized skin, and by fishermen with whom it competed. The landscape of the park is extremely varied, ranging from the canyons dropping off the Argentino, Lao and Raganello rivers (navigable in the most dangerous sections with expert river guides) to the high plains and meadows, which after the snow melt are covered with a spectacular mantle of flowers –

**LEFT AND ABOVE:** wild cats and wolves are rare inhabitants of the southern forests.

snakes, lambs, hares and many species of rodents, but also includes wild cats, weasels and skunks.

Mt Pollino (2,248 metres/7,375 ft) and Serra Dolcedorme (2,267 metres/7,438 ft), both in the Pollino massif, are the park's highest mountains: on a clear day, their peaks offer views over the Ionian, Adriatic and Tyrrhenian seas – the only place in Italy you can see all three seas at once.

The wildest areas of the park are to be found in the Monti di Orsomarso, where the brown bear *(orso* in Italian) of the Apennines once roamed. The resident population of roe deer *(Capreolus capreolus)* is probably thankful for its disappearance. The shy Italian wolf *(Canis lupus italicus)* leaves its tracks in the snow and can be heard howling at the moon, but keeps its distance from hunters, who continue to shoot wolves despite their protected status. In all of Calabria, only about a hundred of them survive. The government compensates farmers for livestock presumed to have been lost to the wolves, but in reality the hens and sheep are killed by the 11,000 or more abandoned dogs that roam the park. Towards the more arid eastern border,

> **BURNING ISSUE**
>
> Thousands of hectares of forest burn every summer; most fires are started deliberately by vandals or on behalf of companies specialising in reforestation.

a small species of vulture has been successfully reintroduced – the black-and-white *capovaccaio (Neophron percnopterus)*, known for its technique of breaking the bones of carcasses by bombarding them with stones from the sky.

There are two more national parks in Calabria. Parco Nazionale della Sila (13,000 hectares/50 sq. miles) and Parco Nazionale d' Aspromonte (80,000 hectares/300 sq. miles) are 100 km (60 miles) apart and made up the former Parco Nazionale della Calabria. The rather small **Parco Nazionale della Sila** has a worthwhile nature trail near the Visitors' Centre at Cupone, which reconstructs the ancient environments and local skills, and contains a

mini-zoo of local species, including roe deer, wild boar, deer and wolves. In the rest of the park, you might see foxes, badgers, weasels, skunks, dormice and black squirrels. At the Visitors' Centre you can also pick up a map illustrating 10 easy itineraries that can all be done in less than a day. The landscape is characterised by gentle highlands and vast spaces, for the most part covered by forests of beech trees, with some poplar and maple. The dark-green *pino laricio* (the Calabrian variety of *Pinus nigra*) reaches a height of more than 50 metres (160 ft) in the Selva di Fallistro. Between December and February, there is good downhill and cross-country skiing (contact the tourist office in Camigliatello Silano for information).

The **Parco Nazionale d'Aspromonte** has the feel of a mountainous island, with granite reliefs nearly 2,000 metres (6,500 ft) high surrounded by the Tyrrhenian and Ionian seas. On the rainy western side, the rocks are covered by lush woods of oak, chestnut, alder, maple, ash, hornbeam and (above 1,200 metres/3,900 ft) by *pino laricio*, beech and white fir; while on the drier eastern side, the rocks often appear bare. Rare animal species here include the wolf, wild cat and Bonelli eagle. More abundant are the royal owl, sparrowhawk and buzzard; squirrels and other small rodents abound.

Many local associations organise unforgettable week-long excursions, providing camping equipment and donkeys, or minibuses for difficult sections.

## Puglia

Although all of Puglia's **Promontorio del Gargano** was made a national park in 1991, only a small part of it can be described as "wild": the **Foresta Umbra** in the interior, which extends for 11,000 hectares (42 sq. miles) at an elevation of 700 metres (2,300 ft) above sea level. Its cool woods of oaks, pines and beeches hide a variety of wildlife (including the roe deer, reintroduced to the area), and a number of marked trails. The nearest tourist information office is in San Severo.

## Sicily

The unique combination of vegetation and volcanic "sculpture" makes the 59,000-hectare

(230-sq.-mile) **Parco dell'Etna** the most interesting of Sicily's protected areas. The fertile lowlands are cultivated with citrus, almonds and hazelnuts; juniper, ash and chestnut take over above 700 metres (2,300 ft), among which is the famous chestnut tree of Cento Cavalli, in Sant'Alfio. According to legend, the tree's 60-metre (200-ft) canopy gave shelter to Queen Joanna of Anjou and her escort of 100 knights. Further up, the forests of beech and *pino laricio* show the scars of the lava flows. This area is home to dormice, foxes, numerous birds and about 70 species of butterfly. Above 3,000 metres (9,800 ft), the landscape is composed of black rocks, ash and pumice stones. The park has any number of exciting areas to explore, but, given the resurgence of volcanic activity, check the options with Catania tourist office. Whether the attraction is a hike around moody lava fields, a botanical ramble or a jeep trip to explore Etna's geology, a guide represents not just a guarantee of greater enjoyment but also guarantee of your safety.

The **Parco dei Nebrodi** extends over 85,000 hectares (330 sq. miles) of the Tyrrhenian coast between Capo d'Orlando and Santo Stefano di Camastra, and features a varied mountainous and coastal landscape. What renders it unique in Sicily are the humid zones: little lakes, marshes and streams between which sit the lakes of Biviere and Trearie, where a number of migratory birds overwinter.

To the west is the 35,000-hectare (135-sq.-mile) **Parco delle Madonie**. Cefalù and the ancient but open-minded mountain village of Castelbuono represent the best bases for exploring the park. Sicily has been slow to develop its green credentials, but bird-watching, hiking, riding, mountain-biking and skiing now show the sporty side of Palermo province. An impressive range of reliable material on activities, routes and farm-stays is available from Palermo tourist office. Also contact the park headquarters in Petralia Sottana (tel: 0921-684011). The growth of bed-and-breakfast and farm-stay holidays in rural Sicily adds to the rugged appeal of the Madonie.

With 200-million-year-old fossils, the rocks here are the oldest on the island. A good network of paths and gravel roads makes it easy to reach the most remote corners. The Sicilian writer Giuseppe di Lampedusa described the area in *The Leopard* as "aridly undulating to the horizon in hillock after hillock... conceived apparently in a delirious moment of creation; a sea suddenly petrified at the instant when a change of wind had flung waves into a frenzy." But the park also has patches of thick forest, as well as shelters and tiny churches cut out of the rocks, imposing farming estates, hermitages and monasteries.

The **Ibleo high plains**, in the extreme southeast of Sicily, are made up of calceous rocks cut by spectacular river canyons *(cave)*. Some are

dry, others lush with vegetation. The most noted is the 14-km (9-mile), **cava d'Ispica** archaeological site, perfumed with capers and herbs.

Finally, **Lo Zingaro**, a wonderful coastal reserve on the rocky northwest coast, is the most user-friendly of all Sicily's nature reserves. It can be reached by boat from the fishing village of Castellammare del Golfo *(see page 283)*. Sicily also has a number of marine reserves, of which the best known are Ustica, beloved by divers, and the Egadi Islands, where the crisis in the fishing industry has prompted the region to take ecotourism more seriously, including the creation of a museum of the sea in Favignana. ❏

**LEFT:** wild violets of the Aspromonte.
**RIGHT:** Red Valerian thrives on the volcanic slopes of Mt Etna.

# PLACES

*A detailed guide to the entire region, with main sites*
*clearly cross-referenced by number to the maps*

The four mainland provinces (Campania, Apulia, Basilicata and Calabria) and the nine Sicilian provinces *(see page 267)* of Southern Italy are set between four seas, which means a beach is never far away. Each coast has its distinct flavour. The Tyrrhenian side is the best known. It begins with the Bay of Naples, which curls round to the Sorrento peninsula so that Capri and the islands are never out of view. Then it takes the switchback corniche down the Amalfi Coast, one of the most dramatic and picturesque in Europe, to the Cilento Coast and Basilicata all the way to the tip of Calabria, where beaches and coves attract more visitors each year.

The opposite Adriatic coast is a succession of ancient ports with bleached Norman churches and castles, which were nurtured by crusaders' zeal. This coast's high point is the Gargano Peninsula, the most dramatic event on Italy's entire east coast. Between the two, the Ionian Sea makes a sandy sweep inside the instep of Italy's familiar "boot", changing its name to the Gulf of Taranto. Much of this stretch seems to have stagnated in time and remains largely neglected.

Outside of the main sights around Naples and in Sicily, don't expect to see much evidence of classical times; wars and earthquakes have taken their toll. The best museum is the Museo Archeologico Nazionale in Naples, which contains many treasures from Pompeii, Herculaneum and Paestum, but local museums, notably in the regional capitals of Bari and Reggio Calabria, have treasures, too. Naples, the capital of the south, is a great seaport and one of the most exciting cities in Europe, where a car is a liability, and a handbag needs to be clutched tightly.

Railways link the main cities and popular resorts, such as Gargano, but in the main the *Mezzogiorno* remains untamed by public transport. To make the most of it, you will need to go your own way. To seek out the Sassi, the cave dwellers of Matera in Basilicata, or the *trulli*, the strange circular houses in Apulia, or to explore the Gargano fully, or see the Albanians in festive mood, needs flexibility. Roads are not always straightforward. The Apennines, Italy's backbone, stretch all the way to the Aspromonte, the highlands on the tip of the toe, making inland roads twist and curve. But the rewards are a diverse and delightful countryside. In the quieter areas, don't expect full tourist facilities, even in the regions now designated national parks. These are not places for the package holidaymaker, but the curious traveller will find rich rewards.  ❑

**PRECEDING PAGES:** viaducts carry the motorway through the rolling hills of Apulia; granite columns with Corinthian capitals (wrongly repositioned in the 19th century) in the Greek Theatre in Taormina, Sicily; the atrium of Salerno Cathedral, built with Corinthian columns taken from the nearby Greek settlement at Paestum.
**LEFT:** overlooking the Cathedral of San Pantalcone in Ravello on the Amalfi coast.

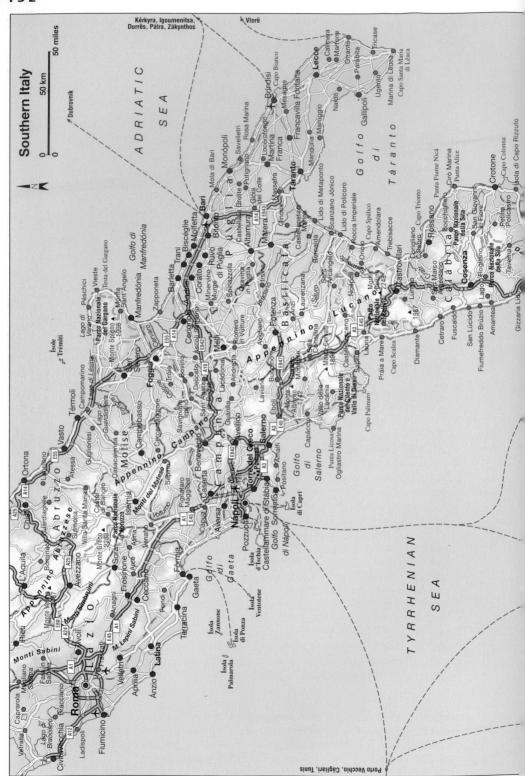

## Southern Italy

N

0     50 km
0     50 miles

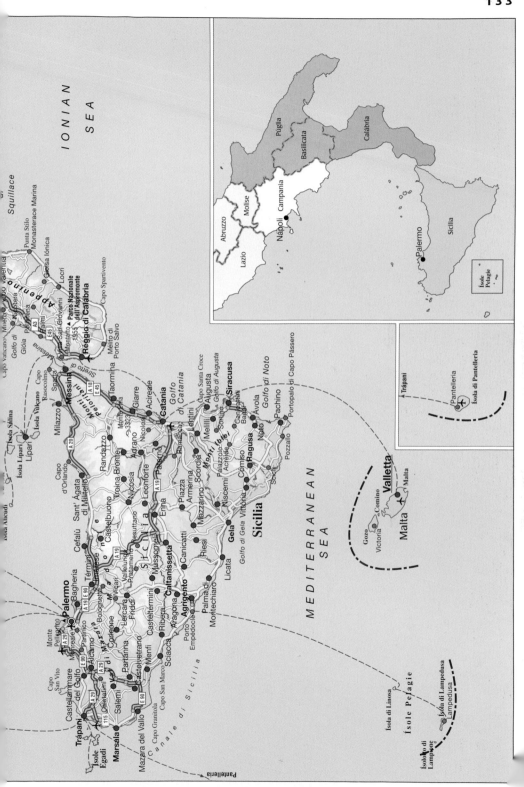

# NAPLES

*Italy's liveliest city is not to be missed. Naples bursts with a passionate and energetic culture, found both in its excellent museums and bustling street life*

Map on page 136

Naples

There has never been a shortage of words describing Naples; it always provokes a reaction. And any selection of quotes about the city and its inhabitants will probably include admiration and disdain in equal measure. So is this mercurial metropolis heaven on earth, or hell's gateway? The writer Peter Nichols puts it like this: "Neapolitans reproduce what must be the nearest equivalent to life in ancient times. The city is one of the great tests: some hate it and some love it. But I think that people who don't like Naples are afraid of something."

Their fear may be the result of the city's lingering reputation for crime and poverty. In truth, this image is the result of media hype as misleading as the romantic image which preceded it. In fact, under the guidance of an enlightened mayor, Naples has been enjoying a cultural renaissance for over a decade. But, above all, the city is a unique feast for the senses; here every aspect of life, including survival itself, is elevated to an art form. There is no better place to encounter this phenomenon than in the city's main thoroughfare, the famous Spaccanapoli.

Negotiating the city is not as fraught with danger as some people, including Neapolitans themselves, would have visitors believe. There are of course certain parts of the city that are probably best avoided by tourists in the evenings (the slum areas of Forcella and Ponticelli, for example), but for the most part Naples is no more threatening than any other major city.

In the rush hour, when the traffic in the congested streets comes to its daily standstill, the best way to get around most of the city is to walk or use public transport. The hills and the harbour and especially the castles and palaces, such as Castel dell'Ovo or Castel Sant' Elmo, provide reliable orientation in the maze of streets in the old part of the city.

Visitors should not be afraid to ask locals for help if they have lost their way. Neopolitans have a reputation for friendliness and hospitality, and most encounters with most Neapolitans are positive, even though the constant advice to keep a firm grip on handbags and camera cases is well-meant, if unnerving. Time and again, Neapolitans will offer to accompany you safely to your destination.

## The old town

Most visitors' first impression of Naples is the noise and confusion of the city's main transport hub, **Piazza Garibaldi ❶**. Every day, many hundreds of thousands of commuters converge here to catch their subway, train, bus or taxi. Don't let the fast-walking crowds, insistent street vendors, zig-zagging scooters

**LEFT:** view over the city to the Bay.
**BELOW:** the best way of getting round town.

and cars discourage you – the notoriously bad Neapolitan traffic is at its worst right here. Be aware that this is prime pickpocketing territory.

The narrow and quieter streets of the historic centre begin at the western end of Piazza Garibaldi. Conquerors of the past would enter the town through **Porta Capuana**, a sturdy Renaissance gate flanked by two mighty Aragonese towers. The open space in front of it, now used as a marketplace, was once the scene of public punishments. From here, the **Forcella** quarter spreads down to **Corso Umberto I ❷**. With a reputation for being the Camorra's main stronghold within central Naples, the area is a favourite for hawkers selling black-market cigarettes and fake brand-name sunglasses and watches.

Via Forcella leads into one of the world's oldest urban streets, originally the Roman *Decumanus Inferior* but these days familiarly known as **Spaccanapoli ❸**. *Spacca* means "split", a reference to the way this long and straight street cuts right through the city. The street changes names as it runs from east to west: Via Vicaria Vecchia, Via San Biagio dei Librai, Via Benedetto Croce and Via Scura. This busy thoroughfare, dotted with historic buildings, churches and squares, is the real heart of the old town. It throngs with Neapolitans out shopping, hanging around chatting, zipping around on mopeds and generally going about their daily lives. At lunchtime there is a lull, but noise levels pick up again after 4 o'clock and by the early evening human traffic is back in full flow.

## San Gennaro's blood

Heading west, make a right turn into Spaccanapoli's main side street, Via Duomo, to pay homage to the patron saint of Naples, San Gennaro (the bishop of Benevento martyred at Pozzuoli's amphitheatre in AD 305). The **Duomo ❹** contains the saint's holy relics – two phials of blood and a gold bust said to contain his skull – housed in the **Cappella del Tesoro**. San Gennaro's fame is due in no small measure to the miracle of the liquefying blood, celebrated in the cathedral twice a year (on the first Saturday of May and 19 September). During the

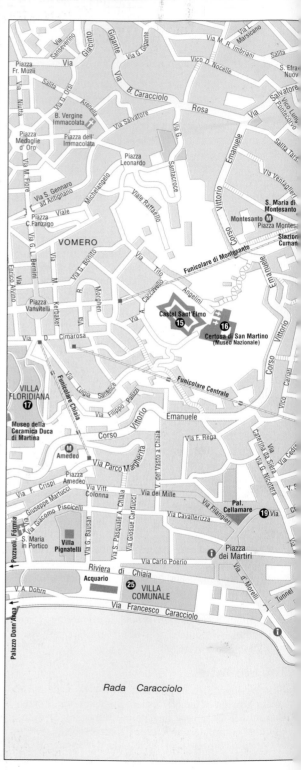

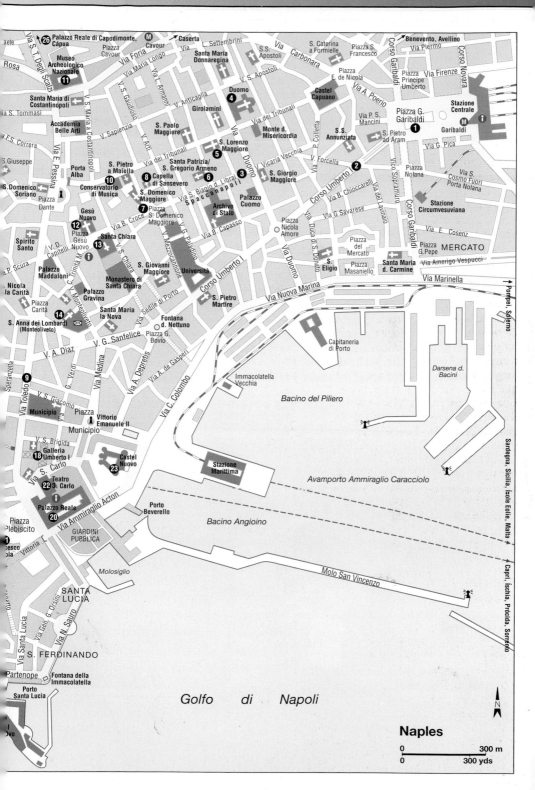

Naples

Golfo di Napoli

0           300 m
0           300 yds

mass, a reliquary containing the saint's blood is tipped to and fro in the midst of prayers, chants and an atmosphere rich with the hopes and fears of thousands of believers, willing the dried blood to liquefy. Amazingly, on most occasions, the blood does indeed appear to liquefy, and is cause for much celebration; the rare exceptions are considered to be a bad omen. No scientist has ever been allowed to test the holy dark-red substance, but the last great eruption of Vesuvius (in 1944) and the earthquake which hit Irpinia northeast of Naples (in 1980) occurred in years that the blood refused to liquefy.

Of little interest in itself, the Duomo (begun in 1294, but with a neo-Gothic façade that dates from the early 20th century) encloses the oldest surviving structure in town, the church of **Santa Restituta**, built by Constantine in 324 with a fine baptistery and columns taken from the Temple of Apollo which stood on the site (excavations visible 9am–noon, 5–7pm).

## San Lorenzo Maggiore and San Gregorio Armeno

Retrace your steps along Via Duomo as far as Via Tribunali. Turn right here and one block down across the road is another Gothic church, **San Lorenzo Maggiore ❺**, home to two large canvases by Calabrian Mattia Preti *(see page 262)* and several medieval sepulchres. Recent excavations have unearthed parts of the Roman *macellum* (food market) and a Christian basilica built on top of it (accessible from the cloister). Continue along **Via di San Gregorio Armeno** to the **Benedectine convent ❻** of the same name, which once served as a repository for the daughters of noble Neapolitan families who were forced to become nuns to save on dowries. The quiet, exotic garden of the pretty **cloister** makes for a pleasant break.

*Naples was founded in the 8th century BC by Greek settlers from nearby Cumae. They had already established a hilltop town known as Parthenope, and as it prospered they built Neapolis (new city) to accommodate the growing population. The chequerboard pattern of streets around Spaccanapoli dates from this period.*

**BELOW:** a *salumeria* selling groceries.

## Piazza San Domenico Maggiore

The Via San Biagio dei Librai leads to **Piazza San Domenico Maggiore ❼**. This attractive pedestrian square is marked by one of the many baroque *guglie* (wooden and stucco spires decorated with putti, flowers and fruit baskets, and carried around town for religious festivals and royal parades). The Neapolitans made these as thanksgiving memorials to the Madonna and saints, in this case for deliverance from the Plague of 1658. No other Italian town developed a taste for "petrifying" *guglie*, and you can see other examples on Piazza del Gesù *(guglia dell'Immacolata)* and next to the Duomo, on Piazzetta Riario Sforza *(guglia of San Gennaro)*.

The 14th-century church of San Domenico Maggiore, much altered due to earthquakes, fires and war damage, has some good examples of Renaissance sculpture and a copy of Caravaggio's *Flagellation* (the original is now at Capodimonte). The square itself is a hangout for students from the nearby university. The café here is perfectly placed for watching the lively comings and goings and admiring the spire.

Around the corner is the baroque **Cappella di Sansevero ❽** (Via Francesco de Sanctis; open Mon and Wed–Sat 10am–5.40pm, Sun 10am–1.10pm, closed Tues; entrance fee), well worth visiting for its air of black magic and virtuoso monuments built for Prince Raimondo di Sangro (1749–71). The most compelling are Corradini's *Pudicizia* (Modesty), Queirolo's *Disinganno* (Disillusion) and Sammartino's masterpiece, the **Cristo Velato** (Veiled Christ).

Carved from a single piece of marble, this statue of a recumbent Christ draped in a translucent veil is a remarkable feat of realism. Prince Raimondo was an alchemist and amateur scientist, who also dabbled in the occult, using the chapel

**TIP**

In Piazza San Domenico Maggiore, the long-established pastry shop Scaturchio is one of the best in town for local favourites like *sfogliatelle ricce* and *cassate*; the *ministeriale* (chocolate with a creamy filling) is a house speciality.

**BELOW:** antiques and bric-a-brac shop with local puppet figures.

as his workshop. According to legend, the two gruesome mannequins in the **crypt** were the result of a macabre experiment, in which he injected two slaves with a liquid to preserve their cardiovascular systems. The prince was eventually excommunicated by the pope for his dubious activities.

### Via Toledo

Naples' grandest thoroughfare and its main shopping area is **Via Toledo ❾**, which descends gently seawards from Piazza Dante to Piazza Plebiscito. Stendhal found it to be "the most populous and gayest street in the world." Officially renamed Via Roma at the birth of the Italian State, locally it is still referred to as Via Toledo. The energetic Spanish viceroy, Don Pedro di Toledo (1532–53), effected the most radical and ambitious urban redevelopment in the city's history, including the construction of new streets, the doubling of the city's habitable space, and the enlargement of defensive structures. Always busy, Via Toledo's peak hours are the late afternoon when Neapolitans gather for their evening *passeggiata*.

Start your own walk along Via Toledo from Piazza Dante at the northern edge of the historical centre, best reached via Piazza San Domenico Maggiore from **Via San Pietro a Maiella**. This quiet street is flanked by shops specialising in musical instruments and sheet music catering to students of the prestigious **Conservatorio di Musica ❿** (take a look at the cloister if open); more music shops await on Via San Sebastiano, proof that Naples is Italy's most musical city.

Piazza Dante is a departure point for buses going south to the Riviera di Chiaia and Mergellina; and you can also catch the No. 161 bus to **Capodimonte** *(see page 146)*.

**BELOW:** a complex catacomb network lies beneath Naples' streets.

## BENEATH THE CITY STREETS

Underneath the thronging, sun-baked city lies another, dark, cold and damp Naples, of which nobody knows the actual dimensions, although to date some 700 cavities have been catalogued. A trip beneath Naples passes through what was once the Greco-Roman Neapolis to the catacombs, cemeteries and branches of the aqueduct, built during the reign of Emperor Augustus, that were used as shelters during World War II air raids.

The **cloister of San Lorenzo** *(see page 138;* tel: 081-290580) is not the city's only gate to this underworld: other portals to Naples' past can be found at **Piazza San Gaetano 68** (tel: 081-296944; www.napolisotterranea.org); on **Via Santa Teresella degli Spagnoli** (tel: 081-400256); and the **Cimitero delle Fontanelle** (church of Maria Santissima del Carmine). On Capodimonte you can visit the **Catacombe di San Gaudioso** (church of Santa María della Sanità; tel: 081-544 1305; booking required) which contain the remains of African bishop St Gaudiosus, who died in AD 452, and the larger **Catacombe di San Gennaro** (entrance from the street that skirts Madre del Buon Consiglio church off Via Capodimonte; open daily; tours at 9.30, 10.15, 11 and 11.45am; entrance fee; tel: 081-741 1071), with early Christian paintings.

## Antiques and antiquities

North of Piazza Dante, on the opposite side of Piazza Bellini, is the attractive **Via Santa Maria a Costantinopoli**. This road, lined with antiques and bric-a-brac shops, leads to the **Museo Archeologico Nazionale** ⓫ (open daily except Tues 9am–7.30pm; entrance fee), one of the world's largest collections of Roman antiquities. The collection includes the Farnese sculptures and a display of everyday objects, frescoes and statues, as well as mosaics from Pompeii, Herculaneum and Stabia. *(For further details of the museum, see pages 148–9.)*

The intersection of Spaccanapoli and Via Toledo is a good place to stop and admire the long, narrow crossroads. From here the Via dei Capitelli leads to Piazza del Gesù Nuovo. Passing the decorative **guglia dell'Immacolata**, built by the Jesuits but financed by "offerings" extorted from the public, you reach **Chiesa del Gesù Nuovo** ⓬. Lined with coloured marbles and gaudy frescoes by baroque painters Solimena and Ribera, the ornate church contrasts starkly with the austerity of **Santa Chiara** ⓭, opposite. In 1943, a bomb destroyed the spectacular 18th-century interior. Reconstruction efforts stripped away the baroque elements and restored the convent to its original French Gothic. Fragments of a Giotto fresco can be seen in the convent choir.

*This majolica figure in Santa Chiara's cloister echoes the colours of mosaics found recently in Herculaneum.*

The **Chiostro delle Clarisse** (open Mon–Sat 9.30am–1pm, 2.30– 5.30pm, Sun 9.30am–1pm; entrance fee) is one of Naples' true wonders. In 1742, the wife of the Bourbon King Charles decided to transform the cloister lawn into a refined garden. The ground level was elevated, a retaining wall was built, and dozens of benches were placed on this wall. Between the benches are 72 octagonal pillars, which support trellised grape vines and wisteria. The walls, benches and pillars were completely covered with majolica tiles of mythological images,

**BELOW:**
the tiled cloister
in Santa Chiara.

*Traffic cop – not the
easiest of jobs to
have in Naples,
particularly given the
current expansion of
the transport network,
from the new metro
to funiculars to
pedestrianisation.*

**BELOW:** the sturdy
medieval fortress of
Castel Sant' Elmo.

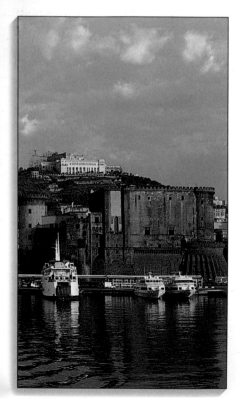

scenes of daily life in the fields, fishermen and sailors. Recent restoration
brought to light medieval frescoes, while the garden was replanted with the
same species grown here in Bourbon times. Within the small museum displaying decorative elements salvaged from the bomb wreckage, an excavated area
reveals part of an old Roman baths complex (1st century BC).

## The Spanish Quarter

Return to Via Toledo and cross to Via P. Scura, then turn into Via Pignasecca
(second left) to visit Naples' most picturesque **food market** (open Mon–Sat
mornings only). The steep and narrow street is a jumble of fruit, fish and tripe
stalls, bakeries, delis and specialist food shops piled high with tinned goods,
pasta, salamis and wheels of cheese, and cut-price clothes and shoe shops.

Via Pignasecca ends at the junction of Via Toledo, Piazza Carità and Piazza
Monteoliveto; the latter leads to the church of **Sant' Anna dei Lombardi** .
The interior is worth a look for its Renaissance sculpture, including the *Pietà*
by Guido Mazzoni, a realistic, life-size representation.

Continuing downhill along Via Toledo, a patchwork of lanes and steep stair-
cases fan out to the right in the area that Don Pedro di Toledo selected to house
the Spanish garrison. In later times, the neighbourhood was colonised by the
poorest Neapolitan families, and dark and unsanitary ground-floor and basement
slums were turned into homes known as the *bassi*. Even today you can sometimes catch a glimpse through the prison-like windows of *mamma* at the stove
and *papà* mending his fishing nets. To a certain extent, the **Quartieri Spagnoli**
still lives up to the romantic cliché of Neapolitan slums, with crumbling houses
held together by colourful washing lines, and *scugnizzi* (street urchins) running
through the streets kicking a football or singing a
song. But to more jaded eyes, thanks largely to rival
factions of the Camorra, crime and degradation over-
shadow the picturesque.

## Funiculì Funiculà

The **Vomero** hill is worth visiting if just for the fun of
a ride on the funicular railway (from the bottom of
Via Toledo) and the great view of the town below.
But this modern neighbourhood also has some key
landmarks, reminders of a more idyllic past, now
turned into three of Naples' finest museums.

Start with **Castel Sant'Elmo** ⑮ (open daily except
Wed 8.30am–7.30pm; entrance fee), a massive
medieval fortress, built in the shape of a star, with a
commanding view of the Bay. Once used as a prison
for political troublemakers, it is now a public exhibition space. Adjoining the fortress is the **Certosa di
San Martino** ⑯, a bit older than the fortress and
given an agreeable baroque restyling. The old Carthusian monastery is now the site of the **Museo
Nazionale di San Martino** (open daily except Wed
8.30am–7.30pm; entrance fee) with 90 rooms which
house paintings, furniture, ceramics, model ships,
coins and costumes illustrating the life and history of
Naples. Highlights include the pharmacy, with antique
glass jars from Murano; the outstanding pinacoteca
of the **Quarto del Priore** (prior's apartment); and t'

well-kept gardens of the **Chiostro Grande** (great cloister). But the most charming section of the museum is the **Presepi Collection,** with a wealth of 18th- and 19th-century nativity scenes composed of statuettes, some the work of famous sculptors. The largest and most famous is the *Presepe Cuciniello*, with its hundreds of tiny statues and objects.

A little to the west stands the **Villa Floridiana** ⑰. Once described as a "baroque chocolate box with neoclassical touches", the villa was originally a wedding present from Ferdinand I, King of the Two Sicilies, to his long-time lover, the Duchess of Floridia, who he married after the death of the queen, by which time they were both grandparents. The villa now houses the **Museo della Ceramica Duca di Martina** (guided tours only 9.30am, 11am, 12.30pm; closed Tues; entrance fee), filled with a fine collection of majolica and porcelain from Europe and the Far East. If bowls and figurines are not your cup of tea, the view of the Bay from the park is worth the detour.

## Around Piazza Plebiscito

Towards the sea end of Via Toledo, opposite the funicular to Vomero, stands the majestic **Galleria Umberto I** ⑱. This is a good introduction to the "royal quarters" of the Piazza Plebiscito, even though the Bourbon dynasty had already succumbed to the new-born Italian State when the gallery was inaugurated in 1890. Although extensively restored in the 1990s, it's hard to imagine how grand the place must have looked at the turn of the 19th century when it was a meeting point of the Neapolitan intelligentsia and aristocracy. Today, a less-than-glamorous collection of shops does not do justice to the fine marble floor and cupola, a triumph of iron and glass nearly 60 metres (200 ft) high.

**TIP**

The Campania ArteCard (www.artecard.it) is a combined 3- or 7-day transport and museum pass to sites including Pompeii and Herculaneum. The card is available at many places including the tourist office in the porticoes of Galleria Umberto I.

**BELOW:** wedding pictures in the Galleria Umberto I.

## CHRISTMAS CRIBS

In the first days of November, the streets between Piazza San Gaetano and Via San Biagio dei Librai become the most bustling and crowded in the city. The stalls that surround the monastery of San Gregorio Armeno fuel the yearly craze for *presepi* (Christmas cribs) that consumes Neapolitans. The seasonal marketplace offers the ingredients for do-it-yourself nativity scenes for all tastes and budgets. The creation of a nativity scene is seen as an art form and you can let your imagination run riot adding papier-mâché mountains, a fountain that spouts water, or a miniature mill with power wheel. Neapolitan *presepi* are unique in Italy because Jesus, Mary, Joseph and the shepherds are often joined by singers, actors, politicians, football players and other contemporary characters. Popular local heroes include movie legend Totò, Pulcinella, Maradona, who played for Napoli in the 1980s, the mayor of Naples and Olympic swimmer Massimiliano Rosolino.

The fine work of Neapolitan craftsmanship and tradition can be observed all year round in nearby craft workshops that specialise in figurines. One of Naples' best-known *presepe* artisans, Giuseppe Ferrigno (Via San Gregorio Armeno 10), turns out 18th-century-style shepherds with terracotta faces, wearing robes cut from period fabrics.

*Teatro San Carlo's opulent auditorium. The theatre is open daily for tours 9am– 5.30pm. The opera season runs from Nov–May, but with concerts year round. The ticket office is in the Galleria opposite.*

**BELOW:** timeless Caffè Gambrinus.

Naples' smartest shopping street, **Via Chiaia** , makes up for the loss. Wrily referred to as the only place in town where goods are genuine, even pizzas here come with an official stamp. Tucked away on Salita Sant'Anna, but clearly visible from Via Chiaia, is the old **Pizzeria Brandi**, credited with the invention of Pizza Margherita *(see page 96)*, a mecca for pizza fans, but not even a flavoursome historical bite can fully redeem what has become a benign tourist trap.

Piazza Plebiscito, thankfully liberated from its role as a car park, now looks grand and spacious. The piazza was laid out in 1602 as part of the hasty construction of the **Palazzo Reale** (open daily except Wed 9am–7pm; entrance fee). It was commissioned from Domenico Fontana by the Spanish Viceroy to host Phillip II, who never came to town. With the exception of the eight portraits of monarchs which were added to the main facade in 1888 to symbolise the eight dynasties that ruled over the city, no king has ever inhabited the palace. The second-floor museum has 30 rooms, each richly decorated and furnished with period furniture and paintings. The highlights here are the ornate private theatre (1768) and the Palatine Chapel with its magnificent altar by Lazzari (1674), master of Neapolitan baroque decoration.

During his seven-year reign, Napoleon's brother-in-law Joachim Murat pulled down a convent to make space for the semicircle of Doric columns pompously named the Foro Murat. At the centre of the colonnade stands the church of **San Francesco di Paola**, built between 1817 and 1846. It was commissioned by Ferdinand I to mark his return from exile, the end of Napoleonic rule and the return of the Bourbon dynasty to power. Modelled on Rome's Pantheon, with a cupola 53 metres (174 ft) high and 34 metres (112 ft) in diameter, the church is a striking sight, especially when floodlit at night.

On the small Piazza Trento e Trieste is the inconspicuous facade of the **Teatro San Carlo** ㉒. Completed on St Charles' Day (4 November), 1737, when Naples was the capital of music in Europe, it was Europe's largest opera house. The theatre quickly earned a reputation for the beauty of its six-tiered auditorium and its fine productions; it is still noted for its perfect acoustics. Nearby is the historic **Caffè Gambrinus**, with its old mirrors and barmen dressed as if they were headed for the opening of the season next door.

From this piazzetta, it's a short walk to **Castel Nuovo** ㉓ (open Mon–Sat 9am–7pm, closed Sun; entrance fee), built in the late 13th century during Charles of Anjou's reign. The awesome, if incongruous, **Triumphal Arch** was added in 1467 to commemorate the entry of King Alfonso I of Aragon (later King of Naples and Sicily) into Naples. The ornate white arch stands in stark contrast to the bulky brown towers that support it on either side. Used as a royal residence until the construction of Palazzo Reale, today Castel Nuovo houses the City Council Chamber, a library, the Palatine Chapel and a **Museo Civico** with paintings and sculptures from suppressed churches and convents.

## Along the waterfront to Posillipo

The waterfront can be reached on foot from Piazza Plebiscito, or from il Vomero via the Funicolare Chiaia, taking in Via Parco Margherita, Via dei Mille and Via Filangieri – a route which passes some attractive shops and Art Deco villas. The smell of the sea leads you to Borgo Marinari, the former fishermens' quarter, now full of sailing clubs and busy trattorias. A bridge connects Via Partenope with the formidable Swabian **Castel dell'Ovo** ㉔ (open Mon–Sat 8am–6pm, Sun 8am–2pm) or "egg-castle", so called because, according to legend, it sits on an

Map on page 136

*In the 19th century, King Ferdinand I's pet crocodile, allegedly fed on a diet of unlucky prisoners, was embalmed and hung on the walls of the Castel Nuovo.*

**BELOW:** French towers and Spanish arch, Castel Nuovo.

Map
on page
136

*Funicular railways
are one of the more
efficient forms of
transport in Naples.*

**BELOW:** elegant
facades by the sea.
**RIGHT:** sun seekers
and Castel dell'Ovo.

egg talisman which belonged to the Roman poet Virgil. The egg is inside a bottle and well protected by an iron cage: should it break, Naples will fall.

Head west along the pedestrianised Via Caracciolo, and spend some time in the **Villa Comunale gardens** ㉕. Come here on Sunday afternoon if you want a taste of Neapolitan life: families gather after lunch in their Sunday best and stroll and chat under the shade of the palms while their children run around and eat ice creams. If you have your own kids in tow, visit Europe's oldest **Aquarium**, built in 1872 (open summer Tues–Sat 9am–6pm, Sun and hols 9.30am–7pm; winter Tues–Sat 9am–5pm, Sun and hols 9am–2pm; entrance fee).

Across the Riviera di Chiaia is the neoclassical **Villa Pignatelli** (open Tues–Sun 8.30am–1.30pm; entrance fee). Once owned by the Rothschild family, it now houses a collection of porcelain and period furniture. Via Caracciolo ends in the Mergellina district, home to groups of fishermen who supply the local seafood market. Piazza Sannazzaro is a popular nightspot, full of pizzerias and inexpensive restaurants *(for more about Neapolitan nightlife, see page 352)*.

Via Posillipo climbs up to an intriguing building, the yellowish **Palazzo Donn'Anna**, built in 1642 from tufa. Once you reach the Parco della Rimembranza and Capo Posillipo, the view is spectacular.

## Capodimonte

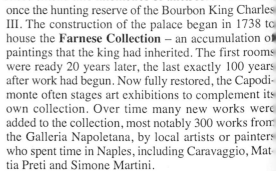

On the north side of the city, the Pompeiian red façade of the **Palazzo Reale di Capodimonte** ㉖ (open daily except Wed 8.30am–7.30pm; entrance fee; accessible by bus from the Stazione Centrale on Piazza Garibaldi, Piazza Municipio, Piazza Dante and the Archaeological Museum) stands against the blue sky and the green fields beyond. These extend into kilometres of thick forest that were once the hunting reserve of the Bourbon King Charles III. The construction of the palace began in 1738 to house the **Farnese Collection** – an accumulation of paintings that the king had inherited. The first rooms were ready 20 years later, the last exactly 100 years after work had begun. Now fully restored, the Capodimonte often stages art exhibitions to complement its own collection. Over time many new works were added to the collection, most notably 300 works from the Galleria Napoletana, by local artists or painters who spent time in Naples, including Caravaggio, Mattia Preti and Simone Martini.

The museum's highlight is the superb collection of 200 paintings by world-famous Italian and Flemish painters – including Masaccio, Botticelli, Bellini, Titian and Van Dyck – which the sharp-eyed Farnese dynasty amassed over three centuries of avid collecting. The museum is too large to be seen in its entirety in just one day, so try to focus on what interests you most: armour, tapestry, porcelain or painting. The magnificent **Salottino di Porcellana** is lined from top to bottom with Capodimonte porcelain tiles made in King Charles III's porcelain factory in 1757. It took two years and more than 3,000 pieces to decorate the walls and ceilings of the queen's parlour. Originally installed in the Royal Palace at Portici, the *salottino* was dismantled in 1866 and reassembled here.

# ART AND ANTIQUITIES OF THE ROMAN ERA

*Naples' national museum ranks among the world's best, housing spectacular finds from Pompeii and Herculaneum, and the colossal Farnese sculptures*

Originally a military barracks, then a university, the vast red *palazzo* north of Spaccanapoli was transformed into an archaeological museum under Bourbon rule. The rooms on the ground floor are devoted to the Farnese Collection – statues that the Bourbon King Charles inherited through his mother from the powerful Farnese family. First-rate copies of older Greek masterpieces are mingled with original Roman creations. Over a varied crowd of heroes and warriors, Aphrodites and Athenas, towers the largest sculpture from antiquity ever found, the *Farnese Bull*, unearthed at the Baths of Caracalla in Rome. The rich collection of mosaics on the mezzanine floor comes from the floors, walls and courtyards of Pompeiian homes. One of the highlights here is the *Battle of Issus*, the remains of a war scene depicting Alexander the Great in his victorious battle against the Persian emperor, Darius (333 BC). Special permanent exhibits include the fine bronze figures from the Villa dei Papiri in Herculaneum (look out for the two athletes whose concentrated expression is almost disconcerting); the Egyptian collection, which contains a mummified crocodile; and the collection of carved precious stones, featuring the *Farnese Bowl*, a giant cameo with fine pink reliefs on a black field (*circa* 150 BC). A recent addition to the museum is a nearly complete fresco cycle detached from the Temple of Isis in Pompeii, with Egyptian landscapes and two episodes from the myth of Io.

▷ **BACCHIC CELEBRATIONS**
After centuries buried in ash, the freshness and colour of Pompeii's artworks are an amazing tribute to the craftsmanship of their ancient makers.

△ **MARBLE LEGEND**
Carved from a single block of marble, the huge *Farnese Bull* depicts the death of Dirce, tied to a bull by Antiope's sons for trying to murder their mother.

▽ **CLASSICAL GIANTS**
The Farnese Collection is a mass of towering sculptures including the statue of Hercules resting on his club (far end).

◁ **EMPERORS AND WARRIORS**
The noseless Emperor Augustus is one of many faces in a formidable line-up of Greek and Roman busts.

▷ **PAESTUM TREASURE**
Exquisite Greek vase portraying the nymphs in the Garden of Hesperides: one picks golden apples for Hercules while another distracts the serpent with offers of food.

## POMPEIIAN EROTICA

After 200 years under lock and key, the museum's so-called "Gabinetto Segreto" (secret room) has recently reopened to the public. It contains erotic images which lift the lid on the racy ancient world. Romans had a taste for eroticism, and prostitution was a flourishing trade. Graphic sex was often depicted in the steam room, with scenes showing nymphs and satyrs disporting themselves, or an over-endowed Priapus simultaneously impaling several victims on his many-pronged member. Frescoes on view in Pompeii and Naples also depict the illicit love of Mars and the sexual antics of Jupiter, who disguised himself as a human to seduce women. Signs displaying male genitalia were considered symbols of good luck, as well as virility and fertility, and were used to ward off evil spirits. In Pompeii, a sign of a penis outside a bakery might also indicate a plentiful supply of fresh loaves, while a goblet adorned with a salacious scene spelt promises of orgies to come.

△ **MOSAIC SCENES**
The delightful parade of cats and cockerels, still lifes, coarse comic actors, brilliant aquatic scenes, and more, fills no less than 24 rooms.

▷ **"SECOND-STYLE" FRESCO**
Wall painting taken from a house in Pompeii depicting Perseus, son of Zeus, and Andromeda, whom he rescued from a sea monster.

△ **BLUE VASE**
Glass cameo amphora from Pompeii, decorated with scenes celebrating the grape harvest.

▷ **MOTHER NATURE**
The many-breasted Artemis of Ephesus, made of alabaster and bronze, represents fertility.

# AROUND THE VOLCANO

*Two of antiquity's finest sites, Pompeii and Herculaneum, sit in the shadow of their fiery nemesis: Vesuvius*

Map on page 152

**N**aples is the best base for visits to the Phlegraean Fields, Caserta and the hills to the east of **Naples ❶**. Trains cover most of Campania, while the roads tend to be crowded, especially in the tourist season. Heading west from Naples, the city's suburbs spread along the scenic coastal drive to Posillipo, Pozzuoli, Bacoli and Roman Cumae. Poets and rich merchants were attracted to the area's salubrious climate, the beauty of its coast, the springs, spas and an eerie volcanic landscape. The ancient Greeks, in awe of this sulphurous terrain, named this stretch of land to the west of Naples the Phlegraean Fields (from the Greek *fleguròs* meaning fire).

Of the 20 or so extinct or long-dormant volcanoes that mark this area, many circular craters are still recognisable, even though their characteristic cones have been lost to time, and the advancing Mediterranean has transformed some into lakes and ports. The landscape is characterised by ample stretches of yellow and grey volcanic rock and sparse, low hills covered with dark green woods, and small lakes.

## Fields of fire

**Agnano Terme ❷** marks the start of the springs and spas. When the muddy Lago d'Agnano was drained in 1870 some 70 thermal springs returned to the surface. Today's Terme di Agnano are known for their restorative and curative powers. Further west the landscape takes on an unusual dimension at the awesome crater of **Solfatara ❸** (open daily 8.30am–1 hour before dusk; entrance fee), in part the inspiration for Dante's *Inferno*. The sulphurous springs were believed to be poisonous discharges from Titans' wounds after their battles with the Gods, while the eruptions were the Titans trying to break free after being buried alive by Jupiter. The mysterious crater has attracted visitors since Roman times. A strong sulphurous smell pervades the area, and as you walk towards the most active hissing steam jets (cordoned off) you can feel the heat rising from the hollow ground. Guides demonstrate this natural phenomenon by throwing a rock to the ground; it falls with a thud which resonates through the labyrinth of underground channels.

Further west is **Lago d'Averno ❹**. Best seen at sunset, it was described by Virgil in the *Aeneid* as the entrance to the underworld. Its name derives from the Greek *àornos* meaning "without birds", presumably because no bird could survive the toxic vapours. Beyond the lake lies Europe's youngest volcano, the 130-metre (430-ft) **Monte Nuovo**, whose cone was created by the 1538 earthquake. It is well worth the climb for the view of the Bay of Naples.

**LEFT:** House of the Faun, Pompeii.
**BELOW:** sulphur spring, Solfatara.

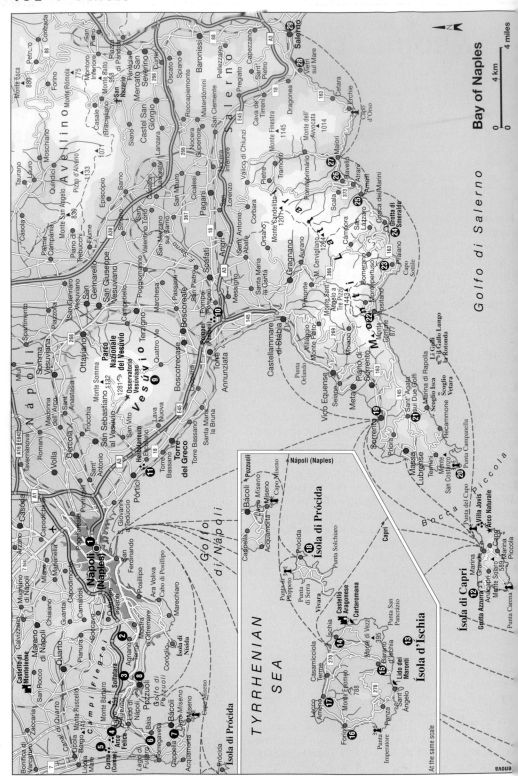

**Bay of Naples**

The most famous sight in **Cumae** ❺ is the Antro della Sibilla. This 130-metre (430-ft) corridor is carved into the hill of the acropolis, thought to be the sacred cave of the Cumaean Sibyl, the prophetess who predicts Rome's destiny in the *Aeneid*, and painted by Michelangelo in the Sistine Chapel. The trapezoidal section of the gallery predates the foundation of Cumae; it was probably once a place to store goods and water. From here, the paved Via Sacra climbs to the scanty remains of the temples of Jupiter and Apollo, both transformed into Christian churches in the early Middle Ages.

The imperial city of **Baia** ❻ was a classical tourist destination, and its licentious habits were described in Petronius' *Satyricon*. Capo Miseno served as an important naval harbour. Unfortunately, most of the splendid villas and Roman buildings sank, lost to *bradisismo*, the rising and settling of sea levels due to pressure from underground heat. Excavations at Baia include the remains of the baths and an imperial palace (open daily 9am–dusk; tel: 081-868 8868; bookings required), with artefacts kept in the Museo Archeologico dei Campi Flegrei, housed in a 16th-century Spanish castle (open daily 9am–6pm; entrance fee; call first, tel: 081-523 3797). This strategically positioned fortress overlooking the Gulf of Pozzuoli was built by the Aragonese, and restructured by Don Pedro de Toledo after the 1538 eruption.

At **Bacoli** ❼, between Baia and Capo Miseno, is the striking Piscina Mirabile, a monumental underwater galleria-cistern carved from the volcanic rock (Via Creco 10; open daily 9am–one hour before sunset; tip required). With a capacity of 12,000 cubic metres (2,650 gallons), this ancient reservoir supplied water for the Roman fleet anchored at Miseno. With five naves supported by 48 pilasters, and the sunlight filtering through an aperture above, it looks more like a basilica than a giant cistern.

Once Rome's main port was **Pozzuoli** ❽, originally known as Puteoli, from the Latin *putere*, "to smell bad", which indeed it does due to the sulphurous vapours. Evidence of the Roman colony is visible everywhere, but Pozzuoli's real claim to fame is the fact that it is the birthplace of screen goddess Sophia Loren. Excavations at the archeological site of **Rione Terra** (open Sat–Sun 9am–2pm, 4–9pm) have uncovered the heart of a once thriving ancient town, including the remains of an Augustan temple, a bakery, a mill and slave lodgings. The 1st-century *macellum* (market) on the seafront was submerged in water until 1985 when the effects of *bradisismo (see above)* left it uncovered.

Another important monument here is the 1st-century Anfiteatro Flavio (open daily 9am–dusk; entrance fee). Once the arena for gladiatorial combats, this was the third largest theatre in Italy and now stages summer concerts. Two of the three levels are still intact, and visitors can wander the underground section, where the scenery and beasts were prepared for the arena.

## Up the fiery mountain

Sorrento and Naples are convenient bases for day trips to the area around Vesuvius and its victims, Pompeii and Herculaneum (Naples' Museo Archeologico

Map on page 152

*Sibyl's Cave, dedicated to the sibyl of Cumae who guided Aeneas through the underworld.*

**BELOW:** Baia's 16th-century castle.

Nazionale holds an impressive collection of objects found during the excavations; *see pages 148–9*). The two towns are served by local buses and trains; if you are travelling by car, they are within easy reach of the Amalfi Coast.

The unmistakeable profile of **Vesuvius** ❾ (Vesuvio) symbolises the Gulf of Naples. The **skyline** between Naples and Pompeii is dominated by its smooth, dark cone, perhaps because the isolated and barren peak rises above an otherwise flat and fertile landscape. Vesuvius is the only active volcano on the European mainland, and an eruption could endanger the lives of 1 million people. Given the risk posed to people in the 18 towns on the slopes, the authorities are offering each family 25,000 euros to move, but few Neapolitans have taken the money – even if this "red zone" is a time bomb and any mass evacuation would be too cumbersome to avoid a second Pompeii.

However, Vesuvius is among the most studied and closely monitored volcanoes in the world. The movement of magma, the chemical composition of the gas and water that flows from it, the micro-quakes and variations in the elevation of its base are constantly analysed from the *Osservatorio Vesuviano* (built in 1845, on the west side of the volcano). It's extremely unlikely that the *Osservatorio* would fail to forecast an eruption in time to evacuate the area, so you can safely climb to the top of the volcano. On a clear day, the view of the Bay, taking in Naples, the islands of Procida, Ischia and Capri is too wonderful to miss.

## Vesuvius' violent history

Vesuvius is a rare example of a pent-up volcano, made up of one cone inside another. The original cone, Monte Somma, once reached a height of

*The violent forces of nature in this part of the world gave birth to several myths. According to one legend, every crater of the Phlegraean Fields was a mouth of Typhon, the hundred-headed dragon that Zeus threw into the Epomeo Volcano on Ischia.*

**BELOW:** Vesuvius, seen from Naples' industrial port.

2,300 metres (7,544 ft). The great eruption of AD 79 opened a second crater within the Somma crater. This "new" crater, Vesuvius, is 1,281 metres (4,200 ft) tall, 200 metres (650 ft) deep, and has a 1,500-metre (4,900-ft) circumference. Modest seismic activity and the occasional belch of smoke from the magma chamber remind us that it is active. The highest point of the Monte Somma crater rises up to the north, beyond the deep semicircular valley known as the Atrio del Gigante. This natural barrier surrounding the 1,132-metre (3,714-ft) Punta del Nasone saved the villages north of the volcano during the eruption of 1631 (the most catastrophic after the one that destroyed Pompeii). But on the south side of the mountain nearly 4,000 people were killed, and for days the smoke darkened the skies as far as Taranto.

The eruption of AD 79 occurred after a long dormant period and must have come as a complete surprise to the local population who no longer considered Vesuvius to be a volcano. The Pompeiians were killed not so much by the lava but by the clouds of toxic gas, lapillus and various particulate matter that rolled over the city, incinerating everything in their path. Since then, Vesuvius has had another 18 violent eruptions. In 1794 the town of Torre del Greco was totally destroyed, but the latest eruption, which happened in 1944, did not cost a single life and marked the end of the once familiar plume of black smoke *(see page 113)*.

## View from the top

The most comfortable ascent of Vesuvius is from the Herculaneum side of the volcano. If you are driving, follow the signs for *l'Osservatorio Vesuviano* until you reach the car park where the road ends at a group of bars and souvenir shops.

**Map on page 152**

**TIP**

The Circumvesuviana railway line runs regular services between Naples and Sorrento, stopping at both Pompeii (called Pompeii Scavi) and Herculaneum (Ercolano). It's a cheap, efficient and stress-free way to get around the bay. www.vesuviana.it.

**BELOW:** looking down into Vesuvius' crater.

From here it's a pleasant, though somewhat slippery, half-hour walk to the crater. Alternatively, there is a bus service from the excavations at Pompeii and Herculaneum to the car park and back (Trasporti Vesuviani, tel: 081-536 5154; about six daily departures from Pompeii and Herculaneum in summer; three in winter; the trip lasts 1 hour 15 mins from Pompeii, 50 mins from Herculaneum).

*The Italian poet Giacomo Leopardi (1798–1837) penned some of his most famous lyrics in the Villa delle Ginestre, one of a string of magnificent coastal villas built along the "Golden Mile" between Naples and Torre del Greco.*

## A Golden Mile of villas

For a change of scene consider visiting the splendid **Ville Vesuviane**, built at the foot of Vesuvius in the 18th century. In 1738, the Bourbon King of Naples Charles III built the **Royal Palace of Portici** (now part of the Agriculture University in Naples; call 081-775 4850 for a tour of the Botanical Gardens housed in the park of the palace), and the royal court soon followed suit, studding the stretch of coastline between Naples and Torre del Greco with 120 fabulous villas.

Surrounded by parks that descend toward the sea, and richly decorated with erotic and trompe l'oeil frescoes in imitation of the recently discovered "Pompeiian style", these villas earned the road the nickname **Miglio d'Oro** ("Golden Mile"). For the most part abandoned, after World War II they were nearly demolished to make way for the urbanisation of the Gulf of Naples. Thanks to a dedicated local group, Ente Ville Vesuviane, 125 villas have been saved, with a number restored and opened to the public. The stars are the elegant 18th-century **Villa Capolieto** (Corso Resine, Ercolano), **Villa La Favorita** next door, with its restored grounds, and the gentrified rustic **Villa Ruggero** nearby. For individual visits to particular villas, or to attend summer concerts in the grounds, contact the Ente Ville Vesuviane, based in Villa Capolieto (tel: 081-732 2134; www.villevesuviane.net).

**BELOW:** Via del Mercurio, looking towards the Forum.

# Pompeii

The main sites in **Pompeii ⑩** (open daily, Nov–Mar 8.30am–5pm; Apr–Oct 8.30am–7.30pm; last admission 90 minutes before closure; entrance fee: a cumulative ticket includes admission to the excavations at Herculaneum and is valid for three days; tel: freephone 800-600601) can be covered in about 2–3 hours. But Pompeii is the kind of place that touches something deep inside many visitors, and it's a good idea to get there early in case you fall victim to its magic. The ideal times of year for a visit are early spring and early autumn. While in winter you may find that you have all of Pompeii to yourself, custodians tend to keep the most interesting structures closed off; remember that a smile, a kind word and a tip go a long way in Italy. The entrance is a short walk from the Pompeii Villa dei Misteri railway station on the Circumvesuviana Naples–Sorrento line.

Founded in the 7th century BC by the Osci, a local Italic people, Pompeii developed under Etruscan and Greek influence until the Samnites took control of Southern Italy in the 5th–3rd century BC. They in turn were defeated in 290 BC by the Romans, who granted Pompeii autonomy. The city grew into the biggest trading centre on the southern coast. It was made a Roman colony in 80 BC, following the so-called "social war" fought by a league of autonomous Italic towns seeking the same civil rights as Roman citizens. In 62 AD, Pompeii was severely damaged by an earthquake and reconstruction work was in full swing when Vesuvius erupted and buried the city 17 years later. By that time Pompeii had become a thoroughly Romanised town of some 20,000 inhabitants, covering about 66 hectares (160 acres).

It wasn't until 1592 that Pompeii saw the light of day again during excavations for a canal. Remains of buildings with painted walls were found and documented, but at the time they were thought to be the ancient city of Stabia. Further excavations of the site didn't begin until 1748 and it was not until 1860 that the site was excavated scientifically with its relics moved to the Museo Archeologico Nazionale. Buried first under a volcano, and then under a tourist avalanche, Pompeii was listed as an endangered site in 2001. This prompted the authorities to devise a master plan to properly conserve Pompeii. As a consequence only about 25 of the 70 villas are open to view at any one time – but these are more than enough to convey the poignancy of the site. Uninterrupted archaeological digs have been going on here since 1748, but only 100 of the site's 163 acres have been explored. Current excavations include an Anglo-American team working on conserving the Villa Imperiale, whose leaking roof was damaging frescoes. The finest fresco restored so far depicts a nymph weeping over the death of Icarus.

## Around the Forum

Start your tour from Porta Marina (near the main entrance), which leads into the **Foro Ⓐ** (Forum) with the ruins of the **Temple of Jupiter** silhouetted against Vesuvius. To the right is the **Macellum** (market hall), with its 12 short pilasters at the centre which supported a wooden shelter that covered a large fountain used for cleaning fish. Opposite stand the brick buildings of the **Public Offices**. Pompeiians were politically active but

**TIP**

Exploring Pompeii in the heat of the day is thirsty work, so bring plenty of bottled water or consider a summer weekend night tour. These must be booked through Arethusa (tel: 081-8575347; www.arethusa.net). For general information on Pompeii and Herculaneum visit www.pompeiisites.org

**BELOW:** murals from the Casa dei Vettii.

# Pompeii

0 ——— 200 m
0 ——— 200 yds

only men were allowed to vote. There were annual electoral campaigns for the two *duoviri iure dicundo* (magistrate-mayors), two *aediles* (assessors for construction, commerce, the games and the baths), as well as the election of the *ordo decurionum* (town council) every five years.

Map on page 158

On the east side of the Forum is the richly decorated gate to the **Building of Eumachia**, a thriving wool factory named after its owner, Venus' priestess. After her death, the building became headquarters of the wool and textile guild: as you step inside, to the right is a small room with overlapping basins designed to collect the urine of passers-by, which was used in the wool-blanching process.

On the west side of the Forum, beyond a locked gate protecting some archaeological finds, is a cubicle which served as a **Public Lavatory**; communal wood and marble seats were set above a canal that runs along three sides of the room. From here, cross Vico dei Soprastanti and, before heading north, take a look at the **Terme del Foro B**. These rather small-scale baths had all the features of larger Roman baths (dressing rooms, gym, and pools with cold, warm and hot water); the decor, now lost, would have included large round mirrors, glass ceilings, silver taps, mosaics, and precious marbles.

*Plaster cast of one of the carbonised bodies found in Pompeii.*

## House of the Faun and House of the Vettii

Take Via della Fortuna to reach the **Casa del Fauno C** (House of the Faun), a luxury villa with four *triclinia* (dining rooms), one for each season of the year, two peristyles (porticoes running along a central garden), and a small bath whose *calidarium* (hot water tub) uses the heat of the oven in the adjacent kitchen. As in most of the villas, the gardens were planted with herbs, bushes and trees, such as mint, camomile, oleander, grapevines, pomegranate and figs. The house is

**BELOW:** bath house with skylight.

## THE FOUR STYLES OF POMPEII

The painted murals found in the buildings in Herculaneum and Pompeii have been divided into four styles that correspond with four distinct periods.

● The **First Style** (3rd century–80 BC), of Hellenistic origin, is the simplest and most sober. It is easily recognisable because of the absence of figurative subjects and the painting technique in glossy stucco. The predominant colours are dark red, black and yellow (see the House of the Faun).

● The **Second Style** (80 BC–Augustus) creates the illusion of "opening the walls of the house". Depth was added to the decorations through gradual use of perspective. The subjects are often inspired by theatrical backdrops with trompe l'oeil scenes of landscapes. There were also large paintings of mythical, heroic or religious subjects (an excellent example is the Villa dei Misteri).

● The **Third Style** (Augustus–AD 62) abandons the use of trompe l'oeil in architectonic elements which now appear stylized. Small panels with different subjects *(pinakes)* had an effect comparable to framed canvases. Beyond the miniature landscapes, there are portraits of daily life, still life, birds and exotic themes.

The **Fourth Style** (Claudius –AD 79) is completely removed from reality, rendering the walls like opulent baroque tapestries, in which the ornamental motifs are crowded together and superimposed upon one another.

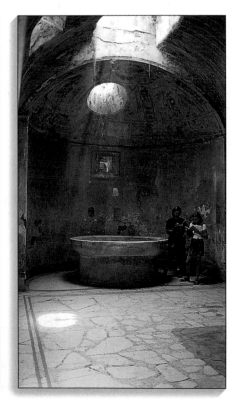

*Cherubs stirring gold; detail from the Amorini fresco which decorates the Casa dei Vettii triclinium.*

named after the statue of a dancing faun which adorned one of the two *atria* (inner courtyards), now replaced by a copy (the original is on display at the Museo Archeologico Nazionale, together with fragments of the impressive mosaic floors; *see page 141*).

At the junction of Vicolo di Mercurio and Vicolo dei Vettii stands the **Casa dei Vettii** , famous for its outstanding paintings. The Vettii, a nouveau-riche family who made a fortune in the wine trade, commissioned these after the earthquake of AD 62. The enigmatic fresco at the entrance (ask custodians if locked) portrays Priapus weighing his gigantic phallus on scales, and a sheep with the attributes of Mercury (the god of earning), both images of wealth. The disproportionately large phallus was a venerated symbol placed at the entrance of practically every home to ward off the evil eye.

Close by, the **House of the Tragic Poet** satisfies both morbid curiosity and aesthetic sense: the floor mosaic of the chained dog, complete with "cave canem" beware-of-the-dog notice, is one of the best-loved mosaics still on site.

## House of the Surgeon to Villa of the Mysteries

**BELOW:** Villa dei Misteri contains many frescoes.

Continue along Vicolo dei Vettii until you hit what is left of the city walls, then turn left to Porta Ercolano. Following the city walls a short way down Via Consolare you will come to one of Pompeii's oldest houses, dating from the 4th century BC, called the **Casa del Chirurgo** (House of the Surgeon) because 40 surgical instruments were found here, including forceps and pliers used to pull teeth (on display at the Museo Archeologico Nazionale). The ancient Romans used medicines based on herbs, spices, roots, honey, vinegar, olive oil and wine; prepared soothing balms from cooked cereals; disinfected wounds with an oint-

ment of lime, baking soda and urine; ate snakes for good health and discovered that the raw leaves of a Pompeiian cabbage eliminated the side effects of heavy eating and drinking. But not all the local pharmacists were trustworthy: in 81 BC a law was passed punishing those who sold dangerous medicines.

Map on page 158

On the other side of Porta Ercolano, **Via dei Sepolcri** is lined with tombs, shops and suburban villas. Roman cemeteries were always located outside the city walls, usually built alongside an important road; in this case the road to Herculaneum. Until the 1st century AD, the Romans cremated their dead and put the ashes in an urn together with a small coin to be used to pay Charon, the boatman who took the dead across the infernal river to the next world.

The cult of the dead was widely observed, and special banquets at the burial place were organised for funerals and anniversaries. The funeral menu always included fava beans, which served as a talisman against the evil spirits of the dead, a tradition that survives throughout Italy as the so-called *fave dei morti* (almond biscuits in the shape of fava beans made around 2 November, the Day of the Dead).

A pleasant walk further down the Via dei Sepolcri leads to one of Pompeii's highlights: the **Villa dei Misteri ❻**, famous for its fabulous frescoes located in the triclinium. The series, 17 metres (56 ft) long and 3 metres (10 ft) high, is the largest surviving painting from antiquity. Its theme is derived from a 4th–3rd-century BC Hellenistic interpretation of the initiation of a young woman, most likely a bride, into the Dionysian cult. Dinner was served in this room. The main meal of the day, it could last as long as seven hours and was often shared with friends. Jugglers, dancers, musicians and beautiful slaves often entertained the diners who ate while reclining on the *triclinia*.

*Pompeii's Casa dei Vettii is decorated with rich murals of mythological scenes.*

**BELOW:** Pompeii street scene.

*Detail of the Neptune and Amphitrite mosaic that gives the house in Herculaneum its name.*

## Bars and brothels

Retrace your steps to the Forum to explore the so-called **Nuovi Scavi** (New Excavations, begun in 1911). The area stretches east for about 500 metres (547 ft) and is crossed by Pompeii's **Via dell'Abbondanza**, once a major thoroughfare lined with shops, houses and drinking spots. The taverns were the equivalent of modern Italian bars. Wine, sometimes served warm with spices, was preserved in large terracotta vases and kept cool in the circular cavities cut out of the marble countertops. Some shops had interior rooms and gardens.

Not far from the Forum, on Vicolo del Lupanare, you'll find the **Lupanar Africani et Victoris ⑥**, one of the city's official brothels (there were 24 others). Ten built-in beds were divided among the two floors; on the wall above the doorways are frescoes depicting the "speciality" of the prostitute who worked there; the customers were in the habit of writing their comments on the walls of the house, as shown by the 120 examples of graffiti that are still visible today. Pompeiians apparently spoke freely about love and sex: prostitution and homosexuality were regular aspects of daily life without stigma or shame. Up Via degli Augustali and to the right on Vico Storto is **Modestus' Bakery**, one of the city's 31 bakeries, complete with oven and grinding mill, where 81 carbonised loaves were found.

Back on Via dell'Abbondanza, further sights include the **Terme Stabiane**, the city's largest baths (damaged by the AD 62 earthquake and not yet restored in AD 79); the **Workshop of Verecundus** (No. 5–7), "maker of cloth, woollen garments and articles in felt"; opposite is the **Fullonica Stephani**, a laundry shop. Two blocks down is the **Thermopolium**, a snack stand which served hot food to take away. Popular items included: *mulsum*, a sort of onion omelette seasoned with wine; chick-pea soup; *moretum*, a flattened roll eaten hot; and pork patties stewed in grape must and *garum*, the famous Roman fermented fish sauce which the Roman poet Martial thought smelled like bad breath.

## To the amphitheatre

Find your way to the **Casa del Menandro ⑪** (to the south on Vico Meridionale), a large house that belonged to a relative of Empress Poppea, and on to the **Orto dei Fuggiaschi** with 13 plaster casts of the carbonised bodies of men, women (including one expecting a baby) and children (near Porta Nocera). To return to Via dell'Abbondanza, skirt the **Grande Palestra ❶** – a huge 141 by 107-metre (460 by 350-ft) square which housed a gym-cum-pool where Pompeiian youth kept fit, practising the famous Roman maxim: *mens sana in corpore sano* (a healthy body in a healthy mind). The world's oldest surviving **Amphitheatre ❶** (early 1st century BC) seated more than 20,000 spectators. It seems that the gladiator games were originally celebrated in honour of the dead, as shown by the funeral paintings of the Osci from the 4th century BC. On Via dell'Abbondanza make sure you see the **House of Octavius Quartio** with the largest and most spectacular garden in town: its now empty T-shaped canal could flood the entire garden, imitating the floods of the Nile.

# Herculaneum

At the foot of Vesuvius' western slopes are the excavations of **Herculaneum**  (open daily, Nov–Mar 8.30am–5pm; Apr–Oct 8.30am–7.30pm; last admission 90 mins before closure; entrance fee). The town was destroyed in AD 79 not by burning lava but by a monstrous avalanche of volcanic material which rolled down Vesuvius in the heavy rain that followed the eruption.

The site was accidentally discovered by an Austrian well-digger in 1709 under 20 metres (65 ft) of petrified mud, which, having perfectly sealed the town beneath, effectively preserved the wood and household utensils that would otherwise have been lost over time. Systematic excavations didn't start until the 1920s, and have so far brought to light only half of the town; further excavation may still yield sensational discoveries, considering that the first large group of carbonised bodies was only found in the early 1990s. Until then, it had been wrongly assumed that Herculaneum's population, unlike that of Pompeii, had managed to escape.

The latest excavations have led to the opening of the **Villa dei Papiri**. This important Roman villa, named after the 1,800 carbonised papyrus scrolls found here in the 18th century, was built by Julius Caesar's father-in-law, and is believed to contain a "lost library" of Latin and Greek literary masterpieces. The finest artefacts, which have mostly been moved to Naples, are limited to sculptures, frescoes and mosaics, which together paint a vivid picture of Roman domestic life and amorous pursuits.

Allow a minimum of two hours to see the highlights of Herculaneum. The entrance is a 10-minute walk downhill from Ercolano station, a stop on the Circumvesuviana Naples–Sorrento line.

Maps:
Area 152
Site 158

*The design of the John Paul Getty Museum in Malibu, California was modelled on Herculaneum's Villa dei Papiri, where any further excavation will require the unpopular expropriation of homes.*

**BELOW:** Roman Herculaneum, with the modern town behind.

### Roman seaside resort

According to legend, the Greek settlement of Herakleia was founded by its patron god Hercules. Like Pompeii, the town passed through periods of Oscan and Samnite domination before becoming a Roman colony in 89 BC. In the 1st century AD, Herculaneum, less commercially successful than Pompeii and about half its size, was a town of some 5,000 residents and a seaside resort favoured by wealthy Romans. A few patricians owned the villas facing the Gulf of Naples, but most houses reflect the middle- and working-class status of their inhabitants, for the most part artisans, artists and fishermen.

The city is laid out in the typical Roman grid pattern, with intersecting streets, known as Decumani and Cardi. All the major sights are along the two central streets, Cardi IV and V, which makes for a pleasant walk. Start from the southern end of Cardo IV, at the **Casa dell'Atrio o Mosaico** (House of the Mosaic Atrium), one of the grandest Herculanean villas, whose *atrium* (the inner courtyard which brought light to the surrounding rooms) still has its lovely black-and-white mosaic floor.

Across the street stands the **Casa a Graticcio**, a two-storey building with a balcony, named after the inexpensive wood-and-plaster technique used to build plebeian houses. You can climb upstairs via the restored inner staircase, which still retains some of the original steps.

Next door is the **Casa del Tramezzo di Legno** (House of the Wooden Partition), another house on two floors, noteworthy for its façade and interior wooden partition with hinges and lamp brackets, which closes the *tablinum* (tiny office) from the *atrium*. The corner shop at No. 10 displays a remarkably well-preserved wooden clothes press.

*In contrast to the houses in Pompeii, where the roofs collapsed under the weight of the hailstorm of ash and pumice stone, Herculaneum's houses and their contents were perfectly preserved in the sea of mud which buried the town.*

**BELOW:**
the Casa a Graticcio and Casa del Tramezzo di Legno.

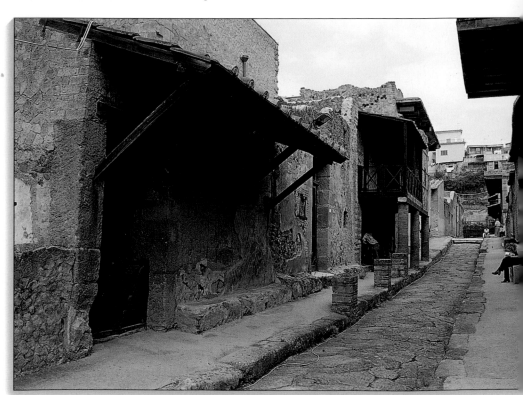

Cross the Decumanus Inferior to the fine **Terme del Foro**, decorated with mosaics depicting marine life which occupy the first block to the left. In the *calidarium* (hot chamber) of the men's baths, the partially collapsed vault reveals the heating pipes and smoke vents. The women's baths are intact.

Returning to the right side of Cardo IV, the **Casa Sannitica** (Samnite House), whose *atrium* features a graceful blind gallery and bronze spouts in the shape of animals, stands at the corner of the Decumanus Inferior.

Two doors down is the **Casa del Mobilio Carbonizzato** (House of the Carbonised Furniture) and the **Casa di Nettuno ed Anfitrite** (House of the Neptune Mosaic), both haunted by the spirit of the owners, whose portraits greet you from the walls. On the ground floor of the second house, past the room stocked with amphorae that was once a **wine shop**, is a small courtyard paved with a beautiful mosaic of Neptune.

Turn right onto the Decumanus Maximus and the entrance of the **Casa del Bicentinario** (House of the Bicentenary), a patrician residence with smaller rooms upstairs, which may have been used by Christian servants or tenants, as the walls are marked with crosses.

The right side of Cardo V is flanked with more houses, while to the left, behind a row of shops with carbonised foods and metal utensils, stretches the large **Palestra** (gymnasium), with a cruciform pool like the one in Pompeii and a central bronze fountain in the shape of a snake. As you cross the Decumanus Inferior, note the corner cereal shop, with a striking marble counter. At the end of Cardo V, to the right, awaits the grandest of all Herculaneum's mansions, the two-storey **Casa dei Cervi** (House of the Deer), with remarkable frescoes and what must once have been a superb garden kissed by sea breezes. ❑

Map on page 152

TIP

Booking is obligatory for the Villa dei Papiri. Tours and online reservations for Herculaneum and Pompeii can be made through Arethusa call centre (tel: 8911 1178).

**BELOW:** the exemplary House of the Mosaic Atrium.

# CAPRI, ISCHIA AND PROCIDA

*Romantic scenery, fine food and natural
beauty make the islands of the Bay of Naples
an international tourist destination*

Maps:
Area 152
Capri 168

Naples

Capri, Ischia and Procida are all blessed with fragrant hills, plunging views, shimmering coves and lush Mediterranean vegetation. But each island has a distinctive feel and charm so, if you are not pressed for time, you should visit them all. Don't make the mistake of going to Ischia hoping to find a less expensive Capri: the first Roman emperor knew what he was doing when he exchanged larger and more fertile Ischia for beautiful Capri. Some 2,000 years later, Capri is still well worth the splurge. But do go to Ischia for the hills, spas and hot-water springs that you won't find on Capri. In laid-back Procida time seems to slow down. Here life is simple: expect lots of sunshine and blue water, good food and pleasant walks far from the madding crowd.

For centuries **Capri ⑫** has been a vacation spot for a rich and sophisticated international crowd, a fact that has in no small measure shaped the recent history of the island. Its charms have been exalted by playwrights, poets and novelists through the ages, from John Dryden (who in 1700 coined the term *romantique* for its wild beauty) to D.H. Lawrence and Graham Greene. It was in turn home to Russian exiles, a gay haunt and a playground of the rich and famous. Apart from its natural beauty, Capri's reputation for glamour and decadence has lured tourists for decades.

**LEFT:** heading for Procida.
**BELOW:** boatman in Marina Corricella.

The "blue island" remains the undisputed queen of the Bay of Naples and one of the few places in Italy which successfully balances the protection of its natural beauty with the demands of a bustling tourist industry. Although Capri is known as a retreat for the jet set, the island's hotels and restaurants are no more expensive than comparable establishments in Rome, Florence or Venice.

In the peak season (July to August and weekends from June to early September), up to 6,000 day-trippers come from Naples and the Amalfi Coast to join the 12,000 residents and some 3,000 hotel guests on the 10 sq.-km (4 sq.-mile) island. Between March and October non-residents are not allowed to bring cars to Capri on the ferry. But even at its busiest, Capri still offers some relatively intimate coves where you can pass the hottest hours of the day.

## Island of goats

It has been said that Capri is Italy's Eden, but to the ancient Greeks it was just another rocky island named Caprea. Its name means "island of the goats" in an ancient Italic language, "of the wild boars" in Greek, and "of the two cities" in Phoenician. Emperor Augustus liked the place: in AD 29 he took Capri in exchange for the Greek colony of Ischia, naming it *Apragòpoli* (the city of the *dolce far niente*, literally "sweet doing nothing"). He had several villas built there, as well

as water cisterns and temples dedicated to the cult of the Nymphs in the grottoes that surround the island, making it a sumptuous imperial park. But his successor, Tiberius, who ruled the Roman Empire from here for 10 years, left a greater mark.

## Around the Piazzetta

*Views of Marina Piccola and the Faraglioni rocks can be seen from Punta Cannone just a 20-minute walk from Capri town.*

It is difficult to believe that such a popular island did not have a proper port until the **Marina Grande Ⓐ** was built in 1931. All boats from the mainland sail in to Marina Grande. Porters are on hand at the jetty to collect bags and transport them in their electric carts up to the hotels. It's a short ride from the port on the *funicolare* up to **Capri Town Ⓑ**, one of the island's two central areas, known for its self-conscious chic. The hub of the town is the little square lined with outdoor cafés known as the Piazzetta.

A short walk from the Piazzetta along Via Vittorio Emanuele and Via Serena brings you in sight of Capri's medieval jewel, the **Certosa di San Giacomo Ⓒ** (open winter Tues–Sat 9am–2pm, Sun 9am–1pm; summer 9am–sunset; free; tel: 081-837 6218 regarding temporary exhibitions). It was founded in 1374 by Count Giacomo Arcucci of Capri, to celebrate the birth of a son and, unlike the other monasteries built for the monks of the order of San Brunone di Colonia *(see page 255)*, no expense was spared. However, in the 16th century it was sacked several times by Saracen pirates, and in 1807 it was suppressed by Napoleon and fell into decline. Partially restored in 1961, the Certosa di San Giacomo has been home to – in the words of its teachers – "the most beautiful school in the world." The works of the visionary painter Karl Wilhelm Diefenbach, who lived on Capri from 1900 until his death in 1913, are on display in the refectory.

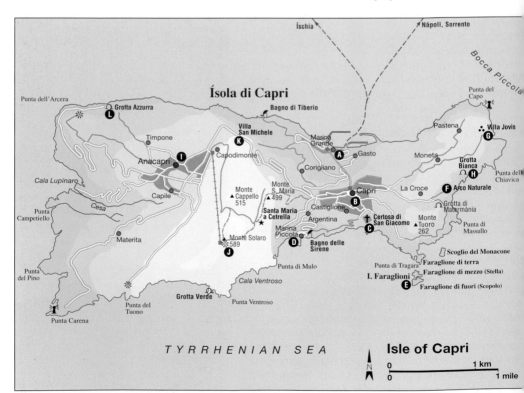

## Scenic walks

Adjacent to La Certosa are the **Giardini di Augusto**, named because they were laid out on the ruins of an ancient Roman settlement. The gardens are planted with a variety of trees and plants and provide an exceptional view over the surrounding area. From here you can take a panoramic walk along the **Via Krupp**, which winds its way down to the sea with different views at every turn. It was financed in 1902 by the German magnate Friedrich A. Krupp to connect the Albergo Quisisana, where he lived, with the **Marina Piccola D**. The marina was built in the 1950s in what was once a bay full of fishing warehouses and landings, and is now home to the trendiest private beaches on Capri and more than a few seaside cafés. Marina Piccola is graced with a picture-postcard view of the **Faraglioni E**, four striking rocks jutting out from the sea (two of them more than 100 metres/330 ft tall), which the Italian Futurist poet Filippo Tommaso Marinetti likened to "an equestrian circus of galloping stones".

One of Capri's most rewarding excursions leads to the **Arco Naturale F** (east of Capri town), a fabulous semicircular opening in the rock which frames the blue-green Cala di Matermania. From the Piazzetta take Via Vittorio Emanuele and continue along Via Camerelle until you reach the **Belvedere di Tragara** with fine views of the Faraglioni, Marina Piccola and Monte Solaro. Continuing east from here, just before the ascent towards the Arco Naturale you'll see the modest house of the eccentric writer and anti-Fascist Curzio Malaparte (1898–1957). Considered a masterpiece of Italian Rationalist architecture, it was designed in the 1930s by Adalberto Libera and Malaparte himself. Countless famous figures were guests at the villa, including Moravia, Togliatti, Cocteau and Camus. On the writer's death it was donated to the People's Republic of China. Later it became the headquarters of a cultural foundation. On occasion it is used for conferences and art exhibits, but is not normally open to the public.

Beyond the Arco is one of Capri's 67 grottoes, **Matermania**, dedicated to the cult of Mater Magna, the goddess of the Earth. From here Via Matermania leads back to Capri town.

## The emperor's legacy

In AD 27, at the age of 68, Tiberius left Rome for Capri, where for the next 10 years he governed the empire using a system of watchtowers that allowed him to communicate with the fleet stationed at Miseno, a coastal town east of Naples. One of Capri's highlights is what remains of Tiberius' favourite residence, **Villa Jovis G** (open daily 9am until one hour before sunset; entrance fee), 2 km (over a mile) from the town centre: follow directions marked on the tiles leading from the Piazzetta to Via Tiberio.

The grandiose multistorey building covered more than 6,000 sq. metres (64,580 sq. ft); the imperial apartments were built with panoramic terraces, with apartments for dignitaries, splendid baths and an astronomical observatory. Just inside the excavation area is the **Salto di Tiberio**, a sheer cliff that plunges to the sea. According to legend, the emperor had his enemies and ex-lovers thrown off the precipice. This

Map on page 168

**TIP**

Boat trips around Capri set off from the Marina Grande. The 1½-hour trip around the rocky coast is a perfect introduction to the island.

**BELOW:** Marina Grande.

*Grotta Meravigliosa, one of a series of dazzling grottoes only accessible by boat.*

vantage point, some 300 metres (1,000 ft) above the sea, offers a spectacular view across the Penisola Sorrentina. Below the villa is Capri's other famous grotto, the **Grotta Bianca** . Discovered by an English couple in 1901 in the Bay of Matermania, a vault-like ceiling covered in white stalactites earned it the nickname *Meravigliosa* (Wonderful).

## Anacapri

Away from the port, **Anacapri** is good for walks and excursions. The island's second centre has a more rustic atmosphere than its rival, with a stark Moorish presence reflected in the whitewashed cube-shaped houses. It sits at the foot of **Monte Solaro**, the highest point on the island (589metres/1,932 ft). The peak of Monte Solaro can be reached by chairlift from Piazza della Vittoria (if you return by foot to Capri town, the beautiful path passes the hermitage of **Santa Maria a Cetrella**).

Of the eight churches scattered around the island, the best one is the 18th-century **Chiesa di San Michele Arcangelo** in Anacapri. Mother Serafina, a Carmelite nun, made a pledge to the Archangel Michael that she would dedicate a sanctuary to him in exchange for a Christian victory over the Turks. The highlight of the church on Piazza San Nicola is the extraordinary majolica floor, with its 2,500 *riggiole* (Neapolitan-style ceramic tiles) in warm pastel colours. The mosaics depict the Expulsion of Adam and Eve from Paradise.

## Villa San Michele

**BELOW:** Villa San Michele, a doctor's dream home.

From Anacapri, take Via Orlandi to Via Axel Munthe and the **Villa San Michele** (open daily, May–Sept 9am–6pm; Oct 9.30am–5pm; Nov–Feb

## THE STORY OF SAN MICHELE

Axel Munthe's *The Story of San Michele* was written at the suggestion of Henry James in a particularly painful moment late in the Swedish doctor's life, when his vision was failing and he suffered from agonising insomnia. He wrote of his life and times and how the villa at Anacapri was built. Having earned a degree in Paris in 1880, at 23 Munthe became the youngest doctor in Europe. In 1890 he opened an office in Rome. Although he counted members of Italy's high aristocracy among his patients (including Princess Vittoria, the future Queen of Sweden), Munthe soon became known for his willingness to treat the neediest patients for free. During World War I, he served on the French Front as the field doctor for the Red Cross.

*The Story of San Michele* "is like a sound vintage of a very good year. It has the full bouquet of an era, a life and a profession; and as you read you are reminded of deep timeless things – nature, the lot of man upon the earth, kindness, and love of wisdom... Like the Confessions of St Augustin or Boswell's *Life of Dr Johnson* it will be read because it is compounded of the agony and the glory, the weakness and the dread, the laughter and the drabness, of humanity." (From the Introduction to the 195 American edition.)

10.30am–3.30pm; Mar 9.30am–4.30pm; Apr 9.30am–5pm; entrance fee; tel: 081-837 1401), designed and built in the late 19th century by the Swedish doctor and writer Axel Munthe (1857–1949). The villa was opened to the public in 1929, soon after the success of *The Story of San Michele (see box, left)*. Today it is owned by the Swedish Government.

The villa was designed to display Munthe's own art collection, and to highlight the beauty of the natural surroundings. "My house must be open to the sun, the wind and the voice of the sea," he wrote, "like a Greek temple with light, light everywhere!" Among the noteworthy objects on display are a Cosmati table, a marble bust of the Emperor Tiberius, a Medusa head and an Egyptian Sphinx. There is an extraordinary view of the Bay of Naples from the colonnade. In the beautiful garden is the *Olivetum*, a pavilion dedicated to the geology, flora and fauna of Capri.

From Villa San Michele you can reach Capri town by descending the so-called **Scala Fenicia** or Phoenician Stairway (actually a Greco-Roman construction). Until 1871, this stairway of 882 steps was the only land connection between the low and high parts of the island.

## The Blue Grotto

In 1826, the Polish poet August Kopisch and the German painter Ernst Fries "rediscovered" the **Grotta Azzurra** ❶ (Blue Grotto), and it soon became a major attraction for those on the Grand Tour. The cave had been known since the time of Tiberius, but for centuries the locals avoided it because they thought it was inhabited by monsters and devils. The entrance to the Grotta Azzurra is low and narrow so visitors arrive in low-slung rowboats. Only one part can be

Map on page 168

VILLA JOVIS

*Tiberius' cliff-hanging retreat on Capri is a miracle of Roman architecture.*

**BELOW:** Villa Jovis, Emperor Tiberius' residence.

**TIP**

The walk or mule ride to the top of Ischia's extinct volcano, Mt Epomeo (788 metres/2,585 ft) is well worth the effort. The path starts from Fontana and climbs to the 15th-century Eremo di San Nicola, a hermitage carved out of the volcanic rock. The views from the top are breathtaking.

**BELOW:** drop off the rocks, Ischia.

visited (three other chambers are inaccessible): the so-called Duomo Azzurro (60 metres/197 ft long, 22 metres/72 ft wide, 14 metres/46 ft high), whose intense blue luminosity is created by the daylight entering through an underwater aperture (the water absorbs the red). Boats to the Blue Grotto go from Marina Grande, buses from Anacapri, or you can walk there in an hour along the Via Grotta Azzurra. It is closed in bad weather.

## Ischia

The extinct volcanoes that form Ischia and Procida, together with Vesuvius and the Solfatara at Pozzuoli, are part of the so-called Phlegraean complex. Less than an hour's hydrofoil ride from Capri, the two islands are separated by just a few kilometres. Nearly five times larger than Capri, **Ischia** ⑬ is the largest of the islands in the Bay of Naples. It may not have the same rugged beauty as its high-profile neighbour, but it has many other advantages. The "Isola Verde" (Green Island) was known in Roman times for its natural hot-water baths and their curative powers and for the fertile, volcanic soil which nurtures noteworthy white wine (Casa d'Ambra is one of the best-known modern producers). The pine woods, olive groves, vineyards, sandy beaches and well-run spas of Ischia make it an ideal resort for the health-conscious and families with children. It is particularly popular with Germans.

Ischia has six small towns which are connected by a 35-km (22-mile) main road that circles the island. Buses are an efficient way to get around; alternatively, you can ride the pricey but charming three-wheeled open taxis or hire a scooter. The tour described below will take at least two full days, longer if you want to treat yourself to some time lounging in a spa or on a beach.

The island's main town is **Ischia** ⑭, with countless cafés, restaurants and nightspots. It consists of **Ischia Porto** – the island's harbour, built into the crater of an extinct volcano – and the historical centre of **Ischia**, named after the causeway that Alfonso I of Aragon had built in 1438 to connect Ischia to the picturesque little island known as the *scoglio* (rock). The highlight is the **Castello Aragonese** (open daily 9am–sunset; entrance fee), built in 474 BC by the *siracusani*. In the 16th century it became the home of the noblewoman and poetess Vittoria Colonna, who turned it into a religious and cultural citadel where Michelangelo was a regular guest. The now empty castle is especially worth visiting when it hosts concerts or art exhibitions. **Cartaromana**, to the south, is Ischia town's best beach.

The road continues south from Ischia town to **Barano d'Ischia** ⑮. This inland hamlet is a good starting point for excursions into the surrounding hills. From Barano, take the road that passes through Testaccio to the **Lido dei Maronti**, Ischia's best-known beach, whose waters are warmed by the hot springs of Olmitello, Nitruoli and Cava Scura (the warmest on the island at 86°C/187°F). If you walk along the 2-km (1-mile) beach, be sure to wear sturdy shoes, as the underground streams can make the sand uncomfortably hot.

The lovely fishing village of **Sant'Angelo** (accessible via the cart road that leads from Maronti beach to Cava Scura) sits on the southernmost tip of the island, with views of the southern coast and Mt Epomeo. Skip the unremarkable village of Serrara Fontana, and head straight for Ischia's wine capital **Panza**, a good departure point for walks to the island's most spectacular coastal panoramas. Beaches along the west coast are well-equipped with sun loungers, umbrellas and refreshment stalls.

*Santa Maria del Soccorso, one of a dozen churches in Forio. See www.ischiaonline.it for information on churches, museums and walks.*

**BELOW:** Ischia Porto.

*Called Pithekoussai (island of the vases) in Greek, for centuries Ischia's economy was based on the production of terracotta, an art still practised in Casamicciola (at the Mennella factory, the oldest workshop on the island), as well as in Ischia Ponte, Barano and Forio.*

Forio ⑯ is the most populous town on the island, with a pretty historical centre and baroque churches. Just outside the town at 35 Via Calise are the impressive gardens of **La Mortella** (open Apr–Oct 9am–8pm Tues, Thur, Sat, and Sun afternoon concerts; tel: 081-986237 to book concerts; www.lamortella.it), carved from an enormous volcanic rock quarry. They were designed by Russel Page, one of the great landscape architects of the 20th century, for the British composer Sir William Walton and his wife, Lady Susanna. There is a teahouse where guests can listen to music by the composer himself. Occasional concerts are held in the recital hall.

The next town is tiny **Lacco Ameno** ⑰, where the Greeks established a settlement in the 8th century BC. Two archaeological museums display remains found in the local necropolis and offshore shipwrecks: Museo Archeologico di Santa Restituta, and the more impressive **Villa Arbusto** (Corso Angelo Rizzoli 210; open Tues–Sun 9.30am–noon, 3–6.30pm; entrance fee; tel: 081-900356). Emerging from the sea opposite Via Roma is the town's emblem, a 10-metre (33-ft) tall block of yellowish volcanic rock called the **Fungo** (mushroom).

Less than 2 km (1 mile) down the road to the east is the popular spa town of **Casamicciola Terme** which has a high concentration of spa hotels. Here Henrik Ibsen began writing *Peer Gynt*. The promontory rising above Lacco Ameno to the west has the island's prettiest beach (Baia di San Montano), a fine day spa and an exclusive hotel *(see below)*.

## Radioactive pools

Ischia's marvellous thermal baths were known to the Greeks and Romans, who found relief from arthritis in the pools of radioactive mud. However, the craze for

the miraculous waters of Ischia really took off in 1558 after a treatise by the Neapolitan doctor Giulio Jasolino, who thought that the mineral waters of the island "restore fertility to sterile women, heal men from exhaustion, comfort the stomach, melt kidney stones, restore the liver, heal scabs and excite the appetite." In those days the poor would take thermal cures: in 1581 the bishop of Ischia, Fabio Polverini, had a hospice built for the diseased poor, and in 1604 some noble Neapolitans financed the Pio Monte della Misericordia at Casamicciola Terme, the first thermal treatment centre free to the public. It was destroyed in an earthquake in the 19th century.

Different springs correspond to different ailments and Italians still consider spa treatments important in the maintenance of good health. The 29 thermal baths, 67 *fumarole* (geysers) and 103 springs (ranging from 15–86°C/ 59–187°F), which bubble to the surface all over the island and in the nearby waters, make Ischia Italy's foremost centre for thermal cures.

## Top thermal spas

The **Giardini Poseidon Terme** (2 km/1 mile south of Forio) has 21 thermal pools as well as a Roman sauna and Japanese bathhouse, all surrounded by lush gardens (tel: 081-908 7111). The **Negombo** botanical park features 12 pools (some filled with sea water) Turkish baths, a beauty centre, and sun treatments with the added attractions of a beach and a season of concerts (Lacco Ameno; open 15 Apr–15 Oct daily 9am–sunset; tel: 081-986152). Many of Ischia's up-market hotels offer spa services to non-residents on a day-care basis, with treatments ranging from wallowing in mud baths to steaming in radioactive waters. The **Regina Isabella** is a hotel with impressive spa facilities (Lacco Ameno; tel: 081-994322; www.reginaisabella.it). In the same area, the **Terme di Augusto** is another prestigious spa hotel (tel: 081-994944; www.termediaugusto.it). If money is no object, Mezzatorre Resort & Spa on the promontory west of Lacco Ameno (tel: 081-986111; www.mezzatorre.it) is the spa hotel of choice.

## Procida

Although closer to the mainland, tiny **Procida** ⓲ feels surprisingly remote. Inhabited by a small community of fishermen and farmers, it remains the most authentic of the islands of the Bay of Naples. The maritime spirit and unspoiled atmosphere of Procida were masterfully captured by Alberto Moravia's companion, the writer Elsa Morante, in her great novel *L'Isola di Arturo*, published in 1957. What the island lacks in shops and tourist services, it more than makes up for in reasonably priced accommodation and, above all, a peaceful night is guaranteed. The only real town is also called Procida, but a number of tiny settlements enliven the rest of the island with scenes of fishermen mending nets at the docks and tomato-laden donkeys plodding up hills. A bridge connects Procida with the tiny island of **Vivara**, a nature reserve.

A common element of settlements all over the island is the collective nature of daily life. This is also evidenced in the local architecture, where an apparently haphazard cascade of cube-shaped pastel-coloured houses held together by stairways, terraces, balconies, arches and courtyards keeps families in close contact (a particularly good example of this is **Corricella**, which is a 15-minute walk south of the town of Procida).

The defensive town of **Terra Murata** was started in the 9th century, in response to Saracen raids along the Italian coast, and completed in the 16th century with the addition of the wall and the **Palazzo-Fortezza d'Avalos**. In 1744, the Bourbons made it their hunting residence. This left the residents with certain benefits, but it also meant the introduction of strict laws against poaching and the prohibition of firearms, dogs and cats. Enforcement was so zealous that the mere presence of pheasant feathers in a home was enough to warrant torture. Palazzo d'Avalos was transformed into a prison in 1818; abandoned in 1988, the building is falling into ruin.

Although it is small (under 4 sq. km/1½ sq. miles), Procida offers a wide choice of beaches. West of the town of Procida are the beaches of **Sirulenza** and **Cannone**. In the opposite direction, near the cemetery, is the charming **Spiaggia del Pozzo Vecchio**.

Next comes the romantic **Spiaggetta degli Innamorati** (Lovers' Beach); you can sunbathe on the comfy volcanic rocks facing the islet of Vivara at **Santa Margherita Vecchia**. The **west coast** is lined with many long, sandy beaches colonised by camps of umbrellas. ❏

*Brightly painted porcelain, made in Ischia.*

**BELOW:** Marina Corricella, Procida.

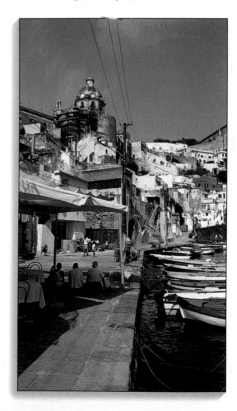

# SORRENTO
# AND THE AMALFI COAST

*Historical towns enhance the beauty of Italy's most*
*spectacular coastline, creating a blend of art and nature*
*that makes the Costiera Amalfitana world-famous*

Map on page 152

Naples

**S**heltered to the south by the Penisola Sorrentina, the Bay of Naples is a mountainous, curling peninsula whose tip is only 8 km (5 miles) from the island of Capri. Between Naples and Castellammare di Stabia the Campania coast appears rather industrialised and overdeveloped, but changes when t meets the reddish rocks of Sorrento. At its southern part is the stunning Costiera Amalfitana (Amalfi Coast).

Although Sorrento makes a good base for visits to the major sites of Naples, Pompeii and the islands, overnighting in the prettier towns of the Costiera will add flavour to your trip. Positano and Amalfi offer a rich combination of fine hotels, shops, beaches and vibrant nightlife (with prices to match), while lofty Ravello offers peaceful refuge from the fray, and attracts classical music lovers during its summer festival. But the beauty of this coastal stretch is no secret to the world, and he area gets pretty overcrowded in the height of the season. The Amalfi Coast is at its best in the spring and autumn. Plan on at least four days to take in the peninsula at a relaxed pace. There's a regular bus service between Sorrento and Salerno via the towns of the Costiera, and during the summer season boat services operate between Sorrento and Positano.

**LEFT:** view of
Sorrento.
**BELOW:** card players
in front of the
Sedile Dominova.

## Sorrento

Believed to have Greek origins and much loved by the Romans as a summer retreat, **Sorrento ⑲** was "rediscovered" by 18th-century Grand Tourists. Casanova, Goethe, Ibsen, Byron, Scott, Stendhal, Nietzsche and Wagner all sought solace from northern puritanism in libertine Sorrento. Nowadays, Sorrento is a cosy place that charms families and tour groups.

The town's past is epitomised in the local anthem *Torna a Surriento* (Come back to Sorrento), begging a young lover to return to "the land of love". Nearly a century after the song was written, Sorrento's orange and lemon groves, its seductive light and deep-blue sea, and the alcoholic euphoria induced by *limoncello* (a sweet liquor made with Amalfi lemons), still work their magic.

There's very little sightseeing in Sorrento. Plan on a few walks around town before resting on the benches of the **Villa Comunale's gardens** with an ice-cream cone as you discuss dinner plans and enjoy the views of Vesuvius and the Bay of Naples. The bulb-like dome emerging from the grounds of the gardens is the bell tower of the baroque church of **San Francesco**, whose medieval cloister, planted with vines and pink bougainvilleas, hosts classical music concerts (*see Culture, page 354*).

*Apart from the inevitable tourist shops crammed with souvenirs, Sorrento has many a chic boutique where you can shop for stylish clothes, perfume and jewellery.*

**BELOW:** coast and mountain backdrop near Sorrento.

The old part of Sorrento centres on **Piazza Tasso**, named after the town's favourite son, the poet Torquato Tasso (1544–95), whose famous poem *La Gerusalemme Liberata*, modelled on Homer's *Iliad* and Virgil's *Aeneid*, is Italy's finest example of a Renaissance epic. From here, Corso Italia leads to the **Duomo**, with its well-crafted choir stalls with typical *intarsio* (inlay work) by local masters, whose skills have been passed down to the rather less refined artisans of the souvenir industry.

On Via Cesareo is the **Sedile Dominova**, an unusual Renaissance loggia with frescoes and a 17th-century majolica dome, which was once the meeting place for the city's governors. Today, it is a club where Sorrentine men gather around baize tables to play cards, read newspapers and talk politics.

The **Museo Correale di Terranova** (open Wed–Mon 9am–2pm, closed Tues; entrance fee) is housed in the former villa of Conte Alfredo di Terranova. Its period furniture and decor conjure up the patrician atmosphere of 18th-century Naples. There are also some good 19th-century paintings, a collection of clocks, majolica from Capodimonte and some local archaeological finds.

Sorrento stands on reddish tufa about 50 metres (160 ft) above the sea. Some of the best hotels are perched on the cliff edge with terraces looking out across the bay – the views are as captivating by day as by night. Many of the hotels have their own lifts that take you down to wooden sunbathing platforms by the sea. Sorrento's beaches are for the most part unremarkable. If you must feel the sand under your feet, try the narrow strips of beach of **Marina Piccola** (right below the Villa Comunale, accessible via a stairway cut out from the rock) and **Marina Grande** (a 15-minute walk or short bus ride from Piazza Tasso); both beachfronts have modest entrance fees and umbrellas and beach

loungers for hire. To find larger and cleaner beaches you need to head further west. If you reach as far as the **Capo di Sorrento**, look out for a path on the right that descends to the sea, leading to the ruins of the Roman villa of **Pollio Felix**.

If you're driving, the most attractive approach to the breathtaking stretch of road known locally as the "Costiera" (officially the SS163) is via **Punta Campanella ⑳**, following the unspoiled western coastline of the Penisola Sorrentina. Coming from Sorrento, instead of continuing on the SS145 towards Sant'Agata sui Due Golfi, follow the signs for Massa Lubrense and the picturesque village of **Termini**. From here, ask for the *"sentiero che va alla Punta"*; a 45-minute walk along a panoramic path brings you to the Punta, which looks straight out to the island of Capri. A Greek temple dedicated to Athena once stood here, but the only remains visible today are of the **Torre di Minerva**, built by the Angevins in the 14th century as a lookout for Saracen pirates. The alarm was sounded with the little bell *(campanella)* in the tower, which gave the Punta its name.

From Termini, another path descends to **Marina di Rapolla**, with a small beach facing three small islands known as **Li Galli**. In the time of the Amalfi maritime republic, criminals were confined here while awaiting judgement. The Russian ballet dancer Rudolf Nureyev lived on one of these islands in a reconstructed Saracen tower.

## The roller-coaster Costiera

With its fine views of the bays of Naples and Salerno, the renowned Amalfi coast road (SS163) begins at **Sant'Agata sui Due Golfi ㉑**. Opened in 1853 by the Bourbon Ferdinand II, the tortuous road hugging the Amalfi Coast was carved and drilled out of the cliffs and seaside hills.

Heading south, the Costiera runs for 69 km (43 miles). It's not an easy drive and can feel twice the distance if you attempt it in one go. The best way to experience the Amalfi coast is to break the journey with visits to the local towns and beaches. Bear in mind that in summer months the traffic can be heavy, especially at the weekends and at night, when the nightclub commuters between Salerno and Positano think nothing of a few hours of bumper-to-bumper on the road. On the other hand, the road empties in the early afternoon while the locals break for lunch and a siesta.

Although SITA buses run hourly from Salerno to Sorrento and back (about one hour each way), a car allows for much more flexibility and easier access to stunning Ravello *(see page 183)*, though there is a regular bus service up the hill from Amalfi. Regular commuters get bored driving along "the most beautiful road in the world" on their own, so this is one of the few areas in Italy that's friendly to hitchhikers.

## Vertical town

The next town after Sant'Agata dei Due Golfi is **Positano ㉒**. The mystique of Positano began after World War II, when it became the favoured getaway of film stars and the *dolce vita* crowd. In 1953, a rapturous John Steinbeck wrote, "Positano bites deep. It is a dream that isn't quite real when you are

Map on page 152

**TIP**

The blue SITA buses that run between Sorrento and Amalfi can get very crowded with local commuters, so if you want to be sure of a seat with a view, avoid peak times and get to the bus stop at least 15 minutes before departure.

**BELOW:** Positano, a favourite of the *dolce vita* crowd.

*The medieval cloister of San Francesco, one of Sorrento's hidden treasures.*

**BELOW:**
Sant' Andrea
Cathedral in Amalfi.
**RIGHT:** chilli and
lemon stall, Amalfi.

there and becomes beckoningly real after you are gone". Positano's appeal did not lie in history or art but in its once clean waters and worldly atmosphere.

As with Rome's Via Veneto, all that has long since faded. What remains of Positano's golden age are the expensive hotels, bespoke clothing and sandal shops, and a vague atmosphere of exclusivity. The town is at its best in late spring and September, when the crowds of day-trippers do not clog the narrow streets. Strange as it may seem, this summer resort becomes quite enchanting over Christmas and in the winter months, when lemon trees are heavy with bright fruit and almond trees are in bloom.

Although the local beaches aren't particularly attractive (the water, though invitingly blue from above, is actually murky when seen up close), a romantic stroll down the Spiaggia Grande (the main beach at the foot of the village) or to the Spiaggia del Fornillo (accessible via a short path that starts from above the hydrofoil pier) is a must, especially as the crimson sunset casts its golden rays all over the beautiful, peaceful landscape.

The hamlet of **Praiano** ㉓ absorbs Positano's tourist overflow, offering a pretty beach squeezed between two cliffs, plus several nearby coves and a 16th-century church. The Costiera continues between steep precipices, including the spectacular gorge called **Vallone di Furore** (which has a tiny, secluded beach) Just past Conca dei Marini, there's a staircase (and an elevator) by a car park that leads down to the **Grotta di Smeraldo** ㉔ (open daily 9am–4pm, weather permitting; entrance fee), a cavern that glows with a green light reflected from the water. It is 60 metres (180 ft) deep, and has stalactites above and stalagmites which can be seen beneath the clear water. The grotto can also be visited by boat direct from Amalfi or Praiano.

## The ancient republic of Amalfi

Amalfi ㉕ is the largest and most lauded town on the Costiera. Its atmospheric hotels, many housed in former villas and medieval convents, and choice of restaurants, *pasticcerie* and *gelaterie* make it an excellent overnight stop.

Amalfi came to be feared as a maritime power as early as the 7th century, when Venice was little more than a confederation of islands dependent on Byzantium; in 839 Amalfi won independence from the Duke of Naples and grew into a thriving republic. In its heyday, the city controlled the whole Costiera territory, its harbour serving as the main trading port in Southern Italy. Amalfitani merchants established trading posts in Byzantium, Asia Minor and Africa. In the Holy Land, they founded the Hospital of St John of Jerusalem from which the Crusader Knights of St John developed. Their symbol, the Maltese cross, is still carved on Amalfi's street corners.

The stunning **Duomo di Sant'Andrea** was founded in the 11th century when the commercial fortunes of Amalfi reached their zenith and the local population had grown to 80,000. The cathedral, which stands at the top of a long flight of steps (a good spot in hot weather to catch an evening breeze) was completely rebuilt in 1203 in the present Moorish-Norman style. The geometrical façade has an attractive pattern of black-and-white stones inlaid with vivid mosaics, and with three tiers of interlacing arches. It is a faithful 19th-century copy of the original, which collapsed. The bronze doors were made in Constantinople in 1066. In the crypt holds the remains of St Andrew the Apostle, spoils from the sack of Constantinople during the Fourth Crusade, led by the Venetians in 1204. Like the miraculous liquefaction of San Gennaro's blood *(see pages 83 and 136)* at the Duomo in Naples, the cult of St Andrew attracts fanaticism among

Map on page 152

**TIP**

In summer, Positano can be reached by ferry from Naples in 40 minutes (www.metrodelmare.com) or otherwise by Circumvesuviana train from Naples to Sorrento, followed by a 40-minute bus trip.

**BELOW:** Piazza Duomo, Amalfi.

*Ravello is a good place to buy Vietri ceramics.*

**BELOW:** Vietri potter.

locals. The Manna of St Andrew, a mysterious oil, is said to seep from his bones. However, not even such a powerful relic was able to save Amalfi from decline. In the 12th century the Amalfitan suffered a Norman invasion and two sieges by their Pisan rivals. Then, in 1343, a storm nearly destroyed the city.

Attached to the Duomo is the **Chiostro del Paradiso** (open daily, summer 9am–8pm; winter 10am–5pm). Built in the 13th century as a burial place for Amalfi's prominent citizens, it was restored in 1908 and is planted with palm trees evocative of a mosque garden and ringed with whitewashed pointed arches resting on double columns. The cloister is now a museum of sculptural and architectural fragments.

The **Municipio** (open Mon–Fri 8am–2pm, 3–8pm), a sombre *palazzo*, is home to the *Tavole Amalfitane*, the Latin book of maritime law that applied until 1570. Adjacent to Piazza Duomo is **Piazza Flavio Gioia**, named after the merchant-navigator traditionally credited with the invention of the compass in the 12th century; the exhibition space under the two tall aisles is all that survives of the republic's **arsenal** (open Mon–Sat 10am–1pm; free; longer opening hours and entrance fee when exhibitions are on).

The rest of Amalfi resembles the *medina* of a Muslim town, with narrow and twisting alleys leading more often than not to dead ends and private homes. If you take a walk to the Valle dei Mulini, you can still see a few water-operated paper mills. Although no longer functioning, they are a reminder of Amalfi's past as one of Italy's most important paper-producing centres, where top-notch manufacturers turned rags and bits of old cloth into high-quality porous paper.

To learn more about this once-thriving trade, visit the small **Museo della Carta** (open Tues–Sun summer 10am–6.30pm; winter 10am–3.30pm; entrance

## VIETRI'S CERAMICS

**D**isplayed on street stalls, piled high in workshops, craft shops and tourist boutiques, and glittering on the majolica cupola and bell tower of the Church of San Giovanni Battista, the famous ceramics of Vietri are omnipresent. Arab forms and techniques of ceramic production were introduced in the Middle Ages by the abbots of the abbey at Cava de' Tirreni, although the vibrant colours and decorative styles you see today show no traces of the Arab influence. Vietri is also known for the nativity figures which were produced here after the Bourbon King, Charles III, closed the factory at Capodimonte *(see page 146)*.

The **Museo della Ceramica Vietrese** (tel: 089-211835 variable opening hours), 2 km (1 mile) from Vietri at Raito has a collection of locally made ceramics from the 17th century to the present day, showing the technical and artistic influence of German ceramicists in the 1920s and 1930s

The best selection of traditional items – plates, platters, vases and coffee services – can be found at the town's largest factory-shop, **Solimene** (Via Madonna degli Angeli 7). At **Carrera** you'll find the works of master ceramicist Ninuccio Carrera (Corso Umberto I, 66), while **Pinto** is the best address for tiles (Corso Umberto I, 31).

fee). The Amatruda family, in business since the 15th century, still makes paper the traditional way, and a good selection of their products can be found at Amalfi nelle Stampe Antiche, on Piazza Duomo, and at La Scuderia del Duca on Largo Cesario Console.

Map on page 152

## An inspiration for Wagner and Vidal

Just past Atrani, at the turn-off for Castiglione, a road to the left climbs up to **Ravello ㉖**, well worth a day's visit. André Gide said that it was "closer to the sky than the seashore" and its romantic aspect has attracted writers down the ages. Boccaccio chose Ravello as the location for the bawdier stories in the *Decameron*, D.H. Lawrence worked on *Lady Chatterley's Lover* here and the American writer Gore Vidal lived in the town for many years.

Built under Amalfitan rule in the 9th century, Ravello's uncompromising location meant that it was often besieged but never conquered. With a population of about 30,000 and a thriving trade with the Near East, the town remained independent until 1813. Wealthy merchants imported Moorish artefacts and architecture, which remain Ravello's glory.

The **Duomo**, dedicated to St Pantaleone, is an 11th-century church. Its austere facade is emboldened by Romanesque bronze doors. Inside, the nave is supported by classical columns and adorned with marble busts. The exquisite Arabic-Byzantine pulpits are richly decorated: the smaller one (1131) has a mosaic depicting Jonah and the Whale; the larger one (1272) supported by six spiral columns boasts mosaics of dragons and birds held aloft by fierce lions. The cathedral square is a location for summer concerts linked to Ravello's music, opera, ballet and art season.

*John Webster's brooding revenge drama,* The Duchess of Malfi, *was based on the tragic life of Joanna of Aragon, the Duke of Amalfi's consort in the 15th century.*

**LEFT:** Ravello countryman.
**BELOW:** Arabic and Byzantine elements, Ravello Cathedral.

Map on page 152

**TIP**

If you are in Ravello during the festival season (June–Aug), go to one of the outdoor concerts at Villa Rufolo for the unforgettable experience of seeing an orchestra playing on a clifftop, with the sunset for a backdrop *(see Culture, page 354)*.

**BELOW:** Villa Cimbrone, Ravello.
**RIGHT:** Cetara.

In the shadow of the cathedral stands **Villa Rufolo** (open daily, May–Sept 9am–8pm; Oct–Apr 9am–6pm; entrance fee), an agglomeration of Norman-Saracen buildings begun in the 13th century by the wealthy Rudolfo dynasty. The corners of the tower are adorned with four statues depicting the seasons, and the ruins are surrounded by lush, exotic gardens where Wagner found inspiration for the magic garden of Klingsor in his opera *Parsifal* in 1880.

**Villa Cimbrone** (open daily, May–Sept 9am–8pm; Oct–Apr 9am–6pm; entrance fee), whose romantic gardens dotted with statues were laid out by an English aristocrat at the turn of the 19th century, has a breathtaking view over the Golfo di Salerno. On a clear day you can see as far as Paestum.

## The Path of the Gods

As beautiful as the Amalfi coast is, the crowds and heat can become oppressive after a while. If you have an extra day to spare, venture out on one of the many walking trails that cut through the heights of the Monti Lattari. One of the best is the **Sentiero degli Dei** – the Path of the Gods. The whole walk goes from the ridge above Ravello down to the Sorrentine Peninsula, but you can walk sections of it. The trail linking the villages of Bomerano (west of Amalfi) and Nocelle (east of Positano), is a gentle three-hour walk through vineyards, lemon groves and wild Mediterranean *macchia* with beautiful views.

## Ravello to Salerno

**Scala**, the next village on from Ravello, has a Duomo with a fine Romanesque doorway and is the birthplace of Fra Gerardo Sasso, who founded the Knights of Malta in the 12th century. **Maiori** ㉗, surrounded by terraced vineyards, offers the Costiera's widest beach. The basilica di **Santa Trofimena** in **Minori** contains the relics of the patron saint of Amalfi; at the edge of town are the ruins of a **Roman villa** (open daily 9am until one hour before sunset; entrance free; tel: 089-852893) with mosaic floors and traces of frescoes.

**Cetara** is a pretty fishing village with a fine 13th century bell tower and a reliable fish restaurant Acquapazza (Corso Garibaldi 38, tel: 089-261606) which prepares popular dishes with anchovies, based on centuries-old recipes.

From **Vietri sul Mare** ㉘, famous for its pottery *(see box, page 182)*, you can take an inland trip to the **Abbazia di Trinità della Cava**, near Cava de' Tirreni, situated in a splendid position with a panoramic view. The church and monastery, rebuilt in baroque style in the 18th century, contrast with the 13th-century original and the Gothic Sala del Capitolo.

The Costiera finishes at **Salerno** ㉙, a workaday port redeemed by a historic centre only half-heartedly restored after it was damaged by Allied bombing in 1943. Its claim to fame is as the capital of the Norman Empire in the 11th century. It is also by reputation the oldest medical school in Europe, supposedly founded by an Arab, a Jew, a Christian and a Turk. However, visitors who wish to savour the romance of the Amalfi coast should ignore Salerno and proceed to the Greek ruins at Paestum *(see page 193)*.

# CAMPANIA

Map on page 188

*Campania's attractions reach beyond the Bay of Naples and Amalfi Coast. Enjoy the stunning scenery of Capua and Caserta to the north and Paestum and the Cilento coast to the south*

The first four chapters in the Places section of this guide have been taken up with the most popular parts of Campania. The region around Naples, the island trio in the bay and the Sorrentine peninsula may well have some of the best-known sights in Italy's south, but they are not the limit of Campania's attractions. To the north, the fertile Capuan plain has many sites of historic interest, most notably Caserta and Capua. Heading south beyond Salerno, towards Basilicata and Calabria, the Cilento coastline from the ancient site of Paestum is a long arc of cliffs, beaches and mini resorts that hug the mountains. The impoverished and neglected state of much of the Neapolitan hinterland cannot be ignored, but as you drive through dramatic mountain and coastal scenery, it's easy to understand why the Romans called this sun-soaked region Campania Felix – the Happy Country.

## On the Capuan Plain

The old Roman town of Capua is today's **Santa Maria Capua Vetere ❶** (off the SS7B road from Naples; not to be confused with Capua, *see below*, which is a few miles further north). Roman Capua is associated with two famous historical events: Hannibal's army wintered there during the Second Punic War (216 BC) and fell prey to the town's notoriously licentious hospitality. It was here, too, that the rebellion of Roman slaves began, led by the gladiator Spartacus, immortalised on the silver screen by Kirk Douglas in Stanley Kubrick's Hollywood epic. All that's left of what was once Italy's largest city after Rome are the ruins of the monumental **amphitheatre**; the rest having been quarried away over the centuries. In addition, a remarkable **Mithraeum** (underground temple of the widespread Persian cult of the god Mithras) features some particularly well-preserved frescoes of Mithras killing a white bull.

One reason for stopping in **Capua ❷** is to see the **Museo Provinciale Campano** (open Tues–Sat 9am–1.30pm; entrance fee; tel: 0823-961402) for its collection of 200 *matres Matutae*, small dolls carved from volcanic rock depicting women holding babies – the widest lap cradling twelve brothers and sisters. The dolls, dating from the 6th century BC to the 1st century AD, were found in the nearby temple of Matuta. They would have been offered up to the Italic goddess of maternity as a plea for fertility, or as thanks after a successful delivery. Capua's **Cathedral** was founded in the 9th century, but only some of the columns and the bell tower survived World War II.

At the foot of Mt Tifata 4 km (2 miles) east of Capua stands the unmissable basilica of **Sant' Angelo in Formis ❸** (on the Napoli–Caserta

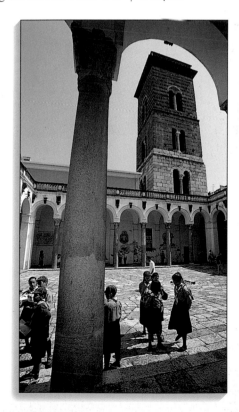

**LEFT:** the "fable in Marble", Reggia di Caserta.
**BELOW:** schoolchildren in Capua.

railway line). Built in 1073, the nave walls are covered with frescoes depicting scenes from the Old and New Testament, including Judgement Day (above the entrance), Christ Pantocrator with the three Archangels (in the apse) and a portrait of Desiderio, the abbot who founded the church. The unknown artists of these superb Byzantine-style frescoes gave an unusual warmth and realism to the figures.

## Versailles' rival

From Sant'Angelo in Formis there's only one road that goes to **Caserta** ❹ (less than 10 km/6 miles away), home of Italy's grandest royal palace, the **Reggia di Caserta** (royal apartments and museum open Wed–Mon 8.30am–7pm; park open Wed–Mon, summer 8.30am–6pm; winter until 2.30pm; English garden closes one hour earlier; entrance fee; tel: 0823-448084). Built by the Bourbon kings in an attempt to outdo the Palace of Versailles, the Reggia measures 247 metres by 184 metres (810 ft by 600 ft), has nearly 2,000 windows and

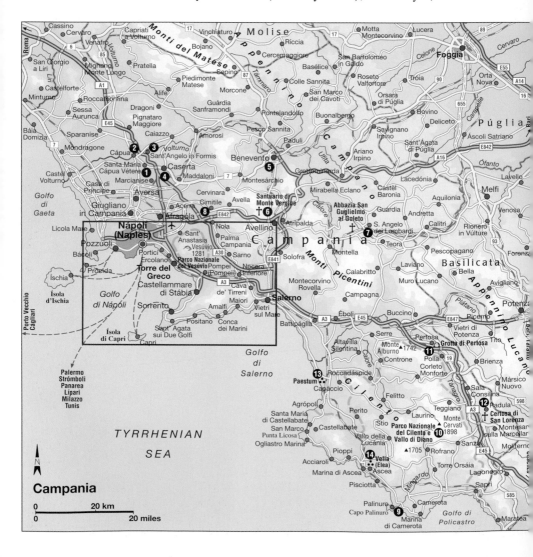

1,200 rooms over five floors connected by 34 stairways and four courtyards. Like Versailles, the palace is surrounded by an immense park (120 hectares/300 acres), which is unusual for an Italian palace. Built on a gentle slope, the park is divided by a long and wide central avenue lined with spectacular waterfalls with basins decorated with life-like sculpture groups of Greek myths and divinities. Among them is the "fable in marble" of Diana and Actaeon: a series of marble "snapshots" showing Actaeon caught spying on the naked goddess and being turned into a stag. An aqueduct was built to bring water to the fountains from 50 km (30 miles) away.

Neither the Bourbon King Charles III, nor the director of the work, the Neapolitan architect Luigi Vanvitelli (1700–73), lived to see the 22-year project completed in 1774. Some 3,000 labourers – made up of prisoners and Muslims kidnapped from the coast of North Africa – were forced to work as slaves. The mammoth building was not universally praised. The English poet and traveller Henry Swinburne, who visited the palace at the time of its completion, thought the facade "gives too much the idea of a monastery". But the interior, he noted, was striking for "the vast dimensions of its apartments, the bold span of their ceilings, the excellence and beauty of the materials employed in building and decorating it, and the strength of the masonry."

The octagonal vestibule of the second floor leads to the **Palatine Chapel** and to the lengthy sequence of royal apartments decorated with paintings and furniture from the 18th and 19th centuries. A salon in the Appartamento Vecchio features an unusual 18th-century *presepe* (nativity scene), with over 1,200 figures. The **Museo dell'Opera e del Territorio**, located in the former dungeons, illustrates the history of the construction of the Reggia and contains a section

*A few kilometres north of Maddaloni on the SS265 stands the Ponti della Valle, an impressive section of the aqueduct built by Luigi Vanvitelli in 1759 to bring water to the fountains of the Reggia di Caserta.*

**BELOW:** magnificent formal garden of the Caserta Palace.

*The Arch of Trajan in Benevento celebrates the emperor's military victories.*

BELOW: sports fans in Avellino.

devoted to daily life in the Bourbon court. Return to the ground floor and cross the second courtyard to reach the charming, horseshoe-shaped **Palatine Theatre**, which has the park as a natural backdrop for the staging of Ferdinando IV's favourite melodramas by Cimarosa and Paisiello. There's also an interesting **English garden** designed by the British botanist John Andrew Graefer for Queen Maria Carolina of Austria, wife of Ferdinando IV. The first camellia in Europe bloomed here. For those who prefer sitting to strolling, a minibus makes a tour of the park.

The Bourbon kings were not only preoccupied with lavish living and promoting their image; they were also a dynasty of enlightened sovereigns who believed in progress and human rights, as illustrated by the utopian project of **San Leucio**, a working-class counterpart to the Reggia di Caserta. In 1785, Ferdinando IV set up a silk factory in the hamlet of San Leucio (follow signs; 2 km/1 mile from Caserta). The workers were given a humane working environment and took pride in their profession, producing fine satins and brocades which became highly sought after in Europe. A special set of laws for the community guaranteed equal working conditions for men and women, education for their children and support for the old and sick.

But this unique social experiment faded with the fall of the Sicilian kingdoms in 1861 and the end of the Bourbons' protectionist regime. The factory went out of business due to high production costs, and the construction of an entire city on this model was never realised. The factory and workers' quarters can only be viewed from the outside, but the shop, **Tessuti Siola Alois** (Piazza Scuderia 8), sells hand-woven silk and handmade braiding.

## Northeast of Naples

**Benevento** ❺, which lies 50 km (30 miles) east of Caserta, was a prosperous Roman town on the Via Appia, the consular road connecting Rome with Brindisi on the Adriatic coast, and one of Italy's most travelled roads. In 571, the city became the southern capital of the power-hungry Lombards and remained their stronghold until 1053, when the duchy passed to the papacy. Completely destroyed by an earthquake in 1688, Benevento suffered heavy damage in World War II. One exceptional monument survived: the 2nd-century Arch of Trajan, one of the finer and better-preserved triumphal arches scattered throughout the former empire that were built to commemorate the reigns and victories of the Roman emperors. The bas-reliefs on the side facing Benevento and Rome glorify Emperor Trajan "at home" (he is welcomed by consuls, offered a thunderbolt by Jupiter, and distributes gifts and benefits to the Roman people), while those on the side facing Brindisi and the overseas provinces celebrate Trajan's policies in the colonies (he is depicted recruiting troops and forming new colonies and being welcomed by river gods).

The next stop is the **Santuario di Monte Vergine** ❻, 40 km (25 miles) south of Benevento (off the SS88 road; take the right-hand fork after Capriglia Irpina). Founded in 1119 on what was once a sacred

Roman site dedicated to the cults of Cybele and Diana, the mountain-top sanctuary preserves its original Gothic three-nave format – despite restructuring in the 17th-century. Twice a year – at Whitsun and in early September – thousands of pilgrims wend their way uphill to the Montevergine Sanctuary, singing hymns as they go.

From the sanctuary, take the road to Avellino, then the SS400 to **Sant' Angelo dei Lombardi** ❼ (also reached by train from Avellino) one of the hill towns in the Irpinia area that was shaken by the violent earthquake of 1980. Its restored historical centre is still pleasant to walk around, but the main attraction here is the 12th-century abbey of **San Guglielmo al Goleto**, 3 km (1 mile) out of town. Under restoration since the earthquake, the forlorn complex shows the scars of neglect and natural disasters, but these contribute to its romantic beauty. The entrance is through two arches which lead to two cloisters. To the left, there's a small structure made up of a lower Romanesque church and an upper Gothic church (reached via an external staircase); a third, larger church was added in the 18th century during a period of vitality at the abbey. The tower on the right was built with the marble from a nearby Roman mausoleum in 1152.

Located halfway between Avellino and Naples is a more interesting religious complex: the medieval basilicas of **Cimitile** ❽ (third road to the right after Schiava on the SS7B road; also served by the Circumvesuviana train line on the Baiano–Napoli route). The complex was originally the pagan and early-Christian burial place for nearby Nola. At sunset the ruined arcades, apses, columns, collapsed ceilings, mosaics and fragments of frescoes make an enchanting sight.

Map on page 188

TIP

The Piana del Lago Laceno (Plain of Lake Laceno), a vast green valley surrounded by mountains and dense forests, is ideal for hiking, biking and horse-trekking. Enquire at Avellino tourist office (Via Due Principati 5, Avellino; tel: 0825-74732/74695).

**BELOW:** Morcone, a small-car town in Campania.

*Certosa di San Lorenzo in Padula, the biggest monastery in the south.*

**BELOW:** Palinuro on the Cilento coast.

## The Cilento coast

The Campania coast from Naples to Salerno is covered in the "Sorrento and Amalfi Coast" chapter *(see page 177)*. From Salerno the landscape is flat and sandy as far as Agropoli, where the rocky Cilento coastline begins. The scenery along this stretch may not be a match for the Amalfi coast, but it has a wild beauty of its own and remains relatively unspoilt. The Cilento coast is characterised by rugged cliffs opening onto small bays, some deserted, others belonging to the quiet resorts dotted along the road: Santa Maria di Castellabate, San Marco, Acciaroli, Pioppi, Marina di Casal Velino, Marina di Ascea, Marina di Pisciotta and Marina di Camerota.

**Capo Palinuro ➒**, the most beautiful corner of the Cilento coast, deserves a special mention. According to legend Aeneas's pilot, Palinurus, was shipwrecked here. The town makes a good base for visits to the local beaches and two great archaeological sites: Paestum, on the Bay of Salerno just before Agropoli *(see page 193)*, and Velia, north of Palinuro between Marina di Casal Verino and Marina di Ascea *(see page 194)*. After Palinuro the coast curves back inwards, becoming the Gulf of Policastro, and leads to the seaside village of Sapri, just before Campania's southern boundary.

Inland, the **Parco del Cilento** (Cilento Park) occupies most of the area bounded by the A3 motorway, and its remotest corners offer some uncrowded hiking routes, particularly around **Monte Cervati ➓** in the Vallo di Diano and on the **Alburni chain** that skirts the northern border of the park. East of Monti Alburni is the **Grotta di Pertosa ⓫**, with impressive stalactites. But its greatest delights are the rolling hills and unspoilt coastline. Nature trails help you appreciate the mix of Mediterranean and Apennine vegetation, and you may be lucky enough to see golden eagles and kites, but you probably won't spot the wolves and polecats which still lurk in remote parts of the park. The ancient Greeks loved the Cilento and it is finally coming back into fashion.

## Carthusian monastery

About 30 km (20 miles) south of Pertosa, along the A3, is **Padula ⓬** and the **Certosa di San Lorenzo** (open daily 9am–8pm; entrance free; tel: 0975-77117), one of Italy's biggest monasteries. The basic structure was completed in the early 14th century, but over the following centuries it underwent many changes as baroque decorations were heaped onto the Gothic and Renaissance foundations. Its floor plan evokes the gridiron which legend says St Lawrence was martyred on.

The largest cloister, lined with monks' cells, is nearly the size of a football pitch. Another of the cloisters, built above the old cemetery, gives access to the kitchens, complete with original frescoes and furnishings. Built in a strategic position, the monastery retained a strong influence over the area until the early 19th century when it was suppressed. One of its most illustrious visitors was Holy Roman Emperor Charles V, who stopped here in 1535. It is said that the monks prepared a special omelette for him using 1,000 eggs.

## Paestum

In the 7th century BC, the Greeks of Sybaris *(see page 239)* founded a colony known as Poseidonia in honour of the sea god Poseidon, which became one of the most dynamic commercial centres in the Mediterranean. After Sybaris fell to Crotone in 510 BC, the city absorbed the surviving Sybarites and all of their wealth. In the half-century that followed, three famous temples were built, later known as the temples of **Paestum** ⓭ (excavations open daily 9am–one hour before sunset; entrance fee; tel: 0828-811023), the Roman name for the city.

A rich and beautiful city, Paestum succumbed to malaria after the fall of Rome and was abandoned after Saracen incursions in the late 9th century. The ruins of Paestum, overgrown and submerged in swamplands, were rediscovered in the mid-18th century, during the construction of a road. Nothing remains of the town apart from late-Roman additions such as the amphitheatre, pool and the exceptionally well-preserved temples, which stand out in magnificent solitude on a grassy patch dotted by oleanders and rose bushes. Built from local travertine marble in Doric style, they glow with a warm, indefinable light that changes hues: mother of pearl under the fast-gathering grey clouds of an impending storm; a blinding ivory glitter at midday; a luscious orange glaze towards sunset.

The most important is the **Tempio di Nettuno** (Temple of Neptune, in reality consecrated either to Hera or Zeus; the temples were misnamed by early archaeologists) dating back to 450 BC. Thought to have been inspired by Athens' Parthenon, it shows all the refinements of the Doric style. If you look closely, none of the columns is straight: the corner columns have slightly oval (rather than round) sections at the top and bottom; those on the longer sides curve

*Acciaroli on the Cilento coast was one of Ernest Hemingway's favourite resorts.*

**BELOW:** Carthusian monastery of San Lorenzo, Padula.

Map on page 188

inwards; while all the columns bulge outwards along the edges and taper in at the top. The miracle of this ancient construction is that, viewed from a distance, all the columns seem straight and the temple perfectly proportioned. The roof is gone, but the 36 external columns are all in place, and the entablatures and pediments are for the most part intact. This gives an especially good sense of how this temple must have looked originally because, unlike the Parthenon and most other Greek buildings, the Temple of Neptune had no sculpted decorations on the outside. The English Romantic poet Shelley was struck by the harmonious blending of the man-made structure with its natural surroundings: "The effect of the jagged outline of the mountains through the groups of enormous columns on one side, and on the other the level horizon of the sea, is inexpressibly grand."

Near the Temple of Neptune is the so-called **Basilica**, in reality another temple to Hera, complete with all of its 50 columns and architraves (third quarter of the 6th century BC). Finally, further north is the **Tempio di Cerere** (Temple of Ceres), more accurately attributed to Athena and built sometime between the other two, which looks like a smaller version of the Temple of Neptune.

Paestum's **Museo Archeologico** (open daily 9am–7pm, closed first and third Mon of the month; entrance fee, combined ticket available) contains some of Southern Italy's rarer objects, including the world's only example of Greek mural paintings, dating from 480 BC. Excavated from one of the necropoli just outside town after World War II, the four panels of the **Tomba del Tuffatore** (Tomb of the Diver) represent scenes of banquets, dancing, games and a young nude diving onto a trampoline (the dive is thought to symbolise the passage from life to the underworld).

**BELOW:**
Cilento beach.
**RIGHT:** Temple of
Neptune, Paestum.

## Philosophical town

Southern Campania's other important archaeological site is **Velia ⓮** (open 9am–one hour before sunset; tel: 0974-972396), one of the last Greek colonies to be founded on the Italian peninsula (mid-6th century BC). Originally, the Greek city of Elea stood on a promontory between two bays, a prime spot which allowed the port to flourish into a fishing and commercial centre of considerable wealth (by the 12th century the bays had completely silted up). Elea became a magnet for intellectuals and gave its name to the Eleatic school of philosophy. Among its most prominent philosophers were Parmenides (*circa* 515–440 BC) noted for his work *On Nature*, written in verse, and his disciple Zeno (born circa 490 BC), renowned for his sly paradoxes. The Eleatic school drew attention to the distinction between information based on the five senses and that based on pure reason, and caused a crisis in Greek philosophy.

Although Velia's ruins were discovered in 1883, excavations didn't start until the 1920s; little remains of the old town, which became a quarry for building material after the fall of Rome. The thing to do here is to climb the beautiful paved street that leads from the *agora* (main square) to the **Porta Rosa**, an arched gateway in the city walls, whose discovery cast doubt on the Romans' title of "inventors of the arch". ☐

# PUGLIA

*This region of wine, wheat, olives and curious* trulli *houses hits a high spot in the Gargano peninsula. Neighbouring Albania and Greece have left their mark, as have Normans and Swabians*

Map on page 200

Puglia is the pointed heel of Italy's boot, running down the length of the Adriatic and forming an instep beside the Ionian Sea. This is one of Italy's largest provinces, and its architecture and landscape make it one of the most diverse. It is a stepping-off point for the Adriatic and the East: crusaders embarked at Bari, the largest city, and the Via Appia – the first great highway from Rome – ends at Brindisi, which is still the main ferry port for Greece 100 km (60 miles) away. Much of this ancient province is flat and fertile, providing an abundance of wheat, wine and olive oil. Here and there are the extraordinary, gaunt stones of the Norman and Swabian castles and churches, Romanesque outposts that the sun has bleached like old bones. The Normans knew the region through pilgrims who returned from the shrine of the Archangel Michael high above the Gargano peninsula – the most attractive stretch on what is the longest coastline of any Italian region.

The Greek colonists founded the modern naval port of Taranto, and the Romans raided for molluscs to make purple dyes. When Rome collapsed, the eastern, Byzantine Empire made Bari a regional power base. But Puglia's most persistent ghost is Frederick II (1220–50), Holy Roman Emperor and the last of the great medieval rulers *(see page 29)*. It is not hard to imagine his hawks hunting in the wide blue skies above his castles.

**PRECEDING PAGES:** the upper Merge in early summer. **LEFT:** *trulli* houses. **BELOW:** Bari trooper.

## Unique architecture

Puglia's refreshingly complex cultural mix sometimes seems at odds with modern Italy. Its unique architecture ranges from beehive *trulli* houses to flamboyant Lecce baroque, with a flavour of the East never far from sight. This broad cultural heritage combines with its southern climate, varied landscape and food to give Puglia a strong, individual character – even when compared with other regions in Southern Italy. Much of the countryside is sparsely populated, because many farmers live away from their land in "farming towns".

Be cautious in the largest centres. In a land where people are friendly and welcoming, there is also a reputation for crime in cities such as Bari. Don't be put off by the initial, ugly prospect of some towns; the most elegant centres disguise themselves on the outside with ill-designed blocks of flats, aberrations in the history of Italian design that, in their unlandscaped and sometimes unfinished state, take on the appearance of a vandalised building site. It is nearly always worth persisting in an effort to reach the *centro storico*, the old town, which is often magical and unspoilt. The recent expansion of the low-cost airlines into Southern Italy has made these little-known gems readily accessible.

*Frederick II's many-towered castle at Lucera, built in 1233.*

## The Tavoliere plain

Entering Puglia from the north you first come across the relatively featureless Tavoliere plain, an important agricultural area centred on **San Severo** surrounded by vines and the busy provincial capital of **Foggia ❶**. Lying at the centre of this important wheat-producing area, it was famous for its underground grain stores called *fovea*, from which the town may have taken its name. Frederick II's heart was kept in a casket here until it was lost in the earthquake of 1731 which destroyed most of the old town. As an important railway junction and air base, it also suffered from wartime bombing. Mainly a commercial centre, Foggia has a fine surviving cathedral, Santa Maria Icona Vetere. Built in 1172, its facade and crypt are all that remain of the original Romanesque building – after the earthquake it was rebuilt in the baroque style.

Other baroque buildings, Chiesa delle Croci, Palazzo de Rosa and the Palazzo della Dogana, are worth seeking out. The Museo Civico (currently being refurbished; tel: 0881-771823 to check if open) contains artefacts from the pre-Greek Daunian period. Foggia's most famous son is Umberto Giardano (1867–1948), composer of *Andrea Chenier* and *Fedora*. The town's autumn opera festival centres on the theatre named after him.

West of Foggia lies the ancient town of **Lucera ❷**. Once the principal town of this area, the importance of this settlement to the successive powers that controlled the region can still be seen in the architecture, in particular the massive **castle**, the finest among the many built in Puglia by Frederick II. Set on a 250-metre (820-ft) hillock, and enclosed by a kilometre-long wall with 24 towers, it has uninterrupted views of the surrounding landscape. The area inside is atmospheric, with a number of relics from the past. In 1233, Frederick, excom-

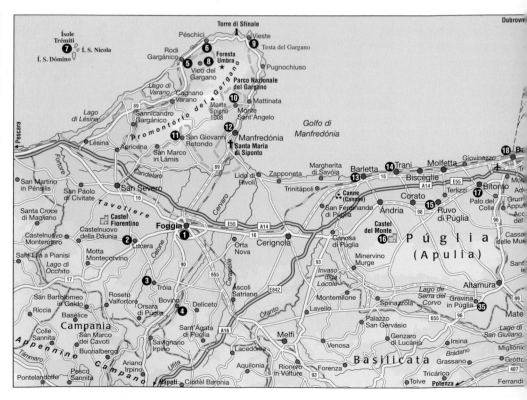

municated by the pope, brought 20,000 Saracen troops here from Sicily to help in his wars with the rest of Italy, and the town must have taken on a distinctly Moorish appearance. Charles of Anjou took the city following Frederick's death and the great mosque that the Saracens had built was replaced by a Gothic cathedral, making it the only Gothic church in Puglia. Its stone altar is thought to be the great banqueting table from Castel Florentino, where Frederick died in 1250; the castle ruins lie 14 km (9 miles) northwest. To the northeast of the town there is a Roman amphitheatre.

South of Lucera is **Troia ❸**, a small town with one of the region's most dramatic cathedrals, completed in 1125, with classical and Eastern influences brought together in unique Puglian style. It has a magnificent rose window and a rich treasury. Just south of Troia lies **Bovino ❹**, less often visited but also with a grand cathedral from the same period. Among its many other historic buildings is a castle which became a ducal palace. A pleasant and unspoilt centre, Bovino is an attractive place to stay to make the most of this hilly and wooded part of Puglia – once famous for its brigands.

## Gargano Peninsula

Travelling east from the plains around Foggia, the landscape changes markedly as Puglia's highest hills signal the approach to the Gargano Peninsula – the most attractive stretch of coastline on Italy's entire eastern seaboard. A private train, the Ferrovia del Gargano, serves the peninsula from San Severo, north of Foggia to Peschici, from where boats ferry visitors to Viesti and Manfredonia.

Contrasting with the flat landscape around Foggia, the Gargano's steep, wooded hills and winding coastal roads above white limestone cliffs offer

Map below

*Who can resist the appeal of a roadside advertisement?*

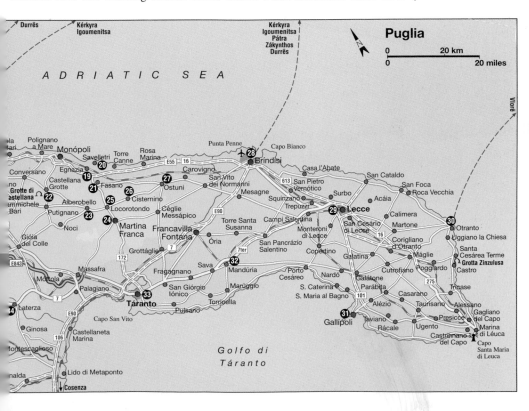

surprises around every corner. The first stop for the delights of the Gargano is in the fishing village of **Rodi Garganico ❺**, at the end of the SS89 from Foggia, which winds down the hillside past olive and carob trees to bring a first close look at the Adriatic's clear, turquoise waters. Below the town, built on bleached cliffs, is a neat harbourside where boats leave for the Tremiti Islands. You might want to stop off at its inviting seafood restaurants. This is a friendly town, unaffected by tourism. The old centre has a small maze of whitewashed houses, and on warm evenings everyone turns out for the *passegiata*. On street corners locals sell wonderful bottled olives, cherries, nuts, oranges and lemons, or whatever else is in season.

East of Rodi there are tempting stretches of beach before the road winds up into the hills towards **Peschici ❻**, perched high above the sea. Its relaxed, easy-going nature and its proximity to many excellent beaches have made the town a popular holiday centre with a number of hotels, restaurants and campsites. The old centre of whitewashed buildings and narrow streets looks almost Greek.

### Summer islands

Depending on the weather conditions and season, boats to the **Tremiti Islands ❼** leave from Peschici every morning – tickets are on sale in the centre of town (boats or hydrofoils also go from Rodi and Manfredonia). With a full day to spare, a visit to these islands is a pleasant day out, but they are best avoided in August. About 30 km (19 miles) off the Gargano coast, this scantly populated archipelago attracts thousands of visitors a year to the crystal-clear seas that lap the rocky shorelines. Those interested in the islands' history tend to head for San Nicola to visit its monastery (founded in 1010 by Benedictines from

**BELOW:** the coast at Rodi Garganico.

Montecassino) or to the landmark Torre del Cavaliere del Crocefisso and the early church of Santa Maria a Mare.

While the coastline offers great attractions, no visit to the Gargano would be complete without a detour inland. From near Peschici, it is a short drive to **Vico del Gargano** ❽, a delightful place where the *centro storico*, signposted as *Terra*, has large fortified walls and towers into which houses have been gradually incorporated over the centuries. Here herbs and tomatoes dry in the sun and working mules are tethered or kept in neighbouring houses that have become en-suite barns. There are some interesting early churches as well as the imposing Palazzo Bella (undergoing EU-funded restoration) and a compact Frederick II castle with a restaurant serving local specialities.

Further inland from Vico is the huge **Foresta Umbra**, last remnant of the primeval forest that once covered Puglia. On weekends and holidays the forest is full of Puglians enjoying elaborate family picnics under the shade of huge oaks and beeches, to the muffled sound of cowbells from the herds that wander the narrow roads through the woods. A circular tour leads to the coast at Peschici passing through Coppo dei Fossi.

From Peschici a pleasant stretch of coast road winds east through olive groves and fragrant pines, passing holiday and camping villages, often tucked away with their own private beaches. The coast has numerous strategic defensive towers such as the Torre di Sfinale, just before **Vieste** ❾. This attractive town has become the holiday capital of the Gargano and on Monday mornings it is further enlivened by an extensive market. The church dates from the 11th century and Frederick built a castle here. Down on the coast the Pizzomunno beach begins beside an enormous pinnacle jutting out of the sea with its town perched

*The inland town of Vico del Gargano, on the way to Foresta Umbra.*

**BELOW:** St Michael's sanctuary in Monte Sant' Angelo.

# THE CULT OF ST MICHAEL

The cult of Michael the Archangel, captain of the heavenly host and scourge of the devil, was probably begun by the Emperor Constantine in the Bosphorus in the 4th century. By the Middle Ages it had become one of the most prolific cults in Europe, and its most important source was Monte Sant' Angelo where the archangel put in several appearances. He first revealed himself in AD 490 to St Laurentius, archbishop of the now lost, great city of nearby Sipontum. At the end of this visit, he left behind his scarlet cloak and the instruction that the site should not be consecrated as he had already done so himself.

Thereafter it became one of the most important pilgrimage sites not only in Italy but in all Europe. In the 8th century St Aubert, a French monk, took a fragment of this cloak back to Brittany where he built the abbey of Mont-St-Michel. Known as the Warrior Angel, St Michael was adopted as protector by the invading Lombards, who built the sanctuary on Monte Sant' Angelo.

It soon became firmly fixed on the pilgrim and crusader routes to the Holy Land. Crusaders and many subsequent believers also adopted the image of St Michael as protective saintly warrior whose effigy, like his worldly manifestations, always appeared in high places.

# Padre Pio

I mages and effigies of Padre Pio abound all over Italy but nowhere more so than in his native Puglia, where he was a priest until his death in 1968. He was born Francesco Forgione in Pietrelcina north of Benevento to a farming family in 1887. As a child he was frail and at the age of 23 he was ordained as a Capuchin priest and sent to Foggia. Contemporaries describe him as extremely emotional and he is reported to have wept copiously during his long hours of prayer. After a brief period of duty as a medical orderly in Naples in World War I, he was discharged from the army due to pulmonary tuberculosis, and was sent to San Giovanni Rotondo where the mountain air was expected to improve his health.

On 17 September 1918, just after the community had finished celebrating the Feast of the Stigmata of St Francis, he went to meditate. The other monks heard a sudden cry and rushing to the choir found him unconscious with blood flowing from wounds in the

palms of his hands. When they took him to his cell they found that his feet were bleeding, too, just as Jesus' hands and feet bled when nailed to the cross. There was also an open wound in his side: Jesus' side was pierced by a Roman soldier to ensure that he was dead. Padre Pio's wounds apparently gave him extreme pain and caused constant bleeding all his life. He nevertheless devoted himself to his faith, and various miracles and acts of healing were attributed to him.

Pope Benedict XV said, "Padre Pio is one of those extraordinary men whom God sends on earth from time to time, to convert mankind". However, Pope Pius XI did not view the cult that grew up around the stigmatised priest so generously and restricted his active ministry. The suspension caused Padre Pio misery, but in 1933 he was reinstated although still prevented from preaching. His presence transformed San Giovanni Rotondo into a world-famous pilgrimage centre. Many regarded him as a worker of miracles and for a large number of people he became known as a healer and even an embodiment of the living God, absolving sinners and guiding them on the path to redemption (see Saints and Superstitions, page 83).

He conceived a major scheme to build a hospital city, and under his inspiration the Casa Sollievo della Sofferenza was built on his underlying principle that "Love is the first ingredient in the relief of suffering".

Beatified by Pope John Paul II in 1999, and canonised in 2002, Padre Pio was, according to the pope, the personification of simplicity, charity and prayer. Padre Pio made lesser claims: "I am a poor brother who prays". Since his death, millions of devotees have visited the monastic church where the latterday saint worshipped for half a century. This onslaught prompted the creation of an immense domed church nearby. Designed by Renzo Piano, and consecrated by the pope in summer 2004, the church acts as a pilgrimage centre, with seating for 6,000 within, and 30,000 on the piazza outside. With Padre Pio's canonisation, his popularity is set to grow, as is the number of international foundations dedicated to him.  ❑

**LEFT:** Padre Pio with the signs of the stigmata on his hands.

above the white cliffs, and beyond it the quieter Scialmarino beach. To the south is the arch of San Felice, one of many arches and caves eroded in the steep, rugged limestone coastline.

From the pleasant, unpretentious town of Mattinata, a road leads inland and twists up 843 metres (2,765 ft) to **Monte Sant' Angelo ⑩**, a town built on the cult of Archangel Michael who appeared inside a grotto *(see page 203)*. This became the **Santuario di San Michele** (open daily, Easter–Sept 7.30am–7pm; Oct–Easter 7.30am–12.30pm, 2.30–5pm; entrance fee), a centre of devotion for pilgrims, crusaders and, today, visitors from all over the world. The Sanctuary, in the middle of the town's attractive old quarter, is approached through a large, richly decorated Gothic portico. Inside, 86 steps lead down to a pair of huge bronze doors made in Constantinople in 1076. These open to the interior, hewn out of solid rock and often packed with pilgrims. Inside there is an 11th-century bishop's throne and other precious works of art, and a museum (open daily 8.30am–12.15pm, 2.30–4.30pm; entrance fee; tel: 0884-561150).

Next door to the Sanctuary stands an unusual 13th-century octagonal bell tower and, below it, steps lead down to the Tomba di Rotari, long thought to be the tomb of an early Lombard ruler.

*Souvenirs of Padre Pio in San Giovanni Rotondo.*

Still further inland, passing through a fertile landscape where shepherds tend their dark sheep, is **San Giovanni Rotondo ⑪**, closely associated with the famous miracle-worker Padre Pio *(see panel on facing page)*.

Back on the coast things start to get rather bleak towards **Manfredonia ⑫**, where a large refinery and other industrial complexes loom as you are entering the poorly signposted town centre. Begun by Manfred, the illegitimate son of Frederick II, the castle of this eponymous town was completed by Charles I of

**BELOW:** the beach and cliffs at Vieste.

Anjou. Now well restored, it looks distinctly out of place among the blocks of flats that surround it. The **National Museum** (open Tues–Sun 8.30am–1pm, 3.30–7.30pm; entrance fee) in the castle has stonework from the ancient Daunii.

**Siponto**, just to the south, was an important Daunian city which was developed by the Romans, and by medieval times was the principal port of northern Puglia. Avoiding the Lido di Siponto, stay on the main road towards Bari and on the left you will find the delightful Romanesque church of Santa Maria di Siponto. Built in the 11th century on the site of a much earlier church, it has an Eastern character and inside there are restored fragments of Byzantine mosaics. Its portal with lions is in the style of many other Puglian Romanesque churches of the 13th century.

## Gargano to Bari

South of the Gargano, between Lido di Rivoli and Margherita di Savoia, the road passes large areas of market gardens followed by extensive saltpans, which are a popular bird-watching spot. At Margherita di Savoia are huge white hills of salt. Production of salt here is the most important in Italy and dates back to the third century BC.

The coast road then approaches the large port city of **Barletta ⓭**, once a departure point for the crusades. The town centre's main attraction is *The Colossus* situated in Corso Vittorio Emanuele. This 5-metre (16-ft) bronze statue, possibly of the 4th-century Emperor Valentinian, is supposed to be the largest surviving Roman bronze figure. Stolen from Constantinople by the Venetians in the 13th century, it was washed up on the shores nearby. Next to it stands the 13th-century Basilica of Santo Sepolcro, built in a mixture of styles, and an

*On the last Sunday in July the "Disfida de Barletta" is re-enacted in the town. This fatal contest, which ended a siege in 1503, pitted 13 French against 13 Italians. The Italians won, as they have done in the re-enactment each year since.*

**BELOW:** Puglian farmhouse.

attractive Puglian-Romanesque Duomo. This was the seat of the Archbishop of Nazareth from 1291 to 1891, and an inscription over the left-hand doorway records the involvement of the crusading King Richard the Lionheart in the building. Watch out for your valuables in the streets of the old town at night.

Beyond Barletta, the olive trees and vineyards multiply and a short distance inland lies the site of the battle of Cannae, where Hannibal famously ambushed and defeated the Romans in 216 BC – overcoming a force twice his size. **Canne di Battaglia** archaeological park (open 8.30am–7.30pm; free) contains an array of ruined buildings and architectural fragments, some bearing Roman inscriptions, and some early painted ceramics.

Back on the coast road lies **Trani ⓮**, where the beautiful cathedral of San Nicola Pellegrino, with a pale stone facade and a tall, leaning campanile, occupies a striking position right next to the clear waters of the Adriatic. The Romanesque carvings around the doorway are particularly fine, as are the bronze doors, from 1179, opening to the interior which includes one of the largest crypts in the world and the 7th-century crypt of St Leucius.

Inland, the cathedral at **Canosa di Puglia** contains a beautiful 12th-century bishop's throne supported by elephants. This string of cathedrals, some of the finest in Puglia, continues through this landscape of rolling hills called Le Murge.

At **Ruvo di Puglia ⓯** there is an excellent rose window and beautifully carved stonework around the door depicting griffons, lions and telamons. The Museo Archeologico Nazionale Jatta (open daily 8.30am–1.30pm and 2.30–7.30pm Fri, Sat and Sun; free) in Piazza Bovio houses a large collection of classical vases for which the town was famous.

If you're visiting one of the large towns by car, it's a good idea to arrive at lunchtime. Shops, churches and museums may close until mid-afternoon, but parking spaces are easier to come by and you can explore the quiet backstreets before the working day resumes.

**BELOW:** Trani's cathedral.

Nearby **Terlizzi** is an attractive town. It specialises in the cultivation of flowers and has some fine buildings. The doorway on the Rosario church, by Anseramo da Trani, was made for a cathedral that was destroyed.

Further west lies a building made famous through its appearance on the wine labels of the local robust red wine. The dramatic outline of **Castel del Monte** ⓰ (guided tours in Italian or English; open daily 10am–1.30pm, 2.30–7.30pm) dominates the landscape of the lower Murge. Frederick II had a penchant for octagons and this angular building has 24-metre (80-ft) octagonal towers at each of its eight corners and eight rooms on each of its two storeys. It may have been built as a hunting lodge, but its purpose is far from clear. It has many architectural quirks, including a classical portal, and academics and fantasists attribute the building with mathematical, mystical and mysterious qualities.

Further along the Adriatic coast from Trani, **Molfetta** does not at first appear to be a promising place to visit, but it does have a nice old centre built around its important fishing port where the Duomo Vecchio stands by the sea. From here the road to Bari passes through almond and olive groves and the town of **Bitonto** ⓱, known for its superior olive oil, and one of the finest Romanesque cathedrals in the region. Its façade is harmonious; the arcaded south side supports an intricately carved gallery and inside there is a beautiful 13th-century pulpit at the entrance to the transept.

## Bari: Puglia's pugnacious capital

Bari ⓲ is the principal town of Puglia, with a university and one of the most modern commercial centres in the south. During the September trade fair, *Fiera del Levante*, its many overpriced hotels fill with business visitors. The fishing

leet is still active, but little of the town's historic importance as a Byzantine maritime power remains in evidence. Its outskirts can seem forbidding, and travellers are often warned by the locals to take care when visiting the narrow backstreets of the Città Vecchia – the old town with its maze of alleys in which to get lost (and to lose your valuables) located on the promontory beside the port, where ferries depart for Greece, Albania, Croatia and Turkey.

Map on page 200

At the centre of the Città Vecchia is the 12th-century cathedral, but a more interesting church, the Basilica di San Nicola, is just to the north. Never fully completed, it was one of the first Norman churches in the south. It has a finely carved doorway, stone altar canopy and a beautiful bishops' throne. The remains of St Nicholas, taken from southern Turkey in 1087, lie in the crypt, and are the source of pilgrimage for both Catholic and Orthodox Christians. Another huge Frederick II castle (open Tues–Sat 9.30am–1pm, 3.30–7pm, Sun 9.30am–1pm; entrance fee) dominates the Città Vecchia. Surrounded by palm trees, it houses an interesting exhibition of church carvings from the region.

Bari also contains two important local museums: the **Pinacoteca Provinciale**, with artworks from the 11th to the 20th century, is housed in the Palazzo della Provincia on Via Spalato, and offers a strong showing by Southern Italian artists (Tues–Sat 9.30am–1pm, 4–7pm, Sun 9.30am–1pm; entrance fee). The Archaeological Museum is currently being revamped and has relocated to the ex-Convento Santa Scolastica in Via Veneria in Bari. The museum will reopen with an expanded collection of classical ceramics and bronzes.

*Greek vase from the Archaeological Museum in Bari.*

## South of Bari

The coast immediately to the east of Bari is not particularly attractive, but just inland is **Conversano**, a comfortable town on a hill overlooking the coast. Its fine baroque churches, cathedral, castle and Monastery of San Benedetto attest to its past importance. The attractions of the coastline resume at **Polignano a Mare**, a former Greek settlement in a spectacular clifftop position, which has a well-preserved old centre and a monastery dedicated to San Vito. Further on, *Monopoli* has an imposing baroque cathedral (open daily 9am–noon, 4–7pm; entrance fee) with a sacristy that exhibits objects of early religious art and Romanesque stone carving from the earlier church on the site.

Southeast from Monopoli, traffic becomes lighter and the surroundings less developed. At **Egnazia** ⓳ there is an important archaeological site of a former settlement of Roman and Messapian origin (open daily 8.30am–6.30pm; entrance fee) and a well-organised modern museum (open same times as above) standing next to the Necropolis. The main archaeological site close to the sea contains extensive remains of houses, two basilicas and a well-preserved section of the Via Traina, a branch of the Via Appia that connected Benevento with Brindisi. It was built between 108 BC and AD 11 out of blocks of limestone on the route of the earlier Via Minucia along which Horace reputedly walked on his famous journey from Rome to Brindisi in 38 BC.

Beyond Egnazia is **Savelletri** ⓴, an enjoyable

**BELOW:** Bari's cathedral.

small fishing port and a tempting place to stay, with several waterside restaurant and a pleasant hotel. It is the value of fish rather than the tourist which is highl prized in this small town. Immaculately painted boats fish close to the shorelin and their catches go to dealers on the quayside and to the numerous loca seafood restaurants.

*Olives are harvested from trees that are several hundred years old.*

### Trulli and the Valle d'Itria

Some of the most interesting parts of central Puglia lie inland. **Fasano** ㉑ known mainly for its safari zoo, has an attractive centre and is a good base fo touring the general area. It has elegant buildings and a large market that take over the southeast side of town on Wednesday mornings. The landscape aroun Fasano is covered with olive trees, some several hundred years old. Another fea ture are the *masserie* – large fortified farmhouses which can be found in man parts of central Puglia. If you want to enjoy a historic experience, the Masseri San Domenico spa near Savalletri dates back to the 14th century and was use by the Knights of Malta; www.imasseria.com.

Further inland the road rises steeply to Selva where there is a panorami view. West of Fasano are the **Grotte di Castellana** ㉒ (open daily 8.30am–7pm entrance fee), some of the most spectacular limestone caves in Italy. Allow tw hours for the guided tour which explores the 3-km (2-mile) "Grotta Bianca route of caves and tunnels containing spectacular stalagmites and stalactite.

The sight that attracts visitors to this part of Puglia more than any other, how ever, is the ***trulli*** area south of Fasano. Here the landscape is covered with cur ous whitewashed buildings with distinctive conical roofs *(see below)*. A **Alberobello** ㉓, *trulli* buildings are dramatically massed together, much to th

**BELOW:**
*trulli* dwellers.

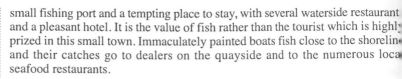

O ften topped with mysterious astrological or religiou symbols, Puglia's *trulli* buildings are found nowhe else in Italy, or the world. The word has no know meaning and their origin is obscure: they may have bee inspired by eastern structures. It has also been suggeste that these buildings, dating from the mid-14th centu evolved to provide a rustic building that could be quickl erected or dismantled in order to avoid punitive taxes permanent homes.

A *trullo* is made of limestone blocks collected fro surrounding fields and placed together using the tim honoured technique of mortar-less or dry-sto construction (although most inhabited ones have h mortar added in recent years). The conical roofs were b up using limestone slabs and inside the loft spac provided storage for hay and the family's food stores. T roof space also draws off the heat, keeping the inter cool. The buildings are not large, and instead constructing larger ones when more space is needed, ot *trulli* are simply added on.

Although rural *trulli* can be found throughout the It Valley, their highest concentration is in Alberobello, whe there are more than 1,500 still standing.

Map
on page
200

elight of the numerous coach loads of tourists who arrive every day in summer
o view the scene. In the surrounding landscape, smaller concentrations of *trulli*
ontinue to provide functional homes and farm buildings, but in Alberobello
ney unashamedly offer themselves to tourists with open houses, rooftop panora-
as, gift shops, restaurants or craft centres. In spite of this commercialism, it is
ill worth a visit, especially early in the morning or late in the day when there
re fewer visitors. If you park in the Lago Martellotta, follow the steps up to
iazza del Popolo where the Belvedere Trulli offers an excellent view over the
onderful concentration of *trulli* houses framed between palm trees.

Back down to the lago, look for Via Monte San Michele and walk up the hill
nong the *trulli* buildings, with endless winding alleys off it making it a delight
o explore. At the top there is even a *trulli* church, the Chiesa a Trullos, as well
s houses advertising panoramas and invitations to see the interiors of everyday
ulli homes. Not all of Alberobello is built in *trullo* style: the attractive town
ntre around the Piazza del Popolo is more conventional but it is a pleasant
ace to join in the evening *passeggiata* or to eat out in one of the numerous
staurants. Here you can sample the local version of the regional ear-shaped
sta, *orecchiette*.

From Alberobello, the back road to Martina Franca is an attractive drive into
aranto Province. In spring the fields around the *trulli* are filled with poppies and
her wild flowers, adding a rich carpet to the vines, olive and cherry trees.
Martina Franca ㉔ is one of Puglia's most attractive towns and offers an allur-
g combination of a slightly Moorish flavour, fine baroque architecture, attrac-
ve shops and restaurants (it is well known as a gastronomic centre) and an
hurried way of life. At its heart is Piazza Roma, entered through the Porta di

**TIP**

Alberobello makes a
good base: treat
yourself to the Hotel
dei Trulli where you
can stay in a *trullo*,
with your own patio in
a garden setting with
swimming pool.
(www.hoteldeitrulli.it;
tel: 080-432 3555). Or
book a *trullo* through
Trullidea (tel: 39-
0804-323860;
www.trullidea.com).

**BELOW:** *trulli*
in Alberobello.

*At Montalbano,
between Fasano and
Ostuni, is the Tavole
Palatine, the
Knights' Table, a
large dolmen
thought to be a
prehistoric tomb.*

Santo Stefano, or Arco di San Antonio, which was rebuilt in 1764 in baroque style. Beneath a group of palm trees there is a cool fountain in front of Palazzo Ducale, making it a pleasant place to linger. A walk down Via Cavour, with its range of shops, leads to the vast Basilica San Martino standing next to the clock tower on Piazza Plebiscito.

On the road north from Martina Franca there is a fine view across a cultivated landscape dotted with *trulli* buildings towards **Locorotondo** ㉕. Perched high up and surrounded by vineyards which produce a well-known *spumante* wine, Locorotondo is the other main town of the *trulli* area. It takes its name, "round place", from the fact that its streets spread from its centre like ripples in a pond. At the top of the town, opposite Porta Napoli, there is a leafy communal garden with an expansive vista of the *trulli* landscape. On the other side of the gate is a graceful baroque library with a clock tower.

Close by, in Via Morelli, is a wonderful arched doorway, and Piazza Fra Giuseppe Andria Rolleo in the middle of town is dominated by the huge baroque facade of the cathedral. Via Giannone passes whitewashed alleys and leads to steps down to Via Cavour and the elegant late-Gothic church of Madonna delle Grazie which has a simple facade and rose window.

## The Salentine Peninsula

**BELOW:**
whitewashed
Ostuni.
**RIGHT:** sun-baked
Locorotondo.

The attractive rocky coast at Torre Canne is popular for offshore fishing, but its pleasant beaches become crowded in summer. The road inland from here to **Cisternino** ㉖ crosses a pleasing landscape of olive trees and, in springtime, wild flowers. The town has attractive gardens with views over surrounding countryside. Nearby is the 13th-century Chiesa Matrice and Torre Civica

Passing through Porta Grenne, next to the tower, Via Basilioni follows a charming route passing a fine baroque balcony to reach Piazza Vittorio Emanuele at the centre of the town. This is a pleasing and atmospheric place with narrow streets running off it, such as Via Regina Elena, where there are many places to eat.

To the east is the charming, whitewashed hill town of **Ostuni** ㉗, which is where the *trulli* area ends and the Salentine Peninsula begins. Its late 15th-century cathedral has a beautiful rose window and doorway as well as gracefully curved and richly carved cornicing. Distinctly Middle Eastern in style, Ostuni's narrow streets and alleyways are a delight to wander around, just to take in the exotic feel of the place.

From Ostuni to Brindisi, as the *trulli* buildings diminish, the towns become less interesting. **Carovigno** is shabby, but has some interesting architectural features and, despite unprepossessing outskirts, San Vito dei Normanni contains interesting rock churches, in particular San Biagio. Soon after midday, when working people have hastened home for lunch and a nap, all these towns fall silent except for the occasional clatter of dinner plates echoing from the windows shuttered against the heat.

From the 2nd century BC, the Via Appia, the great highway from Rome of which virtually nothing can now be seen, entered **Brindisi** ㉘ passing the spot where the smart villa residences of Mesagne now stand. Southern Italy's busiest port was the end of the ancient Roman road and has been the embarkation point for legionnaires, pilgrims, crusaders and traders on their way to the East. The 11th century round church of San Giovanni del Sepolcro is a legacy of the Knights Templars. Beside it, the 15th-century Portico dei Cavalieri

For a view of Brindisi, take a ferry across the harbour to the Monument to Italian Sailors, a piece of chunky Mussolini architecture built in 1933, where a lift rises 30 metres (150 ft) to its summit.

**BELOW:** Brindisi is the end of the road, where ferries set sail for Greece.

*Supporting figure on the facade of Santa Croce, Lecce.*

**BELOW:** Basilica Santa Croce, Lecce.

Templari leads to the provincial archaeological museum with its Greek bronzes (open Mon–Sat 9am–1pm, Tues 3–7pm; free).

Now a busy naval port, Brindisi is the principal point of departure for people taking ferries to Albania and Greece and tickets are advertised everywhere. The attractive, lively seafront is a pleasant area for a wander, but the famous single Roman column – one of two that for centuries marked the end of the Appian Way – has been taken away for lengthy restoration, leaving only a rusty metal barrier and a graffiti-covered plinth to mark the historic spot.

## Lecce's living baroque

Most people stay at Brindisi only if they are taking a ferry, but to the southeast along the SS613 motorway is a town where many find reason to tarry. **Lecce** ㉙ is one of the most important baroque cities in Italy *(see page 109)*. At odds with the surrounding countryside, the sophisticated main centre of the Salentine peninsula is crammed with fine architecture. Around every corner there is a beautiful doorway or balcony, but even these are little preparation for the riot of incredible detail carved into the soft golden stone of Santa Croce, Lecce's celebrated church. Begun in 1549 by the local architect Gabriele Riccardi, it has a well-preserved baroque facade with intricately designed balconies, arches, columns and friezes alive with carved figures, flowers and animals. Next door stands the imposing 17th-century Palazzo dei Celestini.

The centre of Lecce is compact, and a short walk to Piazza Sant'Oronzo – dominated by the missing column from Brindisi's Via Appia, now surmounted by the carved figure of Sant' Oronzo, the Bishop of Lecce martyred in the 1st century. Below this lies the Roman amphitheatre. From here, Via Vittorio Emanuele leads past Sant'Irene, which has a finely detailed baroque interior, to the beautiful Piazza del Duomo. The Duomo as it stands was designed by Giuseppe Zimbalo and completed in 1570, and its entrance is framed on either side by the stone figures standing on balconies. Next to it is the graceful Palazzo Vescovile. A short way down Via Giuseppe Palmieri is the small Piazza Salconieri and the 16th-century Palazzo Balsamo with a wonderful balcony supported by four figures on either side. There is a wide choice of places to eat and drink and, with many other churches to see, such as Gesù and Santa Chiara, a visit is not to be hurried.

Outside Lecce is **Acaia**, a quiet and attractive fortified town entered through a handsome Renaissance gateway. From Acaia, the pleasant drive to the coast brings you to **San Cataldo**, a small seaside resort with a good sandy beach. Further along the coastal route is the popular fishing spot of **Rocca Vecchia** and the crumbling remains of its ancient Messapian site. There are several dolmen scattered around this area.

## The mosaics of Otranto

Close enough to Albania to be able to glimpse its distant coastline on clear days, **Otranto** ㉚, Greek Hydruntum, is Italy's closest port to Greece and Turkey, and it prospered in the heyday of Byzantium and under the Normans. But after the fall of Byzaium in 1480, the town was sacked by a combined Turkish and Venetian fleet, and the Christians were slaughtered by Turks. Last to be slain, it is said, was the Turkish executioner, who had a last-minute conversion after seeing how steadfastly his victims stuck by their faith. Ten years later the Aragonese erected the defensive castle. Nowadays the old town has quiet winding backstreets and an attractive waterfront. It is easy to park near here to walk under the massive fortified Porta Alfonsina and up to the **cathedral**. Behind its graceful facade, the church reveals a splendid mosaic floor, one of the finest in Italy. This extraordinary tapestry in stone, designed in 1165 by a priest named Pantaleone, depicts the months of the year, historical figures and legends, and a host of animals, around a huge tree of life with images of biblical and mythical subjects. A chapel in the south transept holds the bones of those killed by the Turks.

After Otranto a small road continues along the scenic, rugged coastline all the way down to Finibus Terrae (Land's End), taking in some attractive places and viewpoints on the way. At **Santa Cesarea Terme** there are popular spas and a pleasant resort facing a distant view of Albania. South of here a sign points to a short steep road down to the **Grotta Zinzulusa** (open daily 10am–6pm; entrance fee), seaside caves reached by a footpath leading to the rocky inlet. **Castro** is a pleasant town with a castle and attractive marina. There follows a stretch of winding, unspoilt coastline dotted with cacti, palms and olive trees as far as the southern tip. Many people feel a sense of disappointment arriving at **Santa Maria Finibus Terrae** and the lighthouse next to the church marking the most southeasterly tip of Italy. The mournful Masses broadcast on the church's outdoor loudspeakers, the lighthouse surrounded by wire fences, and the car park often crammed with coaches do not encourage the visitor to linger. The great

Map on page 200

*"When the story was finished, I looked on the map of the Kingdom of Naples for a well-sounding name, and that of Otranto was very sonorous".*

– HORACE WALPOLE ON THE WORLD'S FIRST GOTHIC THRILLER, *THE CASTLE OF OTRANTO* (1765)

**BELOW:** Finibus Terrae, land's end.

Puglian aqueduct ends here, and below lies the more cheerful Marina di Leuca where boat excursions can be made to the Grotta di Diavolo.

## The Ionian coast and the Gulf of Taranto

*There is more than one Gallipoli. The name comes from the Greek* kalli polis, *which means "beautiful city".*

Rounding the tip of Puglia, there is little to hold the traveller's interest until reaching **Gallipoli** ③. Built on a small island, this attractive, fortified town typifies the history of Puglia. Greek in origin, it was subdued by the Romans in 265 BC and then occupied by Saracens, Normans and Spanish. The town outgrew its island site and spilled over to the mainland where it has lately developed a busy, unattractive urban sprawl which can be off-putting. But the old town, reached by a bridge, remains lively and full of character and its harbour is still a busy fishing port. The most famous landmark lies on the mainland just on the left before you approach the old town. This is the beautiful Fontana Ellenista which bears witness to the Greek history of the town.

Up the coast from here are new resorts, such as **Santa Maria al Bagno**, **Santa Caterina** and **Porto Cesareo**. Once a quiet fishing village, Porto Cesareo still has a pleasant harbour, but it is now more concerned with the busy summer holiday business and taking advantage of its clear blue waters and good beaches of white sand.

Many of the towns inland are worth visiting. **Galatina** has a Greek flavour and its 14th-century Franciscan church of Santa Caterina d'Alessandria is a legacy of its former wealth. The town is at the centre of an important tobacco and vine-growing area. Further east, **Corigliano d'Otranto** has a fine 16th-century castle with a superb gateway and a richly decorated balcony. **Nardo** is a particularly attractive old town with an untouristy air. At its heart is the Piazza

**BELOW:** fishermen in Gallipoli.

Antonio, centred on the Immacolata Spire Sedile and an unusual Fontana di Torro. Here is another detailed cathedral facade, and the arcaded Piazza Mercato is a pleasant place to stroll. Further north, **Copertino** is a town dominated by its huge castle with a Renaissance portal carved in Lecce stone. It is also the birthplace, in 1603, of Joseph, the flying monk (*see page 86*).

**Grottaglie** is a town with numerous limestone grottoes but its main activity is pottery, which is immediately evident: thousands of terracotta pots are set out to dry in the sun. Ceramics and terracotta have been made here for hundreds of years, though its glazed wares are most notable, including copies of ancient Greek vases, huge plates and pots.

**Sava** is an attractive agricultural town. At the centre of a wine-producing area, it has whitewashed houses, a tufa castle and a medieval bell tower. **Manduria** ㉜, known for its strong local wine, Primitivo di Manduria, is mainly visited for its caves and many miss the attractive town centre. Parking by the clock tower at the end of Via Ferdinando Donno, there is a short walk to the superb early 18th-century Palazzo Corcioli Giannuzzi, where a fine portal leads into a compact courtyard surrounded by a magnificent balcony. There is also a Romanesque cathedral with 16th-century lions guarding the doorway. On the edge of town lies the Zona Archeologica with remains of the old city walls and a necropolis. Nearby is the Fonte di Plinio, a well which Pliny noted in his *Natural History* had a constant water level.

At **Francavilla Fontana** the ornate Palazzo Imperiale is one of several baroque buildings worth visiting. Once the main town of the ancient Messapians, **Oria** was an important stopping point on the Appian Way. It has some fine buildings and shows signs of its early Jewish settlement around the Porta Ebrei.

**Map on page 200**

**TIP**

Grottaglie pottery is famous all over Italy. In the town where it is made, it can be bought far more cheaply.

**BELOW:** crabs and swordfish in Gallipoli's market.

Map
on page
200

*Although Taranto
was famous for its
school of Pythagoran
philosophy and as
the birthplace of
Aistoxenes, who first
notated Western
music, the
Tarrentines liked
their leisure.
According to Strabo,
they had more
holidays than
workdays in the year.*

**BELOW:** pottery
in Grottaglie.
**RIGHT:** cathedral
in Martina Franca.

## Major port and oyster centre

On the approach to **Taranto** ㉝ the sea grows a little murky, but people still have an appetite for the oysters that are cultivated in the shallow waters around this ancient city, which the Spartans founded as Taras in 708 BC. From the east, the city reveals large-scale industry, an unhealthy smell, heavy traffic and sickly-looking trees. With the Mare Piccolo on the inland side and the Mare Grande sheltered from the sea, Taranto consists of three separate parts, all surrounded by water. The busy modern district in the southeast is connected by a swing bridge to the historic centre, sited on a small island. This, in turn, is connected by bridge to the northern part of the city where steelworks and dockyards, Italy's second largest, preside. A main road crosses the Mare Piccolo, bypassing the town completely, which some may wish to do in order to avoid the modern sprawl and the old town's reputation for pickpockets and car crime. Halfway across the lagoon, this road passes Parca Remembranza where the oyster beds and fishing boats, naval docks and the city can be viewed at a distance.

A stop in the city is rewarded by a cathedral with a baroque chapel, a lively fish market and a colourful Old Quarter. The **Museo Nazionale** (Corso Umberto 141; open Tues–Sun 9am–2pm; tel: 0994-532112) in Corso Umberto I on the southern mainland, recalls Taranto's importance as a centre of Magna Graecia. Its huge collection – mainly Greek terracotta and sculpture, and Roman sculpture and mosaics – is second only to the Museo Archeologico Nazionale in Naples. The most popular exhibits are in the Sala degli Ori, which has a fine collection of gold jewellery from the Magna Graecia period.

Northwest of Taranto, the road heads towards Matera in Basilicata *(see page 227)*, which was once part of Puglia. On the way to this town of caves are many subterranean places. Despite its busy, poorly signed, unprepossessing outskirts, **Massafra** has extensive rock-hewn churches made by Greek monks from Asia Minor scattered around its ravine setting. Some are hard to find and it requires persistence to locate the person looking after the keys. Its neighbouring town, **Mottola**, has cave frescoes, notably in the Chiesa di San Nicola.

**Laterza** ㉞, near the Basilicata border, is built in a spectacular canyon-like setting and contains numerous cave dwellings, some of which date back to 2000 BC. There are reputed to be 180 churches carved into the rock, some with Byzantine frescoes. It is not easy to explore these successfully without a guide, but the ravine is an inspiring place to walk and attracts much wildlife, including several types of hawk. This landscape of deep ravines extends all the way to Matera, 10 km (6 miles) to the west. North of this Puglian canyon country is **Altamura** which owes its existence to Frederick II. It has a fine cathedral and its old town is a pleasant place to wander.

In a similar way, **Gravina in Puglia** ㉟, noted for its breed of horses, has a maze of interesting narrow backstreets in the old walled town. There are baroque *palazzi* and the church of Madonna delle Grazie, which has a fine facade. More cave dwellings as well as one of the largest underground churches in Puglia, San Michele dei Grotti, can be found here. ❑

# BASILICATA

*With its forests, sandy coves, castles, ancient troglodyte dwellings and rock-hewn churches, there's plenty to explore in this little-known region*

Even for many Italians, Basilicata is *terra incognita*, regarded by those who have never visited it as economically undeveloped and culturally backward. And though the region lacks the extensive holiday coastlines enjoyed by neighbouring Puglia and Calabria, there is still plenty to see and do.

Basilicata's two established tourist destinations are the chic Tyrrhenian seaside resort of Maratea and the Sassi di Matera, a unique complex of cave homes. But, for all their charm, few would be able to locate them on a map. Even the well-known Parco Nazionale del Pollino, evenly split between Calabria and Basilicata, is more typically associated with Calabria.

Basilicata's unfortunate image is, in part, the lingering consequence of Carlo Levi's landmark documentary novel *Christ Stopped at Eboli*. In 1935 the Fascist regime condemned the writer, painter and political activist to live in the isolated mountains of central Basilicata *(see page 232)*. The title, which refers to a popular local saying, is a reference to the grinding poverty suffered by the region's peasants at a time when much of the rest of Italy was enjoying the benefits of industrial modernisation. In Levi's era, the daily struggle for survival left the people of Basilicata feeling forgotten and abandoned, while the rest of the country assumed that anyone south of Eboli (about 30 km/19 miles from Salerno) lived like a pagan animal.

**PRECEDING PAGES:**
Matera, cave town.
**LEFT:** Rivello, a
typical hill town.
**BELOW:** content in
Lagonegro.

In recent decades, however, Basilicata has emerged from the shadow of poverty. Emigration is no longer the only way to escape misery; the development of successful small industries, supported by European Union money, is rousing Basilicata from its long economic slumber and transforming its agrarian and backward economy. At the same time, the tourist sector is slowly expanding.

## Take to the road

Basilicata is similar to Calabria in spirit, history and landscape. Like its neighbour, it is dominated by a backbone of mountains that descend through dramatic foothills to the sea. But its short (75-km/47-mile) coastline means it doesn't have the island-like atmosphere of Calabria.

One of the best ways to appreciate Basilicata is by car, making several stops rather than basing yourself in one town. Hotels and farm stays are inexpensive and, unless you are heading to the beaches in July and August, reservations are not necessary. A full tour of the region takes a week. For those travelling on foot **Potenza** is a good base for day trips by train to **Melfi** and **Venosa**, the historical towns of the Vulture area.

The short Ionian and Tyrrhenian coastlines are served by the Ferrovie dello Stato (FS state railways), while Matera is on the Ferrovie Calabro-Lucane and

*The castle at Melfi drips with history and houses a museum.*

connected by train to Puglia (but only by bus to Potenza). If you want to fully explore central and southern Basilicata, a car is the best option.

## The Vulture and the castles of Frederick II

A relatively small area around **Melfi ❶**, on the SS93 between Foggia and Potenza, offers one of the region's best combinations of natural landscape and historic sites. It is easily explored by car or public transport.

Melfi itself is a small, unprepossessing town. The Norman conqueror Robert Guiscard was crowned Duke of Puglia and Calabria in the **Castello di Melfi**, and Pope Urban II launched the First Crusade from inside its walls in 1089. The castle, an imposing fortress with a double perimeter wall and eight polygonal towers, was the stronghold for the Holy Roman Emperor Frederick Barbarossa's Swabian dynasty. In 1231 he decreed feudal control over the area from here. The castle is now home to the **Museo Nazionale del Melfese** (open daily 9am–7pm; closed Mon am; entrance fee), displaying Roman and pre-Roman archaeolog-

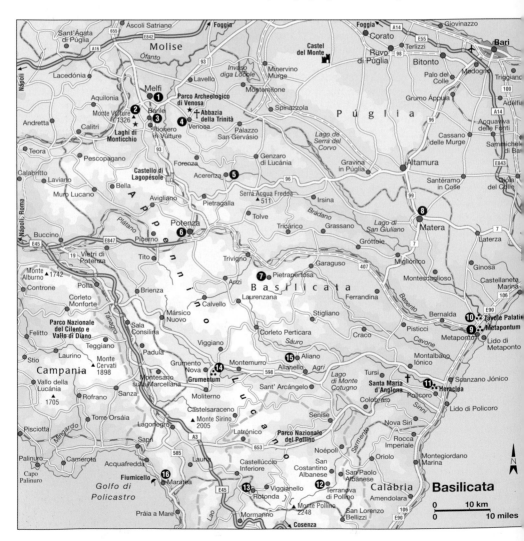

Basilicata

ical finds, Byzantine jewellery and Swabian ceramics. The highlight of the museum is a 2nd-century AD salmon-pink sarcophagus, with its fine details of Greek gods and heroes.

The region around Melfi is dominated by the Vulture massif. At 650 metres (2,130 ft) above sea level, its volcanic craters are filled by two lakes, the **Laghi di Monticchio ②**. A cableway between Lago Grande (big lake) and Lago Piccolo (small lake) rises to Monte Vulture (1,326 metres/4,350 ft). Another splendid view is from the heavily restored Norman Abbazia di San Michele, located on the wooded slopes of the Lago Piccolo crater. From here, the panoramic SS167 road descends to Potenza.

A few miles south of Melfi on SS167 lies **Barile ③**, a humble mountain town of Albanian origins *(see page 258)*, famous for its Easter Processione dei Misteri. On Good Friday afternoon, hundreds of costumed locals pour through the streets, including 33 small children dressed in black, representing Christ's age when he was crucified, three women in white to symbolise the Marys and the character of an eccentric Gypsy woman who goes about town glittering with Arbëreshe (Albanian) gold, loaned by the local women.

## Roman Venusia

Less than an hour away from Melfi is **Venosa ④**. Originally the successful Roman city of Venusia, it has survived thanks to its dominant position above the surrounding territitory. For centuries it was a centre of learning, fought over by the powerful families of the region.

Frederick II's son Manfred was born here, as was the Latin poet Quintus Oratium Flaccus (65–8 BC), who, according to legend, lived in Vico Orazio, where remains of a Roman structure known as the Casa di Orazio are located (not open to the public, but visible from behind the gate). In 1443, Venosa came under the control of Pirro del Balzo (the city was part of his wife's dowry), who enriched it with several monuments. To build the Castello, now home to the **Museo Archeologico** (open Wed–Mon 9am–8pm, Tues 2–8pm; entrance fee), Pirro demolished the cathedral, which was then rebuilt in Piazza del Municipio.

The Via Frusci leads out of the town centre to one of the most interesting areas in Basilicata: **the Parco Archeologico di Venosa**. The park centres on the unfinished Abbazia della Trinità, but it includes Roman and palaeo-Christian remains, Jewish and Christian catacombs, a thermal complex and a 10,000-seater amphitheatre.

The **Abbey** (open May–Sept Wed–Sun 9am–7pm, Tues 2–5pm; Oct–Apr variable; free; tel: 0972-36095), one of the largest projects attempted by the Normans is one of the most intriguing buildings in Southern Italy. It is made up of the so-called *chiesa vecchia* (the old Norman church) and the roofless *chiesa nuova*, a huge basilica (70 metres by 48 metres/ 230 ft by 157 ft) planned by Benedictines in 1135 but never completed. Built of stone from an earlier pagan temple on the site, the abbey is a treasure trove of inscriptions, sarcophagi and frescoes.

Map on page 224

**TIP**

Just 2 km (1 mile) from Melfi, towards Rapolla, is the rock-hewn church of Santa Margherita, with a remarkable 12th-century fresco. If you plan to visit, call the Melfi tourist office on 0972-23975 to make sure that the church will be open.

**BELOW:** the Venosa Archaeological Park.

On the way to Potenza from Venosa you can take the SS169 at San Nicola to Pietragalla, then pick up a tortuous road which leads to **Acerenza ❺**. This claims to be one of Italy's 50 most beautiful towns. The *centro storico* has a Longobard castle and a Franciscan monastery, and the 11th-century cathedral – dubbed "the most Romanesque monument of the Mediterranean" – is home to a fine Renaissance crypt.

West of Acerenza, on the road from Melfi to Potenza, is the pretty rose-coloured **Castello di Lagopesole** (open daily, June–Sept 9.30am–1pm, 4–7pm; Oct–May 9.30am–1pm, 3–5pm; entrance fee), another of Barbarossa's residences.

## Potenza and the Apennine Dolomites

The Byzantine-style symbol of the Virgin in the church of San Francesco in **Potenza ❻**, known locally as the *Madonna del Terremoto* (Madonna of the Earthquake), has had plenty of opportunity to protect the city. Basilicata's capital has suffered more than its fair share of earthquakes, even for a seismically vulnerable southern town.

The last big tremor hit in 1980, and reconstruction has not exactly been miraculous. Built on a spur of rock between two valleys, the historic centre of Potenza looks down on modern suburbs scattered at its feet.

With the exception of the **Museo Archeologico Provinciale** (Via Ciccotti; Sun–Mon 9am–1pm, Tues–Sat 4–7pm; free) which is a 25-minute walk downhill from the centre (or take bus Nos. 3, 5 or 6), and a cluster of fine churches on Via Pretoria, there is little worth seeing. The street takes on a pleasant and relaxed atmosphere during the evening *passeggiata*, which somehow compensates for the relative lack of historic architecture. The Antica Osteria

**TIP**

Potenza and Matera are the only towns fully geared for the traveller in Basilicata. In Matera try the evocative Hotel Sassi, in the middle of the Sasso Barisano (tel: 0835-331009; www.hotelsassi.it).

**BELOW:** Tricorico, a typical hilltop town.

Marconi (Viale Marconi 233; closed Sun eve and Mon; tel: 0971-56900) offers a varied menu of traditional soups and home-made pasta dishes.

South of Potenza stretch the peaks of the remote **Appennino Lucano** range, their bare, pointed rocks and jagged pinnacles sculpted into bizarre forms by the elements. Here, in the "land that time forgot" hides the one-hotel town of **Pietrapertosa** ❼ (southeast of Potenza, off the SS407). Perched at 1,088 metres (3,570 ft), it is Basilicata's highest settlement, reached via a series of nail-biting hairpin bends. The town is overlooked by a romantic fortress carved out of the mountain.

## City of caves

**Matera** ❽ is one of the wonders of Southern Italy. Known as the "City of the Sassi", cave-like habitations have been cut into the steep sides of the ravine Matera rests on. What appear from a distance to be holes in the rock are, in fact, windows and doorways, terraces, alleys and even churches. Once home to the farmers and shepherds of Matera, the Sassi have been recognised by UNESCO as a World Cultural Heritage Site and are currently undergoing restoration and repopulation. The finest example of "cave-architecture" in the Mediterranean, the *sassi* have rightly become the region's main tourist attraction *(see page 228;* contact the tourist office for details, tel: 0835-331983).

Matera has been inhabited since the Stone Age, and its pre-history is well documented in the excellent Museo Ridola *(see page 229)*. The city's Greek and Roman legacy is modest; between the 9th and 10th centuries it suffered repeated invasions by barbarians, Byzantines and Saracens, and was destroyed and rebuilt three times in 130 years. Originally part of Puglia, it was annexed

Map on page 224

*Oil was struck in Basilicata in Val d'Agri in the late 1980s, and until at least 2025 is expected to provide for 10 percent of domestic consumption.*

**BELOW:** the town of drilled stone, Pietrapertosa.

# Sassi Cave Homes

The Sassi (stones) of Matera are the most complete and complex troglodyte dwellings in the Mediterranean region. These cave dwellings, which date from Palaeolithic times, line the steep slope of the ravine above the Torrente Gravina on which Matera is built. They are divided into two distinct quarters: the better-off Sasso Barisano faces northwest; the more impoverished Sasso Caveoso faces northeast. (Caves on the north side of the ravine, once inhabited, were never populated in the same way.)

It is a city within a city, built over the centuries when cave-living was common in the vast surrounding region known as the Murgia. Natural grottoes made simple shelters for families, and were gradually enlarged and enclosed with exterior walls.

Until the beginning of the 20th century, the Sassi cave dwellings were functional if fairly primitive. An ingenious system of tiny canals regulated the flow of rainwater and sewage.

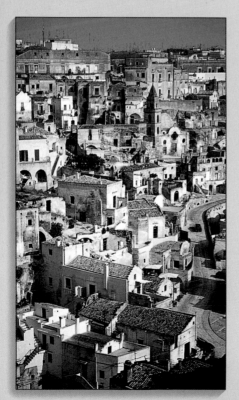

Small hanging gardens and orchards stained the grey volcanic rock of the ravines green, and numerous little churches conferred a sense of dignity to this part of town.

But this was completely lost in the period between the two world wars, when overcrowding and urban decay led to a deterioration in general living conditions. An increase in population meant that caves originally used as stalls, storage areas or cellars became occupied. A hole in the ground without running water or electricity could be home to an entire family (complete with hens and pigs).

In 1950, the Sassi were declared a national disgrace. Of the 2,997 dwellings, 1,641 lacked fresh air and light. As a result of legislation in 1952 to restore the Sassi to a habitable condition, some 15,000 residents left their cave homes and relocated to other parts of town.

Since then, the ancient cavernous *borgo*, which measures 30 hectares (75 acres) has slowly come back to life. No longer considered an emblem of subhuman social conditions, the Sassi are now recognised as an important part of Italy's cultural heritage, a unique habitat worth preserving. In 1993 they were added to the UNESCO list of World Heritage Sites and many of the cave dwellings have been rebuilt and repopulated. The area is slowly being transformed into a "living museum", with the warren of alleys best explored with a local guide (contact Matera Turismo, a group of committed young guides, tel: 0835-334110).

The Sassi's biblical atmosphere has made it an ideal backdrop for films, including Pasolini's 1964 epic *Gospel According to Matthew*, Mel Gibson's *The Passion of Christ,* and in 2006 *The Nativity* (the story of Mary before the birth of Christ). Many of the locals recount stories of minor stardom, as they featured as extras.

The Sassi district has several appealing bed-and-breakfast cave hotels and cosy underground bars. A unique place to stay is Locanda di San Martino, with a deconsecrated church and cosy rooms in cave dwellings all connected by *cunicoli*, secret passages in the rocks (Via di San Fiorentini, tel: 0835-256600; www.locandadisanmartino.it). ❑

**LEFT:** the Sassi area of Matera, once a home for the impoverished, is now being renovated.

by Basilicata in 1663, and served as its capital city. Matera retained this position until 1806, when that role was passed to Potenza.

The great legacy of the Byzantine civilisation in Basilicata is the so-called *chiese rupestri*; these little rock-hewn churches carved out of the tufa resemble surface-level catacombs and feature built-in altars, pilasters, domes and frescoes – all dating from the 9th to the 15th century. Matera has more than 150 *chiese rupestri*, with 48 in the Sassi. The most important and best-preserved are Santa Barbara, Santa Maria de Idris, Santa Lucia alle Malve, San Nicola dei Greci, the Madonna delle Virtù, the Convicinio di Sant'Antonio and Santa Maria della Valle. They are not easy to find or access, so the best way to visit them is with a guide who will often have keys to unguarded churches.

Most of the historic centre of Matera winds through the area of the Sassi *(see opposite)*. From Piazza San Pietro Caveoso, with the eponymous church (rebuilt in the 17th century), Via Buozzi leads to the 17th-century **Palazzo Lanfranchi** (open Mon–Sat 9am–1pm, 4–7pm; free; call ahead to visit, tel: 0835-256211), which houses the Pinacoteca d'Errico – a collection of Italian paintings from the 13th to 18th century – as well as the more interesting Centro Carlo Levi, with impressive canvases immortalising the places and people in his novel *Christ Stopped at Eboli*.

*Frescoes of the Apostles in Santa Maria de Idris.*

The **Museo Ridola** (open Tues–Sun 9am–8pm; entrance fee) on Via Ridola, is a cut above the usual local, dusty archaeological museum, with its first-class display of local objects from Palaeolithic to Roman times.

Further along the street stands the baroque **Chiesa del Purgatorio**, dedicated to the medieval cult of the Holy Souls of Purgatory, with a curvaceous façade and gruesome decorations carved in the tufa of the main doorway.

**BELOW:** the altar of Santa Maria de Idris cave church.

After the rocky, dry environment of the Sassi, the nature reserve of the Lago di San Giuliano is ideal for a picnic and a nap in the shade. If you need a longer break, stay the night at the Agriturismo San Giuliano, a 15-minute walk from the reserve, at Migliònico, about 12 km (8 miles) south of Matera (tel and fax: 0835-559183).

**BELOW:** the Sasso above Torrente Gavina, Matera.

At the junction with Via del Corso is the 17th-century **Chiesa di San Francesco**, with a polyptych by Bartolomeo Vivarini behind the main altar. Piazza del Sedile features a handsome 16th-century building, home to the local conservatoire, and leads into Via Duomo with the Romanesque cathedral, which dates from the 1230s. The façade features a great rose window with small statues of the Archangel Michael, two fancily dressed noblemen and the unusual figure of a man wearing a short gown – a thoughtful homage to the multitude of artisans who worked on the cathedral. The church is dedicated to Matera's patron saint, the Madonna della Bruna, visible in the Byzantine-style fresco above the first altar to the left.

## Christian and pagan rites

The Sagra della Madonna della Bruna, celebrated on 2 July, is the region's most important festival in honour of the Virgin. The curious name of this Madonna – venerated for at least 1,000 years – may derive from Mount Hebron in Judea, where Mary went to find Elizabeth to tell her that she was with child. The name might also allude to the darker skin colour of the Byzantine Madonnas, or to the ancient rites for the agricultural season, in which "bruna" perhaps meant "terra".

The celebration, officially established by Pope Urban VI in 1380, retains many pagan traits. The triumphal float requires up to five months of preparation, during which the friezes and panels in painted and gilded wood featuring views of the Sassi or church façades, as well as the papier-mâché statues representing a different biblical episode every year, must all be built anew. Late in the morning, the 18th-century statue of the Madonna is accompanied by a procession of

shepherds to the town's Piccianello neighbourhood. At sunset the statue is placed on the triumphal carriage, pulled by eight mules harnessed with colourful, festive straps and escorted by horsemen in bright uniforms, who bring it back to the cathedral. The carriage is then attacked by the townspeople, who tear it to pieces in a riotous atmosphere typical of pagan country festivals. A band plays as loudly as it can, while bursts of fireworks reflect against the Sassi.

The evening *passeggiata* takes place along Via del Corso, Via Roma and Via San Biagio; its focal point is the Piazza Vittorio Veneto, which gets cleared of traffic for the occasion. For a memorable meal in a converted cave-dwelling, try Le Botteghe (Piazza San Pietro Barisano 22, tel: 0835-344072, closed Sun eve and Wed). Regional dishes include roast meats and *orecchiette* pasta. Fine local food can also be found at Ristorante Lucanerie (Via S. Stefano 61; closed Sun eve and Mon; tel: 0835-332133).

## Classical sites on the Ionian coast

In Basilicata, the ruins of classical antiquity are concentrated in three areas: at Metaponto and Policoro, both on the Ionian Coast, and at Grumentum, towards the border with Campania.

About 3 km (2 miles) from Lido di Metaponto and its well-appointed beaches are the remains of the Greek colony of **Metapontum ❾**. The Zona Archeologica begins at the junction of the SS106 with the road to modern Metaponto.

This is the only ancient Mediterranean colony where archaeologists have mapped the entire urban layout, including the surrounding agricultural terrain. The first group of ruins includes the remains of a theatre (built on landfill) and traces of the foundations of four temples. More evocative are the so-called

Map on page 224

*The name Basilicata comes from basilikòs, the Byzantine administrator who governed here before the Normans arrived in the 11th century. The region is also known as Lucania, from the Lucani, who lived here in the 5th century BC.*

**BELOW:** the beach at Metaponto.

**Tavole Palatine**  (open daily 9am until one hour before sunset; free; tel: 0835-745327). Situated north of modern Metaponto, just before the SS106 crosses the Bradano river, these are the remains of 15 standing columns from the 6th-century BC Doric Temple of Hera.

The **Museo Archeologico Nazionale** (Via Laverana, about 2 km/1 mile from the Zona Archeologica towards Metaponto; open Tues–Sun 9am–8pm, Mon 2–8pm; entrance fee) has a display of the statuary and ceramics found in the area, but the most interesting items are housed in the Museo Archeologico Provinciale in Potenza *(see page 226)*.

Like Metaponto, Policoro is a new town with little to detain a visitor except a dip in the sea. Excavations are still in progress at the **Parco Archeologico di Policoro** (open daily 9am until one hour before sunset; free), which so far has revealed the acropolis of **Heraclea** ⓫, founded by the rulers of Taranto in the 5th century BC on the site of the even older Siris, one of the richest colonies in Magna Grecia, which was destroyed by its rival cities in 540 BC. The first-rate **Museo della Siritide** (open Wed–Mon 9am–8pm, Tues 2–8pm; entrance fee) contains local finds such as bronzes and statuettes, and a section dedicated to traditional games and sports.

*The 5th-century BC acropolis of Heraclea at Policoro*

## National park with Albanian enclaves

In the southern part of the region is the **Parco Nazionale del Pollino** (www. parcopollino.it). Italy's largest protected area straddles two regions. When compared with the Calabrian section, the Basilicata side of the Pollino range looks rather tame – yet it is no less rich in wildlife and natural beauty *(see Wild Places, page 119)*. This is fine walking country, though the heat can be oppressive in the

**BELOW:** a more prosperous, modern Eboli.

## CARLO LEVI AND EBOLI

Eboli is an undistinguished modern town, but its name is known throughout Italy and beyond thanks to Carlo Levi's classic novel *Christ Stopped at Eboli.* Born to Jewish parents in Turin in 1902, Levi studied medicine and set up an anti-Fascist organisation, Giustizia e Libertà (Justice and Liberty). In 1935 his politics led him to be exiled to Basilicata in the villages of Grassano and Aliano, where he continued to practise as a doctor among a superstitious, poverty-stricken society. (The house in Aliano where he lived is now a museum, *see page 234*.)

From 1939 to 1941 he lived in France, but then returned to Italy and, whilst in hiding from the retreating Nazis, wrote *Christ Stopped at Eboli,* a compelling account of his time in Basilicata. He describes the cave dwellers of Matera who came out of their dark holes to beg – not for money, but for quinine for their malaria. The book was an immediate success when it was published in 1945, and it has never been out of print.

Levi was also an accomplished painter, exhibiting at the Venice Biennale from 1954. He continued to be politically active, as both a journalist and politician, and was a member of the Italian Senate from 1963 until his death in 1975.

summer months. On the eastern side of the park is **Terranova di Pollino** , where wooden handicrafts are still produced by local artisans; here you can buy kitchen tools, walking sticks and various souvenirs, all made by hand. The restaurant Luna Rossa, on Via Marconi 18 (tel: 0973-93254), offers some of the best Pollino food, such as *ferrazzuoli, rascatielli, tapparelle* (local pasta dressed with breadcrumbs and raisins, wild herbs and mushrooms), goat's cheese, lamb and chestnuts.

    **Latronico**, just beyond the western confines of the park, about 10 km (6 miles) away from the A3 and off the SS653, is famous for its alabaster workshops; **Sant'Arcangelo**, a few kilometres above the northern edge of the park, off SS598, is renowned for its wrought-iron workshops.

    The "capital" of the Parco Nazionale del Pollino is **Rotonda** . Close to the Calabrian border and easily accessible from both the A3 and SS19, it makes an excellent base for further explorations. The SS653, which cuts across the park, puts most of the towns within easy reach. Among them, **San Costantino Albanese** and **San Paolo Albanese** (both located in the southeast of Basilicata) have been home to Albanian communities since the mid-16th century. Though not numerous, the Arbëreshe *(see page 258)* in Basilicata rival their Calabrian cousins in maintaining their language and traditions, which are celebrated during their colourful religious festivals. In San Paolo Albanese, the festival of San Rocco takes place on 16 August with a procession led by the *gregna*, a trophy of wheat sheaves carried on the shoulders of four men. In San Costantino Albanese, a series of *nuzazith* (costumed papier-mâché puppets) is set ablaze on the second Sunday in May during the course of celebrations in honour of the Madonna della Stella.

**TIP**

If in the Potenza area, consider visiting the museum of Albanian culture in San Paolo Albanese (open by arrangement 9am–2pm, 3–8pm; tel: 0973-94376/368). For more on the Albanian influence, *see page 258.*

**BELOW:** Piano Ruggio in Pollino National Park.

Map on page 224

## Classical and literary tour

**Grumentum ⓮** (excavations open daily 9am–one hour before sunset; free; Museo dell'Alta Val d'Agri open Tues–Sun 9am–8pm, Mon 2–8pm; entrance fee), near the modern town of Grumento Nova, was a flourishing Roman town. You can visit the ruins of its 1st-century BC amphitheatre, where crowds were entertained for some 600 years, and see the Grande Casa dei Mosaici (3,600 sq. metres/38,750 sq. ft on two floors) with its mosaic floors and wells that were once filled with snow and used as ice houses. The Siri Bronzes, which were dug up here in 1823, are in the British Museum.

From the Val d'Agri, at the junction with Alianello, the road climbs north to the town of **Aliano ⓯**, where Carlo Levi was exiled, and the model for Gagliano in *Christ Stopped at Eboli*. Contact the **Parco Letterario Carlo Levi** (Via Martiri d'Ungheria 1; Thur–Tues 9am–noon, 4–7.30pm; tel and fax: 0835-568529; www.aliano.it) for information about the tour which covers most of the places described in the novel. But Aliano and its surroundings are easily explored on your own, book in hand, as little has changed since 1945. Letters, documents, sketches and other items belonging to the author are on display in the **Museo Carlo Levi** (Via Cisterna; variable opening hours; tel: 0835-568030).

## The brief Tyrrhenian shore

Basilicata's small slice of the high and rocky Tyrrhenian coast between the extensive shores of Calabria and Campania's Cilento coast is a mere 30 km (19 miles) long. Characterised by lush vegetation and a splendid sea, the coastline is riddled with gorges, hidden grottoes and coves. It is best explored from **Maratea ⓰**, where the railway from Rome meets the coast on its way down to Reggio-Calabria. The so-called "city of the 44 churches", which looks out onto the Gulf of Policastro, has become one of the most sought-after hideaways in the south, rivalling Ravello in Campania for its breathtaking views. The unspoilt resort has a charming coastline and boutique hotels, including the luxurious Masseria Serramarina, a world-class spa hotel set in a converted abbey, and the atmospheric Locanda delle Donne Monache, housed in a former convent *(see Travel Tips, page 335)*. The resort itself reveals little of its past as a Greek colony, yet the acropolis once rose from the rock that looms above the modern city, where a huge white marble statue of Christ, with arms outstretched, now stands.

Start your visit from the busy *piazzetta* (Piazza Buraglia), taking Via Cavour to reach the Piazzale di Santa Maria Maggiore. From here, Via Santicelli climbs to the old *borgo*, where pretty little streets and steps wind their way to many attractive churches. The oldest of all is tiny 1,000-year-old San Vito. At the very top of the rock stands the Santuario di San Biagio, built on the site of what was the temple to Minerva.

North of Maratea is the wide beach of Fiumicello, situated next to the rocks of Punta Santa Venere. Many musical events are staged here in the high season. Nearby **Acquafredda** is reputed to be an excellent place for fishing. ❑

**BELOW:** Maratea shopkeeper.
**RIGHT:** the beach at Maratea.

# CALABRIA

*Rome was still a village of shepherds when Pythagoras was teaching philosophy here. Today, beyond miles of shoreline, Calabria is a region of undiscovered beauty*

Map on page 240

Naples

**S**ituated in the toe of Italy's boot, the region of Calabria separates the Ionian and Tyrrhenian Seas, and reaches out to Sicily across the Straits of Messina. For thousands of years its history has been defined by the people who have settled this narrow passage between the eastern and western Mediterranean. Beyond its 780 km (485 miles) of coastline – fully one-fifth of the Italian peninsula – and blue seas rich with fish, Calabria is still a sparsely developed mountainous region. Dense forests, lakes, fast-flowing torrents and unspoiled landscapes set Calabria apart from the rest of Italy.

It was not always so. In the 7th century BC, colonists from nearby Greece landed on the narrow coastal plains of the region, and established some of the most powerful cities of the pre-Roman world: Rhegìon (Reggio Calabria), which participated in the Peloponnesian War as an ally of Athens against Sparta; Lokroi Epizephyrioi (Locri Epizefiri), the first Greek city to adopt a written legal code; Sybaris (Sibari), so opulent and refined that it gave birth to the word "sybaritic"; and Kroton (Crotone), home to the most important medical school in the Western world. But don't come to Calabria in search of ruins; little has been seriously excavated, and archaeology – like so many other aspects of the region – is relatively underdeveloped. The archaeological ruins at Locri Epizefiri, Roccelletta di Borgia and Capo Colonna along the Ionian coast feature some of the remains that have so far been brought to light. Museums in Reggio Calabria, Crotone and Sibari are well stocked with everyday artefacts, statues and the great symbol of the Magna Graecia culture: *pìnakes* – terracotta tablets with vows written to the gods.

## Refuge in the hills

As the Greeks faded from the scene, so did their great cities. The Romans, with their expanding Republic, used Calabria as a much needed source of wood. Their relentless deforestation of the region resulted in environmental change, altering not only the terrain, but also the culture and way of life. Formerly navigable rivers were transformed into spectacular flood torrents known as *fiumare*, which when dry give the landscape a primitive, lunar appearance. Soon after the fall of the Roman Empire, the coastal plains turned to malarial swamps, forcing the local population to take refuge in the inland hills.

In the following centuries the coast, as well as being vulnerable to invasion, was associated with disease – and to this day no traditional Calabrian dish features fresh fish. When the 1950s political reforms forced local landholders to cede their estates to labourers, they withheld the "good" land of the interior – even though the coastal area was perfectly viable.

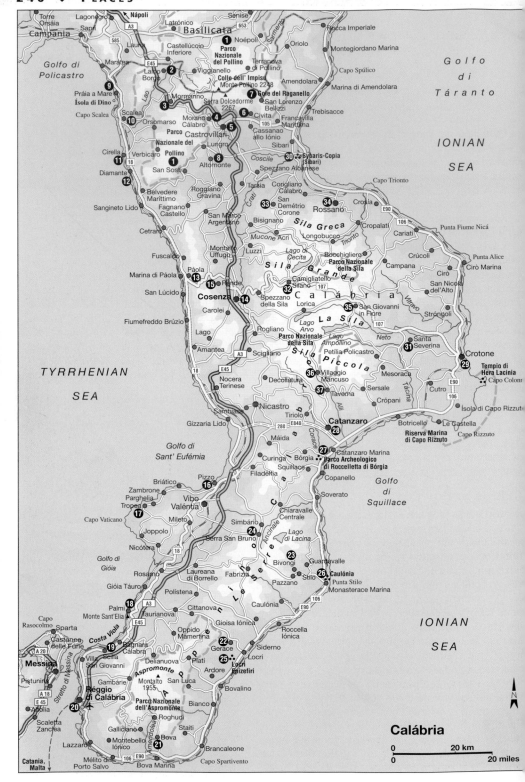

Napoli

Campania

Torre
Orsáia
Sapri
Lagonegro
Maratea
585
Laura
Lauro
Borgo
A3
E45

Latrónico
653
Sénise
Basilicata

① Noépoli
Parco
Nazionale
del Pollino
② Viggianello
Colle dell'Impisu
Monte Pollino 2248
Terranova
di Pollino
Castellúccio
Inferiore

Rocca Imperiale

Oriolo
Montegiordano Marina

Capo Spúlico

Amendolara
Marina di Amendolara

Golfo di
Policastro

Práia a Mare
Ísola di Dino
⑨

Mormanno
Scalea
⑩
Orsomarso
Parco
Nazionale del
Pollino

③
Serra Dolcedorme
2267
⑦ Gole del Raganello
San Lorenzo
Bellizzi
Trebisacce

Capo Scalea

Morano
Cálabro
④
Castrovillari
⑤
Civita
105
Francavilla
Maríttima

Cassanao
allo Iónio
Sibari

Lungro

Golfo
di
Táranto

Capo Trionto

IONIAN
SEA

Cirella
⑪
Verbicaro
18
San Sosti
⑧ Altomonte
Lúngro
Coscile
Spezzano Albanese
⑳ Sybaris-Copia
(Sibari)

Diamante
⑫

Belvedere
Maríttimo
Fagnano
Castello

Roggiano
Gravina
San Marco
Argentano
Bisignano
Tarsia
③③ San
Demétrio
Corone
Coriglíano
Cálabro
③④ Rossanó
Crosia
E90
Cropalati
106
Punta Fiume Nicá
Cariati

Sangineto Lido

Cetraro

Mucone Acri
Longobucco
Sila Greca
Trionto

Crúcoli
Ciró Marina
Punta Alice

Fuscaldo

Marina di Páola
Páola
⑬
⑮ Rende

San Lúcido

Cosenza
⑭

Carolei

Montalto
Uffugo
Luzzi
Lago di
Cécita
Sila
Grande
Camigliatello
Silano
107
⑫ Silano
Spezzano
della Sila
Lorica
Cálabria
Campana

Bocchigliero
Parco Nazionale
della Sila

Ciró
San Nicola
dell'Alto
Strongoli

Fiumefreddo Brúzio

Lago
Lago
Arvo
⑤ San Giovanni
in Fiore
107
La Sila

Santa
Severina
③① 

TYRRHENIAN
SEA

Amantea
Rogliano
Parco Nazionale
della Sila
Lago
Ampóllino
Petília Policastro
Sila
Píccola
③⑥ Villaggio
Mancuso
Mesoraca
Sersale
Taverna
Crópani
Cutro

Scigliano
A3
E45
Decollatura
③⑦
Nocera
Terinese
Sambiase
Nicastro
Tiriolo
Cutro
E90
Santa
Severina
Crotone
⑳
Tempio di
Hera Lacinia
Capo Colonn
Ísola di Capo Rizzut

Gizzaria Lido
Máida
Catanzaro
⑳
280
E848

Golfo di
Sant' Eufémia
Curinga
Filadélfia
⑳ Catanzaro Marina
Squillace
Copanello
Parco Archeologico
di Roccelletta di Bórgia

Briático
Pizzo
⑯
Zambrone
Parghelia
Tropea
⑰
Vibo
Valéntia
Mileto

Bórgia
Soverato

Golfo
di
Squillace

Capo Vaticano
Joppolo
Simbário
⑳
Nicótera
18
Serra San Bruno
Chiaravalle
Centrale
Lago
di Lacina

Golfo di
Gióia
Rosarno
Gióia Táuro
Laureana
di Borrello
Fabrizia
Pazzano
⑳
Bivongi
Stilo
Guardavalle
Caulónia
⑳
Punta Stilo
Monasterace Marina

Polístena
Palmi
⑱
Monte Sant'Elia
A3
Cittanova
Caulónia
106
E90

Capo
Rasocolmo
Sparta
Castanea
delle Fúrie
A 20
Costa Viola
Taurianova
E45
Oppido
Mamertina
Gioisa Iónica
Roccella
Iónica

IONIAN
SEA

Messina
Pistunina
A 18
E 45
Villa
San Giovanni
Scilla
⑲
Bagnara
Cálabra
Delianuova
Pláti
⑳
Gerace
⑳
Locri
Epizefiri
⑳
Siderno
Locri
Ardore

Bova
⑳
Montalto
1955
San Luca
Bovalino

Gambárie
Réggio
di Calábria
⑳
Aspromonte
Parco Nazionale
dell'Aspromonte
Bianco

Apólia
E 18
Scaletta
Zanclea
Roghudi
Staiti

Lazzaro
Gallicianó
Montebello
Iónico
⑳
Brancaleone

Catania,
Malta
Mélito di
Porto Salvo
Bova Marina
106
E90
Capo Spartivento

N

Calábria

0          20 km
0          20 miles

Map on page 240

## Great coastal resorts, fine national parks

Today Calabria offers some of the best seaside resorts in Italy. The Tyrrhenian coast was the first to be developed. The initial boom came in the 1970s with resort towns such as Praia a Mare, Scalea, Pizzo and Tropea, nicknamed "the Capri of Calabria" and a great base for exploring the area.

In the 1990s, development shifted to the Ionian Coast. The area south of Catanzaro is dotted with marinas and picturesque seaside towns perched on the coastal highlands. In the summer months, the towns around the Gulf of Squillace are home to the region's liveliest nightclubs. Accommodation along here ranges from secluded bungalows and *agriturismi* (farm-stays or rural B&Bs) to comfortable, family-run hotels. If you prefer a larger town with more shops and activities, but don't mind a half-hour trip to a clean beach, try Crotone.

To find the quieter, more authentic Calabria, you need to venture into the interland, where the region's ancient towns are stacked on steep slopes. Rising above the remains of castles, these villages have a simple architectural style, and are the best Calabria has to offer.

With the exception of Cosenza, whose historic centre has survived four earthquakes in 200 years, and parts of Catanzaro and Crotone, the major cities of the region are unremarkable, unattractive, unkempt agglomerations. But don't let that put you off. What it lacks in human development, Calabria more than makes up for in natural splendour. Three national parks – the Pollino in the north, the Sila in the centre and the Aspromonte in the south – together form a green belt between the cliffs of the Tyrrhenian Sea and the unspoiled beaches of the Ionian Coast. All of them offer great trails and walks, with English-speaking guides available. In Pollino National Park you can stay overnight in any of its 56 towns, with Civita and Castrovillari offering the added bonus of excellent restaurants.

In Sila National Park, Camigliatello Silano's inexpensive hotels and the self-catering cottages of Villaggio Mancuso are good options. The Aspromonte is scattered with good-quality *agriturismi* (*see Travel Tips, page 332*) and its informal hospitality system, called *ospitalità diffusa* (B&B in private farms and country houses), puts you in touch with the locals and their traditions.

The surprising diversity and drama of the Calabrian landscape lends a cinematographic quality to any visit. From the height of the Isthmus of Catanzaro, the narrowest point of the Italian peninsula, you can pass from the Ionian to the Tyrrhenian coasts in minutes. In a single day from May to September you can swim in limpid waters, rest in the mountains under cool, fresh pine and beech, visit a Byzantine church or folk museum, and stroll along the quiet narrow streets of many abandoned towns. In winter, the peaks of the Sila and Aspromonte are covered in snow and the tourist towns of Camigliatello Silano and Gambarie profit from the regular traffic of local skiers.

## The approach by road

The FS (Italian railways) trains connect the coastal towns and main cities, but a car gives you the best opportunity to enjoy the region fully. Arriving from

*Calabria was the Roman name for what is today the Salento (the southernmost part of Puglia, at the heel of the boot). In the 7th century, the Byzantines applied the same name to the region on the western side of the peninsula.*

**BELOW:** in a Calabrian garden.

*Face at the doorway:
in many inland towns
visitors are scarce.*

the north by car, the best way to enter Calabria is through the Pollino National Park. The Autostrada del Sole (A3) then turns south and passes through Cosenza on its way to Reggio Calabria. Alternatively, you can take the coastal highways *(statali costiere)* but these roads are best avoided in July and August when beach traffic is heavy. Whichever route you take to Cosenza, remember that the city is jammed during peak traffic hours (8–10am, 6–9pm).

If you don't have time to make a stop along the northern Tyrrhenian coast, head down the Autostrada as far as Pizzo, where a beautiful coastline runs alongside the SS522, taking in Tropea and Capo Vaticano. From Nicòtera, you can continue along the coast via the SS18 that passes through Rosarno, or else rejoin the Autostrada, which continues south to Reggio Calabria.

The Ionian Coast is served by the SS106. The Calabrian landscape is so compelling that there are few roads not worth a drive, but – with the exception of freeway A3 – be prepared for slow, careful driving along narrow and twisting mountain roads. Snow chains might be needed in the winter months. Note that there are no toll roads in Calabria.

A complete tour of the region will take at least two weeks. It's advisable to make hotel reservations in advance during high season, which runs from July to August at seaside resorts and national parks, Easter week in national parks and December to February at ski resorts.

## The Olympus of the Apennines

**BELOW:** Pollino National Park.

The Pollino mountain range rises in the north of Calabria – taking its name from the abundance of *pollentes herbae* (medicinal herbs) the ancients collected there. The area has been part of the **Parco Nazionale del Pollino** ❶ since its creation

n 1993 *(see Wild Places, page 119).* The park, home to 172,000 people in 56 owns and villages, stretches for 1,960 sq. km (760 sq. miles) between Calabria and Basilicata, and has a great variety of nature trails. Unless you are accompanied by a guide, a good map is essential.

Starting from Colle dell'Impisu, to the north of Morano Calabro, in a two-hour round trip you can reach the **Piani del Pollino** (Pollino Plains) a delightful alpine meadow with a small lake. **Mount Pollino** is a five-hour round trip, and an eight-hour trip will give you time to tackle the highest peak, **Serra Dolcedorme** (2,267 metres/7,438 ft), named for its shape which suggests the body of a sleeping woman. The evocative landscape of the Pollino moved the English travel writer Norman Douglas (1868–1952) to write in *Old Calabria*: "Silhouetted against the sky in the morning light, these stupendous mountains seem to melt into a fog of amethyst at sunset. A vision of peace."

The symbol of the park is the elegant, tall *pino loricato* - a native species of pine tree that thrives on the **Grande Porta del Pollino** mountain pass. To reach the Grande Porta del Pollino, drive to the Pianoro di Acqua Tremula from San Severino Lucano (15 km/10 miles) or Terranova di Pollino (10 km/6 miles). The trail to the Grande Porta (a four-hour round trip) starts 400 metres (1,300 ft) south of the Pianoro. The best time of year to visit the Pollino is between mid-May and mid-June, when wild flowers – daisies, violets, crocuses, peonies, and orchids – cover the high plains, and the jagged peaks are still flecked with snow.

## owns and villages of the park

Heading south from Basilicata, the first town on the A3 is **Laìno Borgo ❷**, famous for its Good Friday religious procession known as the *Giudaica*, an

TIP

Enquire at one of the visitor centres in the Pollino National Park about the so-called "Literary Park": a trail between Cosenza and Crotone that takes in the places described by Norman Douglas in his novel *Old Calabria* (or check the Literary Parks website: www. parchiletterari.com).

**BELOW:** landscape near Delianuova, Aspromonte.

*Castrovillari hides one of the tastiest attractions in Italy: the Locanda di Alìa, where traditional Mediterranean food is prepared with a flair. Try the ravioli filled with goat's cheese and herbs in a wild anise sauce, the* carne 'ncartarata *(pork in a piquant honey sauce) and the liquorice mousse. There are also rooms to let in the adjoining inn (tel: 0981-46370; www.alia.it).*

**BELOW:**
a red rose in Pizzo.

ancient interpretation of the Passion by locals in costume. Laìno is a good base for visits to the Lao river valley, where rafting and canoe trips are on offer.

Further south, the medieval town of **Mormanno** ❸ is a favourite overnight stop, excellent for climbers and anyone who enjoys strolling through narrow medieval streets. From here it is a quick and easy excursion into the heart of the Pollino mountains. For a great panorama, take the carriage road to the SS19 Campo Tenese exit, and then climb to the Ruggiu plain. Park near the de Gasperi refuge and follow the path to the right for about 25 minutes to reach the Belvedere.

From here, the SS19 leads down to **Morano Calabro** ❹, a sleepy town draped across the mountaintops. Morano's population was severely depleted by emigration in the 1950s. Activity centres on its piazzas, the domain of elderly men who gather every day to exchange news and views. The wildlife museum **Centro "Il Nibbio"** (Vico II Annunziata 11; open daily, June–Sept until 8.30pm; closed 1–4pm; Oct–May until 6pm, closed 1–3pm; entrance fee; tel: 0981 30745; www.ilnibbio.it) has informative displays of the native fauna and flora including a variety of stuffed animals (deer, wolf, porcupine, badger and several dozen birds). Guided tours of the exhibits in English are available on request. The museum entrance looks out across the Sibari plain and on clear days the view extends all the way to the sea.

If you have time, visit some of Morano's churches as well as the small Museo di Civiltà Contadina (next to the Town Hall; irregular opening hours; closed at weekends). It has an interesting display of agricultural implements, artefacts and peasant costumes.

Laid-back **Castrovillari** ❺ is the most populous town in the Pollino area. Its busy shopping street, Strada del Mercato, is flanked by fruit and vegetable stalls and shops, including the Galleria d'Arte Il Coscile, which sells contemporary Calabrian artwork, and a bookstore specialising in books and maps of the region. In Piazza del Comune, sandwiched between two dilapidated baroque palaces, is a tiny museum (entrance through the door to the left of the tourist office; open Mon–Fri 9am–1pm; free) dedicated to the life and work of Castrovillari's most celebrated son, the painter Andrea Alfano (1879–1967).

Founded by Albanian refugees in the 1470s in one of the most beautiful valleys in the Pollino National Park, **Civita** ❻ (off the SS105, 30 minutes from Castrovillari in the direction of Francavilla Marittima) is a town of old narrow streets that have changed little over the centuries. The **Museo Etnico Arbëresh** (open Tues– Fri 4–8pm; but call ahead on 0981 73150; donations welcome), with its small display of Albanian artisan work, is worth a visit, and the Church of Santa Maria Assunta has an unusual icon sculpted in walnut and olive wood.

Nearby, the **Gole del Raganello** ❼, is one of the most spectacular canyons in Italy. Various trails wind their way through the canyon, from easy walks among the broom and wild oleander, to challenging cave explorations that should only be undertaken in the company of an expert guide.

## City of art

At the southern edge of the park – a tortuous drive south from Castrovillari on the SS105 – **Altomonte 8** has emerged as Calabria's "city of art". The residents of this ancient hilltop *borgo* (little village) took it upon themselves to restore its medieval streets, churches and palaces, even raising funds to build an amphitheatre to host the annual Festival Mediterraneo dei Due Mari (Mediterranean Festival of Two Seas). In the wake of the more high profile Festival of Two Worlds (held in Spoleto in Umbria), Altomonte's summer arts festival draws tourists to see open-air art exhibitions, theatre, dance and music performances all focused on Mediterranean culture and traditions.

Altomonte, or "high mountain", enjoys a beautiful natural setting and the town itself has some fine architecture. Don't miss the 14th-century Church of Santa Maria della Consolazione, the only surviving example of Gothic-Angevin style in Calabria. Beyond the gate, to the left of the façade, a panoramic view unfolds; to the right is the entrance to the Dominican Convent (1440), with a small but interesting **Museo Civico** (open Mon–Sat 9am–noon, 4–7pm; entrance fee). Among the collection from the 14th and 15th centuries is a painting by the Gothic master, Simone Martini, and the intriguing *Madonna delle Pere,* an unattributed work featuring a very plain looking Christ child reading a book. If you wish to stay the night in Altomonte the Castello di Altomonte, a Norman castle, is one of Calabria's best historic hotels *(see Travel Tips, page 336).*

## The beaches of the Tyrrhenian Sea

All along its 240-km (150-mile) length, the Tyrrhenian coast is lapped by emerald waters, rocks studded with cedars, hills covered with fig trees and olive

Map on page 240

**TIP**

To reserve a guided tour of the Gole del Raganello contact the bar-restaurant Il Pino Loricato in San Lorenzo Bellizzi, where they also have a list of rooms for rent (Piazza Pio x, tel: 0981-993151).

**BELOW:** Altomonte, the region's "city of art".

groves, stretches of golden sands, and the remains of Greek and Arabic towns. Here, thankfully, the developers haven't made any inroads – at least, not yet. Driving along the coastal road, especially between September and May, it is easy to be hypnotised by the variety of blue and green hues that illuminate this unspoilt landscape.

The SS18 runs parallel to the coast, edging the Parco Nazionale del Pollino for 50 km (30 miles). After it crosses from Basilicata to Calabria, the first stop is **Praia a Mare** ❾. You can rent boats from its large beach to explore the caves and grottoes of **Isola di Dino**, a tiny, uninhabited island just off the shore.

Soon after, the road passes **Scalea** ❿, a picturesque town clinging to the steps of rock (*scale* means stairs). This is a good place to stop for lunch and a stroll along the promenade.

The next town along is **Cirella** ⓫, where the ruins of the old village founded by the Greeks (Cirella Vecchia) are clustered on a hill. This stretch of coast boasts a 4-km (2½-mile) beach. Just offshore lies the Isola di Cirella, another uninhabited island, accessible by boat from Cirella.

A good place to bed down is **Diamante** ⓬, a pretty coastal resort with some nice restaurants. Diamante is known for its murals depicting scenes from Calabrian life, and as the headquarters of the Accademia del Peperoncino (Academy of the Hot Chilli Pepper, on Via Amendola 3), which preaches the virtues of Calabria's most popular spice through its publications (in Italian), national summits, *peperoncino* tastings and "hot" summer camps.

About 30 km (19 miles) south of Diamante on the SS18 is medieval **Paola** ⓭, named after one of Italy's most popular saints. The miracle worker San Francesco da Paola was born here in 1416 and founded the austere mendicant

**TIP**

The Gelateria Pierino, on Diamante's Lungomare, makes wonderful hot chilli ice cream.

**BELOW:**
market near the sea at Diamante.

order of the Minims. The sanctuary that bears his name has a harmonious façade and, despite its isolated location in the river Isca gorge, is a stop on a pilgrimage route. This "route of miracles" dedicated to the saint begins alongside the basilica. To the north, just outside town, is the little underground Chiesa di Sotterra, an early Christian church which has some of the oldest Byzantine frescoes in Calabria. Alternatively you can relax on the beach that skirts Paola's modern expansion, **Marina di Paola**, before you take the SS107 east to Rende and Cosenza.

## Cosenza: without the lightness of being

Saved from earthquakes but shaken by emigration, sultry but hectic **Cosenza** ⓮ can be quite a shock for a visitor accustomed to the relaxed rhythms of the rest of the region. Yet, of the major cities, Cosenza's historical centre is Calabria's best. Dubbed the "Milan of Calabria", the city has developed extensively towards the northeast, an area of suffocating traffic and ongoing construction work. The mountain dwellers of the Sila settled in this part of town, as did those who once lived in the historic centre, which today seems a ghost town. Surrounded by seven hills, perhaps it was not by chance that the Bruzi (the Italic tribes who in the 4th–3rd century BC assumed control of what had been the Greek colonies) chose it as their capital city. The Roman occupation of the city was followed by a long period of decay and barbarian invasions, which ended with the expulsion of the Saracens in 986. Under the Angevins, the Aragonese, the Normans and the Spaniards, Cosenza experienced a cultural and economic rebirth that for centuries made it one of the most sophisticated and lively cities in Southern Italy.

Map on page 240

TIP

The Lavorazione Artigianale Fichi Secchi of Ciccotti Maria Carmela prepares delicious dried figs (a Calabrian speciality), either plain or stuffed with nuts or dipped in chocolate and honey. (Via Rupa 15, Paola, tel: 0982-583255.)

**BELOW:**
San Domenico, Cosenza.

Despite the presence of a university, which draws thousands of young students from the provincial hinterlands, Cosenza seems rather grim. The proverbial hospitality and "lightness of being" of the south has inexplicably disappeared and it's often harder to snatch a smile or a kind response here than elsewhere in Calabria. Neither is it the best place for an overnight stay, as the city's few decent hotels are expensive, ugly and away from the historical centre.

## The old town

Allow half a day for your visit to the historic centre which, unusually for a Calabrian city, is mostly intact. There are a couple of good restaurants and the handsome 19th-century Caffè Renzelli (Piazza Parrasio 17), with its period decor and memorabilia of Italian *Risorgimento* heroes. From Piazza Campanella, where the baroque church of San Domenico stands, Corso Telesio runs uphill towards the 12th-century Duomo. Consecrated by Frederick II in 1222, it contains a 4th-century Roman sarcophagus, containing the body of the Emperor's eldest son, Henry (interred here after his suicide) and the Gothic sepulchre of Isabella of Aragon (died 1270). Contact the Soprintendenza to see two splendid Byzantine works: a gold and enamel reliquary containing a fragment of the Holy Cross, and the icon of the Madonna del Pilerio, protector of the city. For security reasons these are no longer kept inside the Duomo (Piazza Valdesi 13, tel: 0984-75904; free).

Via del Seggio takes you to the Monastery of San Francesco d'Assisi, founded in 1217 but partially remodelled in later centuries. In the beautiful Piazza XV Marzo is the neoclassical Teatro Rendano, famous for its opera, and the Accademia Cosentina, founded in 1514 as a centre of humanist culture and today

*Legend has it that Alaric the Goth, who died of fever in Cosenza in 410, had his tomb built at the confluence of the rivers Crati and Busento, where he was buried with the treasures from the Sack of Rome.*

**BELOW:** Briatico on the Violet Coast.

used as a conference centre. From the piazza, walk up to the formidable Norman Castle (open daily 8am–8pm; free) where you can see the old perimeter walls and the ruins of several rooms.

On the way to Cosenza from Paola is **Rende** ⓯, a pretty hilltown which merits a detour for its views and the Museo Civico (open 9am–1pm, 3–5pm; tel: 0984-443593; free) dedicated to folklore, local traditions, arts, crafts and emigration.

## The Violet Coast

South of Cosenza, a fascinating stretch of coastline winds its way from Pizzo to Palmi, between the Gulf of Sant'Eufemia and the Gulf of Gioia, where the jagged Promontory del Poro reaches into the sea. Here granite crags alternate with secluded coves and narrow stretches of beach. The landscape is dotted with prickly pears, ancient olive trees and gigantic ferns. The promontory's most attractive and safest beaches are at Zambrone, Parghelia, Tropea, Joppolo and Nicotera. Between Tropea and Joppolo is **Capo Vaticano**, one of the most enchanting and unspoiled corners of the region – apart from the campsites which have sprung up alongside some of the larger beaches.

Palmi marks the beginning of the splendid Costa Viola (named after its vivid purple sunsets) which snakes south toward the Straits of Messina. This Tyrrhenian tour is enlivened by the lovely fishing villages – busy resorts in the summer, they are great places for an inexpensive seafood meal. Tropea makes for a chic overnight stop. Other good options are Pizzo and Scilla, while the whole stretch offers plenty of well-equipped campsites.

Stop at **Pizzo** ⓰ for a *tartufo* (chocolate and hazelnut ice cream filled with caramel), a walk through town and a visit to the unsual Chiesetta di Piedigrotta

Map on page 240

*On the Costa Viola, even the onions turn purple: the sweet onions grown here are renowned throughout Italy. Don't miss a chance to try a salad of "cipolle di Tropea" (Tropea onions) tossed together (raw) with ripe tomatoes, fresh hot chilli peppers, oregano and olive oil.*

**BELOW:** deserted beach at Pizzo.

*Fisherman at Scilla, a village that seems to belong to Sicily.*

(open daily 9am–1pm, 3–7.30pm; entrance fee) carved out of the volcanic rock and decorated with statues, including the incongruous figures of John Kennedy and Fidel Castro.

The old town of **Tropea** ⓱, which faces the sea from a sandy cliff, is ideal for an overnight stay. As Calabria's prime resort, Tropea has a well-preserved *centro storico*, numerous restaurants, pizzerias, ice-cream parlours, and irresistible white beaches. On a clear day, Strómboli and the Aeolian Islands are visible from the Belvedere at the end of the main street. Be sure to climb up to the **Church of the Madonna dell'Isola** (open daily 8am–7pm; donations welcome) on the cliff facing the Belvedere with its magical Mediterranean Garden.

## Palmi's folklore museum

The earthquake of 1908 destroyed the historic centre of **Palmi** ⓲, so the main attraction here is the **Museo Civico di Etnografia e Folklore** (open Mon–Fri 8am–2pm, 3–6pm; entrance fee), one of the best museums of its kind in Italy. It is dedicated to agricultural and maritime life, folk art, music, magic and religion. The collection contains more than 3,000 items, including beautifully carved staffs given to maids as love tokens, giant papier-mâché dolls, wooden cake- and bread-moulds and implements designed for catching swordfish. After visiting the museum you might head for the Lido di Palmi, a roomy cove with fine sand.

The Costa Viola ends at **Scilla** ⓳, a charming fishing town, where swordfish *(pesce spada)* is the main source of income. The spirit, dialect and traditions of this town at the entrance to the Straits of Messina make it feel more Sicilian than Calabrian. The view over the straits at sunset is stunning – it will certainly change should the long-awaited suspension bridge ever become a reality. Take

**BELOW:**
piazza café, Tropea.
**RIGHT:** Pizzo
shopping street.

a stroll down to Chianalea and explore the unusual but picturesque fishermen's quarter. The houses are built on the water, so each one has two entrance ways – one facing the sea and the other facing the street.

## The regional capital

**Reggio Calabria** ㉠ (pop. 180,000), is the regional capital. It lies at the end of the motorway and is the main gateway to Sicily – for the moment a half-hour ferry trip away. Plans to build a bridge across the choppy straits, supported by former prime minister Silvio Berlusconi, have been shelved by his successor, Romano Prodi. Completely flattened by the earthquake of 1908, Reggio was rebuilt in the form of a modern urban grid with tree-lined squares. Although parts of the city are run-down, the Bronzi di Riace – extraordinary full-size bronzes of young Greek warriors *(see below)* – are reason enough to stop here. Among Reggio's historic landmarks are the restored Romanesque Duomo, and the walls and towers of the 15th-century Angevin castle which look down on the city. Reggio's flora is another attraction; the city's subtropical microclimate gives rise to a spectacular profusion of exotic plants, with particularly good displays in the gardens of the **Villa Comunale** and on the city side of the **Lungomare Matteotti**, which offers a splendid view of the straits at night.

## Museum of Magna Graecia

The Riace Bronzes are proudly exhibited in an earthquake-proof room of the **Museo Archeologico Nazionale** (open daily 9am–7.30pm; entrance fee). Their exact provenance has yet to be established, but these solemn, well-formed figures – idealised representations of divinity in Greek sculpture – are among the

Map on page 240

*Seminara (about 5 km/3 miles inland off the SS18 at Monte Sant'Elìa) is famous for "babbalutu" (multicoloured bottles in human shapes) and other ceramic objects that protect against the evil eye.*

**BELOW:** pride of the Reggio archaeological museum.

## THE RIACE MIRACLE

On 16 August 1972, a young man on holiday from Rome saw a bronze arm emerge from the Riace Marina in the exact spot where the locals immersed the reliquary of the saints Cosma and Damiano to summon rain. For the faithful, there was no doubt that this was the divine intervention of the two miraculous martyrs. The two "Bronzes of Riace" have brought great fame to the Ionian coastal town. They were sent to Reggio for eight years of restoration, and it was not until 1980 that they were put on display in Florence. The exhibition was a phenomenal success, and the following year the president had the bronzes publicly exhibited at the Quirinale Palace in Rome. They then returned "home" to the Museo Nazionale di Reggio di Calabria. During the first months of exhibition in Reggio, many visitors tried to feel the statues and lifted babies to touch them. The atmosphere was redolent of a Southern Italian pagan-influenced religious festival, when young children participate in divinity through touch.

These glorious, virile 2-metre (7ft 7in) warriors are a patriotic reminder for the Calabrese that their remote toe of the Italian boot was once home to some of the Western world's most important cities in a land of philosophers and artists.

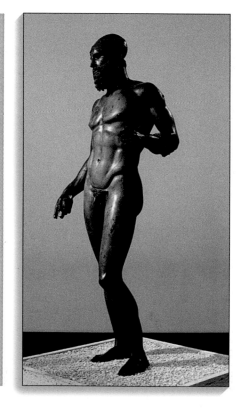

*Interior of the Cattedrale dell' Assunta, Gerace.*

finest surviving sculptures of the ancient world. Stylistic differences imply that they were made 20 years apart, suggesting they were not part of the same sculptural group. The warrior who smiles and tenses his muscles, known as Statue A, is dated to 460–450 BC; the warrior missing an eye (Statue B) seems to have been influenced by the works of Polyclites, dating it to 434–430 BC. The symmetry that renders them a "pair" is, in reality, the result of a restoration of the arms of Statue B – done long after the statue was sculpted, presumably by a Roman-era antiquarian.

On the same floor is the *Testa del Filosofo* (Head of a Philosopher), a masterful portrait of old age in bronze. The work is difficult to date, because its style is not typical of Greek figurative art. Other notable works in the museum's Greek and Roman collection include the mould of a famous engraving of a bull from the Grotta del Romito in the west of the Pollino National Park, a large-scale terracotta sculpture of a horseman carried by a sphinx from the Marafioti Temple at Locri (5th century BC), and the marble *Dioscuri* (the mythological twin brothers Castor and Pollux), also from Locri.

## The Aspromonte

"The Aspromonte deserves its name," writes Norman Douglas, referring to the Italian word *aspro* (sour, rough). It's a tough range to cross, let alone live on, given its susceptibility to natural disasters. Frequent mud slides and floods, a limited electrical supply and basic services have turned many of the *borghi* here into uninhabitable ghost towns and off-the-beaten-track tourist attractions, half-buried by vegetation. Those who inhabit this wild, isolated area between Reggio Calabria and Bova Marina speak a dialect derived from the Greek colonists who settled here more than 2,000 years ago. Graecanico, full of glottal stops, is more redolent of Homer and Plato than modern Greek, and is incomprehensible to other Calabrians.

Despite the arid climate, the *fiumare* – subterranean streams that serve as the region's water source – give life to coniferous forests, chestnut and beech woods and provide irrigation for the local population and their fields. Rivers that run above ground in spring dry up in summer leaving white trails which disappear when the rains return. The largest is the silvery *fiumara* Amendolea, which runs though olive groves, vineyards and citrus, fruit and almond orchards.

Hanging from the high sandstone walls which define its course, two towns capture the traveller's eye: **Gallicianò**, a centre of Hellenistic art and traditions; and, a few miles further upriver, the breathtaking but disquieting **Roghudi**, whose streets and squares are empty, disturbed only by the whistle of swifts. The village was abandoned in 1973 when a catastrophic flood put an end to a century-long battle against depopulation. Now it it is a lonely ghost town.

More than 800 metres (2,600 ft) above sea level, **Bova ㉑** (follow the signs to Bova after passing Bova Marina on the SS106) is the area's cultural capital. In August, it hosts an ethnic music festival, the Paleariza, with a programme of events including an artisan market, gastronomic exhibitions and hiking activities.

To the northeast, nestled between the Aspromonte and the Serre on a nearly inaccessible crag, is the beautiful medieval town of **Gerace** ㉒ (on the scenic SS111). It is best to visit Gerace in the evening, and on foot, to appreciate the romantic sunset views from the grassy ruins of its castle. It is said that in the 10th century the city's inhabitants survived an Arab siege by subsisting on ricotta cheese made from mothers' milk. In still earlier times, a miracle-working saint, San Antonio del Castello, conjured up a spring of pure water in a cave in the cliff that surrounds the castle. The imprint of the saint's knees, they say, can be seen in the floor of the cave.

Gerace is a city of many layers, justifying the phrase, "If you know Gerace, you know Calabria." Its cathedral is the largest in the region. The **Cattedrale dell'Assunta** is 76 metres long and 26 metres wide (250 by 85 ft), with two majestic apses, a Byzantine crypt and three naves lined with 20 columns, some plundered from ancient temples at Locri.

## The Serre

Less charismatic than Aspromonte, less alpine than the Pollino and the Sila ranges, the **Serre** are two mountain chains characterised by extensive fir, beech and alder forests, with an endless variety of wild mushrooms growing in the shade of the trees. A good way into the Serre is via Stilo on the SS110, which sits at the foot of Mount Consolino.

Just outside the town, the **Cattolica di Stilo**, one of the best-preserved Byzantine churches in existence, is a reminder that in medieval times Calabria's rugged interior was a vibrant religious centre. The tiny 9th-century church, built on a square floor plan with five cylindrical cupolas, clings to the flank of Monte

Contact Ugo Sergi, owner of the *agriturismo* Il Bergamotto, for information about donkey trekking in Aspromonte (tel and fax: 0965-727213).

**BELOW:** wild flowers in the Aspromonte.

**TIP**

The Marmarico
Waterfalls can be
reached on foot,
climbing from the
*fiumara* Stilaro coming
from Stilo towards
Bivongi along the
Sentiero del Brigante.
Alternatively, Vincenzo
Murace offers guided
tours of the falls and
San Giovanni Therestis
from Bivongi.
(Tel: 0347-1822574
or 0964-731450.)

**BELOW:** 9th-century
Cattolico di Stilo.
**RIGHT:** San Giovanni
Theristis, Bivongi.

Consolino, just above Stilo, like a miniature castle overlooking its town. Its bright interior is adorned with fragments of frescoes. The four columns supporting the vault are from a pre-Christian temple, but were placed upside-down to symbolise the church's victory over paganism.

Above Stilo is the hamlet of **Bivongi** ㉓, famous for its strong, sweet table wine and a good base for day trips to sights in the Serre. To appreciate the beauty of the lush woods, start with a gentle climb to the **Cascate del Marmarico**, at 90 metres (295 ft) the second highest falls in Italy.

Half an hour from the falls is the delightful 11th-century Byzantine-Norman basilica of **San Giovanni Theristis** (open 16 Sept–June weekends and holidays 10am–noon, 3–5pm; July–15 Sept daily 5pm–sunset; entrance fee). The climate and topology are different here; a sun-baked terrain with an ocean of wild flowers in springtime, it is devoid of vegetation the rest of the year. Set on an isolated hill, the little church was abandoned in the 17th century, then used as a shepherds' shelter and barn. It was rediscovered in 1912 and finally restored in 1994.

To the west of Bivongi on the SS110 and from the same era as San Giovanni Therestis is the subterranean church of **Santa Maria di Monte Stella in Pazzano**. This impressive grotto-sanctuary is carved into the rock about 10 metres (33 ft) below ground level.

## Carthusian monastery

For a more in-depth exploration of the Serre, take the SS110 back towards Pazzano. In the summer this is a particularly pleasant drive through shady tunnels of fir trees. Right in the heart of the peninsula, at 800 metres (2,600 ft) above sea level, surrounded by forests, is another important religious centre –

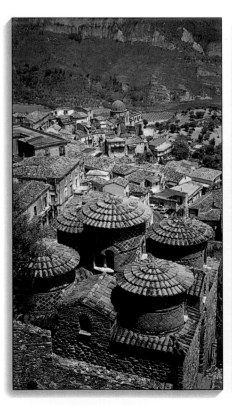

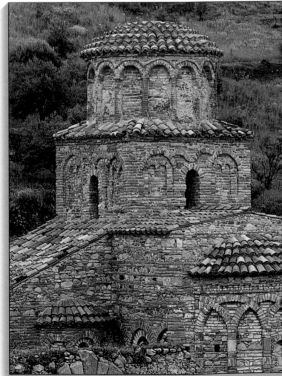

the Carthusian monastery at **Serra San Bruno** ㉔, where you can visit the Museo della Certosa (open May–Oct Tues–Sun 9am–1pm, 3–8pm; Nov–Apr 9.30am–1pm, 3.30–6pm; entrance fee). In this peaceful sanctuary, reconstructed around the ruins of an abbey destroyed by an earthquake in 1783, 16 bearded, white-robed monks live according to the vows of silence, solitude and poverty prescribed in the 11th century by Bruno of Cologne (1030–1110). This was the second charterhouse built by the founder of the Carthusian order – the first was in Grenoble. The monks eat no meat, but make an excellent cheese, which is sold in the town.

## Classical sites along the Ionian shore

Sometimes dotted with seaside towns, sometimes deserted for long stretches, the SS106 that runs along the Ionian Coast is a pleasing drive. Though the "lidos" are for the most part small and unremarkable, there are a number of classical sites en route, with some visible remains.

One of the most prosperous colonies of Magna Graecia, **Locri Epizefiri** ㉕ (Lokroi Epizephyrioi; open daily 9am–7pm; closed first and third Mon of the month; shorter afternoon hours in winter; entrance fee; tel: 0964-390023) once had 40,000 inhabitants. Founded in the 8th century BC, it was protected by 7.5 km (5 miles) of walls, sections of which are still visible. The way in to the excavations is through the Museo Archeologico in Contrada Marasà, which exhibits artefacts found in the area. The most important finds, however, have been transferred to the Museo Nazionale in Reggio *(see page 251)*. Of the four large temples, only a few fragments of the columns and capitals remain, while in the slope of the hill the silhouette of a theatre is visible.

*Map on page 240*

*The locals have a weakness for the meat of the "ghiro", a protected species of dormouse that is illegally trapped and sold at an extraordinary price.*

**BELOW:** necropolis of white goods.

*In the second half of the 7th century BC the Greek colonists of Locri founded Hipponion near what is today Vibo Valentia. Vibo is a modern city with a small historic centre and a worthwhile Museo Archeologico in the Norman-Swabian castle (open daily 9am–7pm; entrance fee). Just outside town, near the cemetery, are the ruins of the Greek perimeter walls.*

**Caulónia** (Kaulonia), about 50 km (30 miles) north of Locri, was an Achean colony. Ancient remains by the beach near Punta Stilo include the foundations of a large Doric temple dedicated to Apollo, and a good stretch of the perimeter walls.

Forty-five kilometres (30 miles) further up the coast, beyond the resorts of Soverato and Copanello, is the entrance to the Parco Archeologico di Rocceletta di **Borgia** (on the road to Borgia just after the junction with the SS106; open daily 8am until one hour before sunset; free). According to some literary sources this was the site of Skylletion, the city founded by Ulysses when he was shipwrecked on his return from the Trojan Wars. More than likely, it was a sub-colony of Kroton. In any case, the only walled structure excavated so far belongs to the Roman Scolacium – you can see parts of the Forum and the Theatre. Also within the park stand the imposing ruins of the Norman basilica of Santa Maria della Roccella.

From here, you can continue along the coast to Crotone or head directly to Sila. The second option will take you through **Catanzaro**, a Byzantine hill-city founded in the 10th century. Unfortunately, earthquakes, war damage and speculative building have left the town almost devoid of character. If you do visit, however, there are several surviving baroque churches worth noting, including dell'Immacolata, del Rosario and dell'Osservanza. The town's most pleasing sight is the Villa Comunale, Catanzaro's public gardens, which are planted along the edge of the city's ravine. The 360-degree view of the Golfo di Squillace and of the Sila Piccola is impressive.

On the road to Crotone, just before Capo Rizzuto, **Le Castella** sits on a picturesque island connected to the mainland by an isthmus. It is one of the 150 or

**BELOW:** horses near Catanzaro.

## PYTHAGORAS AND HIS THEORUM

Pythagoras (*circa* 575-500 BC) was a Greek philosopher and mathematician. He believed that the world could be explained entirely by mathematics, physics and astronomy, a vision summed up in his dictum: "all is number". Known as the "father of numbers", he is most familiar to modern readers for the "Pythagorean Theorem", which, as all schoolchildren can tell you, states that the square of the hypotenuse of a right-angled triangle is equal to the sum of the squares of the other two sides. This theorem was known by the Bablyonians some 1,000 earlier, and although Pythagorus has long been attributed with proving it, this is by no means an established fact.

Pythagoras was born on the island of Samos (off the coast of Turkey) and migrated to Southern Italy, where he established a mystic cult known as the Pythagoreans. This was a select band of followers *(mathematikoi)* devoted to the study of mathematics and philosophy, who led an almost monastic existence. Unusually for the times, women were admitted on a equal footing with men. Since all possessions, including mathematical "discoveries", were communal, one of the students, rather than the great man himself, may have proved the theorem. His highly influential school of mathematics operated for several centuries after his death.

so Norman and Aragonese forts built along the Calabrian coast to fend off Turkish invaders. The restaurant Da Annibale (Via Annibale 3, Le Castella, tel: 0962-795428) is highly recommended, with a short but straight-from-the-fish-market menu and a delicious *pecorino* cheese (often served as dessert).

**Map on page 240**

## Old Greek base

There are many fine hotels on the coastal stretch between Soverato and Le Castella. **Crotone ㉙** – Kroton in the time of Pythagoras – was one of the most important cities in Europe. Nothing survives of the ancient city apart from a column from the temple of Hera Lacinia at Capo Colonna, and some remains in the Museo Archeologico (open daily 9am–7.30pm; closed first and third Mon of the month; entrance fee). The Spanish castle now stands on the site of the acropolis, but Kroton's "suburbs" stretched out to sea. If it were possible to excavate beneath the nearby Montedison industrial complex, archaeologists believe that a large part of the Greek town would be brought to light.

Laid-back, modern Crotone is an agreeable place to base yourself if you are planning to spend some days on the surrounding beaches. It has a busy fishing port, and in May it hosts the Festival dell'Aurora, with concerts, conferences, and performances which pay homage to Pythagoras and Magna Graecia.

The tourist office in Crotone has information on the Riserva Marina di Capo Rizzuto, the largest marine reserve in Europe, running between Torre Brasolo and Capo Donato.

**Sibari ㉚**, or the ancient Greek city of Sybaris (excavations open daily 9am until one hour before sunset; free; tel: 0981-79391), was the richest and oldest Achean colony in Italy. It was founded in 737 BC, and reached its zenith in

*A true Calabrese breakfast, typical of Reggio and the Ionian coast up to Crotone, features several round brioches soaked in a glass of iced almond milk.*

**BELOW:** twisting over the hills near Catanzaro.

# The Albanians

Of the many ethnic groups that live in Italy, the 106,000 Arbëreshe (pronounced are-*bre*-shay) make up one of the largest. There are communities spread across southern Italy and Sicily, with the highest concentration in the Calabrian provinces of Cosenza and Catanzaro.

The Albanian presence on Italian soil dates from the Ottoman invasion of Arbëria (modern Albania) in the 15th century. Entire communities relocated to Southern Italy where the climate, mountainous terrain and abbeys steeped in Byzantine rites resembled the land they had left behind.

The first significant settlements were in Puglia and date from 1461–2, when the ruling Aragonese rewarded the Albanian national hero Giorgio Castriota Skanderbeg with feudal land for the victories he led over the Angevins. Local leaders gave the Arbëreshe land that was untenable or had been devastated by war or natural disasters in exchange

for a share of their produce. The isolated location of these feudal lands and the prohibition imposed on the building cities or fortresses guaranteed that these communities could not join forces or pose a threat.

The fragmented population was held together by their Arbëreshe traditions, which have been tenaciously preserved, above all in the Pollino-Alto area. Of the adult population, 85 percent currently speak a language rooted in modern Albanian, and the first Arbëreshe grammar book has recently been published. In Calabria, many religious communities belong to the Eparchia (the Byzantine equivalent of a diocese) of Lungro, where the Eastern Orthodox rite was instituted in 1919 by Pope Benedict XV for Italo-Albanians.

A particularly interesting aspect of the Arbëreshe culture is the costume. The colourful clothes worn by the women at weddings and on festive occasions `shimmer like multi-coloured mosaics. They are all hand-made in a variety of styles that vary according to location, wealth and social position. The most elaborate are made up of at least 20 pieces, transformed into pleated or frilled gowns, using striking colour combinations, and embellished with lacework, and rich embroidery, shot through with threads of gold.

The best time and place to see these costumes in all their splendour is during Civita's *Vallje*, a lively folk dance through the streets on the Tuesday after Easter, which commemorates a victory against the Turks. Combining a complex choreography with improvised movements, the dancers imprison a member of the public, ideally a *lëtir* (Italian), who symbolically pays his own ransom at the bar while improvised expressions of praise and thanks are sung to him.

Similar costume parades can be seen during Easter week in other traditional Albanian centres (Lungro, Firmo, Acquaformosa, Eianina, Spezzano Albanese, Santa Caterina Albanese, San Demetrio Corone, San Cosmo Albanese, and Santa Sofia d'Epiro).

The Arbëreshe spirit can also be witnessed during the festival of Sant'Atanasio at Santa Sofia d' Epiro, held on the first Sunday in May. ❑

**LEFT:** elaborate costumes are essential in maintaining the Arbëreshe tradition.

530 BC, by which time it was renowned throughout Magna Graecia for its decadent lifestyle – whence the term sybarite for a devotee of luxury. According to the historian Strabone, its dominion extended as far as the Tyrrhenian coast and included 25 cities. Sybaris was eventually destroyed by the rival city of Kroton in 510 BC, when the course of the Crati river was diverted in order to flood any buildings still standing. A second Greek city, Thourioi, supplanted by the Roman capital Copia, was built near the ancient city of Sybaris, and the excavations in the Parco del Cavallo brought to light the Roman phase. The **Museo Archeologico Nazionale della Sibaritide** (open daily 9am–7pm; closed first and third Mon of month; entrance fee) features remains found throughout the area.

## Looking down on the Neto Valley

Inland from Crotone is the *borgo* of **Santa Severina** ㉛, much fought over for its strategic clifftop position, dominating the entire Neto Valley. The town has a long history, having been founded by the Greeks and ruled by the Romans, Byzantines and Arabs. It was liberated by the Venetians, reconquered by the Byzantines and then taken by the Normans, finally becoming an archdiocese under the Angevins and Aragonese. These layers of history are all visible in the foundations, walls and bastions of the formidable Castello, named after Robert Guiscard and thought to have been built after 1073 on the remains of a Byzantine fortress, which was itself built on the ancient city's acropolis.

The enormous Castello has a **museum** (open summer Mon–Fri 9am–1pm, 3–8pm, Sat–Sun 9am–1pm, 3–10pm; winter Tues–Sun 9am–1pm, 3–6pm; entrance fee), which traces the chequered history of Santa Severina. Across the piazza is the well-presented Museo Diocesano (same opening hours as castle

*Signs in both Italian and Albanian.*

**BELOW:** festival in an Albanian town.

museum), which offers a guided tour, while descriptive panels explain everything you will ever need to know about funerary urns and pastoral letters (tickets are sold at the castle). The 13th-century cathedral has been restored and, along with the Byzantine baptistery, is open to the public. Note the design of Piazza del Campo, remodelled in the 1970s by Anselmi and Patanè – a rare example of a historic piazza restored with a modern touch.

## The Sila

Once covered with forests, the scenic **Parco Nazionale della Sila** (from the Latin *silva* for thick wood) is more like a huge plateau than a mountain range. This relatively small national park currently covers 13,000 hectares (32,000 acres), though there are plans to expand the protected area to six times its present size. Touted as the "rugged green heart of the Mediterranean", its pine, beech and oak forests alternate with extensive plains, pastures, lakes and cultivated valleys. In fact, this corner of the deep south is surprisingly reminiscent of parts of Northern Europe, especially in winter.

The area is subdivided into the three mountain clusters: the **Sila Greca** to the north, the **Sila Piccola** to the south and the **Sila Grande** in the middle. From a naturalist's point of view, the best place to explore is the Sila Grande, while the Sila Piccola and the Sila Greca offer several cultural walks. Since the 8th century, communities that follow the Greek-Byzantine rite have settled on the northern slope of the Sila Greca's high plains.

Despite its proximity to the sea and relatively low elevation – averaging around 1,000 metres (3,300 ft) – the Sila range has an alpine climate, offering cross-country skiers Scandinavian-style trails through thick forests and wide open plains.

*The famous carpets with Oriental motifs made in the Sila by Albanians and Armenians can be found in Longobucco and San Giovanni in Fiore, respectively. At Tiriolo, the most beautiful multi-coloured* pezzare *(mats made from fabric remnants) in Calabria are produced.*

**BELOW:** grazing the green Sila.

The entire area is one of the best regions in Calabria for motoring. Each season brings a gift to the Sila: a carpet of wild flowers in spring; refreshing, cool breezes in summer; a riot of coloured leaves and wild mushrooms in autumn; snow in winter. Bars that double as souvenir shops are usually well stocked with guide books and maps of the park trails, but the best tourist information office is at **Camigliatello Silano** ❸❷ (30 km/19 miles east of Cosenza on the SS107). Although there is no lack of places to stay, reservations should be made in advance from November to February and in July and August.

## Albanian town

The isolated village of **San Demetrio Corone** ❸❸ is one of the oldest and most important Albanian settlements in Italy and well worth a trip (a 40-minute drive from Sibari). When the travel writer Norman Douglas came here in 1911, he was told by the amazed inhabitants that he was the first Englishman ever to have set foot in the town. Although tourists are no longer a rarity in these parts, be prepared for the curious stares of barbers, policemen, shopkeepers and women in bright Albanian dresses. The Albanians first fled to Calabria in 1448 to escape persecution by the Arabs. Today they form the largest ethnic minority in the region. They have their own language, literature and dress, and their own Greek Orthodox bishop (for more on Albanian culture see feature on page 258).

As isolated as San Demetrio is in the backhills of the Sila Greca, this was once one of the most important centres of learning in Calabria, the site of the famous Albanian College where the revolutionary poet Girolamo de Rada taught for many years. Inside the college, the little church of Sant' Adriano contains a Norman font and a wonderful mosaic pavement.

**TIP**

For horseriding excursions in the Sila, contact the Club Trekking Val Calamo (Località San Zaccheria, Acrì, north of Camigliatello Silano; tel: 0984-941287 or 0984-401253).

**BELOW:** poppies in the Sila Grande.

Map on page 240

*Calabria holds the Italian title for the region in which the most porcini mushrooms are collected. They grow in the forests of the Sila and of the Serre, along with more than 3,000 other varieties of mushroom.*

**BELOW:**
park rangers.
**RIGHT:** Sila's
Lake Ampollino.

## Byzantine centre

On the Ionian Coast (SS177), overlooking the sea, stands lonely **Rossano** ❸❹ (best reached from the coastal road SS106), the most important city of the south between the 8th and the 11th century. It retains precious examples of the Byzantine-Norman churches which once characterised the area. Most important of these is the Abbazia del Patirion. Built at the beginning of the 12th century, it features three apses studded with yellow, black and orange stone, in accordance with Armenian-Syrian decorative schemes, and an animal-figure floor mosaic. The tiny church *(chiesetta)* of San Marco is perched at the top of town, while in a narrow alley behind the cathedral stands the Chiesetta della Panaghia (of the Holy Saint, or the Madonna), which has remains of Byzantine frescoes. The cathedral is dedicated to Santa Maria Acheropita (the name refers to the 7th/8th-century fresco on a pilaster in the central nave, supposedly painted by an ethereal hand).

The city is home to the famous **Codex Purpureus Rossanensis**, one of the most beautiful illuminated manuscripts of the Greek Gospels, comprising 188 sheets of incredibly thin purplish parchment, with splendid full-page illustrations. It is thought to have been made in Palestine in the 6th century and brought to Calabria the following century. This extraordinary book is displayed in the **Museo Diocesano d'Arte Sacra**, inside the Palazzo Arcivescovile (July–Sept daily 9am–1.30pm, 4.30–8.30pm; winter Tues–Sat 9.30am–12.30pm, 4–7pm, Sun 10am–noon, 4.30–6.30pm, closed Mon; entrance fee; tel: 0983-525263).

## The last of the primeval forest

The Sila Grande takes in high plains, the town of **San Giovanni in Fiore** ❸❺ and the tourist centres of Camigliatello Silano and Lorica. There are ski runs at Monte Curcio and Monte Botte Donato, and artificial lakes at Ampollino, Arvo and Cecita. The 56 trees of the primeval forest of *pino larico* are near Camigliatello Silano in the Riserva di Fallistro. Nicknamed the "Giants of the Sila", the oldest of these pines are more than 2 metres (6 ft) wide and over 40 metres (130 ft) high. One of the most scenic roads is the Strada delle Vette, which goes from the Lago di Cecita to Monte Scuro, Monte Botte Donato and the Lago di Lorica. The best trail (9 km/5 miles) – No. 4 on the park's map – begins in the vicinity of Fossiata at the 5-km mark of the SS282 (direction Bocchigliero), east of the Lago di Cecita, near a picnic area.

Sila Piccola to the south is home to **Villaggio Mancuso** ❸❻, one of the first purpose-built tourist resorts in Italy. Founded in 1929, it still fills up with crowds of Italian visitors who prefer its self-catering – wooden cottages set among trees – to the fancier hotels at Racise, Ciricilla and Trepido (minor resorts located along the SS179). The baroque painter Mattia Preti (1613–99), known as Cavalier Calabrese, was born in **Taverna** ❸❼ (on the SS109B between Catanzaro and Villaggio Mancuso). Although he lived elsewhere, Preti bequeathed a collection of his paintings to the town: the best are hung in the church of San Domenico, with others in the churches of San Martino and Santa Barbara and the Museo Civico (open daily 8am–1pm; entrance fee). ❑

# SICILY

*Across the Straits of Messina lies an island that invented pasta,*
*embraced Moorish culture and had the original Volcano*

To Goethe, Sicily was unique, "clear, authentic and complete." Modern Sicily has its share of scruffy, one-horse towns, inscrutable hill-top villages and industrial sprawl. As a touchstone, Tomasi di Lampedusa's vision of his homeland is more perceptive: "a landscape which knows no mean between sensuous sag and hellish drought; which is never petty, never ordinary, never relaxed."

Sicilian scenery is gruff but seldom graceless. The granary of the ancient world contains citrus groves, pastureland and vineyards as well as endless wheatfields. Trapani's weird lagoons and saltpans seemingly float in the unrelenting heat. Away from the accessible coast, an intriguing volcanic hinterland unfolds in mountains, gorges and the scars of abandoned sulphur mines. Like a dragon in its lair, Etna's smoking breath threatens vineyards and lava-stone castles.

Still, first impressions are safer. After breakfasting in Taormina, Cardinal Newman found it "the nearest thing to paradise." To most tourists, Taormina is still the acceptable face of Sicily, a place of undiluted pleasure where culture shock is absent.

Outside this cosmopolitan pocket, the adventure begins. Sicily is not what it seems. The markets and inlaid street patterns of Mazara del Vallo and Sciacca would not be out of place in Morocco. The perfect medieval town of Erice is a shrine to pagan goddesses, Astarte and Venus. In Sicily, all periods are petrified for posterity. The jewel box of Palermo's Cappella Palatina is a fusion of Arab and Christian. The Arab west of the island is overladen with Spanish finery while the Greek east is truest to the pure classical spirit.

Despite a patina of neglect, Sicily's architectural riches gleam. The island of Mozia retains its Phoenician port and sacrificial burial grounds. Built to "intimidate the gods or scare human beings", the Greek temples of Agrigento, Segesta and Selinunte are a divine reflection of Magna Graecia. The Romans may not have matched these lovely sites but left the vivid mosaics of Piazza Armerina as an imprint of a sated but sophisticated culture.

Cefalù and Monreale cathedrals are a tribute to Byzantine craftsmanship, Arab imagery and Norman scale. Elsewhere, Moorish palaces, Swabian castles and domed churches are interpretations of this inspired Sicilian hybrid. Baroque, the island's last great gasp, explodes in the theatrical fireworks of Noto and Catania. As the cultural capital of the ancient world, Siracusa presides over Greek ruins and Christian catacombs with a luminous grace all its own. Palermo, its psychic opposite, radiates sultry splendour. ❑

**PRECEDING PAGE:** the ferry from Sicily crossing the Straits of Messina approaching Reggio di Calabria.
**LEFT:** soaking up the sun in Terrasini.

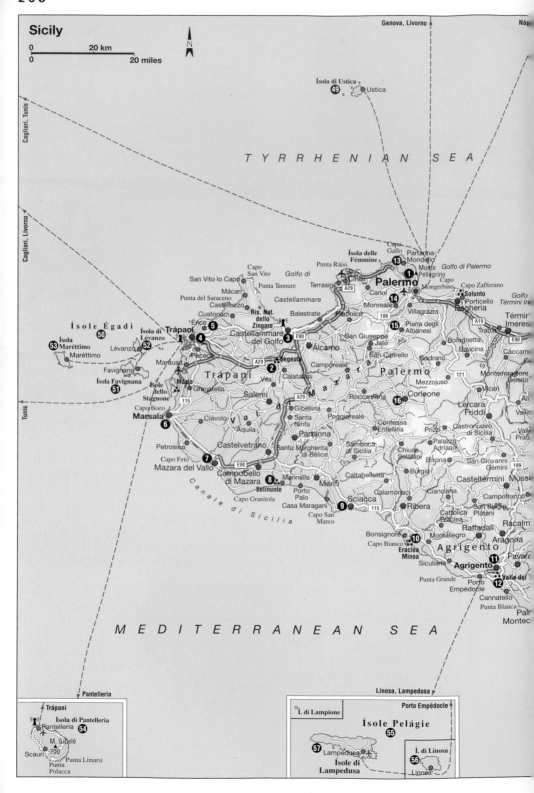

# Sicily

0 — 20 km
0 — 20 miles

N

*Genova, Livorno* ↑
Náp

Cagliari, Tunis

Cagliari, Livorno

Ísola di Ustica
49
Ustica

**T Y R R H E N I A N   S E A**

Capo
Gallo
Ísola delle
Fémmine
13 Partanna-
Mondello
Monte 1
Pellegrino
*Golfo di Palermo*
Capo
Punta Ráisi
San Vito
Capo
Terrasini
Cinisi
**Palermo**
Capo Zafferano
San Vito lo Capo
Punta Tannure
A29
Carini
**Solunto**
*Golfo*
Mácan
*Castellammare*
14
Porticello
*Términ In*
Punta del Saraceno
Balestrate
Monreale
Bagheria
Castelluzzo
Partinico
Villagrázia
**Térmir**
Custonáci
Rís. Nat.
186
Piana degli
Imeres
**Ísole Égadi**
Ísola di
dello
1
Albanesi
A19
50
Lévanzo
Erice
5
Zingaro
San Giuseppe
Bolognetta
E90
Ísola
52
**Trápani**
Castellammare
Jato
Baucina
Cáccam
53 Maréttimo
del Golfo
3
San Cipirello
Lévanzo
4
**Álcamo**
Godrano
Maréttimo
Paceco
Mezzojuso
E90
**Palermo**
Favignana
Maráusa
A29
**Segesta**
121
Montemaggiore
Belsito
Ísola Favignana
**Trápani**
2
Vita
Campóreale
Áli
51
Mázia
Calatafimi
Mezzojuso
Vícari
Granatello
**Salemi**
Ropcamana
**Lercara**
Valle
Ísole
Gibellina
Corleone
**Friddi**
dello
A29
16
Castronuovo
Stagnone
Santa
di Sicília
Valle
**Marsala**
Ciávolo
Ninfa
Contessa
Prizzi
Prati
6
Áquila
Poggioreale
Entellina
Palazzo
**Partanna**
Adriano
Bivona
San Giovanni
Petrosino
Santa Margherita
Sambuca
Gémini
189
di Bélice
di Sicília
Chiusa
**Casteltérmini**
Muss
Capo Feto
7
**Castelvetrano**
Scláfani
Bürgio
Campotranco
**Mazara del Vallo**
E90
Caltabellotta
Cianciana
**Campobello**
Marinella
San Biágio
di Mazara
8
Menfi
Calamónaci
Plátani
*Canale di Sicília*
**Selinunte**
Porto
**Sciacca**
Cattólica
Rácalm
Palo
Éraclea
Capo Granitola
Casa Maragani
9
Ribera
Aragona
Capo San
115
Montállegro
Raffadali
Marco
Bonsignore
10
Siculiana
**Agrigento**
Favare
Capo Bianco
**Éraclea**
11
**Minoa**
Siculiana
**Agrigento**
Punta Grande
Porto
12 Valle dei
Empédocle
Punta Grande
Cannatello
Pal
Punta Blanca
Montec

**M E D I T E R R A N E A N   S E A**

Tunis

Pantelleria

Linosa, Lampedusa

**Trápani**
Porto Empédocle

Ísola di Pantelleria
Pantelleria
54
Í. di Lampione
Porto Empédocle
Í. di Linosa

M. Gibelé
700
**Ísole Pelágie**
55
56

Scauri
Punta Limarsi
Punta
Polacca
57 Lampedusa
**Ísole di
Lampedusa**
Linosa

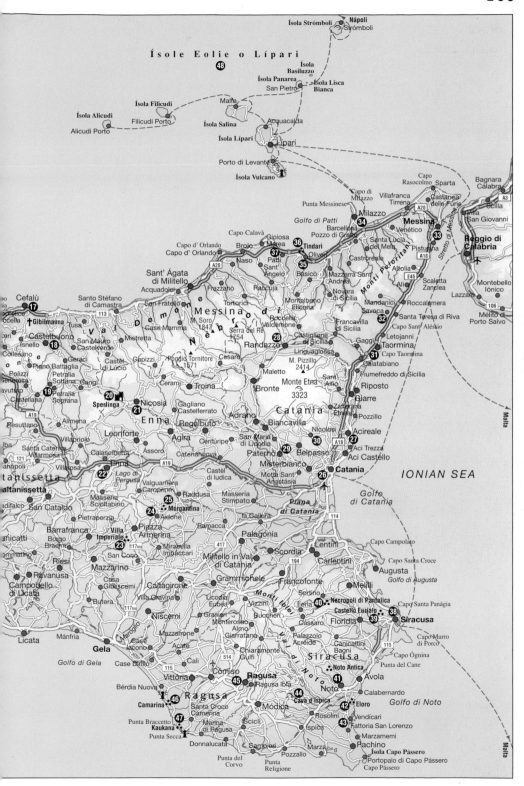

# PALERMO

*Palermo's history is like the persimmon: exotic, ripe, decadent,
and extremely difficult to peel. It's a question of scooping
out the fruit and savouring the sensation*

**P**alermo is both an essay in chaos and a sensuous spice box of a city. Domenico Dolce, one half of the Dolce & Gabbana design duo, is passionate about the spirit of his home town: "Don't go with an itinerary, go with an open heart." This is sound advice for a city that represents an assault on the senses rather than a sweet seduction. Sicily's capital is a synthesis of bomb sites and beauty; with sumptuous Arab-Norman and baroque splendour interspersed with an intriguing Moorish muddle. If Palermo is sweet, it is the cloying oriental sweetness of a Sicilian dessert, and if it is sour, it is with sorrow at the rape perpetrated on the city by ignorant politicians and corrupt speculators. It is sentiments such as these that provoked Gesualdo Bufalino, the Sicilian novelist, to describe his homeland as a place of "light and lamentation".

A Phoenician colony existed from the 8th century BC but not a stone of Punic Palermo remains, nor its original name. The Greeks called the city Panormos (all-haven) for its harbours stretching along a bay known as the Conca d'Oro (the golden shell) because of its glittering citrus groves. As a Roman province, Palermo has revealed scant classical remains compared with its cultured east-coast rivals. Under Byzantine rule, the city developed its principal poles of power: a Byzantine church on the site of the future cathedral; and the Palazzo dei Normanni – the palatial home of the city rulers, later the royal palace and currently the seat of the regional government.

However, it was only with Arab colonisation that Palermo prospered and came into its own. The city was home to Jewish and Lombard merchants, Greek craftsmen and builders, Turkish and Syrian artisans, Persian artists, Berber and Negro slaves. It was the most multiracial population in Europe, and out of such diversity was born the complex city culture that knows many masters. The medieval city had 300 mosques and was ringed by pleasure palaces such as La Ziza, and on the outskirts were palms, vineyards, citrus groves, silk farms and rice paddies. Arab-Norman rule coincided with Palermo's golden age, one of expansion, enlightenment, prosperity and cultural riches. Citizens acquired a love of Arab ornamentation and excess that has never left them.

**LEFT:** traditional Sicilian handcart.
**BELOW:** Palermo panorama.

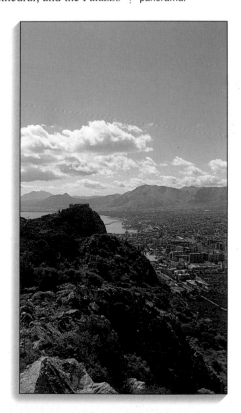

## Decay and renewal

Under Spanish rule, the Arab-Norman city was remodelled along grand arteries but, behind the baroque façades, today's historic centre is a maze of Moorish alleys, confirming the city's deeper affinities. In 1943, Allied bombs destroyed the port and much of the centre, leaving it with gaping holes half-filled with crumbling *palazzi*. The Mafia stepped into the void, later accepting funds from the European

*Racy rider: a motor scooter with class.*

Union to rebuild the devastated city. Instead, corrupt politicians in league with *mafiosi* contractors siphoned off the money. Following the Mafia murders in 1992 of the high-profile public prosecutors Falcone and Borsellino, Palermitans experienced a rare wave of revulsion and public protest. Leoluca Orlando, the anti-corruption mayor, carried forward the momentum and the seeds of civic responsibility were sown, leading to safer streets and a renewed pride in the city's architectural heritage. Orlando saw it as his mission to beautify the city, from planting palms to restoring palaces, and the city is beginning to change. Greater public safety has given a boost to the notoriously low-key Palermitan nightlife, with more bars in the historic centre staying open in the evening. Palermo may not yet be on a par with Naples, but progress has been made.

Palermo is an incredible jumble of periods and styles. No map does justice to the city's confusion. Given that the Spanish grid system is subverted by Moorish blind alleys, squalid bomb sites and rampant urbanisation on the outskirts, it is surprising that the city is so accessible.

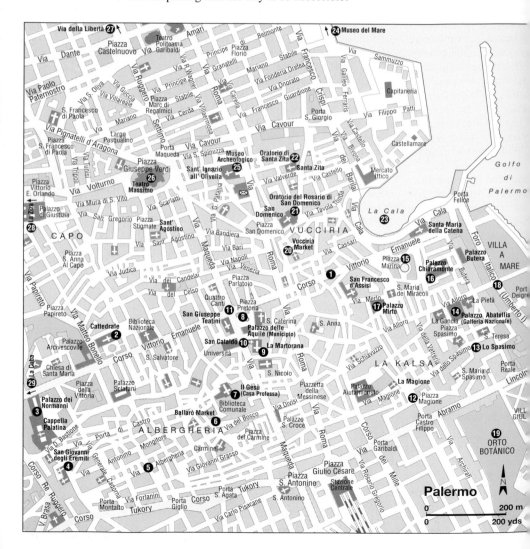

On the junction of Via Maqueda and Corso Vittorio Emanuele, the crossroads of Quattro Canti divides Palermo into its rival quarters. Each reveals a picturesque clutter of decaying mansions, raucous markets and sombre baroque churches with luminous interiors. However, it is the Kasr that represents the public face of historic Palermo. This off-centre heart of the city is the great Arab-Norman nucleus, and contains the city's seats of power, both temporal and spiritual.

Map on page 272

## The Castle and Cathedral quarter

Named after the Arabic for castle, the Kasr quarter contains the cathedral and the royal palace, once the upper castle. Access to the major public monuments is along the time-blackened **Corso V. Emanuele ❶**, the main thoroughfare through the historic centre. Known as the Cassaro, this former Phoenician road was remodelled in 1500 and graced by grandiose city gates at either end. Under the Spanish, the street also acquired a series of patrician palaces which line the route to the cathedral, and are gradually being restored.

The **Cattedrale ❷** (open 8am–6.30pm) is a Sicilian hybrid: mentally erase the cathedral's incongruous dome and focus on the tawny stone, sculpted doorway and crenellated Moorish decoration of the façade. A lovely Catalan-Gothic portico opens onto a peppermint and grey interior, a cool neoclassical shell and the wanly neutered setting for the royal Norman tombs. Borne by crouching lions, the tombs are made of rare pink porphyry and sculpted by Arab masters – the only craftsmen who knew the technique in Norman times. Behind the Duomo emerges the striking geometric design of the Arab-Norman apses, with black-and-white inlays.

**Palazzo dei Normanni ❸** (recommended to call in advance, tel: 091-705 1111; open daily 9am–noon; entrance fee) stands on Piazza Independenza, at the landward end of the Cassaro. Now the seat of the Sicilian Parliament, this eclectic royal palace has been the Sicilian centre of power since Byzantine times. An 18th-century drive leads to the Arab-Norman palace that once rivalled Cairo and Cordoba. The cube-shaped palace has walled gardens overgrown with royal orchids, papyrus, hanging banyan trees, *ficus belgamine* and kapoks. The African kapoks store water in barrel-like trunks and are a favourite with monkeys, a reminder that the Arab emirs bred an exotic menagerie here. The most precious trees are the *cicas*, dwarf palms whose leaves take 50 years to grow.

Leading off a loggia is the **Cappella Palatina** (open Mon–Sat 9–11.45am, 3–5pm; entrance fee), the royal chapel designed by Roger II in 1130 and representing the fusion of Byzantine, Arab, Norman and Sicilian civilisations. This jewel of Arab-Norman art is Palermo's greatest sight. The gold mosaics recall the Crusades when Palermo was a port of departure for the Holy Land. In the penumbra, the mystical Byzantine mosaics slowly emerge. Christ Pantocrator occupies the cupola, surrounded by archangels and saints. On the walls are biblical scenes framed by Islamic decorative devices with the texture of tapestry. Individual masterpieces include the delicate marble

*Staying with a Sicilian prince in a Palermitan palace is now an option. Set close to the cathedral, Palazzo Conte Federico (tel: 091-651 1881; www. contefederico.com) is owned by a descendant of the last Sicilian kings.*

**BELOW:** balcony scene.

**TIP**

Visit the helpful
Palermo tourist office
on Piazza Castelnuovo
34 (tel: 091-53847/
605 8351) to buy a
museum pass offering
combined tickets to
the main attractions,
from the most popular
city museums to the
Monreale Cathedral
cloisters.

paschal candlestick, Corinthian capitals and an inlaid Cosmati marble pulpit. The gold and porphyry throne occupies a dais below a mosaic pointedly entrusting the Norman kings with the Holy Law. The ceiling is unique in a Christian church, a composition of ineffable Oriental splendour. The Normans asked Arab craftsmen to portray paradise and they maliciously obliged with naked maidens, which the Normans prudishly clothed and crowned with haloes. Still, the roof remains a paradise of the senses, where Persian octagonal stars meet Arabian stalactites.

On the floor above is the (rarely open) gilded **Parliamentary Chamber** (1350) and **Royal Apartments**, which reflect the taste of past viceroys. From the balconies stretch views of the Conca d'Oro, the scenic bay surrounded by lemon groves, the port and hills. The finest Moorish rooms depict a profane vision of paradise; the **Sala dei Venti** is open to the winds; and the naturalistic **Sala di Re Ruggero** is frescoed with hunting scenes.

Nearby, just beyond the palm-ringed Piazza della Vittoria, stands the romantic red-domed **San Giovanni degli Eremiti** ❹ (open Mon–Sat 9am–6.30pm, Sun morning only). Now the symbol of Palermo, this Byzantine basilica was converted into a Benedictine abbey and a mosque. Byzantine foundations cede to Arab squinches, filigree windows and Norman cloisters overgrown with jasmine. The shape of the early mosque is still visible, as are stiff frescoes and Muslim arches. The tiny garden is a riot of acanthus, mimosa and pomegranate.

South of Corso Vittorio Emanuele and nudging Via Maqueda is the ramshackle **Albergheria** quarter, once inhabited by Norman court officials and rich Pisan merchants. Approached along **Via Albergheria** ❺, the area is either a squalid slum or an evocation of the old hugger-mugger of backstreet life.

**BELOW:**
Palermo Cathedral.

Although tottering houses propped up by rotten planks are home to illegal immigrants, a dynamic sense of community prevails over scenes of urban decay. An excellent community tour (Albergheria Viaggi, tel: 091-651 8576; minimum of eight people required per tour), led by young volunteers, shows visitors the underside of the area, from a visit to a carob factory to a workshop specialising in painting carts. A visit often ends with the sampling of street snacks in **Ballarò Market 6**, centred on Piazza Carmine, the noisy haunt of artisans and students, housewives and bootleggers. Currently Palermo's liveliest market, Ballarò is authentic and sprawling, with the hurly-burly of exotic food outlets clashing with the second-hand clothes stalls by **Casa Professa 7** (open daily 7.30–11.30am, also open Mon, Wed and Sat 5–6.30pm), also known as Il Gesù. The baroque marble interior of this cloistered Jesuitical church teems with tritons and cherubs.

## Around the Quattro Canti

From Casa Professa, the quaint Via Ponticello leads to Via Maqueda and **Piazza Pretoria 8**, another showpiece. This baroque square is where the city puts on its best public face. It was once nicknamed Piazza Vergogna (Square of Shame) after its saucy nude statues cavorting in the fountain. Amid uproar, this scandalous Mannerist fountain was brought here from Florence. The vast circular basin is peopled by tritons, nymphs and river gods. Reputedly, the local nuns chopped off the noses of the nude gods but stopped short of castration. The fountain was unveiled in 2004, which coincided with the 500th anniversary of the creation of this sculptural masterpiece. Adjoining the square is the **Palazzo delle Aquile**, the mayor's over-restored Gothic city hall, and the towering

**TIP**

For lunch, try Pizzeria Bellini on Piazza Bellini, as good for ice cream or coffee as it is for pizza (closed Mon). Head for Shanghai, on Vicolo Mezzani in the Vucciria market, for rough-and-ready pasta and sardines served without ceremony.

**BELOW:** the Basilica of Giovanni degli Eremiti.

*A cast of heroes in the traditional puppet theatre. For a list of the best ones in Sicily, see Travel Tips page 356.*

presence of **San Giuseppe Teatini** (open Mon–Sat 7.30–11am, 5.30–8pm), a theatrically baroque church decorated with multicoloured marble.

On the adjoining Piazza Bellini stand two delightful domed Arab-Norman churches. **La Martorana** (open Mon–Sat 8am–1pm, 3.30–5.30pm, Sun 8.30am–1pm) was founded in 1143 by George of Antioch, King Roger's Syrian emir and admiral. Although raised in the Orthodox faith, the emir planned La Martorana as a mosque. To complicate matters, he chose Greek Byzantine craftsmen to make the splendid mosaics. The space interweaves Byzantine and Muslim iconography: the Christ Pantocrator is present but so is the figure "8", the Arabic number of perfection. The church featured as a backdrop in the film *The Talented Mr Ripley*, which was partly shot in Sicily. Next door, the triple domed church of **San Cataldo** (open Mon–Sat 9.30am–12.30pm) is one of the last sacred buildings built in the Arab-Norman style. The Oriental impression is confirmed by the brooding Syrian interior. If at first this exquisite space seems sparse, it is only as a reaction to the gilded La Martorana.

There is no escape from the **Quattro Canti** , the notional centre of old Palermo. Known as *"il teatro"* (the city theatre), it offers a cross-section of Palermitan baroque, Arab-Norman splendour and medieval muddle. Behind their forbidding Spanish facades, the four concave-shaped screens of the city conceal chaotic districts, of which La Kalsa is the most subject to restoration.

## Seawards to La Kalsa quarter

**BELOW:** Foro Italico during the feast of Santa Rosalia.

Stretching seawards from Via Maqueda to Foro Italica and the sea is **La Kalsa**, a partly restored quarter with fine museums, austere Catalan-Gothic *palazzi* and vibrant street life. Meaning "pure" or "chosen" in Arabic, La Kalsa is near

longer ironic given that Mother Teresa's mission opened its doors just off the bomb-struck Piazza Magione **⑫**. Wealthy Palermitans were horrified at being lectured by an Albanian nun, even one incarnating sainthood. Her message was that since Palermo was as poor as the Third World, charity should begin at home. The message seems to have struck a chord since the area is now being regenerated, resulting in a greater sense of safety, not to mention the cheerful materialism heralded by new bars and scaffolding-clad palaces close to the gentrified Piazza Marina. Moorish filigree windows and blind arcading announce the ancestry of **La Magione** (open 9.30am–6.30pm), an imposing Cistercian church with a plain Arab-Norman interior. The recent restoration of La Magione extends beyond the complex of basilica, chapels and cloisters to a distinctly un-Palermitan landscaping of the grassy square beyond.

Seawards, in the honeycomb heart of the Kalsa, awaits **Lo Spasimo** **⑬** (open daily 8am–midnight), an open-air cultural entertainment complex set in an atmospheric Catalan-Gothic monastery. Concerts are held in the cloisters and the roofless church, which, given a sultry night and swaying palms, creates a romantic, Moorish atmosphere. With the recent restoration, not only was this early 16th-century monastery rescued from decay, but one of the most deprived districts received a huge boost. Run passionately yet professionally by amateurs, this flagship project employs reformed addicts, alcoholics or offenders. The project also seeks to lead local citizens and children away from the *pensar mafioso*, the mafia path. It provides a healthy overlap between bourgeois Palermitans, who attend the jazz concerts and art exhibitions, and an alienated underclass who can see the benefits in terms of neighbourhood improvements, greater security, employment and culture.

Via della Vetreria leads to **Via Alloro**, the city's patrician centre in the Middle Ages, and **Palazzo Abatellis** **⑭**, Sicily's most beguiling art collection (open daily 9am–1pm, also open Tues–Thur 2.30–7.30pm). Housed in a Catalan-Gothic mansion, the treasures are matched in splendour by their setting. Off a Renaissance courtyard lie Byzantine mosaics, Neapolitan Madonnas, and a geometric Moorish door. Other highlights are a serene bust of Eleanor of Aragon and a haunting da Messina *Annunciation*. The masterpiece is the powerful *Triumph of Death*, a frescoed 15th-century *danse macabre* in which a skeletal grim reaper cuts a swathe through the nobles' earthly pleasures. Before collapsing in Piazza Marina for a reviving drink on the square, admire the church of **La Gancia** (Mon–Sat 9am–noon, 3–6pm). Set beside Palazzo Abatellis, the church is distinguished by its Gothic portal, baroque Serpotta stuccoes and an ornate Renaissance organ, one of the finest in Italy.

**Piazza Marina** **⑮** was a swamp until drained by the Arabs and used as their first citadel. Since then, the square has witnessed the shame and glory of city history. **Palazzo Chiaramonte** **⑯**, a Catalan-Gothic fortress, was a feudal stronghold before becoming the seat of the Inquisition in 1598. Carved on the grim prison walls inside is a poignant plea for *pane, pazienza e tempo* (bread, patience and time). Outside, heretics and dissenters were burned. Commonly

Map on page 272

**TIP**

City nightlife has improved greatly, even though the summer scene moves to Mondello, Palermo's beach resort. In town, Caffe Mazzara (Via Generale Maglicco; open until 11pm) is a chic place for an *aperitif*, ice cream or a double espresso.

**BELOW:** downtown Palermo.

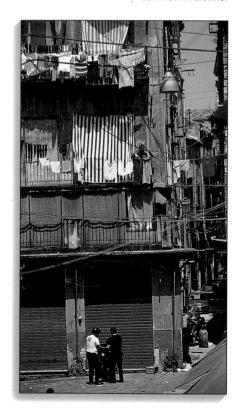

**TIP**

Sample such
Palermitan savoury
snacks as deep-fried
rice balls *(arancini)*,
chick-pea fritters, or
broccoli and
artichokes deep-fried
in batter, followed by
prickly pears,
marzipan sweets,
water ices or
watermelon jelly
scented with jasmine.
Il Golosone, on Piazza
Castelnuovo, is a
simple yet good place
for Sicilian fast food.

**BELOW:** Villa Giulia.

known as the Steri, the mansion belonged to the Spanish viceroys before falling into the hands of Palermo University, who discourage visitors. As one of the few gentrified squares in the old quarter, Piazza Marina is proud of its banyan tree and shady park, around which bric-a-brac traders vie with waiters in their effort to drum up trade.

In neighbouring Via Merlo is **Palazzo Mirto** 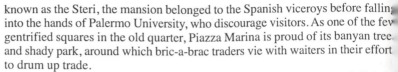, containing a delightful period museum (open Mon–Fri 9am–7pm, Sun 9am–1pm; entrance fee). The mansion is a testament to the eclectic tastes of Palermitan nobles in the 18th century, with chinoiserie and Empire style clashing with neo-Gothic flourishes. Close by is **San Francesco d'Assisi** (open Tues–Fri 9am–4pm, Mon and Sat 9am–noon), Palermo's loveliest Gothic church, its austerity softened by a delicate rose window. Opposite is **Antica Focacceria**, a famous Palermitan inn serving rustic snacks from *panini di panelle* (fried chick pea squares) to *pani cu la meusa* (boiled beef spleen). After feasting on the city's most authentic fast food, cast a glance at the latest restoration triumph, the **Oratorio di San Lorenzo** (tel for visits: 091-582370; open Mon–Fri 9am–noon), set a stone's throw from San Francesco. Described as "a cave of white coral", Serpotta's masterpiece has a porcelain sheen thanks to the *stuccatore*'s innovative technique of mixing marble dust with wet stucco. This Franciscan oratory last hit the headlines in 1969 when Caravaggio's *Nativity* was stolen from within and disappeared without trace.

The **Marina**, Palermo's grand seafront, was, until the *belle époque*, a public parade and a chance for louche encounters. Now known as **Foro Italico**, the stark waterfront has gained some palms and is overlooked by the **Palazzo Butera**, eulogised by Goethe but bombed by the Allies. Beyond is **Villa Giulia**, picturesque formal gardens, and the adjoining **Orto Botánico** (Botanical Gardens; open Mon–Fri 9am–5pm, Sat–Sun 9am–1pm; entrance fee), dotted with pavilions, sphinx statues and a lily pond.

## Vucciria quarter

This dilapidated market district is crammed between La Cala harbour, Corso Vittorio Emanuele and Via Roma. The name is a corruption of the French *boucherie*, thanks to the quantity of flesh on sale in the traditional **Vucciria Market**. The stalls straggle along alleys from Via Roma to **San Domenico** (open daily 7.30am–noon), a vapid baroque church with an impressive façade. Colourful alleys display capers and pine nuts, spices and squirming octopus, skewered giblets and bootleg tapes – charming as night falls and the red awnings are illuminated. Sustenance is necessary, since between San Domenico and the port is devastation. However, the ascendancy of Ballarò Market means that the Vucciria is truly bustling only on Saturday.

Via Bambinai, a former doll-makers' street, has stayed close to its roots: shops sell votive offerings and Christmas crib figures. The street has a baroque jewel in **Oratorio del Rosario di San Domenico** (Mon–Sat 9am–1pm; entrance fee), a theatrical Serpotta chapel, where putti play cellos amid sea shells, eagles and allegorical exotica. Just around the corner, on Via Valverde, lies an equally celebrated oratory, **Oratorio di Santa Zita ㉒**, reached through lush gardens. The oratories were used as social clubs and centres for charitable works, as well as for displays of status. Here, Serpotta's ravishing stuccowork depicts the intercession of the Virgin in the *Battle of Lepanto*.

Beyond the chapel to the south is **La Cala ㉓**, the scruffy portside. Fishing boats bob against a backdrop of bombed *palazzi* whose cellars house immigrant families. However, regeneration is gradually seeping into this semi-derelict quarter, with the restoration of bomb-damaged churches such as **Santa Maria della Catena** (open Mon–Fri 9am–1pm), a Catalan-Gothic church, named after the medieval chain that once shut off the port. The maritime museum is an attempt to reconnect this inward-looking city with the sea. **Museo del Mare ㉔** (open daily 9.30am–noon; entrance fee), set in the former arsenal on Via Cristoforo Colombo, is a maritime showcase with a terrace and sea views.

From the port, retrace your steps to Via Roma and take Via Bara to Piazza Olivella, part of an artisans' quarter of puppet-makers, *pasticcerie* and *trattorie*. By night the area becomes a haunt for students, who frequent bars and clubs that lurk behind baroque courtyards and in medieval backstreets. The baroque **Olivella Church** adjoins the **Museo Archeologico ㉕** (open daily 9am–1.30pm; entrance fee), the essence of classical Sicily encased in a late-Renaissance monastery. The inner courtyard has a tangle of lush vegetation and a lily pond, a showcase for Egyptian and Greek statuary or Phoenician sarcophagi. The superb **Sala di Selinunte** displays one of the main friezes from the classical site of Selinunte *(see page 285)*. In stylised friezes, Athena protects Perseus as he battles with Medusa, Hercules slays dwarves, and Zeus marries a frosty Hera.

Map on page 272

*Consider a drink in the faded grandeur of Hotel des Palmes on Via Roma. Wagner composed part of Parsifal in a gilded salon here in 1882, while the wartime Mafia boss Lucky Luciano held court in the dining room.*

**BELOW:** Teatro Massimo, the city opera house.

## Belle époque and modern quarter

After the labyrinthine alleys of old Palermo, the grid system of the modern city comes as something of a shock. From the Museo Archeologico, Via Orologio leads to the well-restored **Teatro Massimo** ❷❻ (guided visits; tel: 091-605 3111), the city opera house. Designed by the Palermitan Basile in 1864, this is one of the largest opera houses in Europe. The portico, graced by Corinthian columns, is of clear Greek inspiration, while the cylindrical shape of the building and the cupola itself owe more to Roman designs. The interior is equally eclectic, with a grandiose baroque staircase contrasting with floral, decidedly Art Nouveau decor. The opera house was used for the shooting of the climactic scene in Coppola's *The Godfather, Part III*.

Remnants of Palermo's late-flowering *Belle Epoque* can be found north of Via Cavour. The smart shopping street of **Via della Libertà** ❷❼ was once studded with Art Nouveau villas, but most have been demolished or disappeared in fires linked to fraudulent insurance claims. Fashionable bars and the sophistication of the evening *passeggiata* cannot conceal the fact that style has since deserted the quarter. Even so, the attractive landscaped **Giardino Inglese** at the northern end of Via della Libertà is a pleasant spot for a romantic stroll, while **Piazza Castelnuovo**, at the southern end, is the frenetic early-evening meeting place for Palermitan youth.

## The Moorish palace

**BELOW:** resident of the catacombs.

In Norman times, palaces encircled the city "like gold coins around the neck of a bosomy girl". The vivid description given by the Arab poet, Ibn Jubayr, conjures up the pleasure dome of **La Ziza** ❷❽, one of the most impressive legacies

## THE UNDERGROUND CITY

For the ghoulish, the grim catacombs of Palermo represent an unnerving vision of the city. The **Convento dei Cappuccini** (open daily 9am–noon 3–5pm) lies on Via Cappuccini, midway between La Cuba and La Ziza *(see above)*. In macabre Sicilian style superior corpses were mummified here from the 16th century until 1920. In death, the clergy, nobles and bourgeoisie opted for posterity rather than the communal trench: the corpses were displayed according to their sex, status and profession, all dressed in their Sunday best. In these galleries, embalmers have stored more than 8,000 moth-eaten mummies. Fascinating but not for the faint-hearted.

For a bizarre visit to underground Palermo and the 10th-century **water channels** created by the Arabs non-claustrophobic visitors should go on a morning trip with expert potholers, organised by the Sotto-Sopra group (tel: 091-580433). No experience is necessary and all equipment is provided, but take a change of clothes. Visitors are lowered down a deep well-shaft into a waist-high water channel, where they wade behind guides through the winding channels that once provided irrigation for Arab palaces and farmsteads.

of Moorish Palermo. An Arab arch leads to a palace (open Mon–Sat 9am–6.30pm, Sun 9am–1pm; entrance fee) built on the site of a Roman villa, to exploit the existing aqueduct. Fed by canals, the lake was paved with marine-inspired mosaics. La Ziza's most charming spot is the vestibule, adorned by honeycomb vaults, a Saracen fountain and a glorious mosaic frieze of peacocks and huntsmen. In this breezy chamber, the emir and his court listened to the lapping of water. The interior, now a museum of Arab culture, is a mixed success. Critics claim that clumsy restoration has ruined the Arab lines and replaced filigree windows with heavy-framed versions.

On Corso Calatafimi, not far from La Ziza, is **La Cuba** ㉙ (open Mon–Sat 9am–6.30pm), the final piece of the Moorish jigsaw. Once an Arab pleasure pavilion, it is now a roofless ruin marooned in an army barracks. In Arab times, this quaint pavilion was set on a lovely artificial lake within the luxuriant grounds of La Ziza. For those with no taste for the macabre, the return to Palermo is via Porta Nuova, a Spanish gateway decorated with turbaned Moorish giants. For the ghoulish, the grim catacombs represent an unnerving vision of the city *(see panel on facing page).*

## Six days without sleep

The patron saint of Palermo is enshrined in the **Santuaria di Santa Rosalia** in a mountain grotto above the city on San Pellegrino. Santa Rosalia has been affectionately nicknamed La Santuzza (little saint). The sanctuary was built in 1624 after a dreamer had been instructed to find her relics and wave them three times around the city to rid Palermo of the plague. Her saint's day, in July, is a six-day extravaganza, when Palermo barely sleeps.                                        ❑

Map on page 272

*"The city awaits us... early persimmons glowing orange amidst pyramids of bright green cauliflowers, smoking tripods of chestnuts roasting at the curbstones, bloodshed and decaying beauty."*
– From *In Persephone's Island* by Mary Simeti

**Below:** meeting on the theatre steps.

# WEST AND CENTRAL SICILY

*Monreale is the Arab-Norman achievement,
Selinunte and Agrigento are the splendours of Greece,
while inland Corleone is associated with the Mafia*

Map
on page
268

Palermo

**W**estern Sicily is the seafaring and African part of the island. Poignant Mozia is Sicily's greatest Punic site, while the colourful fishing port of Mazara del Vallo could be in Tunisia. Trapani province, in particular, feels tangibly both Phoenician and African yet, paradoxically, produces alcoholic Marsala in the heart of Muslim Sicily. This cultural cornucopia is matched by a landscape of saltpans, vineyards, woods and coastal nature reserves. Despite such resources, the region suffers from degradation, pervasive criminal undercurrents, and a torpor conditioned by centuries of failure. This malaise is most clear in the hinterland, exacerbated by earthquake damage in the centre of the region and the economic collapse of the sulphur-mining industry in the south. The western hinterland is far less promising than the glittering coast.

Easily reached from **Palermo** ❶ along the Palermo–Trapani motorway, **Segesta** ❷ (open daily 9am–dusk; entrance fee) lies in rolling countryside and is one of the most romantic classical sites. Founded by the Elymians, whose language has yet to be transcribed, the settlers claimed to be refugees who escaped the Fall of Troy in Asia Minor, and the Trojan link would explain their hatred of the Greeks, an enmity which led to their role in the razing of nearby Selinunte. Segesta was sacked by Siracusa in 307 BC. Crowning a low hill is a roofless Doric temple. Linked by a minibus service, the Greek theatre on the facing hill has an air of poetic desolation. Recent discoveries have transformed our understanding of the scale of Segesta, with the unearthing of vast Hellenistic fortifications, a necropolis and agora, as well as an 11th-century mosque. An inspirational summer season of classical tragedies, opera, ballet, poetry and jazz is now staged in the Greek temple.

## The coast to San Vito Lo Capo

The coastal road from Palermo runs west to **Castellammare del Golfo** ❸, an overgrown fishing village with panoramic views across the gulf. From the port, a boat ferries visitors to the scenic **Lo Zingaro Nature Reserve** *(see panel on page 284)*. On the headland lies **San Vito lo Capo**, a burgeoning resort noted for its fine coast, its sandy beaches and lively fish restaurants.

**Trapani** ❹, the provincial capital, remains an important port and an embarkation point for the Egadi Islands and the remoter island of Pantelleria *(see pages 316–18)*. Apparently Cronos, one of the Titans, castrated his father Uranus with a sickle and threw his genitals into the sea at Cape Drepanum. The result is modern-day Trapani. It is a patchwork of low lagoons bounded by a thin causeway. The Arab influence reveals itself in local architecture, attitudes and cuisine.

Trapani's traditional industries of coral, tuna fishing and salt linger on. Apart from a fish and fruit

**LEFT:** the romantic site of Segesta.
**BELOW:** steep street in Castellammare del Golfo.

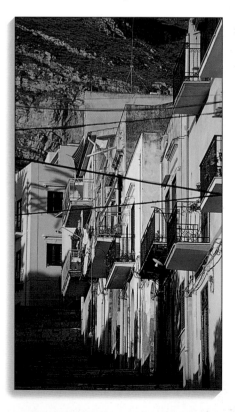

*Fishermen's houses in the provincial capital of Trapani.*

market on Piazza Mercato del Pesce, Trapani offers a graceful Gothic church, a fine arts-and-crafts collection, and a cluster of rather dilapidated baroque *palazzi*.

**Erice** ❺, a medieval walled town just north, makes a much more enticing base than Trapani for exploring the African coast. In spring, the winding road climbs past acacia, wild gladioli and waxy lemon blossom to the legendary Mount Eryx. This mystical city was founded by the Elymni, mysterious settlers of Segesta who worshipped the fertility goddess known as Astarte to the Phoenicians, Aphrodite to the Greeks, and Venus to the Romans. Each spring, she flew off with an escort of doves to her shrine in Sicca Veneria, modern El Kef in Tunisia. Her return signalled the reawakening of nature. In Erice's temple, Romans followed earlier customs of worship, including the cult of sacred prostitution. The battered marble remains of the temple to Venus lie beside a well in the Norman castle (hours variable; tel: 0923-869388) on a rocky outcrop overlooking Torretta Pepoli, a Gothic fantasy created by Count Pepoli. Below stretch ragged turrets, wooded groves and vineyards; a tapestry of saltpans and sea slips all the way to the Egadi Islands and to Cap Bon in Tunisia. Porta Trapani, a medieval gate, leads to a winding cobbled street lined with medieval *palazzi*. Carthaginian walls survive, with Punic symbols. The town is linked to Trapani via a cable car.

## The salty "African coast"

South of Trapani is the "African coast", closer to Tunisia than to mainland Italy. It is known for its saltpans, a reminder of an industry that has flourished since Phoenician and Roman times. **Marsala** ❻ sits on a cape and takes its name from the Arabic Mars-al-Allah, meaning "harbour of God". As Carthaginian

**BELOW:** Lo Zingaro Nature Reserve.

## LO ZINGARO NATURE RESERVE

Lo Zingaro is set on a rocky headland pierced with coves and bays and dotted with clearly marked paths but containing no official roads. Scopello di Sopra, 10 km (6 miles) before Castellammare, marks the southern entrance to the reserve and is a fishing village based around a *baglio*, an imposing medieval farmstead. Apart from a rustic *trattoria* and a chance to buy farm-fresh cheese, the only site of note is the Tonnara, the finest tunnery on the coast. The tunnery overlooks the bay and a shingle beach, one of five, which is popular with swimmers. Above are a couple of rugged Saracen towers, built to combat raids by pirates. The northern entrance to Lo Zingaro lies 11 km (7 miles) southeast of San Vito lo Capo (tel: 0924-35108), just before the ruins of Torre dell'Impiso. The reserve is a glorious home to buzzards and peregrine falcons as well as palms, carobs and euphorbia. The continuing success of the reserve, with a natural history museum, marine laboratory and visitor centre, causes cynical Sicilians to dismiss it as a fabricated Disneyworld, but this comparison bemuses foreigners, who are only too delighted to find a semblance of order in any Sicilian site. The ever-changing coastline can be appreciated by boat, on horseback or on foot.

Lilybaeum, it was the best-defended Punic naval base in Sicily, the only city to resist Greek expansion westwards. The site now houses the Museo Nave Punica (open daily 9am–1pm, Wed, Fri–Sun also open 4–6.30pm; entrance fee), with a reconstructed Punic ship that was sunk off the Egadi Islands. It was manned by 68 oarsmen and has iron nails that have not rusted. Parco Lilybeo (tel: 0923-952535), which covers the adjoining Cape Boeo archaeological zone, is being restyled as "Sicily's Pompeii" thanks to the recent recovery of a Roman ship in the mysterious Stagnone lagoon just beyond the cape, as well as the return from Rome of the "Dancing Satyr" – the legendary Marsala bronze which now joins the Medusa Roman mosaics *in situ*.

Marsala's cathedral is dedicated to St Thomas of Canterbury (Thomas Becket) and pillars destined for Canterbury grace the nave. The Cantine Florio (tel: 0923-781111) is a typical Marsala distillery, most of which are set in *bagli*, traditional walled estates with elegant courtyards.

From Cape Boeo, the coastal road passes saltpans and marshes south to **Mazara del Vallo ❼**, a place of moods rather than specific sights. The fishing port flourished under Arab rule and it still feels like a North African town. A ragged Norman castle overlooks the seafront, while the Norman cathedral has a baroque façade and contains two dramatic Roman sarcophagi. However the best church is the crenellated Norman-Byzantine San Nicolò Regale, at Porta Palermo in the heart of the fishing quarter. One of Italy's largest fishing fleets operates here and the Mazaro river is packed with trawlers. Behind lies the Kasbah, the Tunisian quarter, where North Africans smoke hubble-bubbles.

**Selinunte ❽**, 30 km (20 miles) east of Mazara, is a pocket of Greece in African Sicily. It was founded in 628 BC by colonists from Megara Hyblaea but, as Segesta's sworn enemy, became embroiled in clashes with the Carthaginians and Athenians. After being sacked by Carthage in 409 BC, the city never fully recovered and was destroyed in 250 BC. However, an aerial view of the collapsed columns reveals that they fell like dominoes, evidently the result of an earthquake. A visit to the sprawling site can be followed by a swim off the sandy coast. Framed by temples, the beach at Marinella consists of a dune-fringed shore, with the seafront lined by lively restaurants.

Overlooking the countryside and the sea, the beguiling archaeological site (open daily 9am–7pm; winter until 4pm) is hemmed in by two silted-up rivers and ports. Selinunte is a hauntingly lovely spot. There are half a dozen temples, and within a walled enclosure the acropolis retains some original fortifications, communication trenches and gates. North of the acropolis is the ancient Greek city and, on either side of it lie necropoli which have yet to be excavated. Just 4 km (2 miles) south of Campobello are the **Cave di Cusa**, the classical quarries that provided the stone for Selinunte, now overrun with goats and wild flowers.

The region has suffered several natural disasters, particularly in the inland earthquake zone centred on Calatafimi, Salemi and Gibellina. In 1968 a major earthquake left more than 50,000 people homeless. From Selinunte, an unspoilt coastal route leads eastwards to Agrigento, taking in the classical site of Eraclea

Map on page 268

*Erice has a tradition of dolci ericini, excessively sweet cakes once made by novice nuns. Maria Grammatico's Pasticceria and café in Via Vittorio Emanuele is one of the best in Sicily, selling pasta reale (marzipan), sospiri (sighs) and belli e brutti (beauties and beasts).*

**BELOW:** "Temple A" in the acropolis at Selinunte.

*Santa Maria dei Greci in Agrigento, built over a Greek temple, a medieval tribute to ancient Greek inspiration.*

Minoa. Midway between Selinunte and Eraclea is **Sciacca 9**, a fishing port noted for its sandy beaches and spa waters. This ancient spa town was praised by Pliny and prospered in Arab times. It is a split-level town, with the port overlooked by the natural balcony of the old town. The Moorish quarter is on the highest level, a criss-cross mass of alleys, arches and courtyards home to wary, illegal immigrants. Sciacca lacks spectacular architecture but exhilarating sea views and an engaging ensemble of tawny, weather-beaten buildings justify a visit. On summer evenings the Piazza Scandaliato belongs to Tunisian hawkers flogging exotic clothes or Sciacca ceramics. By contrast, the Terme Selinuntine, an aloof, Art Nouveau establishment, attracts wealthy Italians to its mud baths.

From Sciacca, a winding road climbs inland past farmhouses and deep gorges to Caltabellotta, the loveliest village in Agrigento province, with a cluster of towers and churches framed by spring blossom. Alternatively, from Sciacca the coastal road skirts countryside to the classical site of **Eraclea Minoa 10** (open daily 9am–one hour before sunset; entrance fee). A satellite of Selinunte, it suffered at the hands of the Carthaginians. Eraclea overlooks white cliffs, a crescent of golden sands and a pine grove. Excavations have so far revealed city walls, a Hellenistic theatre, a necropolis and ruined villas.

## Agrigento, home of Greek luxury

The classical splendour of the Valley of the Temples triumphs over the mishmash that is the "modern" city of **Agrigento 11**. Siracusa may have been the most powerful city in Greek Sicily but Agrigento (Akragas) was the most luxurious. Akragas was settled by colonists from Gela in 580 BC, attracted by the abundance of springs and a dreamy, well-fortified site. This most sybaritic of Sicilian cities

was run by tyrants and sacked by the Carthaginians in 406 BC. The city flourished again under the Romans but in AD 535 the Byzantines destroyed all but one of the pagan temples. The medieval city abandoned, Akragas and the classical site were ignored until popularised by Goethe and the 19th-century German Romantics. The city rivalled Athens in the splendour of its temples, but in its hedonistic lifestyle Akragas was the Los Angeles of the ancient world.

The deprived modern city, resting on an economy beholden to the Mafia, relies on a surface gloss of chic bars and jewellery shops. Charmless middle-class apartments gaze across at the temples, often from within the park confines. The "modern" city is not without interest, but if only in the area for a day, head straight for the Valley of the Temples, and restrict a city visit to dinner and an evening stroll. Above Via Atenea, the main street, stands Santo Spirito, a fine Cistercian abbey founded in 1290. Agrigento's commercial spirit triumphs in the form of sweet *dolci di mandorla*, almond and pistachio pastries sold by the resident Cistercian nuns.

Dominating neighbouring Piazza Purgatorio is the baroque church of San Lorenzo, which marks the entrance to the Greek *hypogeum*, the ancient underground water and drainage system. Set among Moorish alleyways further west is Santa Maria dei Greci, a Norman church built over a Greek temple. The cathedral (open 10am–1pm, 4–6pm), which surmounts a ridge in the west of the city where the Greeks had their acropolis, is designed in eclectic style with Arab-Norman, Catalan-Gothic and baroque elements.

Map on page 268

## The Valley of the Temples

The **Valle dei Templi** ⓬ (Valley of the Temples) forms a natural amphitheatre, with a string of Doric temples straddling a ridge south of the city. This is still a valley of wild thyme, fennel, silvery olive groves and almond blossom. This crest of temples was designed to be visible from the sea, both as a beacon for sailors and to show that the gods guarded the sacred city from mortal danger. From the valley, views of the town may offend purists but olive and almond groves mask the modernity. The complex falls into several sections: the main zone (open 8.30am–one hour before dusk) is reached through the adjoining eastern and western gates; there are separate entrances for both the museum and the Hellenistic-Roman quarter. At night the temples are floodlit. In the Eastern Zone the first treasure visible is the Temple of Hercules, dating from 5 BC. Agrigento's oldest temple had similar proportions to the Parthenon in Athens. Villa Aurea, set in olive and almond groves beside the former Golden Gate, belonged to Hardcastle, the Englishman who in the 19th century devotedly excavated the site. At the end of Via Sacra lies the Temple of Concord, dedicated to Demeter, goddess of fertility and peace. After the Theseion in Athens, it is the best-preserved Greek temple in the world. The tawny temple slopes into the valley below, a pastoral scene at odds with its bloody history: on this bulwark thousands were slain in battle against Carthage. Dating from 430 BC, the temple was saved from ruin in the 6th century by being converted into a church, which it remained until 1748, when it was restored to its classical simplicity.

*A sandstone giant, like the ones from the Temple of the Olympian Zeus.*

**BELOW:** almond blossoms in the Valley of the Temples.

The Temple of Hera surmounts a rocky ridge which formed the city ramparts. Known as Juno to the Romans, she was protectress of married couples. Fittingly, Hera is held to be the most romantic of temples, set "high on the hill like an offering to the goddess". Part of the *cella* (inner room of the temple) and 25 columns remain intact; the rest fell over the hill during a landslide. The valley views reflect Pindar's praise of Agrigento as "loveliest of mortal cities".

The Western Zone, which encloses the newly restored Kolymbetra Mediterranean garden, faces the Temple of Olympian Zeus. The size of a football pitch, it is the largest Doric temple ever known. The facade was supported by 38 telamones (giant figures), thereby distributing the weight of the pediment between the columns of the peristyle and the giants. A sandstone copy of a telamon stretches dreamily on the ground, while originals lie in the archaeological museum. West of this temple is a confusing quarter, dotted with shrines dating from pre-Greek times.

The sandy Via Sacra leads to the Temple of Castor and Pollux (or the Dioscuri), named after the twin sons of Zeus. Although it has become the city symbol, the result is theatrical pastiche, erected in 1836 from several temples. Known as the Sanctuary of the Chthonic Divinities, the area conceals sacrificial altars and ditches, a shrine to fertility, immortality and eternal

youth. Pale-coloured beasts were offered to the heavens but black animals were sacrificed to gods of the Underworld. Outside the ancient walls, and half-hidden in an almond grove, is the Temple of Asclepius, dedicated to the god of healing.

Via dei Templi leads past olive groves to the archaeological museum, the Hellenistic-Roman quarter and several pagan shrines. San Nicola, on Via Petrarca, is a Romanesque church built from recycled Greek stone. Next door is a fine archaeological museum (open Tues–Sat 9am–7.30pm, Mon and Sun 9am–1pm; combined ticket), incorporating a church, courtyard and temple foundations. The Graeco-Roman section is the centrepiece, featuring a telamon in all its massive glory. The Hellenistic-Roman quarter (open daily 9am–1pm, 2–6pm) lies opposite, an ancient commercial and residential area laid out on a grid system. The remains of aqueducts, terracotta and stone water channels are visible, as well as vestiges of shops, taverns and patrician villas. Seen in spring, against a backdrop of almond blossom, the view is magical.

## The North Coast and Monreale

In northern Sicily a timeless, clannish yet sparsely populated countryside stretches from Palermo to Enna. Tucked into the fold between coast and mountains is Palermo's Conca d'Oro, formerly the city's summer gardens and citrus groves. By rights, the outskirts should be carpeted with marigolds and lemon trees, but land speculation and Mafia funding have ensured that Palermo's countryside is being encased in concrete.

In a mountain grotto at the top of Monte Pellegrino is the Santuario di Santa Rosalia *(see page 281)*, a kitsch but popular shrine allegedly containing the bones of Palermo's revered patron saint. In the lee of the mountain lies fashion-

*The softness of the people of ancient Agrigento was notorious. At the prospect of war with Carthage, soldiers on watch were under orders to make do with no more than two mattresses, two pillows and a blanket each.*

**BELOW:** Temple of Concord, the Valley of the Temples.

able **Mondello** , a resort pioneered by the Bourbons that had once been a tuna-fishing village. The centre of attraction is the striking ochre-and-maroon Art Nouveau pier, created by a Belgian entrepreneur in the 1890s. On the pier is the Terrazze-Charleston, an exclusive seafood restaurant with a spacious summer terrace and a snooty *maître d'hôtel*.

The cathedral of **Monreale**  (open daily 8am–noon, 3.30–6pm; entrance free), with its views over the Conca d'Oro, is a sumptuous building, the apogee of Arab-Norman art. The cathedral and Benedictine monastery were completed by the time of William II's death in 1189, allegedly inspired by a vision. In truth, his political rivalry with the Englishman, Walter of the Mill, the Palermitan archbishop, fuelled his desire to build a cathedral greater than Palermo's. Ultimately, William triumphed: his white marble sarcophagus lies in Monreale, and his shimmering tapestry is unequalled in Europe. His legacy is a vast cycle of mosaics, second in size only to Santa Sofia in Istanbul.

*Figurative capitals in the cloister of Monreale Cathedral.*

Flanked by severe bell towers, the cathedral is not instantly awe-inspiring, yet the details are exquisite. An arched Romanesque portal, made by a Pisan master, is framed by a greenish bronze door. The portal displays sculpted bands of garlands, figures and beasts alternating with multicoloured mosaics. To the left, a Gagini portico shelters another Romanesque bronze door, enriched by the delicacy of Byzantine inlaid ivory. The apses are the most opulent in Sicily: a poetic abstraction of interlacing limestone and basalt arches, sculpted as delicately as wood. Monreale drew craftsmen from Persia, Africa, Asia, Greece, Venice, Pisa and Provence. The shimmering gold interior fuses Arab purity of volume with Byzantine majesty. The date of the mosaics is disputed: some scholars believe they were finished by 1100; others maintain that while the Byzantines began

**BELOW:** Monreale Cathedral.

*Monreale's biggest tourist trap awaits.*

before then, the Venetians only completed the work by 1250. The highlight is the Creation series on the upper walls in the right of the nave: the delicacy of the flowers, fruit trees and birds singles out these scenes from *Genesis*, and the whole mosaic cycle is a *Biblia pauperum*, a poor-man's Bible.

After admiring the view from the terraces, visit the **cloisters** (open Mon–Sat 9am–6.30pm, Sun 9am–1pm; entrance fee), which express William's love of Islamic art and which are the world's most sumptuous Romanesque example. Every second pair of white marble columns has a vivid zigzag mosaic pattern spiralling up the shaft. The sophistication of these columns suggests a Provençal influence, while the Moorish mood, evoked by mosaic inlays or arabesque carvings, conjures up the Alhambra in Spain.

While Monreale is an anticlimax after the mosaics, a horse-and-cart ride or stroll from the Duomo brings a chance to savour the town's pedestrianised centre of crumbling, baroque churches and shops selling ceramics and ices. As a Mafia-controlled town, it is supremely safe for visitors. It was here that Totò Riina, the former Mafia boss, chose to live quite openly until his arrest in 1993. Local trattorie offer *pasta con le sarde*, a sardine speciality, or dry *biscotti di Monreale*. **Madonna delle Croci**, set on a hill, offers a lingering view from the cathedral to the coast.

**BELOW:** the Mafia town of Corleone, home of a UN-backed anti-Mafia museum and research centre.

## Bandit country

From Monreale south into the interior unfolds a brooding Mafia heartland of gulleys and mountain lairs. Nurtured by the mythology of banditry, the hinterland falls back on ancient suspicion and insularity. As such, the villages south to Corleone are places of subtle mood shifts rather than specific sights or

Map on page 268

scenery. However, **Piana degli Albanesi** ⓯, reached along the SS624, is both an ethnic oddity and representative of this diverse province. The village, which appears suspended above a lake, is home to 15th-century Greek-speaking Albanian immigrants, and encircled by lush pastures and hills. Traditional Byzantine ceremonies include services celebrated in both Albanian and Greek. Local cuisine is a cultural stew such as *dash*, castrated ram, Albanian-Greek style.

**Corleone** ⓰ is perched along the rural SS118, which follows desolate, scorched hills and high verdant plains. The town lies clamped between two rocks, below a weather-beaten escarpment. In the centre looms the Castello, a rocky outcrop topped by a Saracen tower. It was a prison until 1976 but is now home to Franciscan friars. Below, rooftops are stacked in a chromatic range of greys. At first sight, Corleone fails to live up to its infamous reputation but, on closer inspection, an air of watchfulness hangs over the town. Nonetheless, it has a reputation for producing great minds, whether priests, scholars or criminals, and is proud of its anti-Mafia museum, public-spirited youngsters and flourishing B&Bs. Unlike neighbouring towns, Corleone's shops and businesses pay no *pizzo* (protection money) because the town is the stronghold of a powerful Mafia clan. But the arrest in 1993 of Totò Riina, the Corleonese *capo di tutti capi*, merely saw him replaced by another clan member, Bernardo Provenzano, who is still at large, presumably running more than a B&B.

## The road to Cefalù

The coast road from Palermo curves east past fishing villages and coves to **Cefalù** ⓱, one of Sicily's most engaging resorts. Sitting snugly below a headland, Cefalù is Taormina's north-coast rival. The consensus is that Taormina has

**BELOW:** old town and beach, Cefalù.

*Pistachio nuts
ripening, to eat and
to flavour ice cream.*

better hotels, nightlife and atmosphere, but that Cefalù is more compact, peaceful and family-oriented. Out of season, Piazza del Duomo, the town centre, is a delightful sun trap, with a view of the cathedral at the foot of steep cliffs and looming fortifications. The square is also framed by the Corso, a Renaissance seminary and a porticoed *palazzo*. Here, the chic Caffè Duomo is the place for an *aperitivo al fresco*. In summer the town is a delightful tourist trap with quaint craft boutiques selling ceramics and gold jewellery, matched by sophisticated restaurants catering to fastidious French palates. In the evening, the seafront, bastion and Corso become a cavalcade for *passeggiate* and *gelati*.

Cefalù cathedral (open daily 8am–12.30pm, 3.30–7pm), built in 1130 by Roger II, has a bold twin-towered facade and a triple apse with blind arcading. Roger used the see of Cefalù as a counterweight to Monreale and favoured Cefalù as the official mouthpiece of the state church. Inside, a severe nave is flanked by Roman columns surmounted by Romanesque arches – a reminder that a temple lies beneath. A sense of space and majesty is created by the concentration of other-worldly mosaics in the distant dome. These luminous Byzantine mosaics are among the earliest Norman creations and the purest extant depiction of Christ. The rest of the interior is imbued with majesty: the raised choir represents an Oriental element whereas the gold firmament behind Christ is Byzantine.

A warren of alleys leads west from Corso Ruggero, the main street, and reveals Renaissance facades, Gothic parapets and mullioned windows overlooking tiny courtyards. The old port, tangibly Moorish and home to Tunisian fishermen, has been a backdrop in countless films, including *Cinema Paradiso*. An underground spring bubbles up in the arcaded Arab baths, situated at the bottom of curved

steps, beside a lively bar. Via Porto Salvo passes battered churches and flourishing craft shops. From Piazza Duomo, a steepish hill leads down to Museo Mandralisca (open daily 9am–12.30pm, 3.30–6pm; entrance fee) containing Antonello da Messina's *Portrait of an Unknown Man*. A jagged outcrop overhangs the medieval town and is the site of the Citadel, the original Arab settlement and megalithic remains. Marked walks climb through pine groves to the rocky cliffs and views over rust-coloured roofs and an azure sea studded with inlets and beaches.

## Into the Madonie mountains

After Cefalù, coastal olive groves give way to pine woods and rugged valleys. A superior feudal castle towers over **Castelbuono ⑱**, 12 km (8 miles) inland, a prosperous, well-kept place that could be mistaken for Tuscany. Weekend visitors are drawn to the lively atmosphere, well-restored churches and welcoming restaurants. In the centre awaits one of the finest gastronomic experiences in Sicily: Nangalarruni (tel: 0921-671428), celebrated for its mushroom dishes, roast meats and grilled vegetables. Nearby is the Caffè Franconari, which produces some of Italy's finest artisanal *panettone*, exported all over the world.

The rural route south follows the SS286 for 22 km (14 miles) to Geraci and winds up to Gangi, a tortoise-shaped town with a crumbling watchtower, and past the slopes of the Madonie rising to the snowcapped Madonna dell'Alto, at 826 metres (2,707 ft) the highest peak. From here, one can either continue east to Nicosia or complete a circuit back to Cefalù via Petralia and Polizzi. West of Gangi, the SS1 reveals the jagged skyline of **Petralia Soprana** ⑲. Half-hidden in its alleys are striking mansions with baroque or rococo balconies as well as two watchtowers. Now a mountain resort, this former Norman citadel has a trio of Romanesque, Gothic and baroque churches. The Chiesa Matrice is perched on a belvedere and swathed in mist; inside is a precious Arabian altarpiece.

The road west to **Polizzi Generosa** passes *masserie*, feudal farmsteads that were as self-sufficient as most villages. Polizzi is a trekking centre which sustains walkers with pasta and asparagus *(pasta cu l'asparaci)*. From here, the fast A19 returns to the coast, as does the winding route via the ski resort of Piano Battaglia.

## The navel of Sicily

East of Gangi, Palermo province merges into Enna, the desolate, sun-parched centre of the island. This lofty inland province remains resolutely agricultural, producing corn, olives, cheese, nuts and wine – a fitting menu for a place connected with Greek fertility rites. The province suffers from emigration and has pinned its hopes on tourism. The signs are promising; Enna possesses Sicily's greatest Roman villa and a succession of strategic castles and classical sites.

To the north of the provincial capital lies **Sperlinga** ⑳ (open daily 10am–1pm, 2pm–5pm; entrance fee), an intriguing castle with battlemented towers and bastions that stretch to the bottom of the cliff. Below the castle, the rock is riddled with chambers, a secret underground city. Dating from 1082, the Norman castle passed from the Chiaramonte into the hands of the Natali, Princes of Sperlinga.

Map on page 268

**TIP**

Farm stays *(agriturismo)* make an appealing way of exploring the Madonie Mountains. Monaco di Mezzo (tel: 0934-673949), near Petralia Sottana, is one of the best, with rural produce, hiking and horseriding.

**BELOW:** countryside around Enna.

*Flag waver in the annual Palio in Adrano.*

**BELOW:** catching up with news, Enna.

The castle became the Angevins' last stand 200 years later, after the bloody Sicilian Vespers *(see page 31)* in 1282. The French forces held out for more than a year, aided by trap doors that deposited invaders in underground pits. From the crenellations sweeping views overlook oak woods, olive groves and pasture. **Nicosia ㉑**, 8 km (5 miles) southeast of Sperlinga, is set on four hills and ringed by rocky spurs. In the Middle Ages, it was riven by religious rivalry between Roman Catholic newcomers and the indigenous Eastern Orthodox population. After pitched battles, the matter was settled in favour of the natives: the 14th-century San Nicolò triumphed as the city cathedral, with a lacy Catalan-Gothic campanile rooted in a gracious Moorish tower. Leading off Piazza Garibaldi, a square dotted with dingy bars and clubs, are myriad crooked alleys climbing Nicosia's hills.

Further south is Leonforte, a 17th-century Branciforte fiefdom best known for the Granfonte, a magnificent arched fountain on the edge of town. This act of feudal largesse is still appreciated by thirsty donkeys.

## Balcony over Sicily

**Enna ㉒**, a lofty city in the clouds, feels aloof from its rural hinterland and the rest of Sicily. To Ovid, Enna was "where Nature decks herself in all her varied hues, where the ground is beauteous, carpeted with flowers of many tints" – a city in thrall to the cult of Demeter and the myth of Persephone. Enna is still strewn with narcissus in spring, but in winter is often shrouded in mist or blown by wintry gusts. Under the Greeks, Enna was prosperous and relatively independent. Under Roman rule, the old fertility goddesses were worshipped under the new names of Ceres and Proserpine. The vassal city became the breadbasket of Rome, despite several slave revolts. The Arabs also cultivated the region, planting cotton, cane and pistachio nuts, while the Normans focused on reinforcing the city's formidable castle. The Bourbon regime of "hangings and holidays" confirmed Enna's rebellious reputation.

Tradition has it that the cathedral (open daily 9am–1pm, 4–5pm) was begun by Eleanor of Aragon but a fire in 1446 swept away most treasures. Yet the cathedral is a fascinating romp through Enna's mystical past. The carved white pulpit is encrusted with cherubs and rests on a Graeco-Roman base removed from a temple to Demeter, as does the marble stoup nearby, and the wrought-iron sacristy gate once graced a Moorish harem in the Castello di Lombardia.

Along Via Roma are a string of dignified mansions and churches, such as the Catalan-Gothic Palazzo Pollicarini and the baroque Chiesa San Benedetto. Via Roma is pedestrianised for the evening *passeggiata* and contains a good *pasticceria* as well as some cosy restaurants. At the bottom are sweeping views from the belvedere and Torre di Federico II, a tumbledown octagonal tower linked by secret passageways to Castello di Lombardia (open daily 9am–1pm, 3–5pm free) on the hill at the far end of Via Roma. One of the largest medieval castles in Sicily, it began as a Byzantine stronghold, then acquired towers with each wave of invaders. Courtyards lead to the majestic eyrie of Torre Pisano, the tallest of six surviving towers, which commands views over the whole of Sicily.

## Imperial glory

Further south is **Piazza Armerina** and the nearby villa that is Sicily's great wonder of the Roman world. The **Roman Villa** ㉓ (Villa Imperiale; open daily 8.30am–6.30pm; entrance fee) lies 5 km (3 miles) southwest, at **Casale**, where the splendid mosaics triumph as "the last pagan achievement in Sicily executed under the old dispensation." The villa probably first belonged to Diocletian's co-Emperor Maximinian between AD 286 and 305. It was occupied during the Arab period but destroyed by King William in 1160. These fluid, impressionistic mosaics may have inspired the Normans in their designs for Palermo's Palazzo dei Normanni. Whether hunting lodge or country mansion, the villa disappeared under a landslide for 700 years. The vaulting may be lost and the frescoes faded, but the villa's magic lies in the 50 rooms covered in Roman-African mosaics. Their vitality, expressive power and wide-ranging content set them apart. All the scenes excluded from Christian art lie here. The villa highlights intimate pleasures such as child's play and youthful dancing, massage and love-making.

The Museo Archeologico (open daily 8am–6.30pm; entrance fee), set in a 17th-century monastery in the village of **Aidone** ㉔, 10 km (6 miles) north of Piazza Armerina, is an introduction to the site of Morgantina, perhaps the most "legible" site in antiquity. **Morgantina** ㉕ 5 km (3 miles) east (open daily 8am–6.30pm; entrance fee) occupies a rural paradise worthy of Persephone, its slopes covered in trees and framed by grey-blue hills. Its sanctuaries to the Chthonic gods show that the city's focal point was devotion to the cult of Demeter and Persephone. This is a reminder that mystical Enna marked the crossroads of Trinacria, ancient Sicily's three provinces. According to one historian, Enna is the hub of a giant geomantic chart, standing on ley lines which span the island.    ❑

Map on page 268

*In Piazza Armerina, Aidone, Sperlinga and Nicosia, the older inhabitants speak "gallo-italico", a Lombard dialect stemming from northern settlers. They may well be talking about emigration since half the adult population emigrated between 1950 and 1970.*

**BELOW:** Enna, the high point of Sicily.

# EASTERN SICILY

*Here is baroque Catania, chic and timeless Taormina,
the dramatic hinterland of Mount Etna and Siracusa,
the most civilised town on the island*

Map
on page
268

astern Sicily has coasts on three seas: the Tyrrhenian in the north, the Ionian in the east and the Mediterranean in the south. It is the main entry point to the island, and its historic sites at Taormina, Catania and Siracusa attract many visitors. This part of the island is also home to the fuming giant of Mt Etna and more than 20 percent of Sicilians live on the flanks of the volcano. As is the case with Vesuvius, farmers are drawn by the fertile soil, which is ideal for producing sun-drenched fruit, wine and aubergines. Likewise, wealthy city residents have constructed villas for the views, cool summer climate, and for winter skiing on the slopes.

Coastal Catania 26 faces away from the volcanic hinterland and its atavistic spirit and peasant culture. This is commercial Sicily, profiting from its entrepreneurial roots as a Greek trading colony founded by settlers from Naxos in 729 BC. It has budding resorts and exercises strict control over Mt Etna National Park. Yet despite its forward-looking air, the city remains in thrall to the powers of its patron saint, Sant'Agata, and to Mt Etna's whims. The 1669 eruption struck the city centre, while the 1693 earthquake killed two-thirds of the population. However, the subsequent rebuilding transformed the city with a series of trail-blazing baroque palaces, spacious streets and sinuous churches. Visually, Catania is the most homogeneous Sicilian city, stamped with the vision of Vaccarini, an architect influenced by grand Roman baroque. The colour of the volcanic stone seems oppressive at first, but the chiaroscuro effects accentuate the billowing balconies and sweeping S-curves.

**Piazza del Duomo**, the baroque centrepiece, is a dignified composition on a grand scale. In the centre is the city symbol, Fontana dell'Elefante, Vaccarini's fountain: an ancient black volcanic elephant surmounted by an Egyptian obelisk taken from the Roman circus. The cathedral was begun by Count Roger in 1092 but rebuilt after the earthquake. The interior conceals vaulted Roman baths; a Romanesque basilica lies under the nave; while Roman and Byzantine columns line the transepts. Via Crociferi, just west of the Duomo, is Catania's most characteristic street, with its succession of baroque churches and noble *palazzi*. Further north stands Chiesa San Giuliano, distinguished by its graceful loggia. The steep, student-infested Via Sangiuliano ends at San Nicolo ll'Arena, which resembles a grim religious factory rather than a church. As the largest in Sicily, this unfinished, desolate 16th-century work has an eerie, amputated look.

The grandiose **Via Etnea**, the main city thoroughfare, runs parallel to Via Crociferi and climaxes in a stunning view of Mt Etna. The sweeping street passes

*Fishing at Catania.*

the university, baroque churches and a Roman amphitheatre. The street is particularly popular during the evening *passeggiata*, when the locals parade past chic shops selling jewellery, shoes, fruit sorbets and nougat ice cream. Directly south of Via Etnea is Castello Ursino (Mon–Sat 9am–1pm; entrance fee) a well-restored Swabian castle and museum complex built on a steep bastion that commands a view of what was once the harbour.

The main **classical theatres** tend to be in dilapidated areas, where every second turning reveals the odd Roman column or *hypocaust*. Teatro Greco-Romano, off 266 Via Vittorio Emanuele (open daily 9am–1pm, 2.30–5pm; entrance fee), was built over a Greek theatre but retains its Roman underground passages. Next door is the semicircular Odeon, designed for oratory. The intimate site is still hemmed in by a medieval and baroque quarter. In Piazza Stesicoro, off Via Etnea, lies the Anfiteatro Romano (tel: 095-715 0508), the battered remains of the largest amphitheatre in Sicily, the place where St Agata supposedly met her doom and where earthquake ruins were dumped in 1693.

Just south of the Duomo, sandwiched between the cathedral quarter and the port, is **La Pescheria**, the popular morning fish market which makes a fitting farewell to the city. Glistening on slabs of marble lie sea bream and swordfish, mussels and sea urchins, squirming eels and lobsters.

## Cyclops Riviera

Heading north from Catania is a welcome release: sea breezes sweep away images of Catania's scruffy outskirts. The **Coast of Cyclops**, named after the Homeric myth, presents a spectacular seascape of jagged basalt rocks off **Aci Trezza**. Legend has it that these rocks were flung at the fleeing Odysseus by an

Map
on page
268

enraged, blinded Cyclops. In summer, the restaurants are full, and flotillas of fishing craft act as pleasure boats, but essentially these fishing villages remain simple places to sample catches of anchovies and sardines.

**Acireale** ㉗ stands aloof, both from the over-commercialised resorts and the rural hinterland. As Akis, the Greek settlement fared badly in the face of eruptions and earthquakes. However, thanks to the ravages of Etna and the talent of local craftsmen, Acireale is predominantly baroque; an untouristy town admired for its quality of life, sulphur spas and exuberant carnival. The tiny, dark alleys yield rewards in the form of pastry shops and ice-cream parlours. Acireale is credited with inventing sorbets, aided by a profitable monopoly on snow held by the local archbishop until modern times. Castorino, a café in Corso Savoia, is famed for its ice cream, pastries and *pasta reale*, decorated marzipan concoctions. **Santa Venera**, a spa to the south of town, exploits the healing properties of Etna's radioactive waters. Sulphurous lava mud baths have been used to treat rheumatism and skin conditions since Roman times.

## Routes around Etna

The circular journey around the volcano is a game of light and shade, with dark volcanic villages and Norman castles contrasted with the glistening citrus and olive groves, orchards and nut plantations. To appreciate Etna's grandeur, drive around the base or follow a similar route on the Circumetnea single-track railway from Catania or **Giarre-Riposto**, a strange trail which passes lush almond and hazel groves, interspersed with a black lava-stone moonscape.

**Castiglione di Sicilia**, 17 km (10 miles) north, is a stop on the scenic railway. Perched on a crag, this ancient bastion possesses Greek ramparts but is better

**BELOW:** Castiglione di Sicilia.

*Eruptions most commonly occur in Etna's side vents which, in turn, create smaller, secondary cones. The south-eastern crater has been responsible for most eruptions since 1997. A regular nightly spectacle of molten bombs shoots from its cones (see page 112).*

**BELOW:** climbing Etna's lava slopes.

known as a Norman fiefdom. **Francavilla di Sicilia**, just north, is set in a fertile valley of citrus plantations and prickly pears. Founded by King Roger, his ruined castle occupies a lone mound in the valley and once guarded the route to Randazzo. From here, a lovely foray leads to the **Gole dell'Alcantara**, a delightful gorge along the Francavilla–Taormina road.

Continue the anticlockwise drive around Etna to **Randazzo** ㉘, the most atmospheric medieval town on the northern slopes. First settled by Greeks fleeing from Naxos, Randazzo became a summer retreat from the heat of Messina. It remains a self-contained market town, with crenellated churches and medieval walls. For a town in the jaws of Etna, Randazzo has survived magnificently, despite the 1981 eruption which engulfed vineyards, roads and railway lines, leaving the lava flow visible today.

Between Randazzo and Bronte extends a wooded, volcanic landscape south to **Maletto**, noted for its wine and strawberries. Maletto marks the highest point on the Circumetnea line and offers views of recent lava flows. Around **Bronte**, the slopes are covered with small nut trees, a reminder that 80 percent of Italy's pistachio crop comes from these well-tended terraces. **Paternò** ㉙, halfway between Biancavilla and Catania, is famous for cultivating the juiciest oranges in Sicily. This baroque market town also has a fine Norman castle which was used as a Nazi observation post until it drew heavy Allied fire, resulting in the death of 4,000 people. The castle quarter is now the focus for concerts and feasts. East of Paternò is **Nicolosi** ㉚, a charmless ski resort that is the southern gateway to Etna's wine and walking country, offering bracing treks to extinct cones and prehistoric craters. Just east, along the road to **Trecastagni**, the lava beds of 1886 and 1910 are visible.

## ASCENDING ETNA

Circling the volcano is intriguing and safe but an ascent requires caution. The volcano has been in highly eruptive mode since 2001. Eruptions in 2002 destroyed the ski lifts, cable car and tourist office at the Rifugio Sapienza gateway to the volcano. This may rule out the southern approach but the alternatives include taking the northern route, via Linguaglossa, ideally accompanied by an official guide in a four-wheel drive. For advice on current conditions and routes, contact Etna Regional Park in Nicolosi (tel: 095-821111). To discuss options of getting close to Mount Etna, contact Etna Natural Touring (www.naturaltouring.it; tel: 095 64361). For a low-key option, skirt the volcano on the Circumetnea train (www.circumetnea.it; tel: 095-541111).

The sights will depend on volcanic activity and weather conditions, particularly the prevailing winds: it is vital to avoid the gases and volcanic matter emitted from active craters. Blue smoke indicates the presence of magma, while a halo of sulphurous vapour is a rare event. At most, you may see an active crater belching out sulphurous fumes or molten "bombs", or the bottom of the misty cone bubbling with incandescent lava. In periods of intense seismic activity, the volcano spits out molten rock or fireballs, a dramatic sight at night.

## Sicily's most dramatic resort

**Taormina** ③ is Sicily's most dramatic resort, a stirring place celebrated by poets from classical times onwards. Citrus groves carpet the slopes while the cliff face is a tangle of cacti and orchids. Below stretches a craggy coastline and the romantic islet of Isola Bella. The mood may be heightened by sightings of a smouldering volcano or snowcapped peak. May, September and October are the loveliest months in Taormina, with the city enjoying a semblance of solitude.

Taormina was an outpost of Naxos until the Greeks fled the first colony for Taoromenion in 403 BC. Under the Romans, the city acquired a garrison and the new name of Tauromenium, and later became the capital of Byzantine Sicily in the 9th century. Aristocratic leanings later drew Taormina into the Spanish camp, with the Catalan legacy reflected in Taormina's array of richly decorated *palazzi*. In Edwardian times, the terraced resort was a wintering place for frustrated northerners and gay exiles. Today, this haven appeals to romantic couples, sedate shoppers and the cultured middle classes. Yet despite designer glamour and the hordes of blasé cruise-liner passengers, the site's majesty is not manufactured. Nor is the heady decadence and timeless charm. Taormina may now have an internet café, but the locals prefer to pass the time of day chatting from an ancient balcony overlooking the sea. At night, Etna's fiery cone glitters before dissolving into the sea, stars and smoky peaks.

Taormina's *raison d'être* is the **Teatro Greco** (open daily 9am–7pm; winter until 4pm; entrance fee), a setting that is pure drama, hewn out of the hillside. In Greek theatres, sea and sky were the natural backdrop; the Romans preferred proscenium arches. Where the Greeks worshipped nature, the Romans tried to improve on it. The Hellenistic theatre was built under Hieron in the 3rd century

Map on page 268

*"Taormina is the dawn-coast of Europe."*

– D.H. LAWRENCE

**BELOW:** the Graeco-Roman amphitheatre in Taormina.

*Taormina Arte is a*
*season of drama,*
*cinema, ballet and*
*music put on every*
*July to September in*
*the Graeco-Roman*
*theatre. Tickets and*
*information from*
*the tourist office*
*(tel: 0942-23243;*
*www.taormina-*
*arte.com). Recent*
*events include Elton*
*John, opera and*
*Greek drama – not*
*all on the same night.*

**BELOW:** Taormina,
with snowcapped
Etna behind.

BC and enlarged by the Romans in AD 2. Like Tindari's Greek theatre, Taormina's was turned into an arena for gladiatorial combat. Piazza Emanuele lies beyond, a noisy market square built over the Roman forum. Bordering the piazza is a crenellated Catalan-Gothic palace, a medieval gate, and the charming church of Santa Caterina. **Corso Umberto**, the pedestrianised main street, is a feast for shopaholics. The 15th-century *palazzi* are converted into bars, craft shops and boutiques displaying candied fruit, marzipan animals and fresh kumquats, as well as majolica tiles, leather goods and traditional puppets. Just off the Corso lie the arched buttresses of the Naumachia, a hybrid construction which evolved into a Roman gymnasium. For lunch, the restaurant terraces of the adjoining Via Naumachia beckon, with Gambero Rosso (tel: 0942-24863) arguably the best.

Halfway down the Corso, **Piazza Aprile** offers glittering views of Etna and close-ups of preening poseurs at chic cafés. Further along, the baroque fountain on Piazza del Duomo marks the central meeting place. At sunset, or at the first sign of spring sun, kids fetch their footballs, the beautiful people pose, and the town's perma-tanned lounge lizards search for foreign prey. From Taormina, a winding road climbs to Castelmola, a quaint hamlet perched on a limestone peak. Below Taormina, sheer cliffs drop to the islet of **Isola Bella** while, from Via Pirandello, a cable car links the city to the pebbled beach at Mazzaro.

## The Ionian coast

Neighbouring **Giardini-Naxos** is Sicily's fastest-growing resort, and is regarded as a poor man's Taormina. It was founded on an ancient lava flow by Euboans in 735 BC and became a springboard for the colonisation of Catania and the east coast. The archaeological site and museum (open daily 9am–2pm, 3–7pm;

entrance fee) which occupy the promontory of Capo Schiso, reveal Greek lava-stone city walls but the site is still being excavated. **Mazzaro**, linked to Taormina by a cable car, is convenient for families. **Letojanni**, a humble fishing village until the 1960s, is now a bustling resort with riding and water sports.

From Taormina, the motorway hugs the shore north to Messina. Leave the coastal crowds at **Santa Teresa di Riva** for a slice of timeless Sicily, marked by scorched peaks and brooding ravines. Just inland is the battered mountain village of **Savoca** ㉜, best known for its "mummies". The catacombs of the Cappuccino Convento (open daily 9am–noon, 3–5pm; entrance free) contain 32 preserved corpses of monks dating from the 17th century. After this macabre scene, leave the monastery for the evocative medieval village whose roads were repaved with the proceeds of *The Godfather*, filmed on location here.

## City of swordfish

The road hugs the coast to **Messina** ㉝, the ferry port to Reggio on the mainland side of the Straits of Messina. A Phoenician colony settled by the Greeks, Messina thrived for centuries as a seafaring power but was devastated by the calamitous 1908 earthquake which killed 84,000 people in 30 seconds. The shore sank by half a metre and the reverberations were felt in Malta a day later. In 1943, Messina represented the Nazis' last stand, leading to the death of 5,000 people during Allied bombing. Such disasters have engendered a salvage mentality: every recoverable stone has been reused or recreated. Even so, the wide boulevards, grid system and matter-of-factness make Messina the most American-looking Sicilian city. The city's prosperity depends on better communications, although tourism is important, especially with the possible arrival

Map on page 268

**BELOW:** approaching Messina.

*In classical times
Messina was called
Zankle, after its
sickle-shaped
harbour. The name
also reputedly refers
to the sickle with
which Zeus castrated
his father.*

of a suspension bridge over the straits *(see page 75)*. Still, as a touring base, Taormina or a Tyrrhenian coastal resort is infinitely preferable.

The harbour welcomes grey Nato warships and long-prowed *feluccas* in pursuit of swordfish. These creatures, which weigh up to 300 kg (660 lb), are *the* local delicacy. Despite lively cafés and sweeping sea views, mercantile Messina only looks romantic at night, its lights glittering along the harbour front. The Duomo symbolises the stubbornness of the natives. This Norman cathedral has survived medieval fires, earthquakes and wartime American firebombing. The restored Renaissance fountain outside the cathedral is a masterpiece by a pupil of Michelangelo, overshadowed by an incongruous free-standing Flemish belfry. Although several other churches survived the earthquake, the artworks salvaged from the disaster are more significant, and are housed in the **Museo Regionale** (open daily 9am–1.30pm; tel: 090-361292) on Viale della Libertá. This museum is noted for works by two honorary citizens, Antonello da Messina, Southern Italy's greatest Renaissance artist, and Caravaggio, a city resident whose theatricality imbues Sicilian art.

## The Tyrrhenian Coast

This stretch of coast is devoted to popular summer tourism and swordfishing. As a result, the air is heavy with a peculiar combination of petrol fumes and grilled fish. From Messina, tunnels thread through pine and olive groves to **Milazzo** ㉞. The vision of this verdant peninsula is slightly marred by the presence of an oil refinery. Compensations lie in the welcoming breezes and dramatic castle, with views of the jagged green spit stretching towards the Aeolian Islands *(see page 313)*. This is the place to while away the time waiting for a ferry by sampling swordfish or *bottarga* (mullet roe).

**BELOW:** St Martino in Ortygia, Siracusa.

Following the SS113 westwards leads to **Oliveri** ㉟ and the chance to exchange churches for seafood and excellent beaches. Between here and Cefalù is one of the cleanest stretches of coastline on the island. Oliveri itself is a standard Sicilian resort with a Norman-Arab feudal castle and sandy beaches. On the seafront is a converted *tonnara*, the traditional tuna-processing plant, a reminder of life before tourism. Yet the tuna, aubergine and pasta dishes show that life still retains something of its original flavour. Oliveri is on the Golfo di Patti, its bays framed by the moody Nebrodi mountains.

Dominating the headland is **Tindari** ㊱, christened Tyndaris, one of the last Greek colonies in Sicily. The archaeological park (open daily 9am–one hour before sunset; entrance fee), overrun by goats, is pleasingly wild since Italian visitors are more impressed by the sacred Black Madonna housed in the sanctuary bordering the park. **Patti** ㊲ is a historic hill town ringed by new development. The medieval quarter by the cathedral has a quiet charm and several art-filled churches. Patti's greatest attraction is the Roman villa (open daily 9am–one hour before sunset; entrance fee) at Marina di Patti, a late-Imperial villa revealed in 1973. From Patti to **Capo d'Orlando** is a cluster of bland resorts fighting a battle against both coastal ribbon development and the Mafia and currently losing the former but winning the latter.

## Siracusa, a cultured province

South of Catania lies Siracusa, a supremely cultured province, with an ancient savoir-faire that Mafia money cannot mimic or buy. While not beyond Cosa Nostra's reptilian gaze, this southeastern corner of Sicily also has an elegance and grace unmatched by other provinces. The Greeks colonised the province two centuries after settling the rest of eastern Sicily. Since then, Siracusa has rested on its laurels, parading its Hellenistic heart and Levantine soul with the effortless superiority of a born aristocrat. Since short-sightedly destroying a sizeable stretch of coast in the 1950s in the rush for petrochemical riches, this lethargic province has finally come to its senses and started to restore the city of Siracusa, which until recently was declining into genteel decay. Ortygia, the historic heart of the city, may still be swathed in scaffolding for many years to come, but there is a new confidence in the air, and even a discreet new bridge, connecting the island with the modern city.

In its Hellenistic heyday, the classical city of **Siracusa** ③ was the supreme Mediterranean power and it has left us a medley of monuments from all eras. Cicero called it the loveliest city in the world, but Siracusa has also bequeathed us beauty with a baroque heart: the façades in the district of Ortygia are framed by wrought-iron balconies as free as billowing sails. The city was founded in 733 BC by Corinthian settlers who maintained links with Sparta. Although ruled by a succession of cruel but occasionally benevolent tyrants, Siracusa rose to become the supreme power of its age under Dionysius the Elder, who ruled from 405 BC. After the sun set on ancient Greece, Siracusa became a Roman province and was supposedly evangelised by St Peter and St Paul on their way to Rome. The city catacombs are the finest outside the capital.

Map on page 268

*Dionysius, ruler of the city of Siracusa (405–367 BC), personified Sicilian tyranny. His death is said to have been provoked by a heart attack brought on by delight at receiving a (politically expedient) prize for his poetry at the Olympic Games.*

**BELOW:** the Duomo, Siracusa.

*A breadbasket
in Siracusa, a
reminder that Sicily
was once the
breadbasket of
the ancient world.*

The two central areas are the archaeological park of Neapolis and Ortygia, the cultural island at the heart of the ancient city. **Neapolis Archaeological Park:** this ancient quarter is also synonymous with its sprawling park (open daily 9am–12.30pm, 3pm–two hours before dusk; entrance fee) containing rough-hewn quarries, grandiose theatres and tombs. A stroll to the Greek theatre passes the rubble of Hieron II's Altar, built in honour of Zeus. Surrounded by trees, the vast Teatro Greco seats 15,000, and is praised as the masterpiece of ancient Greece. The theatrical tradition survives: dramas by Sophocles and Euripides are still played on the stage once viewed by Plato and Archimedes.

Although partially closed, Via dei Sepolcri, the path of tombs, offers glimpses of tombs and carved niches. Further uphill lie the Grotticelli Necropolis, a warren of Hellenistic and Byzantine tombs, including the supposed Tomb of Archimedes *(see page 24)*. The best catacombs lie nearby, with the entrance opposite the tourist office on Via Sebastiano. The **San Giovanni Catacombs** (open summer 9am–6pm; entrance fee) provide entry to the persecuted world of the early Christians. A reluctant friar shows visitors early Christian sarcophagi, an early drawing of St Peter and a mosaic depicting Original Sin. In the wild garden outside is the shell of San Giovanni Evangelista, Siracusa's first cathedral, dedicated to St Marcian, the city's earliest bishop.

Probably the finest archaeological collection in Sicily lies in the **Museo Archeologico** (open Tues–Sun 9am–1pm; but call 0931-464022; entrance fee) on neighbouring Viale Teocrito, built over a quarry and pagan necropolis. It is divided into prehistoric, classical and regional sections.

A stroll across Ponte Nuovo leads past prettily moored boats and pastel-coloured Venetian *palazzi* to the Darsena, the inner docks, with the atmospheric

**BELOW:** trattoria
in Ortygia.

Ortygia on the far side. This seductive island was dedicated to the huntress Artemis. Via Cappodieci is home to **Palazzo Bellomo** (open daily 9am–1pm; entrance fee) a lovely Catalan-Gothic mansion and the city's compact art gallery. Inside awaits Caravaggio's masterpiece, *The Burial of St Lucy*, and Antonello da Messina's *Annunciation*. From here, a flight of steps leads to the cathedral (open daily 8am–noon, 4–7pm; entrance fee), a temple to Athena masquerading as a Christian church. Ortygia has cosy bars and pubs, *pizzerie* and *birrerie* (beer halls). The evening's summer parade of fashion victims is centred on the western shore, especially the strip between Porta Marina and Fontana Aretusa, a pool which signals the start of bracing sea walks.

## Siracusa's mythical environs

In ancient **Epipolae**, 8 km (5 miles) northwest of Siracusa, you will find **Castello Eurialo** ➌➒ (open daily 9am–one hour before dusk; follow signs to Belvedere). The fort represented the fifth component of the Greek pentapolis and was the most magnificent of Greek military outposts. Inland from Siracusa, the countryside is rocky and parched, Sicily with its roots laid bare.

The rocky tableland is home to **Necropoli di Pantalica** ➍➊. This foremost prehistoric site is best reached via Sortino, following signs for Pantalica Sud. The drive skirts the bleached white Iblean hills before reaching the Anapo Valley and Necropoli di Pantalica (open daily 9am–sunset; entrance fee), set in lush gorges, studded with citrus trees and wild flowers, acanthus and prickly pears. The Anapo river has carved a path through the cliffs and is invitingly cool for swimmers. As the largest Bronze- and Iron-Age cemetery in Sicily, the necropolis has more than 5,000 tombs carved into the cliffs of a limestone plateau.

Map on page 268

TIP

Siracusa has several delightful hotels in the Ortygia district. Even if not staying there, enjoy a heady lunch or romantic dinner on the roof terraces at either of the best stylish waterside hotels, Hotel Des Etrangers (tel: 0931-62671) or the Art Nouveau Grand Hotel (tel: 0931-464600).

**BELOW:**
ice cream in the sun, Siracusa.

**TIP**

In summer, Noto is abandoned by its residents for the undistinguished seaside resorts of Noto Marina or Lido di Avola. This lessens the queues at the chic Mandolfiore *pasticceria* and *gelateria* in Piazza del Carmine.

**BELOW:** San Carlo Borromeo, Noto.

## South from Siracusa

The journey south provides a fair introduction to gentle farming country, with lemon, olive and almond groves giving way to more rugged views of limestone escarpments and rocky gorges. The SS115 leads to **Noto** ④, the finest baroque town in Sicily, both blatantly theatrical and deeply rational. Visitors praise its proportion, symmetry, spaciousness and innate sense of spectacle. Sicilians simply call it "a garden of stone". Yet much is crumbling in the garden and most museums and interiors are closed for eternal "restoration".

Luckily, on this open-air stage, Noto's chief pleasures are on permanent display, charmingly illuminated by antique streetlamps. After Noto Antica was destroyed in the 1693 earthquake, Giuseppe Lanza, a Sicilian-Spanish architect, was entrusted with the urban design. Noto was composed around three parallel axes running horizontally across the hillside. To create interest, he conceived three squares, each enlivened by a scenic church as a backdrop. The design was clothed in warm, golden limestone and used monumental flights of steps to enchant with tricks of perspective. The realisation of this ambitious plan was the work of Gagliardi and Sinatra, both of whom were gifted local architects who also worked in Ragusa province.

On the lower slopes, three scenic squares unfold in a succession of theatrical perspectives sculpted in burnished stone. The lower part of town was designed as the civic and religious centre, whereas the upper town was laid out as a cramped *quartiere popolare*. Paradoxically, the higher the level, the lower the class of the residents. Even so, the two-tiered city looks entirely homogeneous. The Corso sweeps towards Piazza Municipio, Noto's stage set, with the golden grace of the buildings matched by the majestic proportions of the design.

Southeast of Noto lies **Eloro** ㊷, a classical site on the unpolluted coastline that stretches south to Capo Passero. Now in ruins, the Siracusan city of Elorus (open daily 9am–one hour before sunset) was founded at the end of the 6th century BC. Beside this wild site are rocky and sandy beaches which tend to be deserted, but the most appealing beaches await in **Vendicari** ㊸, 6 km (4 miles) south, past citrus and almond groves. As an established nature reserve, the **Vendicari wetlands** are salt marshes popular with nesting and migrating birds, from flamingoes and falcons to herons and storks. Further down the coast lies Marzamemi, an appealing fishing village and low-key resort, noted for its tasty seafood. In summer, Sicilians from Catania and Siracusa flock south to **Pachino** and the sandy beaches around Capo Passero.

From here, it is a short drive west to the Ispica canyon. **Cava d'Ispica** ㊹ (open daily 8am–one hour before dusk) is a 11-km (7-mile) limestone gorge whose ghostly galleries have been inhabited almost continuously since prehistoric times.

## Ragusa province

**Ragusa** ㊺ is the capital of the self-confident agricultural province southwest of Siracusa. It thrives on wine-growing, cattle-breeding and cheese-making, as well as hot-house flowers and genetically modified tomatoes. The town of Ragusa, like Modena and Scicli, is part of a cave-dwelling civilisation. Its mines, both underground and opencast, have produced asphalt that has paved the streets of Berlin, Paris, London and Glasgow. However, Ragusa is a hidden treasure in its own right, rivalled only by Siracusa as the capital of serendipity. Like Ortygia, the partly pedestrianised enclave of **Ragusa Ibla** is the place for aimless wandering, leisurely lunches, and sleepy ruminations amidst a crumbling cityscape.

After the 1693 earthquake reduced medieval Ragusa to rubble, the merchants and landed gentry responded by building Ragusa Alta, the new city on the hill. But the aristocracy refused to desert their charred homes so recreated Ragusa Bassa (Ibla) on the original valley site. In the rivalry between the two centres, Ibla is finally beginning to triumph, with cultural life returning to the historic centre. As a baroque city recreated on a medieval street plan, an old-world intimacy prevails. Gentrification and restoration have reversed the neglect of Ibla in recent years. A number of bars have taken over historic palaces, with tasteful bohemian conversions coexisting with the clubby, patrician side of town. In the evening, in particular, all feudal posturing is banished in favour of food and flirtation.

Santa Maria delle Scale, framed by parched hills, represents the gateway to Ibla. This Gothic church is a balcony over Old Ragusa; 250 steps zigzag down to Ibla, offering a commanding view over isolated farms and the blue-tinged cupola of the cathedral below. The covered passageways, golden mansions and crumbling church make a quaint chiaroscuro introduction to Ibla, part of a picturesque route winding down to the cathedral. After the cosy claustrophobia so far, the spacious Piazza Duomo below comes as a shock. The sloping square is lined with palm trees, baroque mansions and aristocratic clubs but dominated by Gagliardi's San Giorgio, a masterpiece of Sicilian baroque. Giardino Ibleo, an appealing, recently landscaped park, is set on a spur at the eastern end of Ibla. Around the grounds are three ruined churches, victims of the 1693 earthquake: the majolica dome of San Domenico overlooks Gothic San Giacomo, built over a pagan temple, and Chiesa dei Cappuccini, a baroque monastic church.

## Ragusa's coast

An intriguing drive past greenhouses of ripening tomatoes leads to two archaeological sites on the coast. Classical **Camarina**  **46** was founded in 598 BC, a sophisticated piece of urban planning covering three hills at the mouth of the Ippari river. The city of perfect parallel lines was destroyed by the Romans in AD 258. The Antiquarium (open 9am–2pm, 3–7pm; tel: 0932-826004) marks the centre of the site, with an array of city walls, a tower, tombstones and the ruins of Hellenistic villas nearby.

At Punta Secca, the headland just southeast of Camarina, the Roman port of **Kaukana** **47** is slowly being excavated. The port, partly preserved by sand, is a lovely but inscrutable puzzle compounded by the discovery of Hellenistic amphora, Roman coins and Jewish candelabra. Leave the shady umbrella pines for a picnic on the sandy beaches below the headland, or try a fish lunch at the modern resort of Marina di Ragusa, a bustling summer resort. Discreet well-being is indeed the keynote to this relaxed region. ❑

**Map on page 268**

**TIP**

Ragusa province has some of Sicily's best beaches, which are generally free but lack facilities. They range from rocky Cava d'Aliga, to sandy Donnalucata, and the romantic fishing village of Sampieri, while some of the finest shores lie between Camarina and Marina di Ragusa.

**BELOW:** a place to wander, Ragusa Ibla.

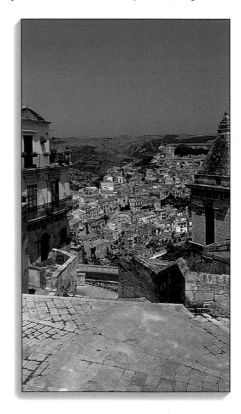

# "LA MATTANZA", A DYING TRADITION

*The ritualistic annual tuna hunt dates from the 9th century but in the wake of commercial fishing it now struggles to survive*

Tuna fishing, along with swordfishing, is rooted in the Sicilian psyche. Nowhere is this more so than in the Egadi island of Favignana, off the west coast of Sicily. It is considered the sea's ultimate challenge to man, as well as the island's traditional livelihood. The warm-blooded, fast-swimming northern bluefin tuna hunt off the coast of Norway but spawn in Sicily's warm spring waters when they reach maturity at 5–8 years of age. Here they are captured in a system of chambered nets introduced by the Arabs in the 9th century. The season lasts May to June and in the past one day could determine the island's fortune for the rest of the year. But numbers are now negligible and the tradition and tourist spectacle struggle to survive. There were once more than 50 coastal tuna traps in Sicily alone. Within the space of one bluefin's lifetime all this has changed. After 40 years of factory-ships, long-line fishing, drift nets, purse seines and sonar, the bluefin tuna, and so La Mattanza along with them, face extinction. In 2003, for the first time in living memory, the nets at Favignana were empty – neither the bluefin nor the swordfish came.

## THE MADONNA GOES TOO

Buoys mark out a 100-metre (330-feet) rectangle on the sea; up to 10 km (6 miles) of nets are suspended between the floats. The helmsman leads the fleet in prayers, aided by an image of the Madonna. The 60-strong crew sings and chants the *cialoma* in guttural Arabic accents. Entreaties are uttered by the *rais*, a Moorish title given to the chief fisherman, who travels in a separate boat and constantly checks the entrance to the *camera della morte*. The eight black boats encircle the nets. As the net is drawn in to the length of a football pitch, the fish circle frantically in the *sarabanda della morte*, the dance of death. The chanting stops and the slaughter begins.

◁ **INVOKING ALLAH**
To the command of *"tira, tira!"* the net is pulled tight. The fishermen's sea shanty chorus of *"aiamola, aiamola"* is derived from *Allah! Che muoia!* (Allah, may it die!).

△ **FATAL ATTACK**
Some tuna are man-sized and their razor-sharp tail fins can kill. Others, however, can die of heart attacks or over-oxygenation.

## A FEW WORDS ON SWORDFISH

Swordfish is the local delicacy par excellence, with prized catches weighing up to 300 kg (660 lbs). Compared with the decimated tuna stocks, this huge fish has fared a little better, with the richest fishing grounds traditionally being off the shores of Sicily, close to the coast of Messina and the island of Pantelleria. Swordfish are pursued in tiny, black, fish-shaped boats, but given the profitability of swordfishing, fast fleets of *feluccas* have gained ground. These 30-ton monsters are equipped with a lookout post and a platform on the prow for the harpoonist. Once the prey is sighted, a blessing is shouted to St Mark and the harpoon gun fired. If the victim is female, the grief-stricken male often thrashes around in sympathy and charges the boat. This final gesture of love leads to the capture of the male in what Sicilians see as "a sublime and mysterious synthesis of love and death." Fatalism, if not forgotten, is double-edged: the unchecked desire for fish looks set to kill off fishing itself.

◁ **THE FINAL CHAMBER**
When the *rais* decides that the currents are right, the shoal is steered through miles of nets into the *camera del morte*, the central "chamber of death". After the slaughter the roiling waters of the chamber are an empty square of bloody pink foam, soon to be carried away by the currents.

△ **GRUELLING WORK**
The fish are stabbed and caught behind the gills with gaff hooks on long poles. A proverb says: "Tuna fishing shortens your arms and silences your tongue."

# SICILY'S ISLANDS

*The Egadi and Aeolian archipelagos represent the main attractions, but divers will be drawn to Ustica and nature lovers to the remote African outposts of Pantelleria and the Pelagie islands*

Map on page 268

The new millennium was welcomed with the brief resurfacing of a long-vanished piece of the British Empire off the coast of Sicily. Graham Island, a submerged volcano first recorded in 10 BC, had not been seen since 1832, but reappeared, amid sulphurous emanations, off the western coast of Sicily. This phantom island, also claimed by Italy and France, last featured in an international dispute in 1987, when a US warplane mistook the tip of the island for a Libyan submarine and dropped depth charges on it. Fortunately, Sicily's remaining "real" islands contain enough explosive drama for such phantoms to pale into insignificance.

Posers can preen on yachts off Panarea, divers can explore underwater wrecks off Ustica, while nature lovers and ramblers can seek out lush Marettimo or barren Lampedusa – Sicily's wild west. On the Moorish islands of Pantelleria and the Pelagie, the kasbah and the curious white-domed *dammusi* houses evoke a distinct sense of North Africa. Pantelleria, a remote lump of volcanic rock, represents a Tunisian outpost far closer to Africa than mainland Italy; even the excellent wine has an exotic flavour. For adventure lovers, the Aeolian Islands are the most dramatic in Sicily, shaped by volcanic eruption and wind erosion. The island of Stromboli, in particular, is a byword for wonderful pyrotechnics.

A four-hour hydrofoil crossing links Naples and Palermo, or Naples and the Aeolian Islands, with far longer ferry crossings also on offer. Palermo, Milazzo, Trapani and Porto Empedocle are the gateways to island life. Within each archipelago, there are good summer connections but island-hopping between archipelagos is difficult. Some islands accept cars, but transport is generally by boat, bicycle or three-wheeled vehicles, able to navigate the tiny alleys.

## Aeolian Islands

The **Aeolian Islands** ㊽, known as the **Isole Eolie** in Italian, form a dazzling archipelago of seven volcanic islands, and represent one of Sicily's most compelling attractions. Named after Aeolus, the god of the winds, these elemental islands still exude an other-worldly air and a sense of isolation, despite their growing popularity. The islands also represent an assault on the senses, from sweet-smelling herbs and acrid sulphurous emissions to mustard-tinted radioactive waters and shores buffeted by the choppiest seas in the Tyrrhenian.

**Lípari** is the largest, best-equipped island and the usual gateway to the archipelago, while **Panarea** is the prettiest, **Salina** the homeliest, and **Filicudi** and **Alicudi** the least developed. For drama, it is difficult to compete with the volcanic activity on **Stromboli**'s seething crater. Other natural wonders include hot

**LEFT:** trip around the Aeolian Islands.
**BELOW:** Lípari shopkeepers.

*Hydrofoils bring the islands closer to the Messina coast, but bear in mind that the islands can be lashed by storms between October and March.*

springs on Lípari and Panarea, with fumeroles (holes emitting volcanic gases) bubbling underwater on **Vulcano** and Stromboli. Apart from pyrotechnics, the archipelago promises sapphire-coloured seas and a dramatic coastline, as well as distinctive honey-coloured wine and food flavoured with capers and olives. Arrival is by hydrofoil or ferry from Naples, Palermo, Cefalù, Messina or Milazzo, with the fastest services from Milazzo *(see Travel Tips, page 329)*.

**Lípari** Ⓐ, the main island in the archipelago, has a dormant volcano but a bustling holiday mood, at one with the local hot springs and fumeroles. **Lípari town** Ⓑ has an appealing port and alleys lined with chic boutiques and open-air cafés. The upper town is a fortified **citadel** perched on lava rock. Centred on the **Castello**, the Spanish-style bastions incorporate urban traces from medieval and Greek eras. The citadel is also home to a heavily remodelled Norman cathedral and the neighbouring **Museo Eoliano** (open daily 9am–1pm, 3–6pm; entrance fee), containing one of the finest Neolithic collections in Europe. **Canneto**, north of the capital, has a sandy beach and lively bars but is better known as the hollowed-out heart of the pumice-mining industry. Campobianco's quarries are the world's best source of pumice. Glossy black obsidian, once used to fashion tools and knives intended for human sacrifice, is also found here.

**Vulcano** Ⓒ, the mythical home of Vulcan, the Roman god of fire, lies just south of Lípari and is the closest island to the Italian mainland. This volcanic outpost rivals Panarea as the most exclusive and expensive island, and has a lively nightlife, luxurious villas, a fine beach, and the drama of the volcano itself. The main crater last erupted in 1890, but there is plenty of secondary activity. It is enough to dock at the small port to be overwhelmed by sulphurous odours and steaming fumaroles. Close to **Porto di Levante**, the only landing place, are the radioactive mud baths known as *fanghi*, essentially a slimy pool of sulphurous mud favoured by wallowing fitness freaks and sufferers from arthritis or rheumatism. The surreal experience is sealed by a dip in the bubbling, occasionally scalding, sea. The **Gran Cratere**, just south, marks the start of the arduous but rewarding ascent of the eerie main crater, best attempted early in the morning or late in the afternoon. The less intrepid can climb Vulcanello, a smaller crater on the northeastern end of the island.

**BELOW:** Lípari town.

**Salina** Ⓓ, the second largest island on the archipelago, lies north of Lípari. This lush island, named after an ancient salt mine, has a plentiful water supply and was the evocative setting for the 1994 movie *Il Postino*. Quieter than Lípari and Vulcano, this welcoming island has a family-oriented feel. **Santa Marina di Salina**, the main port, is pleasant but **Malfa**, in the north, is more picturesque, with a harbour and pebble beach.

**Panarea** Ⓔ, the island north of Lípari, has an elitist reputation, like a miniature Portofino or Sicilian St Tropez. Since the 1960s, when it was discovered by wealthy northerners, this amber-coloured jewel has been a retreat with a *dolce far niente* reputation. While the fashionable yachting fraternity explores the islets and coves by boat, lesser mortals can enjoy the romantic walks, sophisticated nightlife, and the bronze-hued beaches. Tortuous cliffside paths lead past flower-bedecked Moorish-style villas owned by Milanese industrialists to a wilder landscape of rosemary, olives or capers. A stroll from **Punta Milazzese**, a basalt-walled promontory inhabited in prehistoric times, leads to the charming cove of **Cala Junco**, a popular place for snorkelling. Another highlight is the dramatic cliffs, beach, fumeroles and small geysers at **Calcara**.

## The lighthouse of the Mediterranean

**Stromboli ❻**, the easternmost Aeolean island, is black by day but spectacular fireballs and showers of volcanic debris make it incandescently red by night. The ancients called it "the lighthouse of the Mediterranean" and the presence of an active volcano ensures that it remains the most celebrated island. Stromboli further beguiles visitors with whitewashed houses swathed in bougainvillea, and vistas over palm trees, olive and lemon groves. It also has the best nightlife in the archipelago, and pays the price in terms of overpopularity. But boat trips around the craggy coast reveal secluded coves and creeks, as well as black sandy beaches and deep waters for divers.

An excursion to the crater is the high point of most visits. The ascent of the volcano is best at night, and always accompanied by a guide, with three hours allowed for the ascent and two for the descent. **Strombolicchio**, off the north coast, and surrounded by swirling currents, makes an atmospheric boat trip. From afar, this petrified basalt rock looks like a Gothic cathedral or formidable castle. A steep rock staircase rises to a terrace with sheer slopes to the sea.

**Filicudi ❼**, midway between Salina and Alicudi, was named after the prodigious ferns that covered the slopes in classical times, but more common today are the dark-green capers, vineyards and olive groves. The unattractive port is

*In 2003 Stromboli erupted, destroying part of the mountain and unleashing a devastating tidal wave which led to the temporary evacuation of the island and prompted plans for a new system of early-warning buoys to allay local fears.*

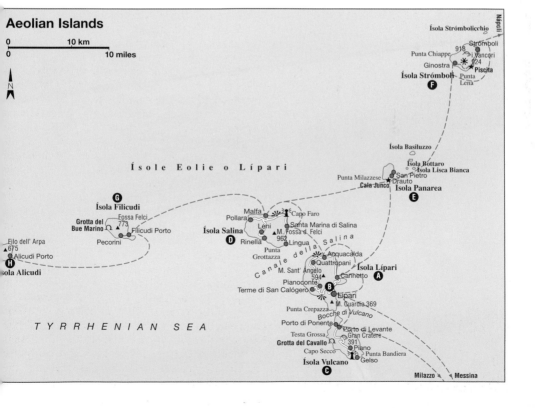

### Aeolian Islands

TYRRHENIAN SEA

not representative of this undeveloped rural island, dotted with flowering cacti and riddled with mule tracks. The most appealing boat trip is to **Grotta del Bue Marino**, a damp cave that was once inhabited by a colony of seals. **Alicudi ⓗ**, Filicudi's sister island, is the most westerly in the archipelago, and remains more interested in catching lobsters than in luring hordes of tourists.

*Sun hats on the upper deck.*

## Ustica

Lying off the north coast, 60 km (40 miles) from Palermo, **Ustica ㊾** is by common consent a diver's paradise. The island is connected by hydrofoil and ferry with both Palermo and Naples, and can be visited on a day trip. This volcanic, turtle-shaped island has tolerated Phoenicians, Saracen pirates and a penal colony, but has flourished as a well-managed marine reserve and resort since the 1960s. Ustica's waters reveal an explosion of colour, from corals, sea sponges and anemones to barracudas, bream, scorpion fish and groupers.

The rugged coastline is riddled with caverns and coves, partly accessible along coastal paths. Landlubbers can visit the fort, lighthouse and aquarium, as well as a marine study centre in a watchtower.

## Egadi Islands

**BELOW:** Favignana, Egadi Islands.

The Egadi Islands ㊿, a small archipelago off the western coast of Sicily, lie in multicoloured waters teeming with marine life. From the docks of Trapani *(see page 283)*, point of departure for the frequent ferries and hydrofoils, the islands resemble dark humps floating on the not-too-distant horizon. Close-up, however, contrasts emerge: **Lévanzo** is rugged and friendly; **Favignana** the liveliest, most developed and family-oriented; while **Maréttimo**, furthest from the main-

land, is the loveliest. As the easiest offshore islands to visit, the Egadi cannot avoid the summer crowds; however, these are focused on tourist-oriented Favignana, leaving Lévanzo and Maréttimo as relatively undiscovered places for boat trips and gentle hiking.

The Egadi have 15,000 years of history and the finest prehistoric cave drawings in Italy. They were once a land bridge linking Africa to mainland Italy and became the springboard for the Arab conquest of Sicily. Arab culture is evident, from the guttural local accent to the cube-shaped architecture. In 1874, the islands were bought by the Florio family, one of Sicily's most famous dynasties of entrepreneurs, who developed the tuna industry.

**Favignana ⑤**, the largest and most populous island, is shaped like a lopsided butterfly and presents itself as the land of tuna, tufa and tourism. Quarrying has made the island a homage to stone; slopes are dotted with tufa houses, and material from the maze-like Cala Rossa built entire Moorish cities. Figs and tomatoes are planted on the floor of abandoned quarries, and sheer stone walls, overgrown with thyme and capers, shelter orange and lemon trees from the sweeping sea winds. The chiselled walls and eroded geometry of seaside quarries such as Cala Rossa and Cavallo make them popular picnic and swimming spots.

The still waters of the harbour reflect the tiled roofs and stone smokestacks of the Tonnara, a tuna fishery converted into a handsome monument to industrial archaeology and soon to be a museum of the sea. On the peak of the island's one hill looms the Arab-Norman **Forte Santa Caterina**, a political prison in Bourbon times and now a forbidden military zone. **Forte San Giacomo**, a Norman castle and Bourbon prison, is a maximum-security prison for Sicily's *mafiosi*.

Maps on pages 268 & 315

**TIP**

Hikers should remember to carry plenty of water, particularly on Maréttimo. On these parched islands, water is more precious than wine.

**BELOW:** Lévanzo.

**Lévanzo** , facing Favignana, is a simpler proposition than the main island, with the tiny port of **Cala Dogana** the sole centre of civilisation. From here, a track passes farmhouses and sheep pens before zigzagging down to the coast. The stony slopes are covered with *macchia mediterranea*: arid, grey-green scrub that blooms in late spring. The Grotta del Genovese, a deep cavern overhanging the rocky shoreline, is the main reason for visiting Lévanzo. One can reach the grotto by boat, and sail and swim from a craft hired at Cala Dogana (or book with the custodian of the caves; tel: 0923-924032). The grotto walls hold Lévanzo's greatest treasure, Mesolithic rock carvings.

**Maréttimo** , the most mysterious, mountainous and greenest of the Egadi, lies to the west, separated from her sister islands by a stretch of sea rich in sunken archaeological treasure. To Sicilian scholars, Maréttimo is a mythical island, nothing less than Odysseus's Ithaca. The little port has no hotel but the fishermen of Maréttimo happily accept guests in their homes.

*Dammusi, the traditional cuboid Arab houses with domed roofs, date back to designs created in Neolithic times by Tunisian settlers to the archipelago. They are designed to keep the interior cool.*

## Pantelleria

Lying off the southwestern coast of Sicily, **Pantelleria**  is closer to Tunisia than to Sicily, and is reached on a five-hour ferry crossing from Trapani, or on a flight from Palermo. Pantelleria's evocative name probably derives from the Arabic "daughter of the winds" after the breezes that buffet this rocky outpost, even in an African August. The landscape is rather bleak, with jagged rocks and coves instead of beaches. Cool, low-domed Moorish *dammusi* houses are surrounded by terraces of capers and grapes; vines are trained low to protect them from being battered by the hot southern winds or cold northern winds.

The volcanic origins of Sicily's biggest island are visible in lava stone, basalt rock, hot springs, and a landscape pitted with "cuddie", small, extinct volcanic craters. A startling scene awaits at **Lago di Venere**: set inside a former crater, the small lake is full of warm, bubbling, sulphurously brown waters, imbued with myriad cures. Steam baths can also be taken in the island grottoes. A rewarding hike from Pantelleria town in the north to the port of **Scauri** allows sightings of traditional *dammusi* houses, terraced vineyards, small settlements and the blackened, lava stone landscape. Dry stone walls enclose orange groves and capers, and are often overlooked by hardy donkeys. Although modern and rather scruffy, Pantelleria town has a lively air as well as an exoticism encapsulated by white-cubed houses and restaurants serving fish couscous. The volcanic soil favours vine-growing, and the island produces prized fortified wines. A museum is being created in the town's castle to house remarkable Hellenistic busts, including one of Julius Caesar, discovered in a cistern in 2003.

**BELOW:** cactus on Pantelleria.

## Pelagie Islands

The **Pelagie Islands**  are a scorching archipelago of three islands lying amid strong currents off the coast of Africa, closer to Tunisia than the Sicilian mainland. Although there are pockets of agriculture, the islands are unnaturally barren due to wanton deforestation and the virtual disappearance of the native olive groves and juniper and carob plantations. Fifty years

Map on page 268

ago, much of this lunar landscape was farmland bounded by dry-stone walls, but today the local economy rests on sponge fishing and canning, supplemented by tourism in Lampedusa. However, the islanders have belatedly realised the error of their unecological ways and started small-scale reafforestation programmes on Lampedusa. In terms of cultural heritage, there are no outstanding sites but the waters are translucent, and rich in marine life, while the rugged native character and cuisine are distinctly Tunisian.

Highlights of a stay include *dammusi* houses, couscous and fish, coastal walks and, except for high summer in Lampedusa, peace and quiet. A curious summer feature is the virtually continuous breezes and chilly nights. These unspoilt islands are reached by ferry from Porto Empedocle near Agrigento (an 8-hour crossing), but direct flights to Lampedusa also operate from Palermo.

**Linosa** ❺❻, the island closest to the shore, can be reached on a day trip from Lampedusa, and represents the tip of a vast submerged volcano. The three visible volcanic cones may now be extinct but the beaches, still strewn with black boulders, can coat the unwary in ash and grit. Even so, in this cauldron of an island, most visitors congregate on the lavic beaches or quickly develop an interest in scuba-diving. On this lump of volcanic rock, there is little to do except rest, roast, swim, trek along dusty paths through vineyards or spot *dammusi*, pastel-coloured cubes with white window frames.

**Lampedusa** ❺❼ is known as "a gift from Africa to Europe", or, due to its recent popularity with illegal immigrants, "the backdoor to Italy". The island was first settled by the Phoenicians and Greeks but was later owned by the Princes of Lampedusa. Weather-beaten Tunisian fishermen live on the south coast, the only inhabited centre. Lampedusa's recent claim to fame is as an American radar base for bombing Libya in 1986 and as an arrival point for boatloads of illegal immigrants (and the occasional drug-runner) who land on remote beaches. In 2003 over 200 illegal immigrants from North Africa died just off the coast of Lampedusa. The island remains Italy's weakest link in terms of security. Sponge fishing represents the mainstay of the island's economy, with a local cannery used to process a wide range of Mediterranean fish. The wonderful marine life is similar to that off the North African coast, with the waters home to shoals of dolphins, monk seals and, in March, the sperm whale migration. Parrot fish and seals abound in the limpid waters, while turtles lay their eggs on **Isola dei Conigli**, an offshore nature reserve named after its rabbit colony.

Lampedusa port has a rabbit warren of a *kasbah* which reeks of spices, sardines, anchovies and goats. Indeed, the port is the best place for sampling such dishes as pasta with sardines, sweet and sour rabbit, or Sicilian candied fruit and spicy desserts. Buses from the port are infrequent and, despite the rocky roads, bicycles and mopeds are a popular way of exploring the interior. A boat trip is the best way of appreciating Lampedusa's secluded grottoes, craggy inlets and sheer limestone cliffs. Lampione, an uninhabited reef, is scorched dry due to man's negligence. Its drama lies underwater: the translucent sea is clean and rich in marine life, from sponge beds to hungry sharks: Sicilian pleasures are notoriously double-edged. ❑

*Despite, or because of, its isolation, Pantelleria is popular with privacy-seeking celebrities from Madonna to Giorgio Armani, who has a villa on the island.*

**BELOW:** Lago di Venere, Pantelleria.

# ✵® INSIGHT GUIDES
# TRAVEL TIPS

# CONTENTS

# Getting Acquainted

**Area:** Italy: 301,308 sq km/ 116,335 sq miles
**Capital:** Rome
**Population:** Italy 58 million; Naples 1,400,000; Bari 353,000; Catania 333,000; Palermo 700,000; Reggio Calabria 180,000
**Language:** Italian
**Religion:** Roman Catholic
**Time Zone:** Central European Time (GMT plus 1 hour; EST plus 6 hours)
**Currency:** The euro (€).
**Weights and Measures:** Metric
**Electricity:** 220 volts. Take an adaptor to operate British three-pin appliances and a transformer to use 100–120-volt appliances
**International Dialling Code:** 39

## Geography

While Southern Italy may appear to be simply the lower portion of the famous boot (and Sicily the triangular-shaped football it is about to kick), the geography of this portion of the peninsula consists of a series of mountain

## Climate

Southern Italy's typically Mediterranean climate leaves it dependably sunnier than Northern Italy. July and August can be unpleasantly hot and humid in all but coastal areas and the mountainous and forested portions of the interior. As with the rest of Italy, late spring and early autumn are the best times to visit, with the weather at its mildest and the crowds at their nadir.

ranges (the southern portion of the Appenines, the Pollino mountains that cover much of Calabria) and the volcanic terrain of Campania and the plains of Puglia. Well-known volcanoes form the landscapes of Naples (Vesuvius), eastern Sicily (Etna), and the entire island of Stromboli.

## Government

Italy's president is elected for a term of seven years by Parliament, which is composed of two houses: the Senate (with 315 members) and the Chamber of Deputies (630 members). The president (currently Giorgio Napolitano, elected in 2006) nominates the prime minister and, on the latter's recommendations, the Cabinet.

After a period of constitutional corruption in the early 1990s, Italy moved from proportional representation towards a "first-past-the-post" system, under which the country elected its first left-wing government, a loose centre-left coalition, in 1996. In 2001 the election was won by Silvio Berlusconi's right-wing Forza Italia coalition, but in 2006 Romano Prodi's centre-left axis took power. As in the US, elected mayors wield considerable power.

The politics of Southern Italy is marked by its historic contrast with the North: it is less developed economically and stigmatised by high unemployment and corruption.

The regions tend to have strong political affiliations, and special autonomous status has been granted to five of them, including Sicily, which has its own parliament and institutions that are organised separately from the Italian state.

## Economy

Southern Italy is notoriously economically underdeveloped, with high unemployment and a long history of corruption, despite decades of subsidies and promises from successive governments to solve the southern problem once and for all. Great strides have been

made recently, however, and progress continues, albeit slower than anyone wants.

Distance from European markets, poor rail and postal services, and the pervasiveness of organised crime all help explain the low productivity statistics for Southern Italy. But the poverty should not be exaggerated. The black economy ensures that major cities meet the national average for consumer spending.

Recent subsidies from the European Union have led to increased manufacturing, but such development has often come at great cost to the natural environment. One industry that continues to grow is tourism.

## Public Holidays

● **January** New Year's Day (1), Epiphany (6)
● **March/April** Good Friday, Easter Monday
● **April** Liberation Day – *Anniversario della Liberazione* (25)
● **May** Labour Day – *Festa del Lavoro* (1)
● **August** Assumption of the Blessed Virgin Mary – *Ferragosto* (15)
● **November** All Saints – *Ognissanti* (1)
● **December** Immaculate Conception of the Blessed Virgin Mary – *Immacolata Concezione* (8), Christmas Day (25), St Stephen's Day (26)

In addition to these national holidays, almost all cities have a holiday to celebrate their own patron saint. Check with the local tourist office for details. Here are a few examples:
● **Festa di San Gennaro in Naples** (1st Sun in May, 19 Sept)
● **Sant'Andrea in Amalfi** (27 June)
● **San Nicola in Bari** (1st weekend in May)
● **Santa Rosalia in Palermo** (15 July)

# Planning the Trip

## Visas and Passports

EU citizens do not need a visa to enter Italy, just a passport or an identification card valid for foreign travel. Visitors from the following countries need a passport but not a visa providing they do not stay for more than three months: Australia, Barbados, Canada, Iceland, Jamaica, Japan, Kenya, South Korea, Kuwait, Malaysia, Maldives, Mexico, Monaco, New Zealand, Niger, Norway, Paraguay, Singapore, Switzerland, Trinidad and Tobago, United States, Uruguay, Venezuela (up to 60 days). Other nationalities should contact their nearest Italian consulate.

You are supposed to register

## Customs Regulations

Used personal effects may be imported and exported without formality. The import of narcotics, weapons and pirated materials is forbidden.

Alcoholic drinks, tobacco and perfume can be imported in limited quantities, depending on your nationality.

Goods on which duty has already been paid in another EU country may be freely imported, provided the amount falls within what might be reasonably described as "for personal use".

For US citizens, the duty-free allowance is: 200 cigarettes, 50 cigars or 3 lb tobacco; 1 US quart of alcoholic beverages and duty-free gifts worth up to $100.

The airports at Naples, Bari, Reggio Calabria, Catania and Palermo have duty-free shops.

with the police within three days of arriving in Italy. In fact, this procedure will be taken care of by your hotel, whatever the level of accommodation. If you are not staying in a hotel, contact the local police station.

## Money Matters

The Italian currency is the euro (€), which is available in 500, 200, 100, 50, 20, 10 and 5 euro notes, and 2-euro, 1-euro, 50-cent, 20-cent, 10-cent, 5-cent, 2-cent and 1-cent coins. There are 100 cents to one euro. It is advisable to bring a limited amount of local currency or obtain some at the airport on arrival, especially if it is the weekend, when banks are closed. Try to avoid changing money in hotels, where the commission tends to be higher than in banks.

**Banks:** Generally open from 8 or 8.30am–1.30pm and for 1½ hours in the afternoon (usually 2.30–4pm).

You will find current exchange rates published in the press and posted in banks.

**Cash machines:** The most convenient way to get money in Italy is to use the ATM machines, which are easily found in all but the most remote towns, accessible 24 hours a day and providing the best exchange rates.

**Credit cards:** In cities, many restaurants, hotels, shops and stores will take major credit cards (Visa, American Express, Diner's Club, MasterCard and Carte Blanche) but most petrol stations require cash. Don't rely on being able to use credit cards in rural areas.

## What to Wear

The Italians are known for their sense of style. This does not mean that one has to dress formally, but you may be barred from entering some churches if dressed in shorts or a short skirt, or if you have uncovered shoulders.

Unless you are going to visit mountain areas, the moderate climate makes heavy clothing

## Travelling with Pets

Pets must be vaccinated against rabies and you should obtain an officially stamped document stating that your animal is healthy. This should be done no more than a month before you arrive in Italy. Visit www.defra.gov.uk for information on the Pet Travel Scheme.

unnecessary in summer. A light jacket will be adequate for summer evenings. In winter (November to March), the climate can be cold and wet in Southern Italy, so bring the appropriate clothing.

## Tourist Offices

**Australia:** Level 4, 46 Market Street, Sydney NSW 2000; tel. (+61) 2-92-621666, email: italia@italiantourism.com.au.
**Canada:** 175 Bloor Street East, Suite 907, South Tower, Toronto, Ontario M4W 3R8; tel. (+1) 416-925 4882; brochure line: (+1) 416-925 3870; www.italiantourism.com.
**UK:** 1 Princes Street, London W1B 2AY; tel: (0)20 7408 1254; free brochure line: 008 0000 482542; www.italiantouristboard.co.uk.
**US:** New York City: Italian Government Tourist Board, Suite 1565: 630 Fifth Avenue NY – 10111; tel: (+1) 212-245 4822/5618; www.italiantourism.com. Chicago: 500 North Michigan Avenue; tel: (+1) 312-644 0996; www.italiantourism.com. Los Angeles: 12400 Wilshire Blvd, Suite 550; tel: (+1) 310-820 1898; www.italiantourism.com.

In Italy, you can call the tourism freephone number for general information, in five languages, about health, transport, safety or tourism offices or sites (tel: 06-49711; open daily 8am–11pm). See also www.enit.it.

## Getting There

### By Air
In addition to the national airline, Alitalia, most major airlines

run direct flights to Italy. Southern Italy has opened up in recent years, spurred on by the expansion of low-cost airlines, such as Ryanair and Easyjet, causing the scheduled airlines to respond with competitive fares. Of the budget airlines operating out of the UK, Ryanair (www.ryanair.com) flies to Bari, Palermo and Trapani; BmiBaby (www.bmibaby.com) goes to Naples; Easyjet (www.easyjet.com) flies to Naples and Palermo; Air Malta (www.airmalta.com) flies from London to Catania, Naples and Reggio Calabria.

From the US, you will tend to fly non-stop to Rome or Milan, then pick up a connecting flight to your final destination.
**Alitalia**: www.alitalia.com; US: www.alitaliausa.com; UK: tel: 0870 544 8259; www.alitalia.co.uk.

All of the above airlines fly to numerous airports across Italy, including Naples. The following are the main airports in Southern Italy:
**Bari: Aeroporto di Bari** (10 km/ 6 miles north of Bari), tel: 080-583 5200 (info). Shuttle bus to the centre of town every half hour.
**Catania: Aeroporto Fontanarossa** (7 km/4½ miles south of Catania), tel: 095-340 505. Bus to central train station about every half hour.
**Naples: Aeroporto Capodichino** (7 km/4½ miles north of Naples), tel: 081-789 6259; www.gesac.it. Frequent buses to Piazza Garibaldi
**Palermo: Aeroporto Falcone-Borsellino** (32 km/20 miles west of Palermo), tel: 091-702 0111; buses every half hour.
**Reggio Calabria/Aeroporto dello Stretto:** (5 km/3 miles from Reggio Calabria), tel: 0965-643291. Buses roughly every hour.
**Trapani Airport (Birgi):** (20 km/ 12 miles south of Trapani), tel: 0923-842502. Flights to Rome and Pantelleria weekdays.
For **Rome airports** see www.adr.it

## By Car

When calculating the cost of travelling to Italy by car, allow for motorway tolls as well as accommodation en route and petrol. Motorists driving through Switzerland will need to purchase a *vignette,* an annual road pass which costs around €30 and can be bought either at the border or at any national tourist office. If you want to travel by toll-free roads in Italy, get hold of the Italian State Tourist Office's *Traveller's Handbook,* which lists them.

The usual route from France to Italy is via the Mont Blanc Tunnel (between Chamonix and Courmayeur) or from Switzerland through the Gran San Bernardo Tunnel (between Bourg St Pierre and Aosta). Some of the many Alpine passes are seasonal, so it is

## Car Trains

The Italian railway *auto al seguito* service can save you the effort of driving and the expense of petrol and toll roads. Vehicles should be no larger than 1.58 metres (5 ft 2 ins) in height, 1.8 metres (5 ft 10 ins) in width, and 7 metres (22 ft 11 ins) in length. A car must be accompanied by at least one passenger on the train. The cost varies with the season, number of travellers (above age 4), and the route (cheaper to buy round trip than two one-way tickets). For example, a Milan–Palermo one-way costs between around €90 and €210.

There are 36 other official routes between the main train stations in Northern Italy (Milan, Turin, Venice, Genoa, Calalzo, Bologna, Florence) and Rome, Naples, Bari, Crotone, Lamezia Terme, Villa San Giovanni, Milazzo, Catania and Palermo. But note that the *auto al seguito* service along these routes only operates on particular periods/ days during the year. Reservations are obligatory, and can be made two months in advance right until the day before departure. Travellers would be wise to check on their insurance coverage and mind valuables, as theft from vehicles carried on this service is not unheard of.

best to check the viability of your route with the tourist board or a motoring organisation before setting off. Alternatively, motorists can head down the French *autoroute* to Nice and cross the border at Ventimiglia on the Riviera.

To take your car into Italy, you will need your current driving licence (with an Italian translation unless it is the standard EU licence), your vehicle registration document (which must be in the driver's name or supported by the owner's written permission for the driver to use the vehicle) and fully comprehensive insurance valid for travel in Italy. You must also carry a warning triangle in case of breakdown.

Improved road access to the south might be on the cards: the controversial plan to link Sicily with mainland Italy via a suspension bridge is still under discussion. Access to Sicily is currently only by sea or air.

### By Coach

National Express Eurolines runs coaches from London Victoria, via Paris and Mont Blanc, to Naples and Rome. To book, contact: Unit 6/7 Colonnades Walk, London SW1W 9SH; tel: 08705 808080; www.nationalexpress.com/eurolines

### By Rail

Rail travel is not a particularly cheap option unless you are visiting different places in Italy as part of the Inter-Rail or Eurail schemes. These provide a month's unlimited train travel in Europe for anyone under the age of 26. They can be an attractive option, especially if you are planning to stop off en route.

For details of rail travel contact:
**UK:** Rail Europe Travel Centre, 178 Piccadilly, London, W1. Mon–Fri 10am–6pm, Sat 10am–5pm; tel: 08708 371371; www.raileurope.co.uk.
See also www.railchoice.co.uk.
**In US and Canada:**
Tel: 1-888-382-RAIL in the US; 1-800-361-RAIL in Canada; www.raileurope.com. See also www.eurail.com.

When travelling from Britain via Paris, it is necessary to change in Paris (from Gare du Nord to Gare de Lyon). EC (Eurocity) and TEE (Trans Europe Express) trains are luxury first-class only trains running between the main European cities. A special supplement is charged and seat reservation is obligatory. Keep in mind that the travel time by train to the south once you cross the border is as follows:

Turin–Naples: 9 hours
Turin–Bari: 10 hours
Milan–Bari: 8½ hours
Milan–Naples: 9 hours
Naples–Reggio Calabria/Catania: 5 hours
Reggio Calabria/Catania–Palermo: 6 hours

For train information, call the same number from anywhere in Italy: 89 20 21. Alternatively, check routes on the official railway website: www.trenitalia.com.

## Package Tours

From the UK, Ireland, or the US, this is usually the easiest and most economical way to visit historic centres. It can be an advantage to travel with a company that has good local representation. Current brochures are generally available from your travel agent.

## Specialist Tours

**Andante Travels**
The Old Barn, Old Road, Alderbury, Salisbury SP5 3AR;
tel: 01722 713800;
fax: 01722 711966;
www.andantetravels.co.uk.
Specialises in archaeological tours.
**ATG Oxford**
69–71 Banbury Road,
Oxford OX2 6PE;
tel: 01865 315678;
fax: 01865 315697/8/9;
www.atg–oxford.co.uk.
Walking holidays which involve exploring the countryside while enjoying excellent Italian food and hospitality.
**Citalia**
The Atrium, London Road, Crawley, West Sussex RH10 9SR;

tel: 0870 901 4013 or
0870 909 7555;
fax: 0870 901 4019;
www.citalia.com.
Covering all kinds of holidays, for a variety of budgets.
**Long Travel**
The Stables, Dudgeley House, All Stretton, Shropshire SY6 6HG;
tel: 01694 722193;
www.long-travel.co.uk.
Travel firm dealing uniquely with Southern Italy. Specialises in agritourism (staying in working farms, albeit in great comfort) and also has a delightful range of fortified manor houses *(masserie)* and villa hotels in the south.
**Magic of Italy**
tel: 0870 888 0228;
www.magicofitaly.co.uk.
Italy-wide specialists who offer a wide range of holidays in the south, including to places off the beaten track.
**Martin Randall Travel**
Voysey House, Barley Mow Passage, London W4 4GF;
tel: 020 8742 3355;
www.martinrandall.com.
Specialises in upmarket art and cultural tours covering themes such as music, art, history, architecture and archaeology.

For **cycling holidays**, the following two companies operate from the US: www.experienceplus.com www.ciclismoclassico.com. This website has details of two hotels in Puglia specially catering for cyclists: www.italybikehotels.it. For cycling maps see www.sustransshop.co.uk.

# Practical Tips

## Business Hours

Shops are open for business 9am–12.30pm and 3.30 or 4pm to 7.30 or 8pm. In areas serving tourists, hours are generally longer than these. Many shops close for one morning or afternoon during the week. Some close on Saturday. Almost everything closes on Sunday and on Monday morning.

## Tipping

Unless otherwise indicated on the menu, service is included. Therefore it is not necessary to tip your waiter. A modest amount of change left on the table is sufficient to express appreciation for good service. Although *pane e coperto*, an outdated cover and bread charge, has been officially eliminated in most cities, some restaurants have been slow in phasing it out. Only in the finest hotels, and for lengthy stays, is a tip for the maids/head waiters necessary.

## Media

The Italian press is concentrated in Milan and Rome. The biggest papers are *La Repubblica* and *Il Corriere della Sera,* which publish regional editions. The main regional newspapers for the south are *Il Mezzogiorno* and *Il Gazetto del Sud* for the whole south (based in Reggio Calabria), *Il Giornale di Sicilia* (based in Palermo) and *La Sicilia* (based in Catania) for all of Sicily, *Il Mattino* for Naples, and *Il Quotidiano* for Reggio Calabria.

Most major cities publish listings magazines which are worth getting, even for visitors with little or no Italian. The best are Naples'

*Qui Napoli* and Palermo's *Agenda*. The local tourist office should also have information on current events.

Controversially, commercial television stations are virtually all owned or controlled by Italy's richest man, ex-premier Silvio Berlusconi, and provide similar, ratings-led fare.

## Postal Services

Post office hours are usually 8am–1.30pm, or 8.30am–2pm, but many towns have a main post office which is open throughout the day. Stamps are also available from tobacconists *(tabacchi)*.

The Italian postal system is notoriously unreliable. It's certainly worth spending the extra to send letters home using the priority service. Mail sent *posta prioritaria* gets delivered within 24 hours in Italy and 48 hours in Europe, while a letter or postcard sent via ordinary post can take days, sometimes weeks. Note that you must drop your mail in the special *"posta prioritaria"* boxes. *Postacelere*, the Italian mail's courier service, offers better rates than comparable private services.

If you want to register a letter, ask to send it *raccomandata*. You can receive mail addressed to a *Posta Restante*, held at the *Fermo Posta* window of the main post office in every town, picking it up personally with identification.

For details about rates and delivery times you can call 803 160 in Italy or visit www.poste.it.

## Telecommunications

Most Italians now have mobile phones glued to their ears (European standard GSM, so Americans will need a tri-or quad-band phone), so public telephones are increasingly scarce these days, but not impossible to find.

Most public telephones *(cabina telefonica)* only accept pre-paid phone cards *(carte telefoniche)*, available from tobacconists and many bars. If you are not carrying a mobile phone, long-distance calls can also be made from main post offices. If you are telephoning to

## Calling Home

To make an international call, dial 00, followed by:

| | |
|---|---|
| **Australia** | 61 |
| **Canada** | 1 |
| **Ireland** | 353 |
| **New Zealand** | 64 |
| **UK** | 44 |
| **US** | 1 |

Then dial the subscriber number, omitting the initial 0.
- European Directory Enquiries: 176
- European operator assistance: 15
- Intercontinental operator assistance: 170

outside Italy, the cheapest time to call is between 10pm–8am and all day Sunday.

### Area Codes in Italy

Remember that for all calls within Italy (even local calls), you must first dial the appropriate area code, which you can obtain free from Information (tel: 12). Unusually, when calling Italy from abroad, you must dial the initial zero of the area code. The area codes of the main cities in this guide are:
**Bari**, tel: 080
**Catania**, tel: 095
**Lecce**, tel: 0832
**Naples**, tel: 081
**Palermo**, tel: 091
**Reggio Calabria**, tel: 0965
**Rome**, tel: 06
**Taormina**, tel: 0942

### Internet

Most hotels will allow you to plug a modem into their phone system; 4- and 5-star hotels should have built-in dataports and/or wireless facilities. All Italian cities now have their fair share of internet cafés, usually located near tourist sites or near the train station.

## Local Tourist Offices

Every major town has an **Azienda di Promozione Turistica** (APT) or **Informazione e Accoglienza Turistica** (IAT). For addresses and phone numbers, check the directory or the *Yellow Pages* under ENIT (Ente

Nazionale per il Turismo –the Italian State Tourist Board). The Yellow Pages website is www.paginegialle.it.

Together with helpful information, APT offices offer a free city map, hotel listings and museum hours. APT offices in the main areas are listed below. A full list of tourist offices, plus general information, can also be found on the Italian State Tourist Board website: www.enit.it.

## CAMPANIA

### Amalfi
Corso Roma 19, tel: 089-871107. Open Mon–Fri 8am–2pm and 3–6pm, Sat 8am–noon.

### Capri
Piazzetta Cerio 11, tel: 081-837 0424; www.capritourism.com

### Ischia and Procida
Via Corso Colonna 108, tel: 081-507 4211. Open Mon–Sat 9am–noon and 2–5pm (shorter hours winter).

### Naples
Palazzo Reale, Piazza Plebiscito, tel: 081-252 5711. There are also smaller offices at Mergellina Funicular Station (tel: 081-761 2102), the Stazione Centrale (main train station, tel: 081-268 779), and the airport.
Naples province, Campania: Piazza dei Martiri 58, tel: 081-405311.

### Paestum
Archaeological site, tel: 0828-811016. Open Mon–Sat 8am–2pm.

### Pompeii
Via Sacra 1, tel: 081-850 7255. Open Mon–Sat 8am–2pm (longer hours in summer).

### Positano
Via del Saracino 4, tel: 089-875067. Open Mon–Fri 8am–2pm, Sat 8am–noon.

### Salerno
Via Roma 258, tel: 089-224744; www.salernoturismo.it Open Mon–Sat 9am–2pm, 3–8pm.

### Sorrento
Via de Maio 35, tel: 081-807 4033; www.sorrentotourism.com. Mon–Sat 9am–2.30pm and 3.30–6.30pm.

## PUGLIA

### Bari
Piazza Aldo Moro 33a, tel: 080-524 2361 (city and province of Bari). Open Mon–Sat 9am–1pm.

### Brindisi
Lungomare Regina Margherita 44, tel: 0831-523072 (city) and 0831-562126 (province of Brindisi). Open Mon–Fri 9am–2pm.

### Foggia
Via Emilio Perrone 17, tel: 0881-723650. Open Mon–Fri 9am–noon.

### Lecce (city)
Corso Vittorio Emanuele II 24, tel: 0832-284092. Open Mon–Fri 9am–1pm and 3–6pm.

### Manfredonia (Gargano Peninsula)
Piazza del Popolo 10, tel: 0884-581998. Open Mon–Sat 9am–1pm.

### Taranto (city)
Corso Umberto 113, tel: 099-453 2392. Open Mon–Sat 9am–2pm.

## BASILICATA

### Maratea
Piazza del Gesù 32, tel: 0973-876908. Open Mon–Fri 9am–1pm.

### Matera
Via Spine Bianche 22, tel: 0835-331817; www.materaturismo.it.

### Potenza
Via del Gallitello 89, tel: 0971-507622. Open Mon–Fri 9am–1pm and 4–6.30pm; Sat 9am–12.30pm.

## CALABRIA

### Catanzaro
City office: Via Spasari 3, Galleria Mancuso, tel: 0961-743901.

Provincial office: Via San Nicola 8, tel: 0961-720260.

### Crotone
Via Torino 148, tel: 0962-23185. Open Mon–Fri 8am–1pm; also Mon and Wed 2–5pm.

### Cosenza
Corso Mazzini 92, tel: 0984-27271. Open Mon–Fri 7.30am–1.30pm; also Mon and Wed 2.30–5pm.

### Reggio Calabria
Stazione Centrale, tel: 0965-27120. Open Mon–Sat 8am–8pm. Airport, tel: 0965-643291. Open Mon–Sat 8am–8pm. Corso Garibaldi 329, tel: 0965-892012. Open Mon–Sat 8am–8pm.

### Tropea
Piazza Ercole, tel: 0963-61475. Open Mon–Sat 9.30am–12.30pm and 4.30–9.30pm.

## SICILY

### Aeolian Islands (Lípari)
Corso Vittorio Emanuele 202, tel: 090-988 0095. Open Mon–Fri 8am–2pm and 4.30–6.30pm (longer hours in summer).

### Agrigento
Via Cesare Battisti 15, tel: 0922-20454. Open Mon–Sat 8.30am–1.30pm; also Wed 4–7pm.

## Useful Websites

Apart from the general Italian State Tourist Board (www.enit.it), the following regions have their own official sites:
**Campania** www.campaniaturismo.it
**Puglia** www.pugliaturismo.com
**Basilicata** www.aptbasilicata.it
**Sicily** www.siciliaturismo.com

Other useful websites include:
www.aptcatania.it
www.inaples.it
www.laterradipuglia.it
www.palermotourism.com
www.parcoetna.it

Valley of the Temples, tel: 0922-26191.

### Catania
Provincial office: Via Cimorosa 10 (off Via Etnea), tel: 095-730 6211. Open 9am–7pm (shorter hours in winter).
City office: Corso Italia 302, tel: 095-373084.
Stazione Centrale, tel: 095-730 6255. Open 9am–7pm (shorter hours in winter).

### Cefalù
Corso Ruggero 7, tel: 0921-421050. Open Mon–Fri 8am–2pm and 4–7pm, Sat 9am–2pm.

### Enna
Via Cavour 15, tel: 0935-680201 (also for Roman Villa at Piazza Armerina.)

### Erice
Viale Conte A. Pepoli 11, tel: 0923-869388. Variable opening times.

### Etna (Nicolosi)
Via Garibaldi 63, tel: 095-901505.

### Marsala
Via XI Maggio 100, tel: 0923-714097. Open Mon–Sat 8am–2pm.

### Messina
Via Calabria 301, tel: 090-674236. Open Mon–Fri 9am–1.30pm and Mon–Thur 3–5pm.

### Noto
Piazza 16 Maggio, tel: 0931-573779. Open Mon–Sat 8am–2pm and 3.30–6.30pm.

### Palermo
Aeroporto Falcone-Borsellino, tel: 091-591698. Open Mon–Fri 8am–midnight, Sat–Sun 8am–8pm. Piazza Castelnuovo 34, tel: 091-702 0289/091-591698. Open Mon–Sat 8am–6pm.

### Ragusa
Via Capitani Bocchieri 33 (Ragusa Ibla), tel: 0932-221511. Open daily 9am–2pm and 3–7pm.

### Siracusa (city)
Via Maestranza 33 (Ortygia),
tel: 0931-65201. Open Mon–Sat
9am–2pm and 4–7pm.

### Taormina
Palazzo Corvaja, off Piazza Vittorio
Emanuele, tel: 0942-23243. Open
Mon–Sat 8am–2pm and 4–7pm.

### Trapani (and the Egadi Islands)
Piazzetta Saturno, tel: 0923-29000.
Open Mon–Sat 8am–8pm,
Sun 9am–noon and 3–6pm.

## Medical Services

In cases of real need, such as
medical aid or ambulances, call the
Public Emergency Assistance
number, **113**. This service operates
on a 24-hour basis, and, in the
principal cities, response will be in
the main foreign languages. For an
ambulance call **118**.

To receive free treatment in
cases of illness or accidents, EU
citizens must obtain (in their
country of residence before arriving
in Italy) the E111 form. The UK
has replaced the E111 with the
European Health Insurance Card
(EHIC; application forms available
at post offices or www.dh.gov.uk).
Note: it won't provide repatriation,
which you may require in the
case of serious illness. Citizens
of non-EU countries must pay
for medical care and medicine.
Health insurance is recommended
for travelling in Italy. Keep receipts
for medical expenses if you want
to claim.

Most hospitals have a 24-hour
emergency department called
*Pronto Soccorso*, but a stay in an
Italian hospital can be a grim
experience. For more minor
complaints, seek out a *farmacia*,
identified by a sign displaying a
red cross within a white circle.
Trained pharmacists give advice
and suggest over-the-counter
drugs, including antibiotics.
Normal opening hours are
9am–1pm and 4–7.30 or 8pm, but
outside these hours the address of
the nearest *farmacia* on duty is
posted in the window.

## Consulates

There is the following limited
local consular representation in
Southern Italy:
**Naples**
**Canada** Via Carducci 29,
tel: 081-401338
**UK** Via dei Mille 40,
tel: 081-4238911
**US** Piazza della Repubblica,
tel: 081-583 8111
**Palermo**
**UK** Via Cavour 117,
tel: 091-326412
**US** Via Vaccarini 1,
tel: 091-305857

## Security and Crime

The vast majority of tourists have
pleasant, trouble-free holidays in
Southern Italy. Although the Mafia
has a strong hold in the region, it is
highly unlikely that the average
tourist will knowingly come into
contact with them.

The main problem for tourists is
petty crime: pickpocketing and bag-
snatching (by young criminals
known as *scippatori* or *scippi*),
together with theft from cars. Theft
of all sorts is more likely in the
tourist areas of Rome, Naples,
Palermo, Catania and Siracusa. You
can greatly reduce the possibility of
theft by taking some elementary
precautions *(see below)*.
Remember, too, that very little
violent theft occurs: the chances of
being mugged are very much higher
in London or New York.

Expect the police to have a
casual attitude to petty crime and
a slightly suspect attitude to a
woman on her own. Expect, also,
to have to prove who you are and
where you are staying before even
beginning to embark on your tale
of woe. In the event of a serious
crime, contact your country's
consulate or embassy as well as
the *Carabinieri*.

### Personal Security
● Don't linger in non-commercial
areas after dark
● Don't carry all your cash

● Use traveller's cheques or
debit/credit cards rather than large
quantities of cash
● Never leave your luggage
unattended
● Keep valuables in the hotel safe
(available at most hotels)
● Deposit your room key at the desk
before going out

### Anti-theft Precautions
Avoid looking like a tourist and do
not wear your wealth ostentatiously:
carry your camera out of sight, and
do not wave money or wallets. If
carrying a handbag, keep it on the
side away from the road (one local
speciality is the motorbike snatch-
and-drive). It is best to leave money
and valuables in the hotel safe. You
should keep a separate record of
credit-card and cheque numbers,
just in case.

### Reporting a Crime
If you are robbed, report it as soon
as possible to the local police. You
will need a copy of the declaration
in order to claim on your insurance.
In Sicily, it is highly likely that part
of your property will be returned.
There is apparently an unspoken
agreement between police and
thieves: provided documents and
credit cards are returned and no
violence is used, the police apply
minimum effort to arresting those
responsible.

### Car Crime
Never leave luggage or valuables
visible in a car; in fact, if possible
leave nothing visible in a car. Cars
are best parked off the street (e.g.
in a hotel car park, of which there
are sadly very few). You must have
all the car documents with you
when driving, but always take them
with you when you park.

## Women Travellers

Difficulties encountered by women
travelling alone in Italy are often
overstated. Women have to put up
with much male attention, but it is
rarely dangerous. Ignoring whistles
and questions is the best way to
get rid of unwanted attention.

# Getting Around

## Public Transport

### BY AIR

Travelling across Southern Italy and Sicily by air is quite feasible, but fairly expensive. Alitali and several smaller national carriers, such as Air One (www. flyairone.it), Meridiana (www. meridiana.it) and Air Sicilia (www. airsicilia.it), offer frequent services between Naples, Bari, Brindisi, Lamezia Terme (in Calabria), Catania, Palermo, Trapani, Lampedusa and Pantelleria. The budget airline blu-express (www.blu-express.com), flies from Rome to Bari, Palermo, Pantelleria and Catania.

### BY RAIL

For the most part, the cheapest, fastest and most convenient way to travel through Southern Italy is by train, with frequent services connecting most destinations. Noteworthy exceptions are the interior of Calabria and Basilicata, where it's best to travel by car.

Train information is available from the *Uffici Informazioni* at most major stations, listed in the telephone directory under *Ferrovie dello Stato*. You can also telephone 89 20 21 (from anywhere in Italy), which operates daily 8am–9pm with English-speaking operators, or visit the official Italian state railway website: www.trenitalia.com.

Local trains are called *Locale, Diretto, Interregionale* and *Espresso*. When travelling long distances or along major lines, the faster *InterCity, EuroCity* and *Eurostar* services are the best bet – the supplementary charge is well worth the time saved and the extra comfort. The *Pendolino* is the fastest, most comfortable train, and requires a supplement and reservation. If you can, buy tickets and make reservations for the *IC/EC/ES* and *Pendolino* in advance; this can be done at any travel agency as well as at the station.

If you are planning to make a number of train journeys, consider buying the inexpensive official train timetable book from any station kiosk. If travelling a fair distance, it is worth reserving a seat as trains tend to be crowded.

Good fare reductions and special offers are available for groups and young travellers, and it is worth making enquiries about these when you arrive in Italy. Train tickets are valid for two months. Passengers must stamp their tickets at the validating machines in the station before boarding. If for some reason that is not possible, you must find the conductor before he finds you.

## Ferries and Hydrofoils

A number of private companies run ferry *(traghetto)* and hydrofoil *(aliscafo)* services between the islands of Southern Italy and the mainland, and also between several cities. Hydrofoils are faster, but more expensive and are affected by choppy seas and high winds (which force them to proceed at ferry speed). Tickets are available from travel agencies and ticket offices at the port, but reserve in advance if you can. There are many websites through which you can book online. In summer, arrive in good time as the ports are chaotic.

The shipping group **Tirrenia** owns Adriatica, Caremar, Saremar, Siremar, Tirrenia and Toremar. For information on crossing times and prices on all of these lines contact Tirrenia:
Tel: (+39) 081-017 1998 (or 892123 within Italy);
www.gruppotirrenia.it.

### *Campania*
#### From Naples
To Capri, call Caremar *(see above)*. To Palermo, by car ferry (11 hrs), call Tirrenia; for the quick crossing (5 hrs), tel: (SNAV) 081-428 5555; www.snav.it.
To Ischia, by hydrofoil (35 mins); by ferry (80 mins), call Caremar or (Lauro) 081-497 2222. To Lípari, call Tirrenia. Naples also has ferry and hydrofoil links to Sorrento and the island of Procida.
#### From Sorrento
To Ischia (30 mins), tel: (Partenopee) 081-551 3236.
To Capri (15 mins), tel: (Alilauro) 081-497 2238; by ferry (20 mins), call Caremar.
There are also regular services to Naples (40 mins) and services to Positano during peak season.

### *Puglia*
#### From the Tremiti Islands
To Termoli, by hydrofoil (50 mins), tel: (Navigazione Libera 081-551 0763; www.navlib.it); by ferry (1 hr 50 mins), call Adriatica.
To Termoli, Vieste (1 hr) and Manfredonia (2 hrs), by hydrofoil, call: Adriatica *(see Tirrenia, above)*.

### *Sicily*
#### From Milazzo
To the Aeolian Islands, by ferry (1½–3 hrs), call Siremar *(above)*; by hydrofoil (45–60 mins), tel: (SNAV) 091-631 7900 or Siremar.
#### From Palermo
To Ustica, by hydrofoil (1 hr), ferry (3 hrs), call Siremar.
To the Aeolian Islands, by hydrofoil (3 hrs), tel: (SNAV) 091-631 7900.
#### From Porto Empedocle
To Lampedusa/Linosa, by ferry (6–8 hrs), call Siremar.
#### Trapani
To Favignana, by hydrofoil (25 mins), call Siremar.
To Pantelleria, ferry (6 hrs), tel: (Ustica) 0923-923103.

## BY COACH

Each province in Italy has its own inter-city bus company, and each company has its own lines. It is worth taking buses, especially when you are going to the mountainous interior, where they are generally faster than the trains. An advantage of buses is that they usually stop in the centre of town, whereas the train stations in rural towns are often quite far from the main piazza. Unfortunately, few of these companies have English-speaking operators, and their information services are limited. Tickets can be bought from tobacconists, who are often well informed on the latest timetables, or check with the tourist office (see page 326).

## TAXIS

Taxis in Italy are relatively expensive; they are found at taxi ranks or ordered by telephone rather than hailed in the street. If you phone for a taxi, you will be charged for the trip the driver makes to reach you.

There is a fixed starting charge and then a charge for every kilometre (and a standing charge for traffic jams). Taxi drivers are obliged to show, if asked, the current list of additional charges. Extra charges are added for night rides (10pm– 7am), luggage, journeys outside town and journeys on Sundays and public holidays. It is a general rule to leave a small tip rounding off the fare to the nearest euro.

### Driving Speeds

The following speed limits apply to cars in Italy:
**Urban areas:** 50 km/h (30 mph)
**Roads outside urban areas:**
90 km/h (55 mph)
**Dual carriageways outside urban areas:** 110 km/h (70 mph)
**Motorways (autostrade):**
130 km/h (80 mph); for cars less than 1,100cc: 110 km/h (70 mph)

### Private Transport

### BY CAR

In Italy, you must drive on the right. The motorways (autostrade) are fast and uncrowded (except in summer), but Italians frequently exceed the speed limit. Nearly all autostrade charge tolls; you must take a ticket as you enter the motorway and pay as you exit.

It is compulsory to wear seat belts at all times and children up to the age of 12 must use a suitable car seat or seat belt.

Pay attention to street signs advising no parking because police are strict on illegal parking and will remove vehicles found in no-parking areas. You'll need plenty of cash to reclaim your car. Try to park in a garage for the night: it will be expensive, but much safer.

**Touring Club Italiano** (TCI) offers information and various discounts (www.touringclub.it/index.asp).

**Hitchhiking** is forbidden on the autostrade and is not advised for women travelling alone.

### Car Rentals

Hiring a car in Italy is an expensive business. Major car rental firms such as Avis, Hertz and Europcar are represented in most cities and at all airports, though local firms offer slightly better rates. Petrol is comparatively expensive too. Agencies are listed in the Yellow Pages under Autonoleggio. Collision damage waiver and recovery in case of breakdown are usually included in the price of hiring a vehicle, but be sure to check exclusions carefully. Additional insurance cover is usually available at fixed rates.

Also, make sure that the price you are quoted includes VAT (IVA), which is levied at 19 percent. To hire a car, you must be over 21 and have a valid driver's licence (an EU licence, an international driving licence or a national driving licence with Italian translation). A deposit equal to the cost of hiring the vehicle is usually required, or a credit-card imprint.

# Where to Stay

### Choosing a Hotel

Southern Italian accommodation tends to be denigrated, but its best upmarket hotels, often set in masserie (fortified farmhouses) or monasteries, rival the best in Northern Italy. In fact, certain pockets of the south have unusual, charming hotels with lovelier scenery and lower prices than the north can offer. The prime locations for boutique hotels in historic buildings are: the islands of Capri and Ischia; Naples; the Amalfi Coast; Taormina in Sicily; Maratea in Basilicata; and Puglia in general, which has a cluster of fabulous spa hotels.

Villa rentals have long been an important part of the Southern Italian appeal, and there is a vast choice of up-market self-catering accommodation.

At the other end of the scale, rural accommodation (agriturismo or aziende agrituristiche) is slowly developing a stronger image, as is bed and breakfast accommodation in the cities, especially in Sicily. While some of the rural accommodation is delightful, much of it is still a hit-and-miss affair, so it is best to rely on recommendations.

Several of the international hotel chains (Hilton, Jolly) are represented in the few major cities in the south, but the likelihood is that you will be staying in privately run establishments. Some of these have banded together with hotels of similar atmosphere, quality and cost into local and national associations. Bear in mind that the number of stars a hotel has been awarded refers only to the facilities and services offered and not their quality.

Although there is a wide variety of hotels to choose from, it is always a good idea to book in advance and get information and confirmation in writing, and stay clear of "representatives" who offer accommodation to tourists coming off the ferry or train. The following listings offer a selection of hotels at all levels. Your travel agent or the local tourist offices in Italy (see page 326) can give you more information on these and other hotels.

## Naples

Hotels in Naples are concentrated along the Lungomare (by the port), in the city centre and up on the hills surrounding the city (many offering panoramic views of the Bay of Naples). Less desirable is the area around the railway station and anything outside the centre of town.

**Caravaggio**
Piazza S.Riario Sforza 157
Tel: 081-211 0066
www.caravaggiohotel.it
This 17th-century building behind the Duomo has 11 comfortable guest rooms. It is within walking distance of the city's most famous sights, churches and monuments. €€–€€€

**Chiaja**
Via Chiaia, 216 (1st floor)
Tel: 081 415555
www.hotelchiaia.it
Charming hotel close to Piazza Plebiscito, popular with visiting musicians and artists performing at the nearby Teatro San Carlo. Good breakfast and very helpful staff. €€

**Grand Hotel Parker's**
Corso Vittorio Emanuele 135
Tel: 081-761 2474
www.grandhotelparkers.com
Established in 1870, this chic hotel is considered to be one of Naples' finest. The rooms are light and airy with wonderful views of the bay. €€€€

**Rex**
Via Palepoli 12
Tel: 081-764 9389
Fax: 081-764 9227
www.hotel-rex.it
Best budget choice among the better hotels along the Borgo

Marinari. The light, airy rooms have wicker furniture and murals; some have a sea view. €€

**Santa Lucia**
Via Partenope 46
Tel: 081-764 0666
www.summithotels.com
Facing Castel dell'Ovo, this refined and elegant hotel right on the harbour has spacious rooms, many with hot tubs. Great sea views. €€€–€€€€

**Splendid**
Via Manzoni 96
Tel: 081-714 1955
Fax: 081-714 6431
www.hotelsplendid.it
In the residential quarter of Posillipo, with views of the bay. Many rooms have private terraces. Convenient for the funicular, which descends to the Lungomare. €€

## The Islands

### Capri

**Bellavista**
Via G. Orlandi 10 (Anacapri)
Tel: 081-837 1463
Fax: 081-838 2719
www.bellavistacapri.com
A simple place to stay in Anacapri, this 15-room hotel was once a private villa. Sports facilities include three tennis courts. €–€€

**Belsito**
Via Matermania 11
Tel: 081-837 0969
Fax: 081-837 6622
www.hotelbelsito.com
A comfortable and simple old-fashioned inn with pleasant surroundings. Terrace restaurant with sea view. €

**Hotel La Canasta**
Via Campo di Teste 6
Tel: 081-837 0561
Fax: 081-837 6675
www.hotel-canasta.com
Family-run hotel with 16 comfortable rooms close to Piazzetta. Swimming pool and garden; lovely views from the terrace restaurant. €€€

**Luna**
Viale Matteotti 3
Tel: 081-837 0433
Fax: 081-837 7459
www.lunahotel.com

### Price Guide

The price categories are based on a double room in high season with breakfast.
€ = under €75
€€ = €75–125
€€€ = €125–250
€€€€ = more than €250

Fantastic 360-degree views, a large swimming pool and peace and quiet are all part of this hotel hidden in the lush vegetation just at the edge of town. €€€€

**Quisisana**
Via Camerelle 2
Tel: 081-837 0788
Fax: 081-837 6080
www.quisi.com
One of Italy's most famous hotels – the height of luxury on one of the world's most luxurious islands. A serious splurge. €€€€

### Ischia

**L'Albergo della Regina Isabella**
Piazza Restituta 1, Lacco Ameno
Tel: 081-994322
www.reginaisabella.it
Rooms range from tasteful, country-house chic to contemporary opulence. Friendly staff and a superb restaurant complement a somewhat clinical spa that is still one of the best on the island. €€€€

**Il Monastero**
Castello Aragonese,
Ischia Ponte
(2 km/1 mile west of the port)
Tel: 081-992435
Fax: 081-991849
www.castelloaragonese.it
Friendly pensione with romantic location high up in the castle precincts. Views over the bay. €€

### Procida

**La Casa sul Mare**
Via Salita Castello 13
Tel: 0932- 651700
www.casasulmare.it
Set in an 18th-century palazzo in the historic centre, this appealing place has views over the fishing port. Rooms are simple but welcoming, with wrought-iron beds. €€

## Sorrento

**Bellevue Syrene**
Piazza della Vittoria 5
Tel: 081-878 1024
Fax: 081-878 3963
www.bellevue.it
Luxurious, elegant seafront hotel.
Handsome, balconied rooms with
wrought-iron beds and views onto
the bay or the hotel garden. Beach
access from garden. €€€–€€€€
**Excelsior Vittoria**
Piazza Tasso 34
Tel: 081-807 1044
Fax: 081-877 1206
www.exvitt.it
Atmospheric hotel in a historic villa,
with luxurious suites in various
styles, from antique to Art Nouveau.
Bathrooms in marble. Fantastic
views of the bay; pool; beauty
centre. €€€€
**Imperial Tramontano**
Via Veneto 1
Tel: 081-878 2588
www.tramontano.com
Elegant hotel perched on the cliff
edge with wonderful views across the
bay. Restaurant with very friendly
staff. Pool and lift to sea level. €€€
**La Badia**
Via Nastro Verde 8
Tel: 081-878 1154
Fax: 081-807 4159
www.hotellabadia.it
A delightful little restored abbey
surrounded by citrus groves on the
clifftops above Sorrento town. Pool,
restaurant, and fabulous views. It's
a steep walk, but there are regular
buses. 40 rooms. €–€€

## Agritourism

*Agriturismo* is a wonderful way to
experience the countryside in
Southern Italy. You stay either in
private guest rooms or apartments
on a working farm or vineyard,
often with an opportunity to enjoy
home cooking on the premises.
Prices average €25 per person
per day, with Calabria and Puglia
offering the best deals at around
€15 per person per day. Ask at
the local tourist office for details
(see page 326).

## The Amalfi Coast

*Amalfi*
**Hotel Cappuccini Convento**
Via Annunziatella 46
Tel: 089-871877
Fax: 089-871886
Another ex-monastery, with the
monastic cells converted into
comfortable guestrooms featuring
period furniture, with garden,
Arab-Norman cloister and fine
views. €€
**Hotel Luna Convento**
Via Pantaleone Comite 33
Tel: 089-871002
Fax: 089-871333
www.lunahotel.it
A converted 13th-century
monastery built on the rocks at the
water's edge. Breakfast is served in
a Byzantine cloister. Good-sized
rooms decorated with antiques and
local crafts, all with view. Swimming
pool with spectacular panorama
over the sea. €€€€

*Positano*
**Hotel Le Agavi**
Località Belvedere Fornillo,
Via Marconi 127
Tel: 089-875733
Fax: 089-876965
www.leagavi.it
Well located just outside Positano
and its tourist hubbub, with all the
amenities, including a swimming
pool, lift to a private beach and, of
course, fantastic views. €€€
**Le Sirenuse**
Via C. Colombo 30
Tel: 089-875066
Fax: 089-811798
www.sirenuse.com
Once the villa of a powerful
Neapolitan family in the centre
of town with panoramic views,
now a luxurious hotel and arguably
the best restaurant on the Amalfi
coast. Pool, gymnasium and beauty
centre. €€€€
**Villa Franca**
Via Pasitea 318
Tel: 089-875655
Fax: 089-875735
www.villafrancahotel.it
First-rate, family-run hotel with 28
well-decorated and comfortable
rooms, most with tiled floors and

arched windows that look out onto
the sea. Pool. €€€

*Ravello*
**Marmorata**
Via Bizantina 3 (Località Marmorata;
7 km/4½ miles south of Ravello)
Tel: 089-877777
Fax: 089-851189
www.marmorata.it
Quiet and well-cared-for hotel a
short car ride from Ravello. Rooms
are decorated with a marine theme,
and most have views. Pool and
private beach. €€€

## Southern Campania

*The Cilento Park*
Overshadowed by the dramatic
Amalfi coast, the Cilento peninsula
has been unfairly neglected until
recently. While not as dramatic, it is
still remarkably unspoilt, and can
be combined with a visit to
Paestum, Castellabate, and a
relaxing beach break on the coast.
**Albergo Il Castello**
Via Amendola 1
Parco del Cilento
Tel/fax: 0974-967169
www.hotelcastello.co.uk
This welcoming old-fashioned hotel
makes an appealing springboard
into the Cilento area. The 17th-
century building is set in the
attractive cobblestone village
of Castellabate, and is just
5 minutes from the coast by car
(or 20 minutes on foot). The 12
bedrooms are airy, welcoming and
designed in low-key rustic style. €€
**Giacaranda**
Contrada Cenito
(Località San Marco)
Tel/fax: 0974-966130
www.giacaranda.it
Fourteen rooms and four
apartments in this lovely, well-
maintained inn. Excellent
restaurant. Tennis court. €€
**Hermitage**
Via Catarozza (Località San Marco)
Tel: 0974-966618
Fax: 0974-966619
www.hermitage.it
Tasteful hotel with modern
amenities and beautiful views of the
Gulf of Salerno. €€

### Palinuro

**King's Residence Hotel**
Baia del Buondormire
Tel: 0974-931324
Fax: 0974-931418
www.hotelkings.it
All the rooms of this comfortable hotel overlook the sea. Guests have free access to a private corner of the panoramic Buondormire beach. Facilities include a garden, swimming pool, sauna and beauty centre. Closed mid-November to mid-January. €€€

**San Paolo**
Via San Paolo
Tel: 0974-938304
Fax: 0974-931214
www.sanpaolohotel.it
Quiet spot in greenery at the edge of town, with simply furnished rooms, panoramic restaurant, piano bar and two pools, one for kids. €€

### Paestum

**Hotel Ariston**
Via Laura 13
Tel: 0828-851333
Fax: 0828-851595
www.hotelariston.com
Located 3 km (2 miles) from the excavations, this modern, full-service hotel (gym, indoor and outdoor pools, sauna and private beach) is good value. €€€

### Vallo della Lucania

**Mimì**
Via de Marsilio 1
Tel: 0974-4302
Fax: 0974-44214
A good address with a restaurant and a garden on the western side of the Cilento National Park, this is a small, family-run hotel. €

## Puglia

### FOGGIA PROVINCE

### Foggia

**Cicolella**
Viale XXIV Maggio 60
Tel: 0881-566111
Fax: 0881-778984
www.hotelcicolella.it
Large hotel close to the railway station; comfortable rooms with marble bathrooms. €€€

### Manfredonia

**Gargano**
Viale Beccarini 2
Tel: 0884-587622
Fax: 0884-586021
A modern hotel in the centre of town, with a swimming pool and good restaurant. All rooms have views onto the Adriatic. €–€€

### Mattinata

The steeply forested 40 km (25 miles) of coast between Viete and Mattinata is an unspoilt and delightful area. Mattinata also provides perfect access to the Gargano peninsula, and one of Italy's finest national parks.
**Baia dei Faraglioni Beach Resort**
Tel: 0884-559584/5
Fax: 0884-559651
www.baiadeifaraglioni.it
Spacious rooms ranging from modest to luxurious, wonderful views, private beach, outdoor pool, gym, sauna, boat trips to see marine caverns. €€€€

### Vieste

**Pizzomunno Vieste Palace Hotel**
Lungomare di Pizzomunno
Tel: 0884-708741
Fax: 0884-707325
The most luxurious place to stay in the Gargano. Five-star amenities include modern, spacious rooms, health farm, private beach, swimming pool, tennis court and gymnasium. Open March to October. €€€€

## BARI PROVINCE

### Bari

**Orchidea**
Via G Petroni 11
Tel: 080-542 1937
Fax: 080-542 6934
www.hotelorchideabari.it
Situated close to the station, this is a simple but reliable family-run 2-star hotel for budget travellers. €
**Palace Hotel**
Via Lombardi 13
Tel: 080-521 6551
Fax: 080-521 1499
www.palacehotelbari.it
Great location, right between the

borgo antico and the modern town. The rooms are tastefully decorated with antiques, and double glazing keeps out the noise. €€€
**Sheraton Nicolaus**
Via Cardinale Ciasca 9
Tel: 080-568 2111
Fax: 080-504 2058
www.sheratonnicolausbari.com
Just outside of town, this is certainly the only modern, high-rise hotel in Southern Italy. All the 4-star amenities you would expect from the Sheraton chain, including a swimming pool. €€€€

### Alberobello

**Dei Trulli**
Via Cadore 32
Tel: 080-432 3555
Fax: 080-432 3560
www.hoteldeitrulli.it
Trulli are circular houses made of whitewashed stone, with conical roofs; in this village you can stay in one of the many trulli which have been converted into apartments. Swimming pool and pleasant countryside. €€–€€€

### Monopoli

**Il Melograno**
Contrada Torricella 345
Tel: 080-690 9030
Fax: 080-747908
www.melograno.com
One of the south's most stylish hotels, close to the fishing port of Monopoli, and convenient for Alberobello. A 17th-century fortified farmhouse luxuriously converted into a charming 5-star hotel surrounded by gardens and olive groves. Its pared-down Mediterranean look is slightly marred by fussy furnishings. The main restaurant serves Puglian dishes and uses olive oil from the

## Price Guide

The price categories are based
on a double room in high season
with breakfast.
€ = under €75
€€ = €75–125
€€€ = €125–250
€€€€ = more than €250

hotel's estate. Sports facilities
include tennis courts, a pool and
private beach. The hotel is linked by
shuttle service to Le Tamerici
Beach Club, with its swimming pool
and sandy beach. €€€€

### Trani
**Royal**
Via de Robertis 29
Tel: 0883-588777
Fax: 0883-582224
www.hotelroyaldam.com
Great value 4-star hotel in the
centre of town, not far from the
railway station. €

## BRINDISI PROVINCE

### Brindisi
**Barsotti**
Via Cavour 1
Tel: 0831-560877
Fax: 0831-563851
Modern, recently refurbished hotel.
Conveniently located in the centre
of town near railway station. Good-
sized rooms are sound-proofed. €€

### Ceglie Messapica
**La Fontanina**
Contrada Palagogna
Tel: 0831-380932
Fax: 0831-380933
www.lafontanina.it
Set not far from Ostuni, this
unpretentious villa is ideal for young
families; comfortable rooms; a
garden of olive and almond trees;
wine-tasting and gastronomic
weekends; pool. €€

### Cisternino
**Villa Cenci**
Via per Ceglie Messapica
(Road to Ceglia Messapica)
Tel: 080-444 8208

www.villacenci.it
Set in a fortified farmhouse in the
countryside near the appealing
village of Cisternino, this retreat
offers either *trulli*-style rooms or
self-catering apartments. Pool and
bar. Open Easter to September. €€

### Ostuni
**Il Frantoio**
SS. 16 Km 874
Tel: 0831-330276
www.trecolline.it
This is a good example of a quality
farm-stay set on an ancient olive
farm close to "the white city" of
Ostuni. The eight lovely rooms
have wrought-iron beds and rustic
antiques; all meals make use of
farm produce. €€
**Novecento**
Contrada Ramunno
Tel: 0831-305666
Fax: 0831-305667
www.hotelnovecento.com
A calming early 20th-century hotel
with comfortable rooms and a cosy
yet efficient atmosphere. €€

### Savelletri di Fasano (between Monopoli and Ostuni)
**Masseria San Domenico**
Strada Litoranea 379
Tel: 080-482 7769
Fax: 080-482 7978
www.imasseria.com
A fortified farmhouse created
around a medieval Knights of Malta
watchtower set in an olive grove;
spa, saltwater pool with waterfall,
private beach, tennis, golf, riding,
gym. This is a discreet, hyper-
efficient 5-star celebrity retreat set
close to the coast. €€€€
**Masseria Torre Coccaro**
Contrada Coccaro
Tel: 080-482 9310
Fax: 080-482 7992
www.gesthotels.com
Set just north of Brindisi, this is a
fortified farmhouse that has been
converted into a chic family-run
luxury hotel which presents
Il Melograno *(see entry on page
333)* with stiff competition. Aveda
spa, pool and Turkish baths,
orchards of almond and carob
trees, as well as individualistic
bedrooms carved into the rock;

elegant antiques and Oriental
carpets. The "Egnathia" restaurant,
set in the former stables, uses
estate-grown organic produce in its
dishes. €€€€

## LECCE PROVINCE

### Gallipoli
**Hotel Palazzo del Corso**
Corso Roma 145
Tel: 0833-264040
Fax: 0833-265052
www.hotelpalazzodelcorso.it
Set in the historic centre, this late
18th-century hotel has been well
restored in tasteful, low-key style,
with exposed arches and brickwork.
Roof garden, solarium, fitness
centre, Jacuzzi and aromatherapy
treatments. €€€–€€€€

### Lecce
**Patria Palace**
Piazzetta Riccardi 13
Tel: 0832-245111
Fax: 0832-245002
www.patriapalacelecce.com
This perfectly central hotel makes it
the best choice in Lecce. Set in an
elegant baroque building enlivened
by Art Nouveau touches, the hotel
also has a good restaurant, Atenze,
serving Puglian specialities. €€€
**President**
Via Salandra 6
Tel: 0832-456111
Fax: 0832-456632
A 4-star modern building and
interior in the newer part of town.
Unremarkable decor, but
serviceable rooms and good
Puglian restaurant. €€€

## OTRANTO PROVINCE

### Marittima di Diso
**Il Convento di Santa Maria di
Costantinopoli**
Tel: 07736-362328
Set in a quaint fishing village just
south of Otranto, this is a bohemian-
chic guesthouse owned by Lord and
Lady McAlpine. The 15th-century
former convent is furnished with
eclectic clutter from around the
world, creating an informal country-

house atmosphere. No TV or phones in rooms; pool. €€€€

## TARANTO PROVINCE

### Taranto
**Grand Hotel Delfino**
Viale Virgilio 66
Tel: 099-732 3232
Fax: 099-730 4654
www.grandhoteldelfino.it
On the waterfront, about 2 km (1 mile) from the old city (città vecchia). Pool, gym; most rooms have a view of the water. €€

## Basilicata

Unlike better-developed Puglia, Basilicata has a shortage of top-quality hotels and restaurants, with the exception of the resort of Maratea, which is now very chic. Even so, the region has a wide range of simple yet genuine rural accommodation and some good inns. If Puglia offers accommodation in quaint beehive-shaped trulli, then UNESCO-listed Matera, Basilicata's main cultural centre, offers unique accommodation in the Sassi, an area of cave-dwellings, some of which have been converted into cosy hotels (see page 228).

### Barile
**Locanda del Palazzo**
Piazza Caracciolo 7
Tel/fax: 0972-771051
www.locandadelpalazzo.com
Set in the heart of town, this well-restored palazzo has comfortable rooms and an excellent restaurant (open eve; and also lunch Tues–Fri, but you need to book). On the menu are local dishes, such as baccalà and ricotta-filled ravioli, all washed down with fine Aglianico wines. €€

### Matera
**Del Campo**
Via Lucrezio 1
Tel: 0835-388844
Fax: 0835-388757
www.hoteldelcampo.it
The nicest place to stay in Matera, this well-run hotel, about 1 km (½ mile) from the Sassi zone, is an

18th-century country house refurbished in modern style. €€€
**Domus**
Via Lombardia 16
Tel: 0835-940 5172
Fax: 0835-335450
www.domusdelbarisano.it
B&B with great views over the Sassi. Rooms or flats available. €
**Hotel I Sassi**
Via San Giovanni Vecchio 89
Tel: 0835-331009
www.hotelsassi.it
Your chance to stay in one of the cave-dwellings – the 15 rooms here have been carved straight out of the rock. Great views from the balcony in each unique room. €€
**Italia**
Via Ridola 5
Tel: 0835-333561
Fax: 0835-330087
A pleasant 3-star hotel right in the heart of the Old Town, the Italia has a patrician old-world atmosphere. Good restaurant. €€
**Locanda di San Martino**
Via Fiorentini 71
Tel: 0835-256600
Fax: 0835-256472
www.locandadisanmartino.it
Set in the heart of the Sassi zone of cave-dwellings, this is the most appealing of Matera's cave-hotels, though it is not for the claustrophobic. Tastefully converted, but remaining in character, this intimate, well-managed, individualistic small hotel incorporates a deconsecrated church and interconnecting tunnels through the rocks. €€
**Domina Degli Argonauti**
Lido di Macchia
Marina di Pisticci
Tel: 0835-470242
Fax: 0835-470240
www.argonauti.com
Summer hotel by the sea with a spa, private beach, huge lido and sailing club. Large modern rooms, all with balcony. Rate is for half-board, two nights minimum. €€€

### Potenza
**Grande Albergo**
Corso XVIII Agosto 1860, 46
Tel: 0971-410220
Fax: 0971-34879

Modern hotel in historic city centre with spacious rooms and impressive views of the valley. €€
**Tourist**
Via Vescovado 4
Tel/fax: 0971-21437
Centrally located, with rustic-style decor. Rooms at the back have views of the valley below. €€

### Melfi
**Hotel Due Pini**
Piazzale Stazione
Tel/fax: 0972-21031
Unremarkable and basic but fairly priced hotel opposite the train station. Restaurant okay. €

### Maratea
Maratea is now one of the most stylish and appealing resorts in the south, with a profusion of atmospheric accommodation. In 2006 the resort retained a prestigious Blue Flag from the EU for the cleanliness of its waters (see www.blueflag.org for criteria). Many of the best hotels are owned by the consortium Mondo Maratea (www.mondomaratea.it).

**Locanda delle Donne Monache**
Via Mazzei 4
Tel: 0973-877487
Fax: 0973-877867
www.mondomaratea.it
A beautifully renovated 18th-century building which originally served as a convent. Spacious rooms are tastefully decorated with period furniture. Terrace, roof garden, swimming pool. Open May to October. €€€
**Santavenere Hotel**
Via Santavenere
www.mondomaratea.it
This 1960s legend (where Burton and Taylor went to romance each other) has been restored to its former glory, with plush rooms and suites overlooking the sea or the large gardens; path to private beach; fitness and beauty centre. €€€€
**Masseria Serramarina**
Contrada Serramarina
Tel: 0496-52323
Fax: 0496-50109
www.masseriaserramarina.it

This world-class 5-star-plus spa hotel is set in a converted abbey and historic fortified farmhouse, complete with health farm and gourmet cuisine in a delightful, discreet rural setting. €€€€

## Calabria

### Reggio Calabria
**Azienda Agrituristica Il Bergamotto**
Condofuri Marina
Tel: 0965-727213
Email: ugosergi@yahoo.it
A hospitable farmhouse with a handful of simple rooms with tiny bathrooms (some rooms also have a mini-kitchen) in the old stables. Delicious Calabrian food is served to guests in summertime: all produce is home-grown, including the wheat for the bread. Owner Ugo Sergi organises donkey trekking in the Aspromonte National Park. €
**Excelsior**
Via Vittorio Veneto 66
Tel: 0965-812211
Fax: 0965-893084
Comfortable, modern, air-conditioned hotel in the centre of town, facing the Museo Nazionale. Some bathrooms with whirlpool bath. Panoramic views from the restaurant. €€€
**Famiglia Franco**
Via XXIV Maggio 51, Bivongi
Tel: 0964-731129
This is not a real hotel but the upper floor of a private house. The rooms (all with private bathrooms) are surprisingly large and comfortable. You can come and go at your convenience, as keys are provided, and privacy is not an issue. €

### Crotone
**Costa Tiziana**
Via per Capo Colonna
Tel: 0962-25601
Fax: 0962-21427
www.costatiziana.it
Resort by the sea a few kilometres south of Crotone. Windsurfing and sailing lessons. Ideal for families, with kids' restaurant, games room, play area and

babysitting service. Mandatory full board in summer. €€–€€€

### Catanzaro
**Grand Hotel**
Piazza Matteotti
Tel: 0961-701256
Fax: 0961-741621
Modern 3-star hotel with 79 serviceable rooms. €€–€€€

---

## COSENZA PROVINCE

### Altomonte
**Il Castello di Altomonte**
Piazza Castello 6
Altomonte (Cosenza)
Tel: 0981-948933
Fax: 0981-948937
www.altomonte.it
A 12th-century Norman castle with a view, this is arguably the fanciest option in the Pollino area. Guest rooms are decorated with wrought iron, while the common areas are decorated with period pieces and armoury. You can sip wine by the glass in the warm cellar or eat Calabrian dishes beneath a vaulted ceiling. €€€

### Amantea
**La Scogliera**
Località Corica
Tel: 0982-46219
Fax: 0982-48670
www.hotellascogliera.net
Set 4 km (2½ miles) from Amantea, this modern, Moorish-style resort hotel has a private sandy beach, suites and some rooms with whirlpool baths; seafood restaurant. Good deals for families and babysitting service. Rate is for full-board. €€€

### Camigliatello Silano
**Hotel Lo Sciatore**
Via Roma 128
Camigliatello Silano (Cosenza)
Tel: 0984-578105
Fax: 0984-579281
Located in the main town of the Sila region just outside the western border of the national park, the Sciatore gets crowded with Italian skiers in the winter months. The restaurant downstairs offers unpretentious Italian fare. €€

### Castrovillari
**La Locanda di Alia**
Via Jetticelle 55
Tel/fax: 0981-46370
www.alia.it
Appealing gentrified-rustic country-house hotel with Mediterranean garden and excellent restaurant (closed Sun). The chef focuses on local produce in dishes such as salmon pastries, fresh pasta, or lamb dishes. €€

### Citadella del Capo
**Palazzo del Capo**
Cittadella del Capo (Cosenza; A3 motorway exits: Lagonegro from Salerno, Falerna from Reggio Calabria)
Tel: 0982-95674
Fax: 0982-95676
www.palazzodelcapo.it
An appealing blend of old charm and modern luxury, including a restaurant and a pool with bar service, this small 5-star hotel is housed in the former mansion of a local aristocratic family. The panoramic view spans the Tyrrhenian coast just north of Paola to the Sila mountains. €€€€

### Cosenza
**Excelsior**
Piazza Matteotti 14
Tel: 0984-74383
Fax: 0984-74384
Simple but serviceable hotel on a main piazza, near the train station. Restaurant, bar, parking; all rooms have bathroom, TV and phone. €–€€

### Morano Calabro
**La Locanda del Parco**
Contrada Mazzicanino
Morano Calabro (Cosenza)
Tel/Fax: 0981-31304
Email: info@lalocandadelparco.it
With a *mamma* shaping pasta dough in a strictly local fashion and fireplaces in the common areas, the "Park's Inn" makes a very homely place to return to after spending your day hiking in the park. Pool and babysitting service. Guided tours on horseback are available all year round. €

### Tropea
**Le Roccette Mare**
Via Mare Piccolo
Tel: 0963-61358
Fax: 0963-61450
www.roccettemare.it
Beachfront 3-star hotel, clean and
comfortable. Half-board required.
Surcharge in August. Closed
November to March. €–€€

## Sicily

The past few years have seen an
explosion of B&B and rural farm
stay *(agriturismo)* accommodation
in Sicily, which has added to visitor
choice. At the forefront of this
development is the Ortygia district
of Siracusa, as well as Palermo
province, Ragusa Ibla, and many of
the offshore islands. Given that it is
a new development, regional
classifications, where they exist,
are often unreliable, so get as
much information as possible about
the place in advance. Since the
Italians have no tradition of B&B
and guesthouses, such places are
generally viewed solely as a cheap
option and many have no aesthetic
appeal or are extremely basic. That
said, there are gems among them,
particularly on the farm-stay
*(agriturismo)* side, which is better-
developed and often guarantees
local produce in abundance.

### PALERMO PROVINCE

Visitors need to choose between
staying in the bustling centre of
Palermo (ideal for seeing the
historic sites) or in the select resort
of Mondello, 10 km (6 miles)
outside town.
   In Palermo city, accommodation
is reasonably priced and easier to
find than in most parts of the
island. It is, however, advisable to
choose a higher grade hotel in
Palermo than you might elsewhere.
For safety's sake, choose a hotel
on a main street.
   There is a large concentration of
hotels at the southern ends of
Via Roma and Via Maqueda,
between the station and Corso

Vittorio Emanuele. Further along the
Corso, the hotels are more expensive. The modern Viale della Libertà
quarter, within walking distance of
the historic centre, is a good choice
from many points of view, offering
safety, convenience and fashionable neighbourhood bars. There are
a few very inexpensive places
around La Kalsa, a colourful part of
town that is up and coming, but still
a little rough round the edges.

### Palermo
**Centrale Palace**
Corso Vittorio Emanuele 327
(at Via Maqueda)
Tel: 091-336666
Fax: 091-334881
www.centralepalacehotel.it
This is the most atmospheric and
appealing hotel in the heart of the
city. The patrician palace has mostly
been well restored, with grand
public rooms, yet still feels like a
stylish private home. The "Ai Tetti"
rooftop restaurant offers panoramic
views over the city centre to Monte
Pellegrino. €€€–€€€€
**Excelsior Palace**
Via Marchese Ugo 3
Tel: 091-7909
Fax: 091-342139
www.excelsiorpalermo.it
Extremely comfortable 4-star hotel,
refurbished in 2005. Centrally
located for sightseeing in town.
Note that the rooms vary
considerably in size, and those on
the top floor have mansard ceilings.
Good restaurant. €€€–€€€€
**Grand Hotel et des Palmes**
Via Roma 398
Tel: 091-602 8111
Fax: 091-331545
One of the oldest hotels in the city,
but well maintained for Palermo. Via
Roma was probably a lot less
congested when Wagner completed
*Parsifal* here in 1882, but double-
glazed windows keep the noise out.
Rooms very variable in size and
quality; ask to see one first. €€€
**Massimo Plaza Hotel**
Via Maqueda 437
Tel: 091-325657
Fax: 091-325711
www.massimoplazahotel.com
Centrally located, facing the Teatro

The price categories are based
on a double room in high season
with breakfast.
**€** = under €75
**€€** = €75–125
**€€€** = €125–250
**€€€€** = more than €250

Massimo and close to the shops,
this is a comfortable small hotel
with friendly and helpful staff.
Bedrooms are sound-proofed and
spacious, while the public rooms
include a bar and reading room.
Breakfast is plentiful – unusual for
an Italian hotel. €€€
**Moderno**
Via Roma 276
Tel: 091-588683
Fax: 091-588260
Good value. Centrally located,
clean, no-frills hotel. €
**Mondello Palace**
Viale Principe di Scalea (Mondello)
Tel: 091-450001
Fax: 091-450657
Modern, luxurious 4-star seafront
hotel surrounded by a garden. Private
beach, swimming pool, restaurant
and bar. Comfortable good-sized
rooms; most offer sea views. €€€
**Politeama Palace Hotel**
Via Piazza Ruggero Settimo 15
Tel: 091-322777
Fax: 091-611 1589
Four-star hotel on Palermo's most
attractive grand piazza. Great location
for sightseeing; rooms are sound-
proofed; good breakfast. Top-floor
rooms have a view of the city. €€€
**Principe di Villafranca**
Via G Turrisi Colonna 4
Tel: 091-611 8523
Fax: 091-588705
www.principedivillafranca.it
This intimate yet patrician
boutique hotel appeals to the
same market as Massimo Plaza
and Centrale Palace *(see entries,
left)*. The hotel has more style
than either of them and features
vaulted ceilings and distinguished
antiques. Bedrooms are soothing
yet contemporary. The restaurant
and bar can both be recommended. €€€

## Price Guide

The price categories are based
on a double room in high season
with breakfast.
€ = under €75
€€ = €75–125
€€€ = €125–250
€€€€ = more than €250

### Villa Igiea Grand Hotel
Via Salita Belmonte 43
Tel: 091-631 2111
Fax: 091-547654
www.summithotels.com
The most stunning place to stay in
Palermo. Built as the palatial
residence of the Florio family in
1908, this 5-star hotel has been
restored to its early 20th-century
Art Nouveau splendour. Set on a
cliff with fantastic views of the city
and the bay. Rooms are richly
decorated with period furniture and
modern amenities. €€€€

### Cefalù
Cefalù vies with Taormina as Sicily's
most appealing resort. Safety,
convenience and good
infrastructure make it an ideal
choice for families or elderly people.
The beaches are closer and far
better than at Taormina. Like
Taormina, the resort feels perfectly
safe and free from petty crime. The
accommodation mainly consists of
pleasant but unremarkable
Mediterranean-style 3-star hotels.
Visitors out of season would do well
to avoid hotels located on the
beach since the beaches tend not
to be very clean in the low season.
### Baia del Capitano
Contrada Mazzaforno
Tel: 0921-420005
Fax: 0921-420163
The best place to stay in the area,
this Mediterranean-style modern
hotel is set in an olive grove about
5 km (3 miles) west of town. Each
small but well-kept room has a
terrace garden and great views.
Pool, tennis courts and a private
beach. €€€
### Kalura
Via Cavallaro 13 (Località Caldura)
Tel: 0921-421354

Fax: 0921-423122
www.hotel-kalura.com
Two km (1¼ miles) west of town,
ensconced in Mediterranean
foliage, the Kalura offers clean,
spacious rooms, each with a
terrace. Swimming pool, private
beach, family-friendly place with
good sports facilities. €€–€€€

### Ustica
This lovely island off Palermo
is extremely popular with swimmers
and nature lovers. It attracts a large
number of German, Scandinavian
and Sicilian visitors. Hotels tend to
fill up fast but there are many
opportunities to rent rooms: call in
at the Marine Park office (Vito
Longo), tel: 091-844 9456, open
June to September only, if the
fishermen at the port haven't
already made you an offer. The
excellent Palermo Tourist Office will
have information on hotels and
rooms to rent.
### Hotel Grotta Azzurra
Contrada San Ferlicchio
Tel: 091-844 9048
Fax: 091-844 9396
www.framonhotels.com
This Mediterranean-style hotel
is the best on the island and is
the best-organised place for
water sports. It also enjoys the
finest sea views, with a natural
grotto below the hotel, as well
as terraced gardens and
"La Cala dei Fenici", a noted
fish restaurant. €€€
### Pensione Clelia
Via Magazzino 7
Tel: 091-844 9039
Fax: 091-844 9459
www.hotelclelia.it
Located on the main square, the
Clelia is the oldest *pensione* in
town. Attached is a wonderful fish
restaurant. €–€€

## TRAPANI PROVINCE

Although the provincial capital
Trapani is relatively pleasant,
mountain-top Erice makes a far
more enticing base for exploring
western Sicily, especially in
summer, when the heat spurs

even the locals to leave Trapani
for the nearby Egadi Islands or
Erice. What's more, Trapani lacks
any really appealing hotels. There
is a cable-car link between Erice
and Trapani, which whisks visitors
between the two centres in about
15 minutes.

### Trapani
### Nuovo Albergo Russo
Via Tintori 4
Tel: 0923-22166
Fax: 0923-26623
Situated close to the cathedral,
this reliable and utterly respectable
low-cost hotel makes a good choice
if you have to stay overnight in
Trapani, before catching the ferry
to the Egadi, for instance. The
decor has changed little since the
1950s but the place is well-kept
and linked to several good
restaurants nearby. €
### Vittoria
Via F. Crispi 246
Tel: 0923-873044
Fax: 0923-29870
Located just off central Piazza
Vittorio Emanuele. Rooms have a
view of the sea or onto a public
garden where summer concerts
are held. €€

### Erice
### Baglio Santa Croce
Tel 0923-891111
Fax: 0923-891112
www.bagliosantacroce.it
As a peaceful converted farmhouse
on the slopes of Mount Erice, the
Baglio is ideal for those wishing to
avoid the bustle of town. Terraced
gardens, sea views and Sicilian
country-style cooking in the inn.
Period features remain, from the
exposed beams and tiled floors to
the simplicity of rooms furnished
with rustic wrought-iron beds. €
### Belvedere San Nicola
Contrada San Nicola
Tel: 0923-860124
Fax: 0923-869139
Set below Erice's lofty fortifications,
this is a family-friendly, new but
traditionally-styled country inn with
simple, tiled bedrooms and a hearty
rustic restaurant *(see entry on page
350)*. Swimming pool; children's

play area; bowls court *(bocce)*; horseriding nearby. **€–€€**

**Hotel Elimo**
Via Vittorio Emanuele 75
Tel: 0923-869377
Fax 0923-869252
www.charmerelax.com
This cosy 17th-century *palazzo* is a perfect retreat from the mists of mountain-top Erice, yet also the best place in which to savour the citadel's other-worldly atmosphere. Family-run by the palace's artistic, patrician owner, Carmelo Tilotta, this boutique hotel is a testament to his care, with spacious public rooms dotted with antiques and eclectic modern art, and a choice of summer terraces. The traditional-looking restaurant is one of the best in Erice, with local dishes given a creative spin by the enthusiastic chef. There is a simpler *enoteca* (wine bar and inn) in the cellars. **€€€**

### Marsala
**New Hotel Palace**
Via Lungomare Mediterraneo 57
Tel: 0923-719492
Fax: 0923-719496
www.newhotelpalace.com
Classical-style villa with spacious grounds. Elegant, frescoed interior with a sophisticated restaurant serving Sicilian specialities and a fine range of wines, including Marsala, naturally. **€€–€€€**

### Pantelleria
**Port Hotel**
Lungomare Borgo Italia 6
Tel: 0923-911299
Fax: 0923-912203
www.pantelleriahotel.it
Modern 3-star hotel with air-conditioned rooms and nice views. Half-board only in August. **€**

### Egadi Islands – Favignana
**Hotel Aegusa**
Via Garibaldi 11
Tel: 0923-922430
Fax: 0923-922440
www.aegusahotel.it
Set on the most popular and most convenient island, this pleasant hotel occupies an old *palazzo*, with

air-conditioned bedrooms in the converted tunnery; reasonable fish restaurant. Closed November to March. Book early for summer. **€€**

---

## AGRIGENTO PROVINCE

### Agrigento
**Colleverde Park Hotel**
Via dei Templi
Tel: 0922-29555
Fax: 0922-29012
www.topsicilia.it
A 4-star hotel set at the start of the Strada Panoramica, with great views across the Valley of the Temples. Rooms are functional but fine; two are equipped for disabled guests; friendly staff. **€€€**

**Domus Aurea**
Contrada Maddalusa,
Valle dei Templi
Tel: 0922-511061
Fax: 0922-598802
www.hoteldomusaurea.it
Called the "Golden House", this villa hotel is run by the neighbouring Foresteria Baglio della Luna *(see entry below)* and shares the same restaurant *(see restaurant entry for Il Dehors, page 350)*. Where the Baglio is rustic and cosy, Domus Aurea is cool and elegant, a small but perfectly formed villa encircled by a Mediterranean garden of citrus trees and palms. Rooms are stylish and most have Jacuzzi baths. Even so, the Baglio should be your first choice. **€€€**

**Foresteria Baglio della Luna**
Contrada Maddalusa,
Valle dei Templi
Tel: 0922-511061
Fax: 0922-598802
www.bagliodellaluna.com
This traditional family-run Sicilian manor house *(baglio)* has been exquisitely restored in gentrified rustic style, and furnished with Sicilian antiques and paintings. Some of the tastefully furnished bedrooms have Jacuzzi baths. Lovely grounds, as well as views over the Valley of the Temples from the terrace and dining room. The gourmet restaurant helps make this Agrigento's top hotel. The location, off the SS640, is

hard to find so arrive in daylight and check directions with the hotel. **€€€**

---

## ENNA PROVINCE

### Enna
**Grande Albergo Sicilia**
Piazza Colajanni 7
Tel: 0935-500850
Fax: 0935-500488
www.hotelsicilianaenna.it
Centrally located and the best of what little there is to choose from in this un-touristy town. Reasonably comfortable hotel; some rooms with views. **€€–€€€**

### Piazza Armerina
This appealing town makes a good stop for visitors wishing to see its famous Roman villa.

**Park Hotel Paradiso**
Contrada Ramalda
Tel: 0935-680841
Fax: 0935-683391
www.parkhotelparadiso.it
This is the most convenient hotel for the Roman villa. The hotel is surrounded by woods and has comfortable rooms and a good restaurant. **€€**

---

## RAGUSA PROVINCE

### Ragusa
**Eremo della Giubiliana**
Contrada Giubiliana (9 km/6 miles toward Marina di Ragusa)
Tel: 0932-669119
Fax: 0932-669129
www.eremodellagiubiliana.it
A fortified medieval hermitage that has been converted into one of Sicily's most delightful hotels. There are also stylish cottages, both old and modern, all with lovely sea views. **€€–€€€**

**Montreal**
Via San Giuseppe 8
Tel: 0932-621133
Fax: 0932-620026
Centrally located 3-star hotel with modern rooms. The best option in Ragusa Alta, but bear in mind that it is quite a steep climb from the old town. **€€**

## SIRACUSA PROVINCE

### Siracusa

Siracusa, in the form of its island core of Ortygia, is such an aesthetically pleasing city that it makes little sense to stay in the bland modern hotels in the new quarter, no matter how comfortable and well-equipped they are. The following recommendations are therefore all for Ortygia, with the exception of one good rural guesthouse just outside the city. The alternative in Ortygia is to stay in a B&B, of which there are many, but without a reliable classification system yet in place in Sicily, it is a hit-and-miss affair.

**Des Etrangers Et Miramare**
Passeggio Adorno 10–12
Tel: 0931-62671
Fax: 0931-65124
Siracusa's only 5-star hotel. Set on the island of Ortygia, this grand and contemporary-looking design hotel was created by merging two historic hotels. Even non residents should sample the panoramic rooftop restaurant which lays claim to being the most romantic in town. The bar and other public rooms are over-designed but the bedrooms are gracious. Spa centre, roof garden and swimming pool, plus tiny private "beach". €€€–€€€€

**Grand Hotel**
Viale Mazzini 12
Tel: 0931-464600
Fax: 0931-464611
www.grandhotelsr.it
Set on the island of Ortygia, this romantic Art Nouveau hotel overlooks the waterfront but has less spectacular views than Des Etrangers (above), although "La Terrazza", its rooftop restaurant, serves impressive cuisine, and is

### Price Guide

The price categories are based on a double room in high season with breakfast.
€ = under €75
€€ = €75–125
€€€ = €125–250
€€€€ = more than €250

especially attractive in summer. The hotel's charm is enhanced by its winter garden and lovely sea views, with the overall effect only slightly marred by cool, blasé service and a disappointing buffet breakfast. €€€–€€€€

**Hotel Gutkowski**
Via Lungomare di Levante 26
Tel: 0931-465861
Fax: 0931-480505
www.guthotel.it
This is a friendly, unpretentious, reasonably priced hotel on the waterfront of Ortygia. The townhouse, a former fishery and craft workshop, has simple bedrooms, some with sea views, and internet access. Good buffet breakfast using local produce. €€

**Hotel Roma**
Via Roma 66
Tel: 0931-465626
Fax: 0931-465535
www.hotelroma.sr.it
Set close to the cathedral in the historic heart of Ortygia, this attractive hotel offers everything except sea views. Carved out of a patrician *palazzo* and tastefully converted to retain plenty of period features, Roma is also proud of its restaurant, "Vittorini". The hotel's staff are exceptionally friendly too. €€–€€€

**Il Limoneto**
Via del Platone 3
Contrada Magrentino
Tel: 0931-717352
Fax: 0931-717728
www.limoneto.it
This is a rural retreat 9 km (5 miles) from the centre of Siracusa, (following the SP14 Mare-Monti road, direction Palazzulo). The setting of orange groves, orchards and rustic-style rooms is enhanced by a warm, house-party atmosphere and tasty home-made dishes. The mezzanine rooms are good for families. €€

## CATANIA PROVINCE

### Catania

**Excelsior Grand Hotel**
Piazza Verga 39
Tel: 095-7476111

Fax: 095-537015
www.thi.it
Expensive but comfortable 4-star Art Deco hotel and restaurant. Centrally located. €€€€

**La Vecchia Palma**
Via Etnea 668
Tel: 095-432025
Fax: 095-431107
www.lavecchiapalma.com
This central baroque *palazzo* has a cosy and cared-for atmosphere; each room is different and some are furnished with antiques; there is a small garden where breakfast is served in fine weather. A good budget choice. €

### Etna (Nicolosi)

**Biancaneve**
Via Etnea 163
Tel: 095-911176
Fax: 095-911194
Three-star hotel with pool and tennis courts. €€–€€€

### Taormina

Most visitors to Sicily wish to visit Taormina, the island's first and foremost resort. Hotels here are among the best in Sicily, and priced accordingly, but you have the choice of charming townhouse hotels, flowery villa-hotels, prestigious contemporary architecture, and even a converted monastery. Given Taormina's popularity, book well in advance and be prepared to accept obligatory half- or full-board in high season. A number of hotels close between November and February.

**Excelsior Palace**
Via Toselli 8
Tel: 0942-23975
Fax: 0942-23978
www.excelsiorpalacetaormina.it
Four-star hotel on a promontory with lovely grounds and a spectacularly sited pool. Rooms face the sea or look on to a lovely garden with Mount Etna beyond. €€€

**Grande Albergo Capotaormina**
Via Nazionale 105
Tel: 0942-572111
Fax: 0942-625467
www.capotaorminahotel.com
Set on the cape below Taormina, this contemporary, well-designed

## Camping

Campsites *(campeggi)* can be found in most areas of Southern Italy, and can be a good option when summer resorts are full. Italy is not a place to set up your own impromptu campsite – both for safety reasons and because of heavy fines.

Campsites charge about €20 for two people with car and tent. Most of them are well equipped with a service area for motorhomes, hot showers and shops selling food and basic necessities; in high season, many offer a shuttle-bus service to the nearest beach and/or town. Facilities like playgrounds, pools, tennis courts, discos, restaurants and pizzerias are often found in the larger campsites, often called

*villaggi turistici* rather than *campeggi*, because they also rent out bungalows and/or small apartments. Note that some places require a minimum stay of three or more nights, and that most *campeggi* are closed between November and Easter.

### Camping Guidebooks

Good guides to campsites include the multilingual *Guida Camping d'Italia* (Guide to Camping in Italy) from Touring Club Italiano (TCI) *(see page 330)*, *Eurocamping Italia-Corsica*, which also includes a detailed map of Italy, and *Guida ai Campeggi in Italia* (Demetra), which has colour pictures of the most popular resorts. Both are in Italian, with international symbols.

avant-garde hotel has great appeal, carved as it is into the rock, allowing for terraces and vistas to surprise at every turn. A lift sweeps you down through a tunnel in the rock to the tiny beach and an appealing free-form seawater pool nearby. There is a choice of three restaurants, with the most charming adjoining the beach. Shuttle service into town, which is 3 km (1¾ miles) up a steep hill. €€€

**Romantik Hotel Villa Ducale**
Via Leonardo da Vinci 60
Tel: 0942-28153
Fax: 0942-28710
www.hotelvilladucale.it
This delightful villa hotel is arguably the most romantic in town, set in a hamlet just above the resort and noted for its charming staff. Typical features include verandahs and terracotta floors; breakfast is served on the terrace overlooking Mount Etna. Closed December to mid-February. €€€

**San Domenico Palace**
Piazza San Domenico 5
Tel: 0942-613111
Fax: 0942-625506
www.thi.it
Once a monastery, the San Domenico is one of the finest hotels in Southern Italy. Magnificent

views toward Etna or the sea. Luxurious rooms decorated with antiques; swimming pool and fine restaurant. €€€€

**Villa Schuler**
Piazzetta Bastione 16
Tel: 0942-23481
Fax: 0942-23522
www.villaschuler.com
Hotel in an old villa set high above the sea, with 21 rooms and six suites. Most rooms have terraces and panoramanic views. Open March to November. The garden villa suite is the best. Shuttle service to beach. €€–€€€

## MESSINA PROVINCE

### Messina

**Jolly dello Stretto**
Via Garibaldi 126
Tel: 090-363860
Fax: 090-590 2526
www.jollyhotels.it
Centrally located just opposite the port. Many rooms with panoramic view of the Strait of Messina. Air conditioning; private beach. €€€

### Castel di Tusa

The fishing village of Castel di Tusa can make a good base for exploring

the Madonie, though it is best-known for Sicily's most talked about design hotel.

**Atelier sul Mare**
Via Cesare Battisti 4
Tel: 0921-334295
Fax: 0921-334283
www.ateliersulmare.com
This is such a cult hotel that visitors come to Sicily especially to stay here. It has been termed an art gallery with beds or an arts-oriented *ashram*. Either way, it's a bold, statement-making enterprise, celebrating everything from pop art to psychedelic wit. This contemporary hotel overlooks the bay and has a mixture of rooms designed with conventional artworks and those designed by previous artists in residence or inspired by celebrity visitors. The results are thought-provoking or outrageous, depending on your artistic sensibility. €€€

### Aeolian Islands (Stromboli)

**La Locanda del Barbablu**
Via Vittorio Emanuele 19
Tel: 090-986118
Fax: 090-986323
www.barbablu.it
Small (six rooms) and intimate, offering bed and breakfast. Excellent home-made food served on an enchanting terrace. Closed November to February. €€

# Where to Eat

## What to Eat

## What to Eat

The gentle lifestyle of Italy is partly a product of its civilised eating habits: eating and drinking in tranquillity at least twice a day are the norm here.

Italian breakfast *(colazione)* is usually light and consists of cappuccino and a *brioche* (pastry), or simply *caffè* (espresso).

For country dwellers, *pranzo* (lunch) tends to be the big meal of the day. It consists of antipasto (hors d'oeuvre), a *primo* (pasta, rice or soup) and a *secondo* (meat or fish with a vegetable – *contorno* – or salad). To follow comes cheese and/or fruit. Italians usually drink coffee after lunch and/or a liqueur, such as *grappa*, *amaro* or *sambuca*.

Traditionally, dinner is similar to lunch, but lighter. However, in the cities people tend to eat less at lunchtime and make dinner the main meal of the day.

### Local Specialities

Every region in Italy has its own typical dishes *(see page 364)*: Naples is the birthplace of pizza, and the nearby *pianura campana* produces the region's famous mozzarella *di bufala*. South from Campania is the region of Calabria, with its long coastline stretching around the tip of the boot. Expect seafood on the menu and hot pepper in sauces. Puglia is a region rich with local cuisine, including *purè di fave e cicoria* (fava-bean spread and chicory) and *orecchiette* (little ear-shaped pasta) with greens, and the creamy *burrata* cheese. Between the two is Basilicata, a long-forgotten region with its own specialities, among which pork and lamb dishes stand out.

The cuisine of Sicily cannot be captured in a sentence. The Greeks, Normans, Arabs, Spanish and French imported all sorts of ingredients and cooking techniques which blended into Italy's most sumptuous, brilliant and varied food scene. Sicily's sweet desserts made with ricotta cheese, such as *cassata siciliana* and *cannoli*, are heavenly. Don't miss fish *cuscus* (couscous) in the western towns and islands, particularly in Trapani and Favignana; swordfish in Palermo and Messina; *caponata* (fried aubergine in a tasty tomato-olive-caper sauce) and *pasta alla norma* (with aubergine and hard ricotta cheese).

## Where to Eat

Italy has thousands of restaurants, trattorias and *osterie*. If you do not want to have a complete meal, you can have a snack at the bar or at *tavole calde* and *rosticcerie* (grills).

If you go to a restaurant, don't order just a salad: the waiters may look down on you and treat you with disdain. If you think a complete meal is too big, forego the antipasto, but take a *primo* and a *secondo* at least.

## Naples

**Cantina di Triunfo**
Riviera di Chiaia 64 (Chiaia)
Tel: 081-668101
This old-style *cantina* run with enthusiasm for good food is a great place for a glass of wine and a light meal. A brief menu (two first courses, two second courses and a few side dishes) is based on what the owners found at the market that day. Open evenings only; closed Sunday and August. €€–€€€

## Price Guide

The price of a three-course meal for one, without wine, is:
€ = below €15
€€ = €15–30
€€€ = €30–45
€€€€ = over €45

## Cake Shops in Naples

**Scaturchio**
Piazza San Domenico Maggiore
Tel: 081-551 6944
This long-established cake shop is one of the best in town for local favourites like almond milk, *babà*, *sfogliatelle*, *cassate*, and chocolate *ministeriale*.
**Pasquale Pintauro**
Via Toledo 275
Here you will find delicious *sfogliatella*, the inimitable Neapolitan pastry with a wavy, crisp shell which looks like a tiny golden fan wrapped around a filling of ricotta and semolina.

**La Chiacchierata**
Piazza Matilde Serao 37 (Galleria Umberto/San Carlo Theatre)
Tel: 081-411465
Join the locals for excellent Neapolitan dishes like rigatoni with ricotta and meat sauce in this conveniently located family-run trattoria. Open for lunch only; closed Sunday. €€
**Ciro a Santa Brigida**
Via Santa Brigida 71 (Galleria Umberto/Toledo)
Tel: 081-552 4072
Full-service restaurant with above-average service and surroundings, this is also considered to be one of the best places in town to sample authentic Neapolitan pizza. Closed Sunday and August. €–€€
**La Mattonella**
Via Nicotera 13 (Chiaia)
Tel: 081-416541
Traditional *osteria* with benches, long tables and a charming marble bar. Try the fried salt cod *(baccalà fritto)* and the Neapolitan version of meatballs *(polpettone)*, and wash it all down with a bottle of local wine. Closed Sunday evening and two weeks in August. €–€€
**Mimi' alla Ferrovia**
Via Alfonso d'Aragona 21 (near the railway station)
Tel: 081-553 8525
Arguably the most famous "Neapolitan" restaurant in Naples and long associated with its famous clientele, Mimi' is still worth the

effort for classic dishes like linguini with seafood and fried anchovies and baby cuttlefish. Closed Sunday and August. €€

**Da Tonino**
Via Santa Teresa a Chaia 47
Tel: 081-421533
Run by the same family for more than a century, Da Tonino is a relic of the traditional *osteria*, where the common Neapolitans came to drink a glass of wine out of the barrel and have a bite of whatever was on the fire. Closed Sunday and August; open for lunch, plus Friday and Saturday dinner between October and May. €€

**La Sacrestia**
Via Orazio 116
Tel: 081-664186
Popular with locals, this restaurant is located on one of the most panoramic streets in the city. €€

### Pizzas and Street Food

Pizza is a must in Naples – the reputed birthplace of one of the world's most beloved foods. You can find wonderful pizzas and other quality, meal-worthy snacks throughout the city, but the following are among the most reliable places to try:

**Brandi**
Salita S. Anna di Palazzo 2
Tel: 081-416928
Famous for (reputedly) inventing the margherita, a pizza in honour of the Queen of Italy, made up of ingredients representing the three colours of the Italian flag: red (tomato sauce), white (cheese) and green (basil). €

**Friggitoria Vomero**
Via Cimarosa 44 (Vomero)
Tel: 081-578 3130
A first-rate Neapolitan fry house (potatoes, bread dough, polenta, aubergine balls, etc) where they charge by the piece and serve in paper bags. Try the *zeppole*, the deep-fried dough balls. Closed Sunday and August. €

**Un Soriso Integrale**
Vico S. Pietro a Majella 6
Tel: 081-455026
Macrobiotic vegetarian restaurant and natural food store in a small courtyard off the southeast corner

of Piazza Bellini. English and French spoken. Open for lunch and for evenings of live music. €

**Da Michele**
Via Sersale 1
Tel: 081-553 9204
Century-old restaurant that serves only two types of pizza – margherita and marinara. No frills, popular and very noisy. Open late. Closed Sunday and August. €

**Timpani e Tempura**
Vico della Quercia
Here they sell rice balls stuffed with salmon or ricotta as well as cheeses, general fried snacks and wine. Ask for a *timballo di ricotta* if you'd like a typical cheesy street snack. €

**Tripperia Fiorenzano**
Via Pignasecca 14 (centre)
Not for the faint-hearted, this tiny place fills with the aroma of stewed lamb's head, pig's feet, tripe and other parts of animals that don't make it to most restaurant tables. €

**Trianon**
Via Coletta 46
Tel: 081-553 9426
Founded in 1932, this is one of the most popular pizza places in the city, especially with the young crowd. Closed Sunday. €

### Cafés and Gelaterie

Naples is known throughout Italy as the city with the best coffee (thought to have something to do with the water), so a good cup of espresso or cappuccino should always be close at hand. Try along the waterfront, particularly out towards Mergellina, where **Ciro** is one of the best cafés. Alternatively, try **Gambrinus** (Piazza Trieste e Trento, tel: 081-417582) overlooking the Teatro San Carlo, an elegant 19th-century *gran caffè*; not cheap, but worth it for its old-world atmosphere.

For great ice cream, try **Gelateria della Scimmia** (Piazza Carità 4, tel: 081-552 0272), which also sells delicious pastries. Also recommended is **Remy Gelo** (Via Galliani 29) in Mergellino.

**Vaco e Press**
Piazza Dante 87
A typical place to eat *arancini* (savoury rice balls), as well as slices of pizza and the full range of Neapolitan fast food. €

### Around the Volcano

#### Pompeii
**President**
Piazza Schettino 12
Tel: 081-850 7245
Updated versions of classic Neapolitan dishes. A menu full of good seafood dishes, a comfortable atmosphere and excellent service; a welcome change from the many standard trattorias and tourist menus that catch the tourist hordes from the ruins. Closed Sunday dinner, Monday and part of August. €€€

#### Herculaneum
**Casa Rossa al Vesuvio**
Via Vesuvio 30 (About 10 km/ 6 miles south of Naples on the road to Herculaneum)
Tel: 081-777 9763
A great stop for lunch before or after visiting the ruins; pizza is the speciality here, baked in the traditional wood-fired oven. At lunch or dinner the views of Naples and the bay are equally idyllic. Closed Tuesday. €

### The Islands

#### Capri
**Canzone del Mare**
Marina Piccola 93
Tel: 081-837 0104
This is the most romantic and exclusive restaurant on Capri, and enjoys a wonderful view over the bay of Marina Piccola. Gracie Fields' former home is now a poolside restaurant serving sophisticated seafood specialities. Open Easter to October, lunch only. €€€

**Da Gelsomina**
Via Migliara 72
Tel: 081-837 1499
Enchanting sea view across the gulf and well loved by Capri habitués. Rabbit, a typical local dish, is served here. €€

**La Rondinella**
Via G. Orlandi 245 (Anacapri)
Tel: 081-837 1223
Good-value rustic trattoria with appetising local specialities like *ravioli alla caprese* with pesto or tomato sauce, and a wide assortment of simple fish dishes. Tables outside. Closed Thursday; open daily in summer. €–€€

### *Ischia*
**Il Focolare**
Località Casamicciola Terme
Via Cretaio al Crocifisso 68
Tel: 081-980604
Located 6 km (4 miles) from the town of Ischia, Il Focolare is an ideal place to sample the local seasonal cuisine. Pasta and bread, all made in-house, are especially good, as is the wild boar and truffles. Open evenings, except at weekends; closed Wednesday (October to May). €€€

**Il Melograno**
Via Giovanni Mazzela 110
(Forio d'Ischia)
Tel: 081-998450
Classic, refined cuisine in an intimate atmosphere, well worth a trip to the village of Forio on the west side of the island. Closed Monday and Tuesday (November to January). €€€–€€€€

**Da Peppina di Renato**
Via Bocca 23 (Forio d'Ischia)
Tel: 081-998312
This informal and cosy trattoria is the place to try the island's non-fish dishes, including pasta in walnut sauce and rabbit. Great views from the terrace. Closed Wednesday (October to March); open only for dinner. €€–€€€

### *Procida*
**Crescenzo**
Via Marina Chiaiolella 33
Tel: 081-896 7255

A family-run restaurant in the portside area with a charming view; the spaghetti with fish sauce is first-rate, as is the *coniglio alla cacciatora* (rabbit prepared with tomatoes according to a local recipe). Pizza is served evenings only. €€–€€€

## Sorrento

**Don Alfonso 1890**
Corso Sant'Agata 11
(Sant'Agata sui Due Golfi)
Tel: 081-878 0026
www.donalfonso1890.com
Widely considered to be the finest restaurant in Southern Italy. Set in Sant'Agata sui Due Golfi, near Sorrento, this gastronomic temple is celebrated all over Italy. It is worth taking the tasting menu. The cuisine is based on creative interpretations of Mediterranean dishes. Closed Monday and Tuesday; mid-January to March. €€€€

**Antica Trattoria**
Via Padre Reginaldo Giuliani 33
Tel: 081-807 1082
A reliable and prestigious local favourite for fresh fish cooked on the grill or delicately sautéed with tomatoes and herbs. Try the octopus cooked with artichokes. Closed Monday and February. €€

**Caruso**
Via Sant'Antonino 12
Tel: 081-807 3156
www.ristorantemuseocaruso.com
Centrally located in Sorrento itself, this is classic Sorrentine food in a refined atmosphere dedicated to the great Italian tenor. Closed Monday (October to March). €€€–€€€€

## The Amalfi Coast

### *Amalfi*
**La Caravella**
Via Matteo Camera 12
Tel: 089-871029
www.ristorantelacaravella.it
This is Amalfi's most celebrated restaurant, and deservedly so. The tasting menu is recommended. Closed Tuesday and November. €€€

**Da Gemma**
Via Fra Gerardo Sasso 9
Tel: 089-871345

Upmarket family-run trattoria that has been serving excellent fish and seafood since 1872. Take a seat in front of the Duomo and enjoy a bowl of fish soup. Closed Wednesday and January. €€€

### *Positano*
**Donna Rosa**
Via Montepertuso 97, Montepertuso
Tel: 089-811806
Five kilometres (3 miles) north of Positano, this is a pleasant restaurant where you'll find vegetable soups and fish served in a variety of ways. Closed Tuesday in winter. €€€–€€€€

**'O Capurale**
Via Regina Giovanna 12
Tel: 089-811188
Wonderful fish at this welcoming down-to-earth trattoria among the riches and glamour of Positano. Closed late October and early February. €–€€

**Il Ritrovo**
Via Montepertuso 77, Montepertuso
Tel: 089-875453
Tables outside in the summer and a roaring fire in the winter, this homely, family-run trattoria features many dishes made with vegetables grown by the proprietors. Closed Wednesday (October to May); mid-January to mid-February. €€

### *Salerno*
**Antica Pizzeria del Vicolo della Neve**
Vicolo della Neve 24
Tel: 089-225705
The oldest trattoria in the city and still worth a stop for excellent home-style cooking in a down-to-earth atmosphere. First-rate pizza and *calzone*. Closed Wednesday and over Christmas; open for dinner only. €

**Al Cenacolo**
Piazza Alfano 1, 4/6
Tel: 089-238818
Salerno's best restaurant; refined cuisine in a low-key setting in the centre of town. The food is based on traditional and age-old recipes, and the menu changes with the seasons. Closed Sunday dinner and Monday; two weeks in August and Christmas to New Year. €€€

**La Botte Piccola**
Traversa E. da Corbilla
Tel: 089-254101
An intimate, family-run restaurant where you'll find home-made pasta dressed with seasonal vegetables and a good choice of traditional meat and fish dishes. Open for dinner only. €€

## Southern Campania

### Agròpoli
**Il Ceppo**
Via Madonna del Carmine 31
Tel: 0974-843036
www.hotelristoranteilceppo.com
Family-run gentrified-rustic-style restaurant with adjoining hotel. Fish dishes and country-style dishes from the Cilento make up most of the menu, but pizza is also served in the evenings. Don't miss the tasty local cheeses, including a superb mozzarella *di bufala*. Closed Monday. €€–€€€

### Palinuro
**Carmelo**
Isca, 2 km (about a mile) east of Palinuro on the SS562
Tel: 0974-931138
In this long-established, family-run restaurant you can sample some of the best local cuisine, based on fish and fresh pasta. Outside dining in fine weather. Closed Wednesday and Christmas; summer open daily. €€

### San Giovanni a Piro
**U' Zifaro**
Lungomare Marconi 43
Tel: 0974-986397
Tables outside in summer, where you can dine with a view of the port. Varied all-fish menu made every which way, including fried fish and fish baked whole in a crust of salt. Save room for dessert, with wonderful fruit ice cream and *cassatine* (ricotta-filled pasty topped with icing) brought from Sicily. Closed Sunday and Monday in winter, and December to January. €€

### Santa Maria di Castellabate
**La Taverna del Pescatore**
Via Lamia
Tel: 0974-968293

Fantastically well-preserved town in the Cilento area. Cilento-style cuisine is on offer, with great *zuppa di pesce* (fish soup) and a wonderful array of local seafood. Best wine list in Southern Campania. Closed Monday. €€

### Ravello
**Cumpa' Cosimo**
Via Roma 44
Tel: 089-857156
Much-loved local trattoria, judging by the dozens of framed pictures on the walls of happy customers over the past decades. Closed Monday and November to February. €€
**Palazzo della Marra**
Via della Marra 7
Tel: 089-858302
Welcoming restaurant inside a restored historic *palazzo*. Creative, unusual take on traditional cuisine. Amalfitan dishes with a twist, such as steamed fish with marrow and chicory. Closed Tuesday from October to March. €€€

## Puglia

Puglian cuisine is renowned for being distinctive, genuine and varied. Some of the best places are farms that have gone up-market without betraying their country traditions. Also check the Puglia hotels section, as many hotels and even simple farm-stays have good restaurants.

### FOGGIA PROVINCE

### Foggia
**Locanda di Mali**
Via Arpi 86–88
Tel: 0881-723937
Set in a historic *palazzo*, this restaurant is good for modern twists on classic seafood and meat dishes. Closed Sunday evening and Monday lunch. €€
**Osteria del Zio Aldo**
Via Arpi 62
Tel: 0881-708104
This family-run trattoria serves reliable Puglian dishes, from pasta dishes to octopus salad or kid and potatoes. Good cheeseboard. Closed Sunday and part of August. €

**Trilussa**
Via Tenente Lorio 50
Tel: 0881-709253
Good pizzeria with the best bruschetta (toasted bread with various toppings) in Puglia. Closed Wednesday; open for dinner only. €
**Il Ventaglio**
Via Postiglione 6
Tel: 0881-661500
Set in an elegant 19th-century villa on the outskirts of town, this is a trusty place for refined Puglian cuisine, including seafood ravioli and seasonal vegetable dishes. Closed Sunday evening and Monday. €€€

### San Giovanni Rotondo
**Osteria Antica Piazzetta**
Via A. Mercato 13
Tel: 0882-451920
Set in the historic centre, this authentic trattoria serves simple local dishes, including mixed grills, fish caught that day, local salami and home-made pasta. Closed Wednesday. €

### Tremiti Islands
**Hotel Gabbiano**
Piazza Belvedere
Isola San Domino
Tel: 0882-463410
www.hotel-gabbiano.com
Solid fare at the restaurant of this hotel near the port; the mixed grill is especially recommended. Outside dining in the garden with a panoramic view. Transfer service to the port. €€

### BARI PROVINCE

### Bari
**Alberosole ESP/G**
Corso Vittorio Emanuele 13
Tel: 080-523 5446
On the main street that divides the ancient and modern parts of the city, this first-rate restaurant is one of Bari's best for Puglian dishes prepared with confidence. Warm, efficient service. Closed Monday and August. €€–€€€
**La Taverna Verde**
Largo Adua 18
Tel: 080-554 0870

Simple, much-loved restaurant just off the Lungomare. Excellent *favè e cicoria* (fava-bean purée with sautéed chicory). Closed Sunday evening and August. €€

**Terranima**
Via Putignani 213
Tel: 080-521 9725
Step back in time into this intriguing restaurant, with its 19th-century decor and a brief menu made up of traditional Puglian specialities. Charming period setting and old-fashioned air. Closed Sunday dinner and mid-July to mid-August. €€

*Alberobello*
**La Cantina**
Via Lippolis 9
Tel: 080-432 3473
Among the many tourist restaurants in the town famous for *trulli*, this is a simple trattoria recommended for a good plate of *orecchiete* pasta, served simply with mushrooms or asparagus, according to the season. Closed Tuesday and August. €–€€

*Locorotondo*
**Ristorante Taverna Del Duc**
Tel: 080-431 3007
This inn is set in a village famous for its wine, so call into the Cantina del Locorotondo first; then sample delicious Puglian specialities such as pasta, fresh fish, charcoal-grilled lamb, and sweet pastries. €€

*Trani*
**Torrente Antico**
Via Fusco 3
Tel: 0883-487911
An acclaimed restaurant well worth a stop on your way up or down the coast. Not only is the food creative and delicious, but the wine list is one of the best in the region. Closed Sunday dinner and Monday. €€€

### BRINDISI PROVINCE

*Brindisi*
**Trattoria Pantagruele**
Via Salita di Ripalta 1
Tel: 0831-560605
Very handy for the port, this no-nonsense restaurant offers the standard local dishes prepared with care. There is ample choice of grilled meat as well as fish, and the tasty home-made desserts are worth trying. Outside seating too. Closed Saturday lunch, Sunday and August. €–€€

*Carovigno*
**Osteria Gia Sotto l'Arco**
Corso Vittorio Emanuele 71
Tel: 0831-996286
Set in a Bourbon palace in the historic centre, this elegant gourmet restaurant is one of Puglia's best. It serves pasta, seafood and rabbit stew. Closed Monday. €€

*Ceglie Messapica*
**Fornello da Ricci**
Contrada Montevicoli
Tel: 0831-377104
This is one of celebrity chef Antonio Carluccio's favourite restaurants, and he's from Puglia so he should know. Set in an old farmhouse with a pergola and terrace, the estate serves hearty regional dishes such as Carluccio's favourite, *fava e cicoria*, a purée of broad beans infused with garlic and wild chicory. Tricky to find the place but worth it. Closed Monday evening and Tuesday. €€

*Ostuni*
**L'Osteria del Tempo Perso**
Via Tanzarella Vitale 47
Tel: 0831-304819
Set close to the cathedral, this traditional inn is set in a former bakery and is noted for its huge range of dependable home-made Puglian antipasti and roast meats. Closed Monday. €€

### LECCE PROVINCE

*Lecce*
**Cucina Casereccia**
Via Costadura 9
Tel: 0832-245189
The name of this plain trattoria means "homemade cuisine" and just about says it all. Closed Sunday dinner and Monday; two weeks in September. €

**Picton**
Via Idomeneo 14
Tel: 0832-332383
Inventive, often wild, combinations in this restaurant make a refreshing change in this otherwise tradition-bound part of the country. Closed Monday and part of June. €€–€€€

### TARANTO PROVINCE

*Taranto*
**Ponte Vecchio**
Piazza Fontana 61
Tel: 0994-706374
Smart fish and seafood restaurant with a summer terrace. Dishes include pasta with clams or lobster. Closed Tuesday. €€

*Martina Franca*
**Il Ritrovo degli Amici**
Corso Messapia 8
Tel: 080-483 9249
This pleasant restaurant is the best place to try this wonderful town's famous salamis and sausages, as well as other local specialities. Closed Sunday dinner, Monday and February. €€

### Basilicata

### MATERA PROVINCE

*Maratea*
**Taverna Rovita**
Via Rovita 13
Tel: 0973-876588
Just off the main piazza in Maratea Alta. Eat your spaghetti *al pecorano* (with tomatoes, ricotta cheese and basil) and other classic local dishes in simple terracotta bowls. Closed Tuesday and mid-January to mid-March. €€–€€€

*Matera*
Ask Matera tourist office (Via Spine Bianche 22, tel: 0835-331817) for the names of good food shops, dairies and wine estates which run food- and wine-tastings. Do sample the region's top wine, the volcanically tinged Aglianico di Vulture.
**Il Casino del Diavolo**
Via La Martella 48
Tel: 0835-261986

A local favourite, this restaurant set in an olive grove on the outskirts of town features an ample selection of local specialities laid out along a long buffet. Eat in the garden in summer. Closed Monday. €–€€

**Le Botteghe**
Piazza San Pietro Barisano 22
Tel: 0835-344072
Traditional cuisine served in a comfortable restaurant carved out of a *sassi* cave. Dishes include vegetable pasta, roast meats and lamb with mushrooms. Closed Sunday evening and Wednesday. €€

**La Latteria**
Via Duni 2
Tel: 0835-312058
This simple inn serves cheeses, salami, soups and antipasti, as well as offering wine-tasting in another part. Open all day in summer. €

**Trattoria Lucana**
Via Lucana 48
Tel: 0835-336117
Try the wonderful bruschetta made with hearty local bread, and pasta served with seasonal vegetables and sausage. Closed Sunday in winter. €€

## POTENZA PROVINCE

*Potenza*
**Antica Osteria Marconi**
Viale Marconi 233
Tel: 0971-56900
Arguably the best restaurant in Basilicata. Don't miss the fresh pasta and the *minestra di fave e cicoria* (broad bean and chicory soup). A tempting wine list features the best of the region's production. Charming location, with terrace for summer and cosy brick-and-wood dining room for winter. Closed Sunday dinner, Monday and August. €€

### Price Guide

The price of a three-course meal for one, without wine, is:
€ = below €15
€€ = €15–30
€€€ = €30–45
€€€€ = over €45

**Due Torri**
Via Due Torri 6
Tel: 0971-411661
Relaxing restaurant set inside a fortified building in the old part of town. Try the home-made *strascinati* pasta with kid sauce, followed by grilled meat and pecorino cheese. Good service and solid wine list. Closed Sunday. €€

*Melfi*
**Agriturismo La Villa**
Località Cavallerizza
Tel: 0972-236008
Farm-restaurant offering home-grown specialities from the Vulture area, using estate-grown olive oil, vegetables and cured meats, as well as the renowned Aglianico di Vulture wine. Closed Sunday evening and Monday; best to call in advance. €€

**Novecento**
Contrada Incoronata
Tel: 0972-237470
Set in a classical-style villa on a hill, the cuisine is traditional and strongly flavoured, using local cheeses and salami as well as roast meats. Good selection of Aglianico wines. Closed Sunday evening and Monday. €€

**Vaddone**
Contrada Santa Abruzzese (Melfi)
Tel: 0972-243323
Rustic family restaurant with wonderful local salami and cheeses. The pasta *maquarnara* (with meat sauce and local pecorino cheese) is a winner. Closed Sunday dinner and Monday. €–€€

*Rionero in Vulture*
**Il Cantinone**
Via Forcella 22
Tel: 0972-722443
A traditional *enoteca*, or wine bar, and the ideal place to sample different Aglianico di Vulture wines and many other regional Italian wines. Closed Tuesday. €

**La Pergola**
Via Lavista
Hotel in the centre of town renowned for its restaurant, which specialises in game and mushroom dishes, all accompanied by regional wines. €€

*Rotonda*
**Da Peppe**
Corso Garibaldi 13
Tel: 0973-661251
After working up an appetite exploring the Parco Nazionale del Pollino, you can treat yourself to a hearty dinner here. Set in a 19th-century *palazzo*, this atmospheric inn serves fine vegetable dishes as well as pork, lamb and rabbit. Closed Monday. €€

### Calabria

## CATANZARO PROVINCE

*Catanzaro*
**Da Pepe**
Vico I – Piazza Roma 6
One of several places in town to sample *morzello*, Catanzaro's typical dish: a spicy sauce cooked slowly in an enormous pot, in which veal tripe and innards are stewed. The dish is served in a soft pitta bread and eaten on the spot. Closed Sunday. €

**La Fattoria**
Via Magna Grecia 83 (7 km/ 4½ miles from Catanzaro, in the direction of Catanzaro Lido)
Tel: 0961-782809
Once an olive-oil press, this restaurant is a great place to sample different Calabrian dishes from a well-prepared and inviting buffet. If you have room, there's also an impressive selection of local cheeses. €€

*Civita*
**Agora'**
Piazza Municipio 30
Tel: 0981-73410
Simple, family-run, traditional restaurant specialising in the local, Albanian-influenced cuisine. The lamb and kid dishes are wonderful. Closed Monday. €–€€

## COSENZA PROVINCE

*Cosenza*
**Da Giocondo**
Via Piave 53
Tel: 0984-29810
Reliable restaurant in the old part

## Price Guide

The price of a three-course meal for one, without wine, is:
€ = below €15
€€ = €15–30
€€€ = €30–45
€€€€ = over €45

of town. Don't miss the pickled mushrooms, the local cheeses (from the Sila), and the *maccheroni* in kid sauce or the gnocchi and swordfish. Closed Sunday evening and August. €€

### Castrovillari
**La Locanda di Alia**
Via Jetticelle 55
Tel: 0981-46370
A restaurant renowned for some of the best food in Calabria, its ever-changing menu is sure to be full of dishes that combine traditional recipes with touches of creative fancy. Reservations recommended. Closed Sunday and Christmas to New Year. *(See Where to Stay, page 336.)* €€€

## CROTONE PROVINCE

### Crotone
**Casa di Rosa**
Viale Cristofaro Colombo 117
Tel: 0962-21946
Simple, small restaurant located above the Porto Vecchio, with a wide selection of fish on the menu. Try the *spaghettoni con cozze e pomodorini al forno* (baked with mussels and cherry tomatoes) and the fried fish. Reservations recommended. Closed Sunday and mid-December to mid-January. €€–€€€
**Da Ercole**
Viale Gramsci 122
Tel: 0962-901425
At the southern end of town, this fish restaurant is the place to enjoy sea urchins and *scrine*, a local mollusc found only here. Outside dining in summer. Reservations recommended. Closed Wednesday in winter. €€€

### Isola di Capo Rizzuto
**Da Annibale**
Via Duomo 35 (Le Castella)
Tel: 0962-795004
One of the best fish restaurants in the Catanzaro area and well attended by locals, Annibale remains affordable. Trust the waiters, who tend to bring you the catch of the day rather than the menu. Ask for a taste of their special pecorino cheese at the end of the meal. €€–€€€

## REGGIO CALABRIA PROVINCE

### Reggio Calabria
**Baylik**
Vico Leone 3
Tel: 0965-48624
Established fish restaurant close to the port where you can dine until midnight on the catch of the day. The star turn is the swordfish served with pumpkin flowers. Closed Thursday and part of August. €€
**Taverna degli Ulivi**
Via Eremo Botte 32
Tel: 0965-891461
Ignore the pizza served here and opt instead for the *maccarruni I casa* (traditional Calabrian hand-made pasta with meat sauce). Wonderful grilled meat and sausages. Closed Sunday. €€

## VIBO VALENTIA PROVINCE

### Vibo Valentia
**Approdo**
Via Roma 22 (Località Vibo Marina, 10 km/6 miles from Vibo Valentia)
Tel: 0963-572640
Acclaimed fish restaurant near Vibo Marina. Try the *fileja* (home-made pasta) with mussels, shrimp and courgettes, and the anchovy and aubergine tart. First-rate service and warm welcome. Closed Monday in winter. €€€

### Tropea
**Osteria del Pescatore**
Via del Monte 7
Tel: 0963-603018

You'll find this traditional *osteria* set inside a noble *palazzo* behind the Duomo in the centre of Tropea. The short menu features a few pasta choices and a selection of grilled or fried fish. Closed Wednesday (except summer). €€

## Sicily

Expect there to be considerable seasonal variations in opening times: many of the best city restaurants tend to close for part of July and August, while resort restaurants are often closed in winter.

## PALERMO PROVINCE

### Palermo
Palermo offers the most varied dining experience in Sicily, with its many restaurants sited in the historic centre, in the blander new Viale Libertà district, or in Mondello, Palermo's seaside resort, where the city decamps in summer. In general, dining standards are high in Palermo province, particularly in the Madonie mountains and in Cefalù.
**Antica Focacceria San Francesco**
Via Paternostro 58
Tel: 091-320264
The historic shop to drop into for your fill of Palermitan street food, including pizza Palermitan-style (*sfincioni*) or *milza* (spleen) sandwiches, fried rice and cheese balls (called *arancini di riso*), and chickpea fritters. €
**Bye Bye Blues**
Via del Garofalo 23 (Mondello)
Tel: 091-684 1415
Well worth the trip from Palermo (or further), this welcoming Mondello restaurant offers by far the best food in the area. Ever-changing menu based on fresh fish and seasonal vegetables. Open for dinner only; closed Tuesday. €€€–€€€€
**Capricci di Sicilia**
Via Istituto Pignatelli 6
(off Piazza Sturzo)
Tel: 091-327777
Simple, rustic and informal, this is the best place to stop for lunch after a walk through the Borgo

Vecchio and Piazza Politeama; try a delectable bowl of spaghetti dressed with a sea urchin sauce and traditional Sicilian aubergine rolls. Also try the *polpette*, fish balls made with fresh sardines. €€

**Charleston–Le Terrazze**
Viale Regina Elena (Mondello)
Tel: 091-450171
Situated on the pier at Mondello, this is where the smart set eat out in summer. The Art Nouveau dining room is the setting for seafood dishes such as risotto, calamari with fava beans, or swordfish roulades. Closed Wednesday (November to January). €€€–€€€€

**Santandrea**
Piazza Sant'Andrea 4
Tel: 091-334999
Set in the colourful Kalsa district, just behind the raucous Vucciria market, this reliable restaurant makes use of market produce and presents it beautifully. Try the vegetable antipasti, spaghetti with fresh sardines, and rich chocolate tart. Closed Tuesday in winter and Sunday in summer, also Monday lunch. €€–€€€

**Shanghai**
Vicolo dei Mezzani 34
Tel: 091-589702
Crumbling little restaurant on a small terrace above the bustling Vucciria market, from which the food is hauled up in wicker baskets. A memorable simple meal. No credit cards. €

**Ostaria dei Vespri**
Piazza Croce dei Vespri 6
Tel: 091-617 1631
Set in the former stables of Palazzo Gangi, next door, linked to the famous novel and film *Il Gattopardo* (The Leopard). Great wine selection at this inn, with a limited but appetising menu that always includes marinated fish and pasta with swordfish sauce. Outside seating in an attractive piazza. Closed Sunday and August. €€€

**Il Ristorantino**
Piazza de Gasperi 19
Tel: 091-512861
Popular restaurant in a residential part of town, where locals enjoy warm, excellent service and good food such as swordfish (*pesce*

*spada)* or aubergine-filled ravioli. Great selection of dependable Sicilian and Italian wines. Closed Monday and August. €€€

**La Scuderia**
Viale del Fante 9
Tel: 091-520323
Worth the trip to the foot of Monte Pellegrino, a few miles out of town, to enjoy a view of the city from the terrace and the usual array of reliable Sicilian specialities. Closed Sunday and August. €€€–€€€€

### Castelbuono

Castelbuono is a well known gastronomic centre for the Madonie mountains and much of rural Palermo province. This attractive, well-kept village is the place to indulge in tastings and hearty meals.

**Nangalarruni**
Via Alberghi/Via della Confraternita 5
Tel: 0921-671428
www.ristorantenangalarruni.it
This is hearty mountain fare and the best in the Madonie area. Set in the historic centre, this rustic restaurant is well-known for its mushroom and vegetable pasta dishes, as well as meaty specialities such as suckling pig or kid served with saffron. Closed Wednesday. €€

**La Fiasconeria**
Piazza Margherita
Tel: 0921-671231
This is one of the best *pasticcerie* (pastry shops) in Sicily and sells home-made *panettone* in such flavours as fruits of the forest (*frutti di bosco)* and almonds (*di mandorle)*, as well as offering free tastings of the pastries and *fico d'india* or almond liqueurs at the family bar opposite. €

**Romitaggio**
Località San Giulielmo
Tel: 0921-671323
Set in the countryside 5 km (3 miles) outside Castelbuono, this inn occupies a former monastery and the frescoed stone walls make an atmospheric backdrop to meals. Dishes are based on local mountain specialities using fresh pasta, cheeses, roast pork and full-bodied wines from Palermo province. Closed Wednesday and mid-June to mid-July. €€

### Cefalù

**La Brace**
Via XXV Novembre 10
Tel: 0921-423570
Pleasant little restaurant near the Duomo. Nice mix of classic Sicilian and more innovative cuisine, including ricotta and pistachio tart. Good selection of local wines. Closed Monday and mid-December to mid-January. €€

**Ostaria del Duomo**
Via del Seminario 5
Tel: 0921-421838
Lovely open-air setting overlooking the Duomo. Authentic *caponata* (aubergine stew) and *carpaccio di pesce* (thinly sliced raw fish, lightly marinated). Also seafood spaghetti. Closed Monday (except in summer) and January. €€

### Ustica

**Mamma Lia**
Via S. Giacomo 1
Tel: 091-844 9407
The island's most popular restaurant. Try the soup made from local lentils or the pasta with fennel and sardines, followed by swordfish croquettes. Bookings required. Closed October to March. €€

**Da Mario**
Piazza Umberto I 21
Tel: 091-844 9505
Local fish dishes in a pleasant, family-run trattoria. Try the spaghetti with sea urchin and shrimps with the local Albanella wine. Outside dining in summer on the town's main piazza. Closed Monday and January. €€

## TRAPANI PROVINCE

### Trapani

**Ai Lumi**
Corso Vittorio Emanuele 75
Tel: 0923-872418
Set in the historic centre, a thick wooden door on the town's main drag hides this cosy rustic restaurant with wooden tables, memorabilia on the walls, and the best seafood in town. If you happen to be here during tuna season (May to June) you can try *lattume* (tuna roe). Closed Sunday. €€

**Trattoria del Porto**
Via Staiti 45
Tel: 0923-547822
The TV blares the latest news and soccer scores from this brightly lit, family-run trattoria opposite the hydrofoil to the Egadi Islands. Fish couscous and spaghetti *alla trapanese* (with a pesto sauce made of almonds) are local favourites. Closed Monday. €€

*Erice*
**Belvedere San Nicola**
Contrada San Nicola
Tel: 0923-860124
Rustic fare abounds at this family-friendly country inn located just below Erice's walls. Enjoy grilled fish and meats as well as ultra-fresh fruit and vegetables while overlooking the distant sea. Closed Wednesday. €–€€

**Caffè Maria Grammatico**
Via Vittorio Emanuele 4
This is a bar, pastry shop, ice-cream parlour, tearoom, and simple restaurant for a light lunch. It is run by Maria Grammatico, Sicily's best-known pastry chef, whose pastry shop is next door. She supplies the best bars all over Sicily and also runs teaching courses in Sicily and San Francisco. Set in a patrician palace, the cosy tearooms occupy the first floor, and serve many of the sweet pastries Maria learnt from the nuns during her disquieting girlhood spent in a nearby convent. (For the full story, read *Bitter Almonds*, Maria's intriguing memoirs, in English, which has recipes too; *see Further Reading, page 368.*) €

**Elimo**
Via Vittorio Emanuele 73
Tel: 0923-869377
Fax: 0923-869252
This patrician palace in the centre of town is home to a cosy hotel

**Price Guide**

The price of a three-course meal for one, without wine, is:
€ = below €15
€€ = €15–30
€€€ = €30–45
€€€€ = over €45

*(see Where to Stay, page 339)* as well as to a noted restaurant and a wine bar. The individualistic yet traditional restaurant is one of the best in Erice, with local dishes given a creative spin by the enthusiastic chef. Typical dishes include *tagliolini alla verdure*, pasta with capers, mushrooms and marrow (squash), followed by fillet steak. La Filosofia dei Sapori is a simpler *enoteca* (wine bar and inn) that serves a wide range of top Sicilian wines, including Cerasuolo, Sicily's best red. Restaurant €€, wine bar €

**Monte San Giuliano**
Vicolo San Rocco
Tel: 0923-869595
Established and endearing rustic inn which is hidden away in Erice's maze of alleys below Piazza Umberto. Although the inn is noted for its fresh seafood, equally good is the couscous, a reminder of western Sicily's Moorish past, or the pasta, especially *pesto alla trapanese* with garlic, basil and fresh tomatoes. Closed Monday. €€

*Marsala*
**Fonte d'Oro**
Via Curatolo
Tel: 0923-719586
This is an appealing and fashionable seafood restaurant which combines a friendly atmosphere with a passion for fish: try the grilled swordfish, *fritto misto* (mixed grill), stuffed squid, or just rely upon the catch of the day. €€

**Trattoria Garibaldi**
Piazza dell'Addolorata 35
Tel: 0923-953006.
A reliable if slightly tired-looking trattoria in the historic centre. On offer is fresh pasta with lobster or sardines, seafood couscous, and grilled sea bass. Closed Saturday lunch; also Sunday in winter. €€

*Pantelleria*
**La Nicchia**
Contrada Sicauri Basso
Tel: 0923-916342
Wonderful informal restaurant set in a Moorish *dammuso* house with outside dining and a view of the sea. Try the delicious house speciality,

spaghetti with shrimps, capers and tomatoes. Open evenings only; closed Wednesday. €€–€€€

## AGRIGENTO PROVINCE

*Agrigento*
**Il Dehors**
Foresteria Baglio della Luna, Contrada Maddalusa, Valle dei Templi
Tel: 0922-511061
www.bagliodellaluna.com
Set in a charming manor house hotel *(see Where to Stay, page 339)*, this is the chicest restaurant in Agrigento, and classed as one of the top five in Sicily. The internationally renowned Italian chef favours a creative version of nouvelle cuisine, using seasonal Sicilian ingredients. While exquisite, portions are on the small side, so best to take a full tasting menu. Bookings required. €€€–€€€€

**Leon d'Oro**
Via Emporium 102 (Località San Leone)
Tel: 0922-414400
Well worth the short drive (about 8 km/5 miles) west of the town centre, this much-loved restaurant serves good seafood. Excellent spaghetti with swordfish and mint sauce. Outside dining. Closed Monday and November. €€

**Trattoria dei Templi**
Via Panoramica dei Templi 15
Tel: 0922-403110
This gentrified rustic retreat is convenient for the Valley of the Temples and, although popular with tourists, attracts locals too. A vaulted ceiling and terracotta-tiled floor provide the backdrop to pasta *alla norma* (with aubergines) and *panzerotti della casa*, ravioli stuffed with white fish in a seafood sauce. Closed Friday (and Sunday in July and August). €€

**Villa Athena**
Via Passeggiata Archeologica 33
Tel: 0922-596288
www.hotelvillaathena.com
This overrated 18th-century villa-hotel used to be the finest in town but rested on its laurels because of its unparalleled views over the exquisite Temple of Concordia. But

this is still the place for a romantic dinner on the terrace, with seafood, lobster risotto or herb-flavoured roast meats enlivened by views over the temple. If you do overindulge, then stay overnight in room 205, which has a magical view over the moonlit temple. Book in summer. €€€

## ENNA PROVINCE

### Enna
**Ariston**
Via Roma 353
Tel: 0935-26038
Reliable and central local restaurant for Sicilian standards like rigatoni *alla norma* (with aubergine and salted ricotta). Good grilled meat and fish. Efficient service. Closed Sunday and August. €€

## SIRACUSA PROVINCE

### Siracusa
**Archimede**
Via Gemmellaro 8
Tel: 0931-69701
Located off the central piazza of the same name, this is the oldest restaurant in the city, and a good place to sample from a changing menu of traditional dishes. Utterly reliable and cosy, it also has a pizzeria. Closed Sunday. €€
**Des Etrangers Et Miramare**
Passeggio Adorno 10
Tel: 0931-62671
In Ortygia, the city's top waterfront hotel boasts a panoramic rooftop restaurant which is arguably the most romantic dining room in town, and a rival to La Terrazza *(see entry below)*. Bookings required. €€€
**Don Camillo**
Via Maestranza 96
Tel: 0931-67133
Set on one of Ortygia's most intriguing streets, this chic restaurant specialises in sharp but light reinterpretations of classic Sicilian seafood cuisine, matched by a great wine list. The stylish atmosphere is complemented by the vaulted dining room, dotted with plants. Closed Sunday. Best to book in advance. €€–€€€

**Jonico – A Rutta E Ciauli**
Riviera Dionisio il Grande 194
Tel: 0931-65540
Worth a visit for the fabulous Art Deco interior and stunning view from the roof terrace (outside dining in summer). Varied menu of fish and pasta dishes, including spaghetti with wild fennel or the swordfish rolled in raisins and pine nuts. Pizza in the evenings. Closed Tuesday. €€–€€€
**La Siciliana**
Via Savoia 17
Tel: 0931-68944
A handy pizzeria and trattoria in the old part of town, a stone's throw from the Tempio di Apollo. Outside dining. Good for pizza, mixed grills or Sicilian pasta dishes. Closed Monday. €
**La Terrazza**
Grand Hotel
Viale Mazzini 12
Tel: 0931-464600
In Ortygia, this romantic rooftop restaurant is the best thing about the stand-offish Grand Hotel *(see Where to Stay, page 340)*. Apart from waterfront views and the rooftop summer terrace, this cool, Art Nouveau-inspired, glassed-in eyrie showcases Sicilian cuisine and is professionally served, albeit with little warmth. Bookings required. €€€

## CATANIA PROVINCE

### Catania
**Il Cantine del Cugno Mezzano**
Via Museo Biscari 8
Tel: 095-715 8710
Centrally located in one of Catania's grandest baroque *pallazi*, this wine bar *(enoteca)* has a limited menu of delicious and creative dishes such as almond soup with clams. Outside seating and great selection of wines. Open for dinner only. Closed Monday and August. €–€€
**Metró**
Via dei Crociferi 76
Tel: 095-322098
Sit outside on a pedestrian street in the shadow of baroque buildings and enjoy food inspired by ancient recipes, such as meatballs

flavoured with pomegranate. The home-made desserts are worth saving room for. Restaurant stays open until after midnight, which is quite unusual for Sicily. Closed Saturday and Sunday. €€
**Osteria I Tre Bicchieri**
Via San Giuseppe al Duomo
Tel: 095-715 3540
Set not far from the cathedral square, behind the university, this sophisticated spot offers one of the best dining experiences in Sicily. The vaulted dining room boasts the best of creative Mediterranean cuisine. Typical dishes include pasta with squid and octopus, timbale with cuttlefish, and grilled sole. Open evenings only; closed Sunday. €€€–€€€€

### Nicolosi
**Etna**
Via Etnea 93
Tel: 095-911937
Traditional Etna cuisine in a post-modern restaurant and pizzeria. Try the grilled wild boar. Closed Monday and February. €€

### Taormina
**Al Duomo**
Vico Ebrei 11
Tel: 0942-625656
Efficient service; elegant restaurant. Delicious pasta with fried courgettes and ricotta. Some of the finest eating in Taormina. Closed Monday (except in summer) and February. €€€
**Bella Blu**
Via Pirandello 28
Tel: 0942-24239
This buzzing restaurant/pizzeria/ piano bar and disco is included as much for atmosphere as for cuisine as it's an entertaining and chic place to spend an evening. Specialities include grills and barbecued meats as well as pasta with sardines. Book in summer. €
**La Giara**
Vicolo Floresta 1
Tel: 0942-23360
Elegant restaurant. Specialities include spaghetti with swordfish roe. Open evenings only; closed Monday (except in summer) and January to March. €€€–€€€€

## Price Guide

The price of a three-course meal for one, without wine, is:
€ = below €15
€€ = €15–30
€€€ = €30–45
€€€€ = over €45

### Granduca
Corso Umberto 172
Tel: 0942-24983
This chic, atmospheric old-fashioned grand restaurant offers lovely views over the bay. Closed Tuesday in winter. Bookings required. €€€

### Nautilus
Via San Pancrazio 48
Tel: 0942-625024
Creative and delicious food – influenced by the owner's experience working aboard an Oriental cruise liner. Outside dining on a terrace near the church. Open evenings only; closed Sunday, and January to February. €€€

---

## MESSINA PROVINCE

### Messina

### Le Due Sorelle
Piazza Municipio 4
Tel: 090-44720
Traditional Mediterranean cuisine with creative touches from India and North Africa including couscous. Great wine list and dining outside on the piazza. Closed August; weekends open for dinner only. €€

# Nightlife

Clubs go in and out of fashion (or in and out of business) at a fast rate, so it's a good idea to check with the local tourist office and ask around (hotels, local bars, etc) for the latest nightspots. Bear in mind that during the summer months many clubs and discos set up on the beach or by the water.

## Naples

Neapolitan nightlife is concentrated in the chaotic but characteristic historic centre, the area stretching towards the sea, and the Pozzuoli district by the port. The Borgo Marinaro area, which used to be patronised by pensioners, is now popular with all ages, although the bars and trattorias are just the same as they were 30 years ago.

### CLASSIC CAFES, WINE BARS & LIVE MUSIC

As well as classic cafés, such as the legendary Gambrinus, Naples has a decent range of bars, including several atmospheric vinerie. Note that most places here close on Monday. As far as nightlife is concerned, Naples is a city of fads but in recent years the centre of nightlife has seen a shift out to Posillipo and Mergellina, even if a number of chic places retain their appeal in the up-market Chiaia area. The following is a mixture of classic and happening places, but do check on the ground.

### Around Midnight
Via Bondo 32
Tel: 081-558 2838
Naples hasn't escaped the global craze for fake Irish pubs but this is

a spirited, very southern version, with live music, generally Celtic-inspired, cheerfully mismatched by extrovert non-Celtic behaviour.

### Caffè Gambrinus
Via Chiaia 1–2, Piazza Plebiscito
Tel: 081-414133/417582.
This is the city's most famous bar, adorned with gilt-and-plaster reliefs. Although it's crowded, the terrace makes a good spot for watching the world go by, sipping an aperitivo or coffee. Open from early morning until 10 or 11pm.

### La Taverna del Cavaliere
Vico dei Banchi 6
This typical Neapolitan hybrid is a so-called "resto-pub" (both a bar and restaurant) with live music of every description in the evening, as well as a casual, rustic-looking restaurant for light suppers. Closed Monday, no booking.

### Murat Live Club
Via Bellini 8
Tel: 081-544 5919
Set in the San Carlo Arena district, this is a reliable choice for live music, especially jazz, including modern and contemporary. Sets tend to begin at around 10pm.

### Vinarium
Via Cappella Vecchia 7
Tel: 041-764 4114
Conveniently located in the city centre, this classic wine bar is particularly popular with trendy professionals over 30. The atmosphere is smart/casual, with a pleasant, relaxing feel despite the relative formality of the surroundings. From here, it is just a quick stroll to Via Carlo Poerio, which is bursting with small bars, pubs and wine bars.

### La Vineria
Via Palladino 8
This atmospheric wine bar set close to Piazza San Domenico Maggiore was once a student haunt, but now attracts a wider cross-section. The atmosphere is "intellectual yet homely", a mood enhanced by low lighting and wood and marble fixtures and fittings. Closed Monday.

### Virgilio
Via Tito Lucresio Caro 6
Tel: 081-575 5262
This is now a club and piano bar for twenty and thirty-somethings.

However, in true Neapolitan style, different sets of people go on different nights, with Thursday a typical night for *per bene* (well-bred) thirty-somethings. There are sea views from the terrace of this Posillipo haunt.

**Yes Brazil Pub**
Via Posillipo 405
Tel (Italian mobile): 338 641 8587
This is a cool, laid-back place that favours live Latin music in the evenings, especially Brazilian.

## The Islands

### Capri
Nightlife in Capri is vibrant: clubs, bars and cafés with live music stay open late. If a quiet, romantic walk is more appealing, there's a path from Anacapri to the Belvedere Migliara or you can walk from Capri town to the Belvedere Cannone and the view of the Faraglioni at Tragara. Here are a few suggested nightspots. To see and be seen, it is enough to sit in the Piazzetta in the heart of town and drink an aperitif at any of the eternally chic cafés, of which the most fashion-

## Clubs & Bars

Although the following are among the most stylish or fashionable places for dancing in Naples, note that the city is not known for cutting-edge clubs and avant-garde music. Most venues tend to play a similar mainstream mix of classics from the 1970s and '80s right through to rap, house music or the current chart hits. Most places close on Monday. Given that clubs change all the time, pick up a copy of the latest *Qui Napoli* listings magazine (in English and Italian) or, if you read Italian, consult the website www.napolinapoli.com. There is a more limited selection of venues (in Italian and other languages) on the official Naples site www.inaples.it.

**Chez Moi**
Via di Parco Margherita 20
Tel: 081-407526
Set in the chic Chiaia area, this is

able has long been QuisiBar, the terrace of the Quisiana hotel.
**Relais Le Palme** – Popular piano bar in the centrally located hotel of the same name. Open late. Via Vittorio Emanuele 39, tel: 081-837 0133.
**Taverna Guarracino** – Neapolitan folk music and sing-alongs. Via Castello 7, tel: 081-837 0514.
**Taverna Anema e Core** – Live, mostly contemporary music. Very popular with the chic crowd. Via Sella Orta 39/e, tel: 081-837 6461.
**Number Two** – Dancing till dawn (long after the other clubs have closed). Via Camerelle 1, tel: 081-837 7078.
**Lanterna Verde** – Set in a grand villa hotel, this discreet yet romantic bar and panoramic restaurant is the place to enjoy a quiet time away from the crowds. Hotel San Michele (Anacapri), tel: 081-837 1427.

### Ischia
**Blu Jane** – The island's biggest dance club, set on the beach. Ischia Porto, Via Pagoda, tel: 081-993296.

an intimate, established club for all ages, depending on the night.
**Dug Out**
Tel: 081-662183; www.dugout.it
Set in the trendy Mergellina area, this disco is a real dug-out, a cavern in a courtyard carved out of the tufa rock. Call to check what "night" it is before setting out.
**La Mela**
Via dei Mille 40b
Tel: 081-410270/413881
Set in the up-market Chiaia area, this is a place for "Napoli-bene", monied types, whether latter-day yuppies or Italy's unique take on preppies. This is a smart, trendy place. However, given allegations of Mafia involvement in the club, there are occasional shootings, after which the place is closed for a while. Whatever its dubious associations, many locals miss it when it's gone.

**Dolce Vita** – A varied programme from a piano-bar atmosphere to jazz, blues or house music. Hotel Zi Carmela,Via Monsignor Filippo Schioppa 27, Forio, tel: 081-998423, www.zicarmela.com.

## Sorrento

**Artis Domus** – Set in the historical centre, this is a popular summer disco for all ages, but culture-lovers prefer the Sorrento Summer Music Festival. Via San Nicola.

## Puglia, Basilicata & Calabria

None of these regions is noted for having any distinctive nightlife (although Calabria and Puglia have much to offer in the way of high culture, in the form of opera and classical concerts). All these regions have their fair share of standard beach-resort discos but little more, with the exception of the chic resort of Maratea. In general, if staying in these regions, your best bet is to follow discerning locals by enjoying the evening *passeggiata* (see panel, page 354) before settling down to a good dinner and rounding off the evening in a cosy bar. This is as true of the big cities, such as Bari, as it is of typical seaside resorts, such as Tropea.

## Sicily

### Palermo
Palermo at night is nowhere near as lively as Naples. Even so, Palermitan nightlife has been transformed for the better recently, both in terms of safety and variety. Whereas the historic district used to be out of bounds to most security-conscious visitors, it now feels far safer, with a wider range of bars, clubs and cultural centres. Still, it is best to be clear where you are heading, and ideally go in company. Slightly timorous visitors will feel more at home in the grand hotel bars, which often have (admittedly sedate) live music.
    In the historic heart, lively nightspots include the Piazza

Marina area, which has numerous bars and restaurants. In the "new" part of town, the liveliest squares are Piazza Castelnuovo and Piazza Verdi (home to Teatro Massimo, where the opera scenes in *The Godfather* were filmed). The pedestrianised Via Principe di Belmonte has several smart bars, as does the elegant Via Libertà nearby. In summer, much nightlife moves to the resort of Mondello, 10 km (6 miles) away, which abounds in bars and clubs.

### Catania

Catania, even more than Palermo, has reclaimed the historic city centre and made it safer and more inviting at night, especially in the lively Via Etnea area. To find out what's on, pick up *Lapis*, a free listings magazine available from hotels and the tourist office.

### Taormina

**Palazzo San Domenico** (Piazza San Domenico) is the place to drop into for a late romantic drink in the bar and torch-lit gardens of a medieval monastery converted into a lovely hotel. Other recommended cocktail spots are **Caffe Wunderbar** (Piazza IX Aprile), which is great for people-watching or looking out over the bay, or **Mocambo Bar**, also on the main drag (Piazza IX Aprile). **Bella Blu** (Via Pirandello 28, tel: 0942-24239) is a buzzing twenty- or thirty-something place for a night out *(see entry, page 351)* with a piano bar, disco and chic restaurant.

**Club Septimo** (Via San Pancrazio 50; tel: 0942-62522) is a smart nightclub for thirty- to forty-somethings, while **Tout Va** (Via Pirandello 70, tel: 0942-23824) is younger, both more chaotic and more cool, an open-air dance club with views of the sea. **Ziggy's Bar/ Le Perroquet** (Piazza San Domenico, tel: 0942-24808) is Sicily's main gay-friendly nightclub.

# Culture

## Campania

### Naples

The **San Carlo Opera House** in Naples is Italy's largest, and rivals Milan's La Scala for its near-perfect acoustics (tel: 081-797 2111; www.teatrosancarlo.it). Dress is formal, especially for opening night. The season runs from January to mid-July. Another music venue is the **Teatro delle Palme** (Via Vetriera 12, tel: 081-418134), where a classical-music season runs from January to April. Naples' summer season is one of Italy's liveliest: from rock and pop concerts to traditional Neapolitan and classical music. Most events take place under the stars in the **Villa Comunale**, out of town in the **Ville Vesuviane**.

Naples, like the rest of the south, is awash with prestigious music festivals and stages more than anywhere else in Italy, from classical to jazz, blues and ethnic music *(see Festivals, page 356)*. Also try the charming **Teatro Trianon** (tel: 081-225 8285; www.teatrotrianon.it) for Neapolitan music and song. Classical concerts are held in various churches, palaces and villas, including the church of **Santo Marcellino** (tel: 081-253 7192) and in **Palazzo Doria D'Angri** (tel: 081-790 1000). To find out what's on, pick up *Qui Napoli*, the free monthly listings magazine in Italian and English, or see the official Naples website (www.inaples.it), which is in Italian and other languages.

To save money on museum entry, buy the Campania Artecard (tel: freephone 800-600601 or buy at the airport or in big hotels). This integrated museum and public transport card provides up to three days of discounted travel and museum entry.

### Salerno

The **Teatro Giuseppe Verdi** (Via Indipendenza, tel: 089-662141) stages opera, ballet and concerts from October to May.

### Ravello

From June to September, the focus of the music scene is **Villa Rufolo's gardens** where concerts are held on a cliff, with the sunset as a dramatic backdrop (tel: 089-857133). This is part of the broader Ravello Festival (tel: 089-858149; www.ravellofestival.com), which runs from June to September.

### Amalfi

Throughout the summer, Amalfi's **Duomo and Cloister** house international visiting orchestras and artists.

## Puglia

### Bari

The magnificent **Teatro Petruzzelli** is the city's main opera house. Another important venue for classical music is the **Teatro Nicolò Piccinni** on Corso Vittorio Emanuele (tel: 080-558 6906).

### Lecce

A **baroque music festival** is held in churches throughout the town in September. Plans are underway to use the restored Roman Amphitheatre in Piazza Sant'Oronzo as a venue for concerts and plays.

## La Passeggiata

The *passeggiata* (evening or Sunday stroll) is an Italian institution that is still popular in Sicily. Mondello is the place to see a nightly parade of Milanese fashion. On summer nights, the offshore islands come alive. In particular, Ustica, the Egadi Islands (especially Lévanzo) and the Aeolian Islands (especially Lípari) are awash with strollers admiring one another.

### The Gargano

In the summer, the Gargano has a vibrant cultural scene.

## Calabria

### Reggio Calabria

The Conservatorio Cilea (Via Aschenez, tel: 0965-812223, call mornings) provides up-to-date information about music events throughout town. The city's cultural scene livens up in the summer, with performances staged under the stars at the **Villa Comunale** and at the **Lido Comunale**. In July and August, a floating platform is anchored in front of the Lungomare where movies (often dubbed but sometimes in the original English) are screened al-fresco.

### Crotone

Every year in May, Crotone hosts the *Festival dell'Aurora*, a schedule of concerts, conferences, and theatrical pieces focused on Pythagorean themes and those of Magna Graecia.

### Altomonte

Altomonte hosts the *Festival Mediterraneo dei Due Mari* (Mediterranean Festival of Two Seas) every year in July and August, focusing on Mediterranean culture and traditions.

### Bova

In August, Bova hosts an important ethnic music festival, the *Paleariza*, where you can also buy artisanal products and local gastronomical items (for information contact GAL Area Grecanica, Piazza Roma 2, tel: 0965-762230).

## Sicily

### Palermo

Palermo's **Teatro Massimo** (ticket office Piazza Giuseppe Verdi, tel: 091-605 3515; www.teatro massimo.it; guided tours Monday to Friday 9am–1pm) organises concerts, operas and ballets all year round. The centrally located **Politeama** theatre (tel: 091-605 3315) also stages opera and classical concerts from November

to May, but the stunningly restored Teatro Massimo is far more impressive. In summer, mainstream classical concerts and operas are staged by the Teatro Massimo team in the gardens of the Teatro del Parco di Villa Castelnuovo in Viale del Fante 70 (tel: 091-605 3301).

For an alternative look at local culture, visit **Lo Spasimo** (Via dello Spasimo, tel: 091-616486), a strange and poignant cultural centre in the middle of the partially bomb-struck La Kalsa area. The Spasimo centre stages excellent summer concerts beside the evocative ruins of a Norman Gothic church. To find out what's on in Palermo, pick up a copy of the (free) *Agenda* (in English and Italian) from Palermo tourist office or visit www.palermotourism.com.

### Catania

The **Teatro Massimo Bellini** (Piazza Teatro Massimo, tel: 095-730 6111) is also a widely recognised venue for opera and ballet. Bellini's *Norma* premiered here in 1890. In the summer, performances are held in the open air at the Giardino Bellini.

### Taormina

In Taormina, the **Teatro Antico** (Greek Theatre) and the nearby **Palazzo dei Congressi** (Via Timeo 1) are the main venues for the *International Taormina Arts Festival*, embracing classical music, ballet and theatre, and also for the famous *Taormina Film Festival*. The former runs from June to September, with the Film Festival held in July. Contact the tourist office for details (Palazzo Corvaja, Piazza Santa Caterina, tel: 0942-23243). If you're visiting in winter, look out for *Natale a Taormina*, a series of free Christmas concerts held in the Duomo and other churches in December and January.

## Further Information

For up-to-date information on events and venues, contact the local tourist office *(see page 326)*.

## Literary Parks

This is a popular concept in the south, and a way to develop historically neglected areas in which the region abounds without damaging the environment. These "literary parks" can cover a real geographical area or a series of itineraries linked to a particular author. Sicily possesses the lion's share of such literary parks (including ones inspired by Pirandello, Giuseppe di Lampedusa and Giovanni Verga) but there are also parks dedicated to Carlo Levi in Basilicata (*see page 223*; www.parcolevi.it) and a newish park dedicated to Norman Douglas in Calabria *(see page 243)*. For a full list of parks see www.parchiletterari.it.

## Classical Sites

**Pompeii**, **Siracusa**, **Segesta** and **Taormina** are the major classical sites where events are staged in or around the temples or Greek theatres in summer, from ballet and opera to popular music and even Greek tragedies (in Siracusa).

# Festivals

(see page 88).

## Special Events

The Italian year is packed with special events, some linked to the Catholic calendar, others to the harvest season. Many involve processions, public performances, religious ceremonies, ceremonial races and competitions, elaborate costumes, singing, dancing and, of course, communal meals *(see page 88)*.

## Calendar

### February
**Early February**: Almond Blossom Festival – music and folk dancing (Agrigento).
**3–5 February**: Festa di Sant'Agata – procession of wooden floats through the city (Catania).
**End February**: Carnevale – celebrated with costumes and street festivals in Manfredonia (Puglia), Trapani, Acireale and Sciacca.
**Feb–May**: The Scarlatti concert season in Naples showcases young international classically trained musicians (tel: 081-406011).

### March
**Sunday following 19 March**: Festa di San Giuseppe, in Salemi. Celebrations include bread sculptures.
**March–April**: 'Ndrezzata on Ischia (at Buonopane near Barano): the frenetic dance known as 'Ndrezzata ("intertwined") takes place. Dancers wear traditional costumes and are armed with rolling pins.

### April
**Easter Week**: Notable celebrations in Trapani, Naples and Palermo. Dramatic processions and

celebrations also in Taranto, Ruvo di Puglia, Bari, Lecce, Enna, Messina, Ragusa, Marsala, Erice and Prizzi, where there is a pagan "Dance of the Devils".
In the Albanian town of Laino Borgo in Calabria, the *Giudaica*, a passion play, is staged in the streets, and has been ever since 1557.

### May
**Saturday preceding first Sunday**: Festival of San Gennaro in Naples – liquefaction of the saint's blood.
**First Sunday**: Festa di Santa Lucia, the patron saint, in Siracusa.
**4 May**: Festa di San Francesco da Paola at Paola.
**7–9 May**: Festival of San Nicola di Bari, with a procession, fireworks, concerts, and a blessing of the sea, all in Bari. Festival of Saint Cataldo in Taranto, with similar celebrations, from the castle bastions.
**15 May**: Festa di San Vito in Positano, with fireworks.

### Summer-long Festivals (June–September)
These festivals often run for the whole summer, but check locally.
**Sorrento Summer Music Festival** is based in the cloisters of San Francesco, and features classical, sacred and jazz concerts (www.estatemusicalesorrentina.it).
**Pompeiian Summer** features classical concerts among the ruins of Pompeii (call the tourist office, tel: 081-850 7255, or the organisers, tel: 081-542 2136).
**Flavian Nights** is a summer music festival staged in the restored Roman amphitheatre of Pozzuoli (tel: 081-526 1481).
**Arena Flegrea** is a concert season in the Phlegraean Fields which features Italian and international artists (tel: 081-725 8000).
**Midnight in the Parks** is the free summer season of music, cinema and theatre that takes place in 24 parks and public spaces around Naples (tel: 081-795 4180).
**Leuciana Festival** takes place in San Leucio, near Caserta and features music, theatre and dance (www.comune.caserta.it/belvedere).

**Neapolis** festival of rock and music in the former steelworks of Bagnoli, near Naples (www.neapolis.it).

### June
● Plays, films and concerts in Taormina's Greek theatre.
● Classical drama staged in Greek theatres, especially in Siracusa and Segesta.
**22 June**: Corpus Christi procession in Brindisi, led by the archbishop riding a white horse.
**27 June**: Festa di San Andrea (patron saint of Amalfi) – processions and street celebrations in Amalfi; Festa dei Gigli in Nola, near Naples – procession of towering floats, recalling the homecoming of a local bishop in the 4th century.

## Sicilian Puppet Theatre

Traditional plays performed by puppets *(see page 89)* can still be seen in the towns listed.

### Palermo
**Cuticchio**, Via Bara all'Olivella 95, tel: 091-323400. Modern versions of traditional puppet theatre (closed August).
**Opera dei Pupi**, Vicolo Ragusi 6, tel: 091-329194. Two or three shows weekly at 9pm.
**Teatro Bradamante**, Via Lombardia 25, tel: 091-625 9223. A free show at 10pm most Fridays in summer.
**Museo delle Marionette**, Via Butera 1, tel: 091-328060. Free shows.

### Monreale
**Munna**, Cortile Manin 15, tel: 091-640542. Performances on Sundays in summer.

### Acireale
**Turi Grasso**, Via Nazionale 95, tel: 095-764 8035.

### Siracusa
**Piccolo Teatro dei Pupi**, Via della Giudecca 17, tel: 0931-21136. There are usually performances at 11am or 9.30pm.

**Every four years:** Amalfi hosts a dramatic regatta staged in period costume between teams representing what were once the four maritime republics that dominated the Italian peninsula (Pisa, Genoa, Amalfi and Venice). The regatta will next come to Amalfi in June 2009.

### July

**Early to mid-July:** Renaissance music festival in Erice.
**Early July:** Sagra del Pesce Spada (swordfish festival) at Bagnara Calabra to celebrate the end of the local fishing season.
**2 July:** Festa della Madonna della Bruna in Matera.
**12–15 July:** Festa of Santa Rosalia, Palermo – procession to the sanctuary on Mount Pellegrino.
**26 July:** Festa di Sant' Anna, Ischia – a torchlight procession of hundreds of boats, transformed into floats.
**Late July/early August:** Festival of the Itria Valley, Martina Franca – concerts and opera.

### August

**Early August:** Settimana Pirandelliana, in Agrigento – opera and ballet performances.
**13 August:** Palio dei Normanni, Piazza Armerina in Sicily – fierce jousting competition among the various neighbourhoods of town.
**15 August:** Procession of the Varia in Palmi – giant papier-mâché models are carried aloft. Procession of the Grande Vara in Messina – a giant float representing the Assumption is pulled across town.

### September

**Early September:** Traditional Neapolitan music festival at Piedigrotta, with fireworks.
**Mid-September:** Couscous festival in San Vito lo Capo, near Trapani.
**19 September:** Festa di San Gennaro, in Naples – the faithful gather to watch the liquefaction of the saint's blood (see page 136).

### November

**1–2 November:** All Saints' Day, celebrated all over Italy, but with particular intensity in Sicily, where it feels more pagan than Hallowe'en, a real Festival of the Dead.
**10 November:** Festa di San Trifone, Adelfia, Bari – children dressed as angels ride on horseback.

### December

**8 December:** Sausage and polenta festival, San Bartolomeo in Galdo, Benevento.
**Christmas:** Particularly beautiful public celebrations in Bari, Naples, Siracusa, Puglia, and all over the south. Watch out for a delightful tradition, now making a comeback, of *zampognari*, or bagpipers, who descend from the mountain regions of Calabria playing adaptations of old hill tunes such as *Cantata dei Pastori*. These shepherd musicians claim that it was bagpipe music that soothed Mary during labour. Figures of the *zampognari* are very popular in nativity scenes.

# Outdoor Activities

## Hiking and Camping

The **national parks** in Southern Italy are more like protected wilderness areas than parks. Visitors' centres, campsites and well-marked trails are few and far between. See the chapter on Southern Italy's Wild Places *(page 119)* for descriptions. Website: www.parks.it

### Parco Nazionale del Pollino
Equally split between Basilicata and Calabria, this is Italy's largest national park and the richest repository of wildlife in Southern Italy.

### Sentiero Italia
This is a national trail project running all through the *Mezzogiorno*, beginning in Calabria's Parco Nazionale d'Aspromonte. It runs along the spine of the Apennines with refuges at strategic points along the way where hikers can stay the night.

### Parco Nazionale della Sila
Relatively small, this national park has an informative visitors' centre at Cupone, where you can pick up a map of 10 easy one-day itineraries. Contact the tourist office in Camigliatello Silano for information.

### Parco Nazionale d'Aspromonte
This is the area around the toe of Italy, a wall of ragged peaks looming over the narrow coastal plain. In summer, a good starting point for hikers is Gambarie, with views over the straits and Sicily. In winter, Gambarie is Calabria's ski resort.

### Promontorio del Gargano
The Gargano Peninsula was declared a national park in 1991, though only the Foresta Umbra is "wild".

## SICILY

### Parco dell'Etna

Founded in 1981, this national park is the most interesting of Sicily's protected areas. Accurate, timely information on Mount Etna is hard to come by without visiting a local tourist office or travel agency. Conditions and entry points to the park are all subject to change, depending on volcanic activity. If you read Italian, see the websites of Catania province (www.apt.catania.it) and Mount Etna Regional Park (www.parcoetna.it). Also see the chapter on Eastern Sicily *(page 297).*

### Parco delle Madonie

With 200-million-year-old fossils, the rocks here are the oldest on the island. There is a good network of paths and gravel roads for hikers. This is one of the most accessible parks in Southern Italy.

## Sports

### Soccer

The national obsession is felt in the south as strongly as in the north. The Serie A (Premiership) championship is played from September to May. At the time of writing, the teams from Lecce, Reggio Calabria, Palermo and Messina are in Serie A, and Napoli, Catania, Salerno, Bari and Avellino are in Serie B. If you would like to go to a match, be sure to call the tourist office for ticket information well in advance of your visit.

### Other Sports

Almost all other sport is enjoyed in Southern Italy, including basketball, golf, water polo, cycling, tennis, horseracing, rugby, rowing and sailing, and skiing. If you are interested in buying tickets for any match or event, buy the pink *Gazzetta dello Sport* newspaper, which lists everything you need to know about sport in Italy.

# Shopping

## Shopping Areas

### NAPLES AND AROUND

You needn't walk too far through central Naples or any touristy part of Campania to find the region's most famous products: coral jewellery from the world's coral capital, Torre del Greco, and leather goods. Most of the leather shoes and bags that make Northern Italy famous are actually manufactured here. Be warned that street sellers are not likely to have authentic merchandise.

Naples also has its share of great antiques shops, mostly on Via Santa Maria di Costantinopoli, where at No. 102 Mario Raffone (tel: 081-459667) sells artisanal prints of Mount Vesuvius and figures from Nativity scenes. Don't miss Via San Gregorio Armeno, which is lined with shops selling hand-carved figures for Nativity scenes, a cottage industry in Naples. Look for some of the year's noteworthy figures (athletes, movie stars, politicians), who are often represented. In Naples, the main shopping area is around Piazza dei Martiri, along Via Chiaia, Via Roma and pedestrian-only Via Calabritto. The Galleria Umberto (Via San Carlo) is definitely worth a look, as much for its glorious architecture as for the stores inside. Marinella (Riviera di Chiaia 287/a, tel: 081-245 1182) sells unusual ties. Adele Improta on Via Carlo Doria 8 (tel: 081-544 9753) has a delightful shop that specialises in talismans and amulets to ward off evil spirits. For unsual antique wooden toys, gadgets and ceramics try Amacord 900, Via Giacomo Poscicilli 77b (near Piazza Amedeo, tel: 081-549 8276). And for a legendary local

bookshop visit Colonnese on Via San Pietro a Maiella 33.

Torre del Greco (15 km/9 miles east of Naples on the Circum-vesuviana train line) teems with over 60 coral workshops selling cameos, objects and jewellery carved not only out of coral, but also turtle shell, turquoise, jade and other semi-precious stones. Keep an eye out for the wood inlay *(intarsia)* made in nearby Sorrento.

### CAPRI

The other shopping centre of Campania is Capri, whose hordes of big-spending tourists have brought all of Italy's most famous boutiques to the island. Between the Piazzetta, Via Vittorio Emanuele and Via Camerelle, you will find the world's most prestigious names in shoes, clothing and jewellery, antiques shops, and even an artisanal perfume workshop called Carthusia. In addition, Capri is known for its particular style of hand-made sandals and informal, summery clothing available from small shops all over the island. The town of Capri is small enough to explore on foot, but don't miss the backstreets, where the locals shop. There is a *limoncello* factory at Via Roma 79, where you can buy the sweet lemon-flavoured liqueur for which Campania is famous. But bear in mind that most boutique items in Capri, Taormina, Maratea and other chic resorts are overpriced so it is wise to restrict yourself to splashing out on unique hand-crafted objects (often jewellery or ceramics) rather than the familiar designer brands.

### AMALFI COAST

The sunny ceramics of the Amalfi Coast – produced in the town of Vietri sul Mare – are famous throughout Italy and well worth a look. Look for a *bottega* (workshop) or shop that sells ceramics of *produzione propria* (their own production), rather than a general gift shop, for the best selection and prices *(see box on page 182 for good addresses).* In Amalfi, the gift shops clustered around the Duomo sell artisanal paper made by the town's last surviving paper mill.

## SOUTH OF NAPLES

Apart from Bari, Catania and Palermo, what the towns south of Naples lack in swanky designer stores, they occasionally make up for in artisan shops. In big and small places, it usually pays to attend the open-air market (held at least once a week in every town), where interesting items are available at low prices.

### Calabria
The craftsmanship in Calabria is particularly appealing. In Acri (north of Cosenza), Giovanni Garotto keeps alive the art of building folk guitars and lutes (tel: 0984-953161); for beautiful blankets and tablecloths made from broom, visit To Argalio, Via Pasubio, in Bova Marina, run by

Laura Crisopulli (tel: 0965-761316); in Reggio Calabria, Fabrizio Romeo creates briar pipes (home tel: 0965-57447). Keep an eye open for hand-woven fabric and carpets, whose Oriental patterns testify to Calabria's strong Greek, Arabic, Byzantine and Albanian cultural legacies. In Badolato and Tiriolo, in the province of Catanzaro, long and narrow silk shawls with silver and gold embroidery called *vancali* are woven. Tiriolo is also the capital of *pezzare*, attractive mats made from remnants of fabric from industrial production. Longobucco, in the Greek Sila, is known for silk blankets and tapestry; San Giovanni in Fiore, in the Sila Grande, for its Armenian-style carpets; and in Seminara near Palmi, Paolo Condurso makes some of the region's best ceramics (Corso Barlam 30, tel: 0966-317123).

### Basilicata
In Basilicata, it's worth taking a detour to visit the smaller towns where you can find original hand-

made artefacts: the small towns of Avigliano, Forenza, Francavilla sul Sinni, Montalbano Ionico, Nemoli, San Mauro Forte, Terranova di Pollino and Valsinni specialise in wooden handicrafts, while ironwork can be found in Lagonegrese, Grassano, Sant'Arcangelo, Trecchina and Tricarico. Grottole, Matera, Melfi and Venosa have a century-old tradition of earthenware production, as does Grottaglie (near Taranto in Puglia), where the prices and huge dimensions of terracotta flowerpots and amphorae are hard to beat.

Inexpensive, oven-proof pottery is also produced in Grottaglie.

## SICILY

Southern Italy's most sophisticated ceramics come from Sicily. To add lots of character to your dining table, try to create your own unique set of plates and cups by choosing among items sold by the piece

## Shopping for Food

Some of the most delicious foods from Southern Italy are made to last and travel well, so they are ideal for bringing home as souvenirs.

Below are some good addresses and more general advice on where to find what, but the list is by no means exhaustive.

### Sicily
The world's tastiest almonds and pistachios are used to make several kinds of pastries and sweet treats, called *da riposto* (to conserve in the cupboard): soft macaroons, cookies, *frutta martorana* (marzipan shapes decorated like fruit), *pasta reale* (marzipan), and *torrone* (nougat). For almond pastry and *frutta martorana* in Erice there's the famous **Pasticceria Grammatico** (Via Vittorio Emanuele 14 and Via Guarnotte 1, tel: 0923-869390), established by Maria Grammatico who learned her trade while

growing up in a local convent (*see Where to Eat, page 350*).

In Noto, the **Caffè Sicilia** (Corso Vittorio Emanuele 125, tel: 0931-835013), in business since 1892, makes arguably Sicily's best (and probably Italy's most expensive) *torrone*: choose between plain almonds, toasted almonds, pistachios and sesame seeds. Caffè Sicilia also has a selection of rare jams: quince, mulberry, prickly pear and *azzeruoli* (a local variety of wild apple).

Trapani and the Egadi islands offer a variety of tuna products, from various cuts of tuna preserved in olive oil to *ficazza*, a sort of spicy sausage.

If you plan on trying your hand at Sicilian cuisine back home, don't leave without buying some capers in salt.

The area around Castelvetrano is known for its excellent extra-virgin olive oil that rivals the best in Tuscany and Liguria.

### Calabria
A speciality of Calabria is dried figs, which come in all shapes and sizes. Get them plain, strung together, stuffed with orange and almonds or dipped in chocolate and honey at the **Premiata Lavorazione Ficchi Secchi** (Viale Stazione 142, Belmonte Calabro, tel: 0982-47017). Another good address is **Lavorazione Artigianale Fichi Secchi** of Ciccotti Maria Carmela (Via Rupa 15, Paola, tel: 0982-583255).

Top-quality dried porcini mushrooms are sold in the Sila and Serre regions.

The Amarelli family has been in the liquorice business for over 250 years. Although their liquorice sweets are available elsewhere in Italy, you'll find more variety than you thought possible on display at their shop, **Liquirizia Amarelli**, in Rossano Calabro (Contrada Amarelli), tel: 0983-511219.

## Clothing Size Chart

**Women's dresses:**

| Italian | UK | US |
|---------|----|----|
| 38 | 8 | 6 |
| 40 | 10 | 8 |
| 42 | 12 | 10 |
| 44 | 14 | 12 |

**Men's shirts:**

| Italian | UK | US |
|---------|----|----|
| 36 | 14 | 14 |
| 38 | 15 | 15 |
| 41 | 16 | 16 |
| 43 | 17 | 17 |

rather than buying a full set. The region's most important centres of production are: Collesano (30 km/ 19 miles south of Cefalù) for bottles and lamps; Sciacca and Santo Stefano di Camastra (40 km/ 25 miles east of Cefalù) for vividly coloured pottery; Caltagirone for tastefully decorated pottery and tiles. Giovanni di Blasi in Taormina, Corso Umberto 103, tel: 0942-24671, has them all.

Siracusa is famous for hand-made papyrus paper, either plain or painted with Egyptian scenes, but beware of commercially produced items which don't feel silky to the touch – a reliable address is Galleria Bellomo at Via Capodieci 15, tel: 0931-61340.

Erice, near Trapani, boasts numerous good crafts shops, including Altieri 1882 at Via Cordici 11, tel: 0923-869431, one of the best places for Sicilian ceramics.

### Palermo

The main shopping area in Palermo is around Piazza Castelnuovo: Via Roma and Via Maqueda are lined with boutiques that become more up-market as you approach the piazza and nearby Via della Libertà. The curious should not miss the outdoor markets in the Vucciria and Ballarò neighbourhoods. The Ballarò market is currently far livelier, even if the Vucciria is more colourful. On Sunday afternoon, there is a fun bric-a-brac market on Piazza Marina.

# Language

In large cities and tourist centres you will find many people who speak English, French or German. Nevertheless, it is well worth buying a good phrase book or dictionary. The following will help you get started. Since this glossary is aimed at non-linguists, we have opted for the simplest options rather than the most elegant Italian.

## Basic Communication

**Yes** *Sì*
**No** *No*
**Thank you** *Grazie*
**Many thanks** *Mille grazie/tante grazie/molte grazie*
**You're welcome** *Prego*
**Alright/Okay/That's fine** *Va bene*
**Please** *Per favore/per cortesia.*

## Days and Dates

**morning/afternoon/evening** *la mattina, il pomeriggio, la sera*
**yesterday/today/tomorrow** *ieri/oggi/domani*
**the day after tomorrow** *dopodomani*
**now/early/late** *adesso/presto/ritardo*
**a minute** *un minuto*
**an hour** *un'ora*
**half an hour** *un mezz'ora*
**a day** *un giorno*
**a week** *una settimana*
**Monday** *lunedì*
**Tuesday** *martedì*
**Wednesday** *mercoledì*
**Thursday** *giovedì*
**Friday** *venerdì*
**Saturday** *sabato*
**Sunday** *domenica*
**first** *il primo/la prima*
**second** *il secondo/la seconda*
**third** *il terzo/la terza*

**Excuse me** (to get attention) *Scusi* (singular), *Scusate* (plural)
**Excuse me** (to get through a crowd) *Permesso*
**Excuse me** (to attract attention, e.g. of a waiter) *Senta!*
**Excuse me** (sorry) *Mi scusi*
**Wait a minute!** *Aspetta!*
**Could you help me?** (formal) *Potrebbe aiutarmi?*
**Certainly** *Ma certo*
**Can I help you?** (formal) *Posso aiutarla?*
**Can you show me...?** *Può indicarmi...?*
**Can you help me?** *Può aiutarmi, per cortesia?*
**I need ...** *Ho bisogno di ...*
**I'm lost** *Mi sono perso*
**I'm sorry** *Mi dispiace*
**I don't know** *Non lo so*
**I don't understand** *Non capisco*
**Do you speak English/French/ German?** *Parla inglese/francese/ tedesco?*
**Could you speak more slowly, please?** *Può parlare piú lentamente, per favore?*
**Could you repeat that please?** *Può ripetere, per piacere?*
**slowly/quietly** *piano*
**here/there** *qui/lá*
**What?** *Cosa?*
**When/why/where?** *Quando/perchè/dove?*
**Where is the lavatory?** *Dov'è il bagno?*

## Greetings

**Hello** (Good day) *Buon giorno*
**Good afternoon/evening** *Buona sera*
**Good night** *Buona notte*
**Goodbye** *Arrivederci*
**Hello/Hi/Goodbye** (familiar) *Ciao*
**Mr/Mrs/Miss** *Signor/Signora/ Signorina*
**Pleased to meet you** (formal) *Piacere di conoscerla*
**I am English/American** *Sono inglese/americano*
**Irish/Scottish/Welsh** *irlandese/scozzese/gallese*
**Canadian/Australian** *canadese/australiano*
**I'm here on holiday** *Sono qui in vacanza*
**Is it your first trip to Sorrento?** *É il Suo primo viaggio a Sorrento?*

**Do you like it here?** (formal)
*Si trova bene qui?*
**How are you** (formal/informal)?
*Come sta/come stai?*
**Fine thanks** *Bene, grazie*
**See you later** *A più tardi*
**See you soon** *A presto*
**Take care** *Stia bene*
New acquaintances may ask you:
**Do you like Italy/Naples/my city
or town?** *Le piace Italia/Napoli/la
mia città?*
**I like it a lot** (is the correct
answer) *Mi piace moltissimo.*
**It's wonderful** (an alternative
answer) *È meravigliosa/favolosa.*
(Both responses can be applied to
food, beaches, the view, etc.)

## Telephone Calls

**the area code** *il prefisso
telefonico*
**I'd like to make a reverse charges
call** *Vorrei fare una telefonata a
carico del destinatario*
**May I use your telephone, please?**
*Posso usare il telefono?*
**Hello** (on the telephone) *Pronto*
**My name is** *Mi chiamo/Sono*
**May I speak to... ?** *Posso parlare
con...?*
**Sorry, he/she isn't in** *Mi dispiace,
è fuori*
**I'll try again later** *Riproverò più tardi*
**Can I leave a message?** *Posso
lasciare un messaggio?*
**Please tell him I called** *Gli dica,
per favore, che ho telefonato*
**A local call** *una telefonata locale*
**Can you speak up please?** *Può
parlare più forte, per favore?*

## In the Hotel

**Do you have any vacant rooms?**
*Avete camere libere?*
**I have a reservation** *Ho fatto una
prenotazione*
**I'd like...** *Vorrei...*
**a single/double room** (with a double
bed) *una camera singola/doppia
(con letto matrimoniale)*
**a room with twin beds** *una camera
a due letti*
**a room with a bath/shower** *una
camera con bagno/doccia*
**for one night** *per una notte*
**on the first floor** *al primo piano*

## Pronunciation and Grammar Tips

Italian speakers claim that pronunciation is straightforward: you pronounce it as it is written. This is approximately true but there are a couple of important rules for English speakers to bear in mind: *c* before *i* or *e* is pronounced "ch", e.g. *ciao, mi dispiace, la coincidenza*. *Ch* before *i* or *e* is pronounced as "k", e.g. *la chiesa*. Likewise, *sci* or *sce* are pronounced as in "sheep" or "shed" respectively. *Gn* in Italian is rather like the sound in "onion", while *gl* is softened to resemble the sound in "bullion".

Nouns are either masculine (*il*, plural *i*) or feminine (*la*, plural *le*). Plurals of nouns are most often formed by changing an *o* to an *i* and an *a* to an *e*, e.g. *il panino, i panini*; *la chiesa, le chiese*.

Words are stressed on the penultimate syllable unless an accent indicates otherwise.

Like many languages, Italian has formal and informal words for "You". In the singular, *Tu* is informal while *Lei* is more polite. Confusingly, in some parts of Italy or in some circumstances, you will also hear *Voi* used as a singular polite form. (In general, *Voi* is reserved for "You" plural, however.) For visitors, it is simplest and most respectful to use the formal form unless invited to do otherwise.

There is, of course, rather more to the language than that, but you can get a surprisingly long way towards making friends by learning how to pronounce a few basic phrases.

**We have one with a double bed**
*Ne abbiamo una matrimoniale.*
**Can I see the room?** *Posso vedere
la camera?*
**Could you show me another room
please?** *Potrebbe mostrarmi
un'altra camera?*
**How much is it?** *Quanto costa?*
**Is breakfast included?** *É compresa
la prima colazione?*
**Is everything included?** *É tutto
compreso?*
**half/full board** *mezza pensione/
pensione completa*
**It's expensive** *É caro*
**Do you have a room with a balcony/
view of the sea?** *C'è una camera
con balcone/con vista sul mare?*
**Is it a quiet room?** *É una stanza
tranquilla?*
**The room is too hot/cold/noisy/
small** *La camera è troppo calda/
fredda/rumorosa/piccola*
**What time does the hotel close?**
*A che ora chiude l'albergo?*
**I'll take it** *La prendo*
**What time is breakfast?** *A che ora
è la prima colazione?*
**Come in!** *Avanti!*
**Can I have the bill, please?** *Posso
avere il conto, per favore.*
**Can you call me a taxi please?**
*Può chiamarmi un taxi, per favore?*

**dining room** *la sala da pranzo*
**key** *la chiave*
**lift** *l'ascensore*
**towel** *l'asciugamano*
**toilet paper** *la carta igienica*
**pull/push** *tirare/spingere*

## Eating Out

### DRINKS &
### BAR SNACKS

**I'd like...** *Vorrei...*
**coffee** *un caffè* (*espresso*: small,
strong and black)
*un cappuccino* (with hot, frothy milk)
*un caffelatte* (like *café au lait*)
*un caffè lungo* (weak, often served
in a tall glass)
*un corretto* (laced with alcohol,
usually brandy or grappa)
**tea** *un tè*
**lemon tea** *un tè al limone*
**herbal tea** *una tisana*
**hot chocolate** *una cioccolata calda*
**orange/lemon juice** (bottled)
*un succo d'arancia/di limone*
**fresh orange/lemon juice** *una
spremuta di arancia/di limone*
**orangeade** *un'aranciata*
**water (mineral)** *acqua* (*minerale*)
**fizzy/still mineral water** *acqua
minerale gasata/naturale*

## Bar Notices

*Prezzo al tavolo/in terrazza*
**Price at a table/terrace** (often double what you pay standing at the bar)
*Si paga alla cassa* **Pay at the cash desk**
*Si prende lo scontrino alla cassa* **Pay at the cash desk, then take the receipt** *(lo scontrino)* **to the bar to be served.** This is common procedure.
*Signori/Uomini* **Gentlemen** (lavatories)
*Signore/Donne* **Ladies** (lavatories)

**a glass of mineral water** *un bicchiere di minerale*
**with/without ice** *con/senza ghiaccio*
**red/white wine** *vino rosso/bianco*
**beer** (draught) *una birra (alla spina)*
**a gin and tonic** *un gin tonic*
**a bitter (Vermouth, etc.)** *un amaro*
**milk** *latte*
**a (half) litre** *un (mezzo) litro*
**bottle** *una bottiglia*
**ice cream** *un gelato*
**pastry** *una pasta*
**sandwich** *un tramezzino*
**roll** *un panino*
**Anything else?** *Desidera qualcos'altro?*
**Cheers** *Salute*
**Let me pay** *Offro io*
**That's very kind of you** *Grazie, molto gentile*

## IN A RESTAURANT

**I'd like to book a table** *Vorrei riservare un tavolo*
**Have you got a table for...** *Avete un tavolo per ...*
**I have a reservation** *Ho fatto una prenotazione*
**lunch/supper** *il pranzo/la cena*
**I'm a vegetarian** *Sono vegetariano/a*
**Is there a vegetarian dish?** *C'è un piatto vegetariano?*
**May we have the menu?** *Ci dà il menu, per favore?*
**wine list** *la lista dei vini*
**What would you like?** *Che cosa prende?*

**What would you recommend?** *Che cosa ci raccomanda?*
**home-made** *fatto in casa*
**What would you like as a main course/dessert?** *Che cosa prende di secondo/di dolce?*
**What would you like to drink?** *Che cosa desidera da bere?*
**a carafe of red/white wine** *una caraffa di vino rosso/bianco*
**fixed-price menu** *il menu a prezzo fisso*
**dish of the day** *il piatto del giorno*
**cover charge** *il coperto/pane e coperto*
**That's enough; no more, thanks** *Basta (così)*
**The bill, please** *Il conto per favore*
**Is service included?** *Il servizio è incluso?*
**Where is the lavatory?** *Dov'è il bagno?*
**Keep the change** *Va bene così*
**I've enjoyed the meal** *Mi è piaciuto molto*

## Menu Decoder

### ANTIPASTI (HORS D'OEUVRES)

*antipasto misto* **mixed hors d'oeuvres** (may include cold cuts, cheeses and roast vegetables – ask, however)
*buffet freddo* **cold buffet**
*caponata* **mixed aubergine, olives and tomatoes**
*insalata caprese* **tomato and mozzarella salad**
*insalata di mare* **seafood salad**
*insalata mista/verde* **mixed/ green salad**
*melanzane alla parmigiana* **fried or baked aubergine (with Parmesan cheese and tomato)**
*misti toscani* **croutons with liver pâté, salami and cured ham**
*mortadella/salame* **salami**
*pancetta* **bacon**
*peperonata* **vegetable stew with peppers, onions and tomatoes**

### PRIMI (FIRST COURSES)

*il brodetto* **fish soup**
*il brodo* **consommé**
*i crespolini* **savoury pancakes**
*fagliolini* **green beans**

*gli gnocchi* **potato dumplings**
*la minestra* **soup**
*il minestrone* **thick vegetable soup**
*pasta e fagioli* **pasta and bean soup**
*il prosciutto (cotto/crudo)* **ham (cooked/cured)**
*i supplí* **rice croquettes**
*la zuppa* **soup**

### SECONDI (MAIN COURSES)

Typical main courses are fish-, seafood- or meat-based, with accompaniments *(contorni)* that vary greatly from region to region.

#### La Carne (Meat)

*allo spiedo* **on the spit**
*arrosto* **roast meat**
*i ferri* **grilled**
*al forno* **baked**
*al girarrosto* **spit-roasted**
*alla griglia* **grilled**
*involtini* **skewered veal, ham, etc.**
*stagionato* **hung, well-aged**
*stufato* **braised, stewed**
*ben cotto* **well-done** (steak, etc.)
*al puntino* **medium** (steak, etc.)
*al sangue* **rare** (steak, etc.)
*l'agnello* **lamb**
*la bresaola* **dried salted beef**
*la bistecca* **steak**
*il capriolo/cervo* **venison**
*il carpaccio* **lean beef fillet**
*il cinghiale* **wild boar**
*il coniglio* **rabbit**
*il controfiletto* **sirloin steak**
*le cotolette* **cutlets**
*il fagiano* **pheasant**
*il fegato* **liver**
*il filetto* **fillet**
*la lepre* **hare**
*il maiale* **pork**
*il manzo* **beef**
*l'ossobuco* **shin of veal**
*la porchetta* **roast suckling pig**
*il pollo* **chicken**
*le polpette* **meatballs**
*il polpettone* **meat loaf**
*la salsiccia* **sausage**
*saltimbocca (alla romana)* **veal escalopes with ham**
*le scaloppine* **escalopes**
*lo stufato* **stew**
*il sugo* **sauce**
*il tacchino* **turkey**
*il vitello* **veal**

### Frutti di Mare (Seafood)

Beware the word "surgelati",
meaning frozen rather than fresh.

*affumicato* **smoked**
*alle brace* **charcoal grilled/barbecued**
*alla griglia* **grilled**
*fritto* **fried**
*ripieno* **stuffed**
*al vapore* **steamed**
*le acciughe* **anchovies**
*l'aragosta* **lobster**
*il baccalà* **dried salted cod**
*i bianchetti* **whitebait**
*il branzino* **sea bass**
*i calamari* **squid**
*i calamaretti* **baby squid**
*la carpa* **carp**
*i crostacei* **shellfish**
*le cozze* **mussels**
*il fritto misto* **mixed fried fish**
*i gamberi* **prawns**
*i gamberetti* **shrimps**
*il granchio* **crab**
*il merluzzo* **cod**
*le ostriche* **oysters**
*il pesce* **fish**
*il pesce spada* **swordfish**
*il polipo* **octopus**
*il risotto di mare* **seafood risotto**
*le sarde* **sardines**
*la sogliola* **sole**
*le seppie* **cuttlefish**
*la triglia* **red mullet**
*la trota* **trout**

*il tonno* **tuna**
*le vongole* **clams**

### I Legumi/La Verdura (vegetables)

*a scelta* **of your choice**
*i contorni* **accompaniments**
*ripieno* **stuffed**
*gli asparagi* **asparagus**
*la bietola* **similar to spinach**
*il carciofo* **artichoke**
*le carote* **carrots**
*i carciofini* **artichoke hearts**
*il cavolo* **cabbage**
*la cicoria* **chicory**
*la cipolla* **onion**
*i funghi* **mushrooms**
*i fagioli* **beans**
*i fagiolini* **French (green) beans**
*le fave* **broad beans**
*il finocchio* **fennel**
*l'indivia* **endive/chicory**
*l'insalata mista* **mixed salad**
*l'insalata verde* **green salad**
*la melanzana* **aubergine**
*le patate* **potatoes**
*le patatine fritte* **chips/French fries**
*i peperoni* **peppers**
*i piselli* **peas**
*i pomodori* **tomatoes**
*le primizie* **spring vegetables**
*il radicchio* **red, slightly bitter lettuce**
*la rughetta* **rocket**
*gli spinaci* **spinach**

*la verdura* **green vegetables**
*la zucca* **pumpkin/squash**
*gli zucchini* **courgettes**

## I DOLCI (DESSERTS)

*al carrello* **(desserts) from the trolley**
*un semifreddo* **semi-frozen dessert (many types)**
*la bavarese* **mousse**
*la cassata* **Sicilian ice cream with candied peel**
*le frittelle* **fritters**
*un gelato (di lampone/limone)* **(raspberry/lemon) ice cream**
*una granita* **water ice**
*una macedonia di frutta* **fruit salad**
*il tartufo (nero)* **(chocolate) ice-cream dessert**
*il tiramisù* **cold, creamy cheese and coffee liqueur dessert**
*la torta* **cake/tart**
*lo zabaglione* **sweet dessert made with eggs and Marsala wine**
*la zuppa inglese* **trifle**

### La Frutta (Fruit)

*le albicocche* **apricots**
*le arance* **oranges**
*le banane* **bananas**
*il cocomero* **watermelon**
*le ciliegie* **cherries**
*i fichi* **figs**

## Specialities of Southern Italy

The following is a list of dishes, sauces, drinks and desserts commonly found in Southern Italy:
**Alla puttanesca** tomato sauce with garlic, olives, parsley and capers.
**Alla sorrentina** tomato sauce with fresh basil and mozzarella.
**Bottarga** cured fish eggs, grated over spaghetti or salads.
**Braciole (brasciole)** 'rolls', either meat or aubergine, with various stuffings (not to be confused with the Italian word for 'chops').
**Brioche** sweet roll sold in bars and *gelaterie* (ice-cream parlours); eaten plain, soaked in iced *latte di mandorla (see below)* or with an ice-cream filling.
**Calzone** bread dough filled with vegetables, cheese, sausages, eggs, olives, etc., either *al forno*

(baked) or *fritti* (deep-fried). Not to be confused with the folded pizza.
**Capocollo** spiced cured pork; often cured in red wine and/or smoked.
**Caprese** tomato salad with mozzarella and basil leaves.
**Cavatelli (cavatieddi or cecatelli)** tiny wheat dumplings.
**Ciambotta (ciambrotta or cianfotta)** vegetarian dish prepared in various ways but always featuring peppers, potatoes, aubergines, onion, celery and olives.
**Fritto di paranza** mixed platter of fried fish and seafood.
**Granita** home-made ice slush sold in bars and *gelaterie*; flavours include *limone* (lemon), *caffè*, *mandorle* (almond), *fragole* (strawberry), *gelso* (mulberry).
**Latte di mandorla** almond milk.

**Minestra maritata** "married soup" – made with vegetables and meat.
**Pancotto** light vegetable soup thickened with stale bread.
**Panzanella** salad made with stale bread and raw vegetables dressed with olive oil and vinegar; in Campania it's typically made with tomatoes, onion, peppers, garlic, anchovy and olives.
**Ragù** braised meat; spices and condiments may differ, but the idea is always to use the (meatless) sauce for pasta followed by the meat served as a main course. Not to be confused with Northern Italy's *ragù* (bolognaise sauce).
**Stoccafisso** dried cod, prepared in a number of ways, including baked with potatoes and/or other vegetables.

## Regional Specialities

### Campania

**A scapece** vegetables or fish prepared *a scapece* are first deep-fried then marinated in vinegar, garlic, herbs and spices.

**Babà** cake soaked in a light rum syrup served with whipped cream.

**Friarielli** leafy vegetables of the beet family with a slightly bitter taste.

**Impepata di cozze** sautéed mussels with parsley, lemon juice and freshly ground black pepper.

**Parmigiana di melanzane** baked dish made with layers of fried aubergine slices, tomato sauce, mozzarella, basil, parmesan and hard-boiled eggs (optional).

**Pesce all'acqua pazza** fish poached in "crazy water" (water flavoured with sautéed onion, white wine and fresh tomatoes).

**Sartù** thin shell of pilau rice filled with tiny meatballs, sausage, peas, hard-boiled eggs, mozzarella and (optional) chicken liver, baked to a golden crust and served with *ragù*.

**Sfogliatella riccia** pastry with a crisp fan-shaped shell filled with ricotta and semolina.

### Puglia

**Alici arracanate** fresh anchovies baked with breadcrumbs, fresh mint and oregano, capers and garlic.

**Alici in tortiera** as above, but with parsley and garlic.

**Burrata** popular cheese from Andria, like mozzarella with a cream filling.

**Carteddate (cartellate)** deep-fried, crisp pastry dipped in honey and sprinkled with cinnamon.

**Ciceri e tria** tagliatelle with chickpeas and onion.

**Friselle (frisedde, frise)** wheat or barley bread topped with fresh tomatoes and basil, or tossed in *panzanella*-style salads.

**'Ncapriata (purè di fave e cicoria)** dried fava-bean purée served with chicory and a side dish of olive oil.

**Orecchiette** "little ears"; pasta traditionally served with *cime di rapa* (local name for *friarielli* – see above) and anchovies.

**Tiella di riso e cozze** baked rice dish with potatoes and mussels.

### Basilicata

**Gnummerieddi (gnomirelli)** baked or grilled lamb (or kid) intestines stuffed with offal, often sprinkled with pecorino cheese.

**Lagane e fagioli** wide pasta strips with beans, garlic and chilli.

**Strascinati (strascenate)** Small squares of pasta dressed with tomato sauce and pecorino cheese.

### Calabria

**Carne 'ncantarata** salt-cured pork with tomato sauce and chicory and fennel seeds or honey and spices.

**Ferrazzuoli** fresh pasta in a meat sauce made with pork, lamb, veal, turkey, onion and tomatoes.

**Lagane** wide and short eggless *fettuccine* often tossed in bean or chickpea soup, dressed with ricotta and freshly ground black pepper, or boiled in milk and sprinkled with pecorino cheese.

**Morseddu (mursiello, suffrittu)** pork offal stewed in red wine and tomato sauce, sprinkled with oregano and spread on *pitta (see below)* or bread.

**Pesce stocco** Calabrian for *stoccafisso*.

**Pitta** Calabrian for *pizza bianca* (thick plain pizza sprinkled with salt), sold in bakeries.

**Pitta 'nchiusa** pastry filled with raisins, walnuts, cinnamon and *vino cotto* (reduced wine).

**Sagne** short for lasagne; *sagne chine* are baked with tiny meatballs, hard-boiled eggs, pecorino cheese, mozzarella, scamorza cheese and, in season, also with artichokes, peas and mushrooms.

### Sicily

**Arancini** deep-fried, crispy balls ("little oranges") of risotto made with meat sauce, cheese and peas.

**Cannoli siciliani** crisp flaky pastry filled with sweetened ricotta; in Palermo, bits of bitter chocolate and candied fruit are added to the filling.

**Caponata** fried aubergine slices in a sweet and sour tomato sauce with olives and capers.

**Cassata siciliana** dessert made with layers of sponge cake, sweet ricotta cream, pieces of bitter chocolate and candied fruit, covered with a pistachio-flavoured almond icing.

**Coniglio a 'stimpirata** rabbit stew with olives, pine nuts and raisins.

**Cuscus(u)** Sicilian for couscous, always prepared with fish.

**Farsu magru** large veal (or beef) roll stuffed with hard-boiled eggs, cheese, prosciutto (cured ham), sausage, peas, and pine nuts and raisins (optional), braised in a tomato sauce and served sliced.

**Impanata siracusana** baked *calzone (see opposite)* stuffed with broccoli, sausage and *primosale* cheese, or with potatoes and onion.

**Involtini di pesce spada** swordfish rolls with breadcrumbs, cheese, capers, olives and parsley, grilled on skewers with onion and bay leaves.

**Panelle** deep-fried polenta squares.

**Pasta alla Norma** rigatoni with fried aubergine, tomatoes and a sprinkling of hard ricotta.

**Pasta busiata** short and thick macaroni; in Trapani, it's coated in a pesto made with basil, tomatoes, garlic, olive oil and almonds.

**Pasta con le sarde** pasta with fresh sardines, wild fennel greens, anchovy paste, capers, onion, pine nuts, raisins and saffron (optional); ground toasted almonds are passed around instead of parmesan.

**Pasta 'ncasciata** short pasta baked with meatballs, fried aubergine, hard-boiled eggs, peas, salami and *caciocavallo* cheese.

**Pesce spada alla ghiotta** swordfish steaks poached in a tomato sauce with onion, celery, olives and capers.

**Salmoriglio** condiment made with olive oil, garlic, lemon juice, parsley and oregano poured on grilled fish.

**Sarde a beccafico** fresh sardines baked on a bed of bay leaves with breadcrumbs, pine nuts, raisins, anchovies and cinnamon, sprinkled with fresh orange and lemon juice.

**Scacciata** like *impanata (see above)* but with a basic filling of anchovy and cheese, to which vegetables might be added.

le fragole **strawberries**
i frutti di bosco **forest fruits**
i lamponi **raspberries**
la mela **apple**
il melone **melon**
la pesca **peach**
la pera **pear**
il pompelmo **grapefruit**
le uve **grapes**

## BASIC FOODS

l'aceto **vinegar**
l'aglio **garlic**
il burro **butter**
il formaggio **cheese**
la frittata **omelette**
i grissini **bread sticks**
l'olio **oil**
la marmellata **jam**
il pane **bread**
il parmegiano **parmesan cheese**
il pepe **pepper**
il riso **rice**
il sale **salt**
la senape **mustard**
le uova **eggs**
lo zucchero **sugar**

## Sightseeing

aperto/a **open**
chiuso/a **closed**
chiuso per la festa **closed for the festival**
chiuso per ferie **closed for the holidays**
chiuso per restauro **closed for restoration**
**Is it possible to see the church?** É possibile visitare la chiesa?
Entrata/uscita **Entrance/exit**
**Where can I find the custodian/sacristan/key?** Dove posso trovare il custode/il sacrestano/la chiave?

## At the Shops

**What time do you open/close?** A che ora apre/chiude?
**Closed for the holidays** Chiuso per ferie (typical sign)
**Pull/push** Tirare/spingere (sign on doors)
**Entrance/exit** Entrata/uscita
**Can I help you?** Posso aiutarLa? (formal)

**What would you like?** Che cosa desidera?
**I'm just looking** Sto soltanto guardando
**How much does it cost?** Quant'è, per favore?
**How much is this?** Quanto viene?
**Do you take credit cards?** Accettate carte di credito?
**I'd like...** Vorrei...
**this one/that one** questo/quello
**I'd like that one, please** Vorrei quello lì, per cortesia
**Have you got ...?** Avete ...?
**Can I try it on?** Posso provare?
**the size** (for clothes) la taglia
**What size do you take?** Qual'é a sua taglia?
**the size** (for shoes) il numero
**Is there/do you have ...?** C'è ...?
**Yes, of course** Sì, certo
**No, we don't (there isn't)** Non c'è
**That's too expensive** É troppo caro
**Please write it down for me** Me lo scriva, per favore
**cheap** economico
**Don't you have anything cheaper?** Ha niente che costa di meno?
**It's too small/big** É troppo piccolo/grande
**brown/blue/black** marrone/blu/nero
**green/red/white/yellow** verde/rosso/bianco/giallo
**pink/grey/gold/silver** rosa/grigio/oro/argento
**No thank you, I don't like it** Grazie, ma non è di mio gusto
**I (don't) like it** (Non) mi piace
**I'll take it/I'll leave it** Lo prendo/Lo lascio
**This is faulty. Can I have a replacement/refund?** C'è un difetto. Me lo potrebbe cambiare/rimborsare?
**Anything else?** Altro?
**The cash desk is over there** Si accomodi alla cassa
**Give me some of those** Mi dia alcuni di quelli lì
**a (half) kilo** un (mezzo) chilo
**100 grams** un etto
**200 grams** due etti
**more/less** più/meno
**with/without** con/senza
**a little** un pochino
**That's enough** Basta così

## TYPES OF SHOPS

**antiques dealer** l'antiquario
**bakery/cake shop** la panetteria/pasticceria
**bank** la banca
**bookshop** la libreria
**boutique/clothes shop** il negozio di moda
**bureau de change** il cambio
**butcher's** la macelleria
**chemist's** la farmacia
**delicatessen** la salumeria
**department store** il grande magazzino
**dry cleaner's** la tintoria
**fishmonger's** la pescheria
**food shop** l'alimentari
**florist** il fioraio
**grocer's** l'alimentari
**greengrocer's** il fruttivendolo
**hairdresser's** (women) il parrucchiere
**ice-cream parlour** la gelateria
**jeweller's** il gioielliere
**leather shop** la pelletteria
**market** il mercato
**newsstand** l'edicola
**post office** l'ufficio postale
**shoe shop** il negozio di scarpe
**stationer's** la cartoleria
**supermarket** il supermercato
**tobacconist** il tabaccaio (also usually sells travel tickets, stamps, phone cards)
**travel agency** l'agenzia di viaggi (also usually books domestic and international train tickets).

## Travelling

**airport** l'aeroporto
**arrivals/departures** arrivi/partenze
**boat** la barca
**bus** l'autobus/il pullman
**bus stop** la fermata dell'autobus
**car** la macchina
**connection** la coincidenza
**ferry** il traghetto
**ferry terminal** la stazione marittima
**first/second class** la prima/seconda classe
**flight** il volo
**left-luggage office** il deposito bagagli
**motorway** l'autostrada
**no smoking** vietato fumare
**platform** il binario

**porter** *il facchino*
**railway station** *la stazione dei treni*
*(ferrovia)*
**return ticket** *un biglietto di andata*
*e ritorno*
**single ticket** *un biglietto di sola*
*andata*
**reservation** *prenotazione*
**sleeping car** *la carrozza letti/*
*il vagone letto/la cuccetta*
**smokers/non-smokers** *fumatori/*
*non-fumatori*
**stop** *la fermata*
**taxi** *il taxi*
**ticket office** *la biglietteria*
**train** *il treno*

### Road Signs

*Accendere le luci in galleria*
**Lights on in tunnel**
*Alt* **Stop**
*Autostrada* **Motorway**
*Attenzione* **Caution**
*Avanti* **Go/walk**
*Caduta massi* **Danger of falling rocks**
*Casello* **Toll gate**
*Dare la precedenza* **Give way**
*Deviazione* **Diversion**
*Divieto di campeggio* **No camping**
**allowed**
*Divieto di sosta/Sosta vietata*
**No parking**
*Divieto di passaggio* **No entry**
*Dogana* **Customs**
*Entrata* **Entrance**
*Galleria* **Tunnel**
*Guasto* **Out of order** (e.g. phone box)
*Incrocio* **Crossroads**
*Limite di velocità* **Speed limit**

## Numbers

| | |
|---|---|
| 1 *Uno* | 17 *Diciassette* |
| 2 *Due* | 18 *Diciotto* |
| 3 *Tre* | 19 *Diciannove* |
| 4 *Quattro* | 20 *Venti* |
| 5 *Cinque* | 30 *Trenta* |
| 6 *Sei* | 40 *Quaranta* |
| 7 *Sette* | 50 *Cinquanta* |
| 8 *Otto* | 60 *Sessanta* |
| 9 *Nove* | 70 *Settanta* |
| 10 *Dieci* | 80 *Ottanta* |
| 11 *Undici* | 90 *Novanta* |
| 12 *Dodici* | 100 *Cento* |
| 13 *Tredici* | 200 *Duecento* |
| 14 *Quattordici* | 500 *Cinquecento* |
| 15 *Quindici* | 1,000 *Mille* |
| 16 *Sedici* | 2,000 *Duemila* |

*Passaggio a livello* **Railway crossing**
*Parcheggio* **Parking**
*Pericolo* **Danger**
*Pronto Soccorso* **First aid**
*Rallentare* **Slow down**
*Rimozione forzata* **Parked cars will**
**be towed away**
*Semaforo* **Traffic lights**
*Senso unico* **One-way street**
*Sentiero* **Footpath**
*Solo uscita* **No entry**
*Strada interrotta* **Road blocked**
*Strada chiusa* **Road closed**
*Strada senza uscita/Vicolo cieco*
**Dead end**
*Tangenziale* **Ring road/bypass**
*Traffico di transito* **Through traffic**
*Uscita* **Exit**
*Uscita (autocarri)* **Exit for lorries**
*Vietato il sorpasso* **No overtaking**
*Vietato il transito* **No thoroughfare**

## AT THE AIRPORT

**I'd like to book a flight to Naples**
*Vorrei prenotare un volo per*
*Napoli*
**Are there any seats available?**
*Ci sono ancora posti liberi?*
**Have you got any hand luggage?**
*Ha bagagli a mano?*
**I'll take this hand luggage with me**
*Questo lo tengo come bagaglio*
*a mano*
**My suitcase has got lost** *La mia*
*valigia è andata persa*
**My suitcase has been damaged**
*La mia valigia è rovinata*
**The flight has been delayed**
*Il volo è rimandato*
**The flight has been cancelled**
*Il volo è stato cancellato*
**I can put you on the waiting list**
*Posso metterla sulla lista d'attesa*

## AT THE STATION

**Can you help me please?** *Mi può*
*aiutare, per favore?*
**Where can I buy tickets?** *Dove*
*posso fare i biglietti?*
**at the ticket office/at the counter**
*alla biglietteria/allo sportello*
**What time does the train leave?**
*A che ora parte il treno?*
**What time does the train arrive?**
*A che ora arriva il treno?*

## Conversion Charts

**Metric–Imperial:**
1 centimetre = 0.4 inch
1 metre = 3 ft 3 inches
1 kilometre = 0.62 mile
1 gram = 0.04 ounce
1 kilogram = 2.2 pounds
1 litre = 1.76 UK pints

**Imperial–Metric:**
1 inch = 2.54 centimetres
1 foot = 30 centimetres
1 ounce = 28 grams
1 pound = 0.45 kilogram
1 pint = 0.57 litre
1 UK gallon = 4.55 litres
1 US gallon = 3.78 litres

**Can I book a seat?** *Posso*
*prenotare un posto?*
**Is this seat free/taken?**
*É libero/occupato questo posto?*
**I'm afraid this is my seat** *É il mio*
*posto, mi dispiace*
**You'll have to pay a supplement**
*Deve pagare un supplemento*
**Do I have to change?** *Devo*
*cambiare?*
**Where does it stop?** *Dove si ferma?*
**You need to change in Naples**
*Bisogna cambiare a Napoli*
**Which platform does the train**
**leave from?** *Da quale binario parte*
*il treno?*
**The train leaves from platform one**
*Il treno parte dal binario uno*
**When is the next train/bus/**
**ferry for Naples?** *Quando parte il*
*prossimo treno/pullman/*
*traghetto per Napoli?*
**How long does the crossing take?**
*Quanto dura la traversata?*
**What time does the bus leave for**
**Sorrento?** *Quando parte l'autobus*
*per Sorrento?*
**How long will it take to get there?**
*Quanto tempo ci vuole per*
*arrivare?*
**Will we arrive on time?** *Arriveremo*
*puntuali?*
**Next stop please** *La prossima*
*fermata per favore*
**Is this the right stop?** *É la fermata*
*giusta?*
**The train is late** *Il treno è in ritardo*
**Can you tell me where to get off?**
*Mi può dire dove devo scendere?*

## DIRECTIONS

right/left  *a destra/a sinistra*
first left/second right  *la prima a sinistra/la seconda a destra*
Turn to the right/left  *Gira a destra/sinistra*
Go straight on  *Va sempre diritto*
Go straight on until the traffic lights  *Va sempre diritto fino al semaforo*
Is it far away/nearby?  *É lontano/ vicino?*
It's five minutes' walk  *Cinque minuti a piedi*
It's 10 minutes by car  *Dieci minuti con la macchina*
opposite/next to  *di fronte/ accanto a*
up/down  *su/giú*
traffic lights  *il semaforo*
junction  *l'incrocio, il bivio*
building  *il palazzo*
Where is ...?  *Dov'è ...?*
Where are ...?  *Dove sono ...?*
Where is the nearest bank/ petrol station/bus stop/hotel/ garage?  *Dov'è la banca/la stazione di servizio/la fermata di autobus/l'albergo/ l'officina più vicino/a?*
How long does it take to get to ...?  *Quanto tempo ci vuole per andare a ...?*
Can you show me where I am on the map?  *Può indicarmi sulla cartina dove mi trovo?*

### Emergencies

Help! *Aiuto!*
Stop! *Fermate!*
I've had an accident  *Ho avuto un incidente*
Watch out! *Attenzione!*
Please call ...  *Per favore, chiami ...*
... a doctor  *... un medico*
... an ambulance  *... un'ambulanza*
... the police  *... la Polizia*
... the fire brigade  *... i pompieri*
Where is the telephone?  *Dov'è il telefono?*
Where is the nearest hospital?  *Dov'è l'ospedale più vicino?*
I would like to report a theft  *Vorrei denunciare un furto*
Thank you very much for your help  *Grazie dell'aiuto*

### Tourist Signs

Most regions in Italy have handy signs indicating the key tourist sights in any given area:

*Abbazia (Badia)* **Abbey**
*Basilica* **Church**
*Belvedere* **Viewpoint**
*Biblioteca* **Library**
*Castello* **Castle**
*Centro storico* **Old town/ historic centre**
*Chiesa* **Church**
*Duomo/Cattedrale* **Cathedral**
*Fiume* **River**
*Giardino* **Garden**

You're on the wrong road  *Lei è sulla strada sbagliata*

### ON THE ROAD

Where can I rent a car?  *Dove posso noleggiare una macchina?*
Is comprehensive insurance included?  *É completamente assicurata?*
Is it insured for another driver?  *É assicurata per un altro guidatore?*
By what time must I return it?  *A che ora devo consegnarla?*
underground car park  *il garage sotterraneo*
driving licence  *la patente (di guida)*
petrol  *la benzina*
petrol station/garage  *la stazione di servizio*
oil  *l'olio*
Fill it up please  *Faccia il pieno, per favore*
lead free/unleaded/diesel  *senza piombo/benzina verde/diesel*
My car won't start  *La mia macchina non s'accende*
My car has broken down  *La mia macchina è guasta*
How long will it take to repair?  *Quanto tempo ci vorrà per la riparazione?*
Can you check the ...?  *Può controllare ...?*
There's something wrong (with/in the) ...  *C'è un difetto (nel/nella/ nei/nelle) ...*
... accelerator  *l'acceleratore*
... brakes  *i freni*

*Lago* **Lake**
*Mercato* **Market**
*Monastero* **Monastery**
*Monumenti* **Monuments**
*Museo* **Museum**
*Parco* **Park**
*Pinacoteca* **Art gallery**
*Ponte* **Bridge**
*Ruderi* **Ruins**
*Scavi* **Excavations/ archaeological site**
*Spiaggia* **Beach**
*Tempio* **Temple**
*Torre* **Tower**
*Ufficio turistico* **Tourist office**

... engine  *il motore*
... exhaust  *lo scarico/ scappamento*
... fanbelt  *la cinghia del ventilatore*
... gearbox  *la scatola del cambio*
... headlights  *le luci*
... radiator  *il radiatore*
... spark plugs  *le candele*
... tyre(s)  *la gomma (le gomme)*
... windscreen  *il parabrezza*

### Health

Is there a chemist's nearby?  *C'è una farmacia qui vicino?*
Which chemist is open at night?  *Quale farmacia fa il turno di notte?*
I don't feel well  *Non mi sento bene*
I feel ill  *Sto male/Mi sento male*
Where does it hurt?  *Dove Le fa male?*
It hurts here  *Ho dolore qui*
I suffer from ...  *Soffro di ...*
I have a headache  *Ho mal di testa*
I have a sore throat  *Ho mal di gola*
I have a stomachache  *Ho mal di pancia*
Have you got something for sea sickness?  *Ha/Avete qualcosa contro il mal di mare?*
antiseptic cream  *la crema antisettica*
insect repellent  *l'insettifugo*
mosquitoes  *le zanzare*
pharmacy  *la farmacia*
sunburn  *scottatura da sole*
sunburn cream  *la crema antisolare*
sticking plaster  *il cerotto*
upset stomach pills  *le pillole per male di stomaco*
wasps  *le vespe*

# Further Reading

## History and Culture

**The Decameron:** Giovanni Boccaccio. *The Sixth Tale of the Fifth Day* is a raunchy tale set on Ischia.
**Easter in Sicily:** Antonino Buttitta, Sicilian Tourist Service, Palermo. An introduction to Sicilian festivals.
**Thus Spake Bellavista:** Luciano da Crescenzo, Picador. Romanticised short tales about Neapolitan life.
**Siren Island, Summer Islands, South Wind** and **Old Calabria:** Norman Douglas. Atmospheric travel books on Southern Italy.
**Graziella:** Alphonse de Lamartine, AC Mclurg, Chicago. The Romantic poet's affair with a fisherman's daughter on the island of Procida.
**History of Sicily:** Finley and Mack Smith, Chatto & Windus. The best overall Sicilian history.
**The Story of San Michele:** Axel Munthe. Story of the Swedish doctor's life and building of his villa on the island.
**Christ Stopped at Eboli:** Carlo Levi. Classic story of a year spent in a poverty-stricken community of Southern Italy.
**Naples '44:** Norman Lewis. Account of the author's experiences in Naples between 1943–44.

## Literature

**Volevo i Pantaloni:** Lara Cardella, Mondadori. Bizarre story of a young girl's struggle with rural prejudice.
**La forma dell'acqua, Il cane di terracotta, Il ladro di merendine, La voce del violino:** Andrea Camilleri, Sellerio. These four detective stories written in Sicilian vernacular language have become bestsellers in Italy.
**The Last Leopard: A Life of Giuseppe di Lampedusa:** David Gilmour, Quartet.

**Sicilian Carousel:** D.H. Lawrence, Marlowe.
**Six Characters in Search of an Author:** Luigi Pirandello, Methuen.
**The Mask of Apollo:** Mary Renault, Sceptre. A novel set in ancient Siracusa.
**The Leopard:** Giuseppe Tomasi di Lampedusa, Collins.
**I Malavoglia (House by the Medlar Tree):** Giovanni Verga, Dedalus.
**Conversation in Sicily:** Elio Vittorini, Quartet.
**Kingdom in the South:** John Julius Norwich. The Norman period (out of print, available through libraries).

## Feedback

We do our best to ensure the information in our books is as accurate and up-to-date as possible. The books are updated on a regular basis, using local contacts, who painstakingly add, amend and correct as required. However, some mistakes and omissions are inevitable and we are ultimately reliant on our readers to put us in the picture.

We would welcome your feedback on any details related to your experiences using the book "on the road". Maybe we recommended a hotel that you liked (or another that you didn't), as well as interesting new attractions, or facts and figures you have found out about the country itself. The more details you can give us (particularly with regard to addresses, e-mails and telephone numbers), the better.

We will acknowledge all contributions, and we'll offer an Insight Guide to the best letters received.

Please write to us at:
**Insight Guides
PO Box 7910
London SE1 1WE
United Kingdom**
Or send e-mail to:
**insight@apaguide.co.uk**

## Crime and Society

**The Dark Heart of Italy:** Tobias Jones, Faber. A provocative portrait of Italy highlighting the interplay between politics, society and crime.
**Men of Honour, the Truth about the Mafia:** Giovanni Falcone, Little Brown. Judge Falcone's testament.
**Mafia Women:** Clare Longrigg, Vintage. A courageous investigation into the changing role of women in Cosa Nostra. Compulsive reading.
**Ten Pains of Death:** Gavin Maxwell, Alan Sutton. An account of the people the author met while living in Scopello in the 1950s.
**Midnight in Sicily:** Peter Robb, Panther. Insights on art, food, history, travel and the Mafia.
**The Mafia:** Clare Sterling, Grafton. Analysis of the Mafia, particularly the "Pizza Connection".
**Excellent Cadavers: the Mafia and the death of the first Italian Republic:** Alexander Stille, Pantheon Books.

## Travel and General

**Bitter Almonds:** Mary Taylor Simeti and Maria Grammatico, Transworld. Poignant memoir of a much-feted Sicilian chef and former nun, and a collection of her recipes.
**Italian Journey 1786–1788:** J.W. Goethe, Penguin. Evocations of Naples in the 18th century.
**Voyage en Sicile:** Guy de Maupassant. Edrisi, Palermo.
**Journeys to the Underworld:** Fiona Pitt-Kethley, Abacus. Bawdy account of the poet's island adventures.
**On Persephone's Island:** Mary Taylor Simeti, Penguin.
**Sicilian Food:** Mary Taylor Simeti, Random Century (first published as **Pomp and Sustenance**).
**Old Calabria:** Norman Douglas, Marlboro Press/Northwestern.

## Other Insight Guides

The 550 books and maps published by Insight Guides include comprehensive coverage of Italy. **Insight Guides** to *Italy, Florence, Rome, Northern Italy, Tuscany, Venice, Sardinia* and *Sicily.*

Thoroughly updated and expanded, the bestselling *Insight Guide: Rome* lifts the lid on Italy's capital.

*Insight Guide: Tuscany* explores one of Italy's best-loved regions.

**Insight Compact Guides** are handy on-the-spot reference guides packed with detailed information on sights and museums. *Insight Compact Guide Venice* is excellent for practical on-the-spot information.

The new *Insight Guide: Sicily* is packed with up-to-date information, revealing background essays and sumptuous photography.

**Insight Pocket Guides** are itinerary-based guides written by on-the-spot authors and accompanied by full-colour pullout maps. Italian titles in the series include *Tuscany, Florence, Milan, Rome, Venice, Sardinia* and *Sicily*.

*Insight Pocket Guide: Florence* provides tailor-made tours of Italy's art capital. Perfect for a short break. Includes a pullout map.

Also available:
**Insight Fleximaps** to Florence, Milan, Italian Lakes, Rome, Sicily, Tuscany.
**Insight Phrase Book: Italian**

# ART & PHOTO CREDITS

## Picture Spreads

**INSIGHT GUIDE**
## SOUTHERN ITALY

*Cartographic Editor* **Zoë Goodwin**
*Production* **Linton Donaldson**
*Design Consultants*
**Carlotta Junger, Graham Mitchener**
*Picture Research* **Hilary Genin, Britta Jaschinski, Susannah Stone**

**Map Production** Phoenix Mapping
© 2006 Apa Publications GmbH & Co.
Verlag KG (Singapore branch)

# Index

*Numbers in italics refer to photographs*

# INSIGHT GUIDES

*The classic series that puts you in the picture*

**INSIGHT GUIDES**
*www.insightguides.com*